A Unifying Approach to the Theories and Practice of Psychotherapy and Counseling

Michael W. York

G. David Cooper

Allyn and Bacon

Boston ■ London ■ Toronto ■ Sydney ■ Tokyo ■ Singapore

We dedicate this book to Janet Ann York
whose aid was invaluable.

Senior Editor: *Rebecca Pascal*
Editor-in-Chief, Social Sciences: *Karen Hanson*
Editorial Assistant: *Whitney Brown*
Marketing Manager: *Caroline Croley*
Production Administrator: *Deborah Brown*
Cover Administrator: *Linda Knowles*
Composition Buyer: *Linda Cox*
Manufacturing Buyer: *Megan Cochran*
Editorial-Production Service: *Susan McNally*

Library of Congress Cataloging-in-Publication Data

York, Michael W.
    A unifying approach to the theories and practice of psychotherapy and counseling /
Michael W. York, G. David Cooper.
        p. cm.
    Includes bibliographical references (p.) and indexes.
    ISBN 0-205-27609-1
    1. Psychotherapy. 2. Mental health counseling. 3. Psychotherapy—Case Studies. 4.
    Mental health counseling—Case studies. I. Cooper, G. David. II. Title

    RC480.Y67 2000
    616.89′14—dc21

                                                                                    00-044801

Printed in the United States of America

10 9 8 7 6 5 4 3 2 1   05 04 03 02 01 00

CONTENTS

iii

PREFACE

When we first began to work on a text about psychotherapy and counseling, behavioral and cognitive approaches were just beginning to be considered as alternatives to psychoanalysis and client-centered therapy. The first author (a graduate student in the early sixties) badgered the second author to tell him what type of therapy was "true." The first author asked if he should do client-centered therapy, apply one of the new behavioral approaches, try Albert Ellis's rational emotive therapy, and on and on. Probably in self-defense the second author stated that whatever one did in therapy, whatever approach one used, one ought to be able to say why it worked and with whom it worked. This was the beginning of our attempt to make sense out of the multiplicity of theories and techniques of psychotherapy and counseling.

For over thirty years we have been trying to piece together what works and with whom, and to develop a systematic integration of theories and techniques of psychotherapy and counseling. Types of therapies have multiplied until there are now hundreds of them. We think we have been somewhat successful in describing what approaches work and with whom. However, our quest for a unified theory of psychosocial strategies is far from completed. We hope the reader will find our presentation a powerful first step in its development.

This book is directed to graduate students who still ask these questions and to practicing professionals who have not yet found adequate answers to them. The theory and techniques are organized such that the treatment of less distressed or disturbed clients is considered first and then the treatment of increasingly more seriously disturbed clients is discussed. Numerous case histories, some with excerpts from therapy sessions are included. Significant details in the case histories have been changed to fully protect the confidentiality of the individuals described. We will use interchangeably the terms client and patient (and occasionally client/patient) throughout the current text, as well as counselor and psychotherapist (and occasionally counselor/therapist).

Throughout the text we discuss difficulties in the current psychiatric classification system, the *Diagnostic and Statistical Manual*, 4th Ed. (DSM-IV). However, it is necessary for mental health students and practitioners to have their own copy of the DSM-IV and become thoroughly familiar with it and subsequent revisions. As of the publication date for this text a web site was available for the DSM-IV diagnostic categories and numerical codes (http://psy.utmb.edu/disorder/dsm4/dsmnum.ht). In addition, the student needs to become familiar with the psychoactive drugs currently in use and their common risk factors and side effects (see Appendix 2). We have also listed three web sites in Appendix 2 to update the student or practitioner on psychoactive drugs now in use.

There are many people who have aided us in the development of this text. The first author would like to express appreciation to all of his students who were exposed to earlier versions in graduate courses in psychotherapy and counseling. We both would like to thank our colleagues Alan Towbin, C. H. Patterson, Richard O'Brien, James Monahan, and Arnold Hyman, among others, for their detailed reviews. Their many suggestions and corrections greatly improved the clarity and accuracy of this text. Special thanks go to Theodore Riggar who wrote the initial draft of Chapter 1 and to Barbara Jarmon for her work on the section on frail elderly in Chapter 4. Many students helped with the cross-checking of references, notably Seanne Tyson, Orit Whitman, Steve Hardy, and Tarek Mandour. We would also like to acknowledge the Library of the University of New Haven staff for their aid, especially Evelina Woodruff, Marian Sachdeva, June Cheng, Juan Li, and Hanko Dobi. Our thanks also to Liane Turman and Hanna Monahan for their help in typing this manuscript. Our thanks also go to the Allyn and Bacon production team with whom we worked, Deborah Brown, Julia Collins, and Susan McNally. And, finally, we would especially like to acknowledge Georgia Lee McElhaney for her extensive editing of this text, and Steven Skrabacz for his work on its graphics.

1 Critical Issues in Psychotherapy

Psychosocial interventions, whether psychotherapy, counseling, or other psychosocial approaches, are the primary function of many nurses, social workers, psychologists, and psychiatrists. The purpose of this text is to offer a systematic integration of the theories and techniques of psychosocial intervention. In essence, the practitioner wants to know what works with whom and under what circumstances. One means of determining what works and with whom is to require that techniques be clearly specified. What is it one does when one performs "psychotherapy?" Older "schools" of psychotherapy and counseling were often unclear about what psychotherapy or counseling was. Some approaches were technique driven (behavioral and cognitive therapies) and some were relationship driven (humanistic therapies and psychoanalysis). However, most therapists have recognized the importance of defining what the practitioner is doing and establishing a working relationship with one's clients or patients. Miller, Luborsky, Barber, and Dorherty (1993) and Silverman (1996) stated that one means to specify technique was to develop treatment manuals, although Silverman was somewhat skeptical about the mechanical use of manuals. They also stated that most outcome research about psychotherapy effectiveness was defined by manuals.

For us, the major problem in manual-driven therapy is that the importance of the relationship between the therapist and the client or patient is often made secondary to therapeutic technique, or is described as yet another technique. We hold that technique, though important, must not subsume the interpersonal relationship between the therapist and the person with whom he or she is working. The rush to find the "cure" for "this disease" or "that disease" could easily lead one to ignore the importance of the *therapeutic relationship*.

In this age of managed care we need to be aware of the danger of prematurely "prescribing" specific therapies. Reid (1989) suggested a set of intervention techniques based on DSM-III-R diagnoses. It is not difficult to imagine insurance companies refusing to pay for any treatment but the "right" one. It seems to us that for psychotherapy and counseling a great deal of the effectiveness of the treatment[1] still depends upon the judgment and expertise of the individual practitioners.

Yet the literature of psychology and counseling and the experiences of practicing therapists may have reached the point where a general and systematic integration of approaches to psychotherapy and counseling can occur. Patterson and Watkins (1996, p. 489) stated that "it would appear that the objective of the field of psychotherapy would be to develop a universal theory or system. Few would agree that such an objective is possible, or even desirable. Yet there is an interest in attempting to integrate different methods if not theories." Our position is closer to that of Patterson (1989; Patterson & Watkins, 1996, p. 490) who stated that "The objective of any movement toward eclecticism or integration must be the development of a single comprehensive system of psychotherapy including philosophical and theoretical foundations." However, Rigazio-DiGilio, Goncalves, and Ivey (1996), and Stubbs and Bozararth (1994) concluded that such a comprehensive integration cannot easily be achieved, if at all. We will attempt to convince them and the reader that not only can a comprehensive system be framed, but also that it is necessary to do so now.

Attempts at theoretical integration have not been convincing. Dollard and Miller (1950), Kendall (1982), Apfelbaum (1981), and Wachtel (1977) all attempted theoretical syntheses. For Dollard and Miller and Wachtel, integration was aimed at synthesizing behavioral and psychoanalytic approaches to psychotherapy. Their attempts and those of Kendall and Apfelbaum failed in part because they focused their integration too narrowly. In addition the vast array of research on psychotherapy effectiveness had not yet reached a point at which empirically verified psychotherapeutic approaches could be organized.

If it is now time for a unifying approach of the theories and techniques of psychotherapy and counseling, what form might that organization take? Frank (1961) stated that whatever successful therapists were doing, they were doing the same thing. There are at least two different ways that Frank's remark could be interpreted. First, that one could identify the common elements shared by effective therapists, as suggested by Frank and clearly defined by Patterson and Watkins (1996). Our problem with this approach is that differential analysis of treatment effectiveness is submerged in general effects. Boddington and Lavender (1995) reported that all of the types of psychotherapy that they had analyzed were effective. They noted that this was yet another example of the dodo bird effect, in other words, "everybody has won so all shall have prizes" (Luborsky, 1995). This conclusion boggles the mind and leaves unanswered the question of what a therapist does in particular with a particular person. While we hold that the therapeutic relationship and other factors not specific to technique are essential parts of any successful therapeutic approach, it does not follow that such non-specific factors account for all of the variance in successful psychotherapy and counseling.

A second interpretation of Frank's remark is that successful therapists employ similar techniques with people who have similar problems. Patterson and Watkins (1996) have pointed out that there are so many different techniques, theories, therapist characteristics, process variables, and ways one might put all of this together, that the inductive construction of such a theory is a virtual impossibility. However, in our estimation they did not rule out a theory based on an explicit set of assumptions (postulates) as opposed to one based on unguided inductive synthesis.

There are seven basic assumptions structuring our theoretical system:

1. Human development of thinking, feeling, and acting follows an orderly process. The interruption of that process (defined as *fixation*), either by environmental stress stimuli or physiological factors or some combination of the two, causes psychological disorders.
2. Successful therapists either select people for whom their approach works or modify their approach.
3. The earlier the disruption in the developmental process the more severe is the psychological disorder that emerges.
4. For severer disorders longer treatment is required.
5. The severer the disorder the more structure the therapist must provide.
6. Effective therapy must deal concretely with the issues and difficulties of the specific client or patient.
7. All effective psychotherapy occurs in the context of an effective therapeutic relationship.

In Chapter 2 we offer the first part of our theoretical integration. Chapter 14 explores issues in classification and causal analysis necessary for an integrated theory. There are many additional factors that have delayed both technical and theoretical integration of psychotherapy and counseling approaches. First, what Eysenck (1960) called the lateral development of psychotherapy and counseling led to the proliferation of techniques and theories without the collegial cooperation required to develop scientifically validated approaches.

A second and related problem is that many proponents of approaches to psychotherapy and counseling viewed other approaches as either worthless or invalid and rarely cited or became familiar with each other's literature. Singer (1974) and Patterson and Watkins (1996) underscored the importance of the need for psychologists and psychiatrists to become familiar with theoretical and technical approaches outside of any narrow orientation. Within the fields of psychology and psychiatry, historical accidents were related to the chaotic fragmentation of the fields of psychotherapy and counseling. As an example, Freud's emphasis on sexuality was readily accepted by a segment of the Viennese population but found little acceptance in England or the United States until much later. Finally, the current emphasis on physiological causes and treatment of psychological distress threatens to reduce psychotherapy and counseling to a secondary and perhaps irrelevant status as a means of treating troubled people.

It is possible to begin to meet some of the challenges to a successful integration of the theories of psychotherapy and counseling. If both are to continue as viable approaches in the treatment of troubled people, such integration is required. The myriad number of therapies and theories of psychopathology that exist confuse the public and lead to a general sense of unease about whether there really is such a thing as psychotherapy. The authors' intentions in developing a theoretical integration is both to aid the practitioner in making sound clinical judgments and ultimately to inform the public about what kinds of psychosocial interventions are required for treating psychological disorders.

Lateral Development of Psychotherapy and Counseling

It is obvious even to the most casual observers that the development of techniques and theories of psychotherapy and counseling has not enjoyed a simple evolution. Those of us who are interested in psychological ideology are able to note changes in the framework of concepts with the values and beliefs that are current at a particular time in a particular culture. Far too often, psychotherapy (here broadly defined to include group therapy and counseling), its practice and its principles, has been more concerned with fads rather than with facts.

Paris (1973) pointed out that traditional clinical psychotherapy was divided into a number of ideological camps. He found that allegiance to any traditional system carried the possible danger of sacrificing the care of clients and patients to attain theoretical consistency. Indeed, one could extend Paris's arguments to directive psychotherapy, humanistic counseling, and many of the approaches to psychotherapy and counseling described in manuals and texts (Klerman, Weissman, Rounsaville, & Chevron, 1984; Beck, 1976; Ivey & Gluckstern, 1992), which have themselves become doctrinaire (London, 1972; Russell, 1974; and Drozd & Goldfried, 1996).

Paris's resolution of the issue of how to select the correct psychotherapeutic technique was to declare that therapists must accept the uncertainties of the eclectic position and abandon attempts to develop a universal theoretical approach. Such an injunction is little more than the admission of ignorance and is not likely to be of any concrete aid to the practitioner of psychotherapy or counseling. The eclectic "solution" fails because it offers ever-changing guidelines for treatment to the practitioner and fails to provide any sense of direction to the theoretician. Eysenck (1960a) argued that psychology, particularly that part devoted to psychotherapy and counseling, developed laterally rather than vertically. Eysenck supported the notion that a combination of experience, scientific methodology, and collegial cooperation could have led to vertical growth; in other words, to the progressive development of psychotherapeutic techniques, each of which complemented the other and each of which was exact, systematic, and effective.

The history of psychotherapy and counseling shows a rather different development. This development Eysenck called lateral because categories of behavioral difficulties, during the period from 1900 to 1960, had grown wider and techniques used to treat them had become increasingly heterogeneous. This proliferation of techniques and theories of psychotherapy continues and threatens to lead to a tower of Babel. Each proponent of a particular approach, whether behavioral, humanistic, psychoanalytic, or medical, had proposed that his or her approach was the only possible one that an effective therapist could adopt. Serious conflicts that reduced collegial cooperation arose between traditional verbal psychotherapy and directive techniques, principally those included under the heading of behavior modification or cognitive therapy, and more generally between psychosocial and medical approaches to the treatment of psychological distress.

Another conflict of some importance involves counseling psychology and clinical psychology. Advocates of counseling psychology, often disenchanted with the psychoanalytic emphasis on pathology rather than on health, separated rather early from psychoanalytic theory and practice. It is fair, we think, to characterize counseling approaches as basically humanistic and optimistic as opposed to psychoanalytic determinism and pessimism.

Perhaps the most important and troubling issue is the current emphasis on medication instead of psychosocial intervention of any kind. It is widely held that psychologically disturbed people are mentally ill and therefore require medication. In practice this means that the person receives only medication and the evaluation process is focused on producing a DSM-IV label with a recommendation for "appropriate" medication to treat the "mental illness."

Historical Overview

The Origins of Clinical Psychology/Psychotherapy

The first of the "traditional" psychotherapy practices was developed scarcely a century ago by Josef Breuer and Sigmund Freud. The development of psychoanalytic theory and practice has continued and its main tenets and methods are well known, frequently used, and have been recorded at length and in detail (Walker, 1957). All of the current psychodynamic approaches to diagnosis and treatment have their initiation in Freudian theory, and newer procedures and practices are usually presented as modifications of it (Henry, Strupp, Schacht, & Gaston, 1994). In such techniques, it is a tenet to search beyond the presenting behavior of the patient for the underlying causes of that behavior (Eysenck, 1960b). The symptom is considered to be a defense mechanism that protects the organism against, or temporarily resolves, the underlying conflicts. Traditionally, the symptom itself should not be directly attacked by the therapist but rather attention should be directed to exposing, analyzing, and resolving the underlying conflict. Treating the underlying cause rather than the symptom is one characteristic of the medical model.

It is understandable that Breuer and Freud would have implicitly adapted part of the medical model. Both were physicians with neurological practices. Perhaps it is unfortunate that both therefore adhered to the medical model of "emotional illness" and sought to treat the "causes" of the "illness" rather than attend directly to the thoughts, feelings, and behavior of troubled people. Indeed, according to Yates (1970), practitioners' dissatisfaction with the psychodynamic approach and the assumed medical model for "emotional illness" was widespread and based at least in part on rejection of the appropriateness or accuracy of this model.

Behavior modification and more directive therapy approaches grew out of a different background than the medical tradition that framed the work of Freud and Breuer (Breuer & Freud, 1955). Behaviorism was developed in universities and focused on overt behavior, not upon symptoms and underlying physiological disorders. The behavioristic-experimental trends begun by Pavlov (1927, 1928) and popularized by Watson (1925, 1928) and Skinner (1953, 1961) collided abruptly with much that was routinely accepted by traditional psychotherapists. Watson (1914, 1916) was among the first psychologists to call himself a behaviorist and stated that behavioral techniques could be used with people to produce desired behavior patterns. Or, to paraphrase Watson (1928), give me a child of normal intelligence and I will give you a doctor, a lawyer, or an Indian chief.

The clash between the analytic and more traditional approaches and the more directive approaches characterized by behavior modification advocates may no longer be significant and is possibly coming to an end. As London (1972) stated,

> . . . With the era of polemics virtually ended, and Skinner (1971) citing Freud over and over again in his latest work, and the American Psychoanalytic Association at a recent convention casually incorporating behavior modification into its discourses on psychotherapy, the political utility of learning theory, so called for the definition of the field, is ended. It was never really theory anyhow, as we used it, but ideology for professional purposes and mostly metaphor for clinical ones. It is time now, I think, for the remedial branch of this business to stop worrying about its scientific pretensions, in the theoretical sense, as long as

it keeps its functional nose clean, and to devise a kind of engineering subsidiary, or more precisely, a systems analysis approach to its own operations. We have gotten about as much mileage as we are going to out of old principles, even correct ones, but we have barely begun to work the new technology. (p. 914)

In the light of London's arguments, it seems appropriate and necessary to determine, through the literature, the relative strengths and weaknesses of some of the major models for psychotherapy and counseling. A second and less empirical part of our literature review is a consideration of some of the therapeutic approaches for which success has been claimed. Although these approaches fail to meet the criteria of Chambless and Hollon (1998) for empirically verified methods, we believe that it is essential not to ignore earlier approaches simply because they lack the patina of current scientific respectability. We simply don't know enough to exclude whole traditions without more research.

The Origins of Counseling Psychology/Counseling

Counseling psychology had a different genesis from clinical psychology, deriving its existence neither from the medical/psychoanalytic tradition of Freud and Breuer nor from the behaviorist tradition of Watson and Skinner. It is fair to say that its birth was from the first pragmatic and eclectic, focused not upon troubled people but rather upon people who were seeking aid in reaching life decisions with which they could comfortably live.

The name most frequently associated with the birth of counseling psychology is Frank Parsons (1909). His major emphasis was on determining individual traits that would lead to success in a particular occupation. With the development of the Army Alpha and Army Beta group tests of intelligence during World War I, an emphasis on assessment and testing began to define counseling psychology. The testing approach remained consistent with the life-decisions and vocational-choice approach of earlier counseling psychologists. Dissatisfaction with such a limited role and its own occupational consequences may have contributed to Carl Rogers's (1942) redefinition of counseling, which stated that counseling was not to be limited to placing a person in the right "niche" but rather was to aid the client in realizing his or her own potential. Rogers (1951) emphasized growth, not pathology, the use of the client's strengths, not weaknesses, and the belief that each human being—when provided with the appropriate interpersonal climate—will move toward self-actualization (defined as the need for any person to be all that he or she can be). This humanistic orientation is consistent with many of the positions advocated by existential and Gestalt therapists.

It has become increasingly difficult to maintain clear boundaries between counseling and clinical psychology. Distinctions between counseling and clinical psychology may be more apparent than real and are very probably unnecessary. We suggest that a unified approach needs to be developed which does justice to both the contributions of counseling psychology and clinical psychology. Neither set of insights or techniques can be abandoned because both approaches are required to address the totality of human distress with which mental health personnel deal.

Research in Psychotherapy and Counseling: An Overview

Eysenck's Attack on "Traditional" Psychotherapy

It is impracticable to review thoroughly in this chapter all of the outcome studies and other kinds of studies on psychotherapeutic technique and theory (again defined broadly, to include counseling approaches and any other psychosocial intervention strategies) that have appeared in the past forty years. A sampling is provided, derived from the work of Eysenck and the reviews of Strupp and Bergin (1969), Meltzoff and Kornreich (1970), Bergin and Garfield (1971, 1994), and Volume 51 of *American Psychologist* (1996). Also included are findings reported in specific outcome studies and meta-analysis studies. Meta-analysis is a statistical method that combines the results of any number of similar studies and arrives at a conclusion about the significance of the outcome across those studies.

H. J. Eysenck (1952a, 1952b, 1958, 1960a, 1960b, 1965, 1967, 1995), a pioneer in research on the question of the effectiveness of traditional psychotherapy, has examined the effectiveness of numerous outcome studies. From his investigations, Eysenck argued that traditional therapy developed inadequately due to certain critical problems or assumptions, which purported or entailed that traditional psychotherapy:

1. was based on inconsistent theory never properly formulated in postulate form;
2. was derived from clinical observation made without necessary control observations or experiments;
3. considered symptoms the visible offshoot of unconscious causes;
4. regarded symptoms as evidence of repression;
5. assumed that symptoms are determined by defense mechanisms;
6. assumed that all treatments of disorders must be historically based;
7. proposed that cures are achieved by handling the underlying dynamics, not by treating the symptom itself; and
8. regarded the interpretation of symptoms, dreams, acts, and so forth, as an important element of diagnosis and treatment.

(Adapted from Eysenck, 1960b)

It is clear from Eysenck's paper (1960b) that the focal point of his attack was the efficacy of traditional psychoanalytic psychotherapy, although he also condemned client-centered counseling approaches in the same analysis. Few analysts, and virtually no eclectically oriented or client-centered therapists, would now argue that symptom treatment as described by Eysenck (and summarized in items 3–8) applies to all clients or patients. Therefore, Eysenck created a straw man ("traditional therapy") to attack rather than deal directly with therapy effectiveness. The polemic nature of some of his arguments will become clear as we subject them to close analysis.

In 1952 Eysenck began his analysis of traditional psychotherapy. In this famous study, he reported that the claimed rates of cure for "neurotics" by traditional therapists, either psychoanalytic or eclectic, were lower than the spontaneous remission rate reported for neurotics at mental hospitals. Eysenck maintained that the best that could be said for traditional therapy was that it did not seem to do any appreciable harm.

In 1960 Eysenck followed the 1952 study with several important articles. He (1960b) concluded that there was no satisfactory evidence that psychotherapy benefited people suffering from neurotic conditions. According to Eysenck, there was no reason to suppose that vague traditional psychotherapeutic techniques were capable of producing relief from neurotic disorders. Eysenck concluded that roughly two-thirds of neurotic patients recovered or improved within about two years of the onset of their illness, whether or not they were treated by psychotherapy. Eysenck held that these results were stable from one investigation to another regardless of type of patient treated, standard of recovery employed, or method of "traditional" therapy used (Eysenck, 1960a, 1960b; Rachman & Eysenck, 1965).

The interpretation of the findings cited by Rachman and Eysenck (1965) may be more illusory than real. The criteria used by therapists claiming success or failure were so different that raw numbers of clients (or patients) showing "improvement" across therapists and treatment approaches (or even no treatment) have no meaning. Some therapists have claimed success only when the client was free of symptoms, expressing satisfaction with his or her life, and effectively coping vocationally and socially; whereas another therapist has claimed success when the client only hallucinated when alone. Success may be claimed if clients or patients are discharged from a hospital. Patients in institutional settings were often called improved and released when there was an increased demand for hospital beds. Even now the demand by HMOs for release of all hospitalized patients as soon as possible underlines the notion that release from a hospital may not be equivalent to full recovery.

Finally, one might question if hospital personnel can tell whether or not a mentally ill patient has improved. For instance, Rosenhan (1973) demonstrated that personnel in neuropsychiatric in-hospital settings were not able to determine which patients were "normal" or "abnormal." If hospital personnel cannot tell when a patient is improved, how could Eysenck claim that "spontaneous remission" of untreated hospitalized "neurotics" was higher than the cure rates for "traditional" psychotherapy?

The second argument raised by Eysenck was that no study using a proper no-treatment control group had reported that traditional psychotherapy worked. The studies reporting negative results that Eysenck (1961) cited as paragons of research design excellence—the Cambridge–Somerville study (Powers & Witmer, 1951), the Brill–Beebe study (1955), and the Barron and Leary study (1955)—were themselves hopelessly confounded from an experimental point of view. In the Cambridge–Somerville study juvenile offenders were randomly assigned to "experimental" or "control groups." Counselors chosen for the experimental group were individuals whose training and commitment were often inadequate (McCord & McCord, 1956). Juvenile offenders in the control group received no treatment. In this study, it is questionable whether there was any psychotherapy at all. With such poorly trained counselors it is not surprising that no significant differences were reported. Certainly there was no consistent firm but kind treatment of these troubled adolescents (McCord & McCord, 1956). The patients in the Brill–Beebe study were all classified as suffering from "traumatic war psychosis," referring to what was then also called combat fatigue, which in these cases did not produce the long-term effects characteristic of posttraumatic stress disorder. However, traumatic war psychosis was sufficiently severe that the soldier was removed from combat. Removal from combat and the supportive treatment of such veterans led to an approximately 90% cessation of symptoms. One may question whether there was, in this study, any real no-treatment control group at all. In the Barron and Leary study, Minnesota Multiphasic Personality Inventory profiles before and after therapy were compared and no significant differences reported. (The MMPI is an objective paper and pencil test.) However, no attempt to control for differential therapist effectiveness was included in this study. Again, this is hardly compelling evidence against traditional psychotherapy.

Most surprising is Eysenck's attack on the Rogers and Dymond study (1954). As the reader can see from Figure 1.1, their experimental design was perhaps the finest example of an early no-treatment control group study of the effects of psychotherapy. One might challenge Rogers on his use of "ideal self" versus "actual self" differences as his criterion, but not, we think, for his experimental design.

Eysenck (1960b) argued that the effect of the Rogers and Dymond (1954) study could be accounted for by the placebo effect. It has been observed (Roethlisberger & Dickson, 1939) that if you pay special attention to people, their performance improves. Therefore, Eysenck concluded that special attention rather than psychoanalytic or client-centered therapy probably accounted for any changes in client behavior. On the other hand, if one considers attention and caring as important components of effective therapy *of any kind,* such an effect is not a confounding variable but rather

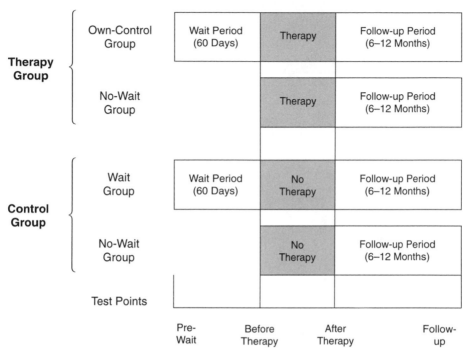

FIGURE 1.1 Experimental Design for the First Block. The Rogers and Dymond Study. Adapted from Rogers and Dymond (1954).

an important focal point for developing a workable technology of psychotherapy.

Eysenck remains the best known of the critics of the "talking cure," but by no means the only critic. Perhaps the most damning attack on psychotherapy (and this attack includes behavior modification techniques as well as traditional psychotherapy) was that of Masson (1988). Masson stated that because of a power imbalance between therapist and patient, the therapist automatically imposes his or her values upon the patient. Masson then attacked Freud, Jung, and Rosen, respectively, as individuals whose very humanity was questionable. York (1994) reviewed an edition of Jung's lectures (*Thus Spoke Zarathustra,* Jarrett, 1988), which he presented from 1931 to 1936, and could find no evidence to support Masson's contention that Jung was anti-Semitic. In these lectures Jung was critical of Hitler and Stalin and their actions in Germany and Russia. Masson's attack on Jung as being in sympathy with Hitler could not be supported with these data. These kinds of attacks on therapy of one kind or another have continued. For instance, Dawes (1994) in his book *House of Cards* stated that there was little evidence to validate psychotherapeutic techniques and often cited Masson to support his arguments. Currently, Eisner (2000) proclaimed that psychology was dead. Often these attacks on psychotherapy have not been balanced, reasoned, or objective but rather have reflected some strong emotional antipathy for the process itself.

It is inappropriate to universally condemn without empirical basis. However, it is also inappropriate to praise or support approaches without empirical basis. As overbearing as Eysenck was in his damnation of traditional psychotherapy, he was even more generous in supporting behaviorally oriented therapists. He did not apply the same yardstick to these studies as he did to traditional therapy. He cited Ellis (1957), Rosen (1953), and Wolpe (1958) as demonstrating that behaviorally oriented psychotherapy was effective. Many of those studies did not report comparisons with a no-treatment control group. Finally, he ignored damaging studies or reviews (such as Lloyd & Abel, 1970; Russell, 1974; Brody, 1990; Gossette & O'Brien, 1992, 1993) where success due to behaviorally oriented or cognitive therapists was limited. Indeed, if we are to take Russell (1974) seriously, the most one could say about behavior or cognitive therapies is, as Bergin stated about traditional therapies, "It now seems apparent that psychotherapy practiced over the past 40 years has had an average effect that is modestly positive" (Bergin & Garfield, 1971, p. 283).

Alternatives to Eysenck: Research on Psychotherapy and Counseling

A review of Strupp and Bergin (1969) on the effectiveness of traditional psychotherapy presented a more balanced analysis than that of Eysenck or his colleagues. The work of Strupp and Bergin is presented in summary in Bergin and Garfield (1971). This summary was based on an extensive bibliography of research on the effectiveness of psychotherapy, and the gross number of patients considered was in the tens of thousands. The evidence cited yielded the general conclusion that psychotherapy on the average had modestly positive effects (Bergin & Garfield, 1971, 1994).

Bergin and Garfield (1971) concluded that something potent or efficacious must be operating in some portion of the therapy that was routinely done, even though average effects were only moderately impressive when diverse cases and change scores were lumped together. The Strupp and Bergin (1969) survey, based on 501 outcome studies published from 1916 through 1967, additionally found that the more homogeneous the technique and the sample of patients, and the more specific the criterion, the better the results. The Meltzoff and Kornreich (1970) study of 101 outcome studies provided additional evidence that psychotherapy was more effective than no treatment at all. They also concluded that there was something in some techniques that did in fact work.

More recently, and more modestly, Bergin and Lambert (1978) also concluded that psychotherapy (again broadly defined to include any one-on-

one intervention) was, in general, more effective than no treatment at all. Their conclusions were similar to those drawn by Smith and Glass (1977). Smith and Glass based their conclusions on meta-analysis and found that, in general, the summary's results favored psychotherapy as opposed to no treatment. Eysenck (1995) and Sohn (1995) criticized meta-analysis techniques in general and the Lipsey and Wilson (1993) meta-analysis study in particular. A problem with meta-analysis was that this statistical procedure lumped dissimilar studies together and obscured differences among them. Lipsey and Wilson (1995) responded to Sohn that the purpose of their study was to find common effects in studies of psychotherapy that could logically be grouped together. They stated that their analysis was not intended to identify differences but rather to indicate that therapy was, on the whole, effective.

Seligman (1995) reported that, in general, psychotherapy was effective. He cited a survey study reported in *Consumer Reports,* which indicated that ". . . patients benefited from psychotherapy, that long term treatment did significantly better than short term treatment, and that psychotherapy alone did not differ in effectiveness from medication plus psychotherapy. Furthermore, no specific type of psychotherapy was consistently superior to any other type of psychotherapy; psychologists, psychiatrists, and social workers did not differ in their effectiveness as treaters. . ." (1995, p. 15). Seligman cited several methodological virtues in the *Consumer Reports* survey (CR survey), including the use of a very large sample (equivalent to that of the Framingham study [Dawber, 1980] on heart disease) and the consideration of the duration of treatment with respect to successful/unsuccessful psychotherapy outcomes.

Seligman was aware of the limitations of the survey approach but was able to handle them sufficiently well to be confident that the CR survey supported the efficacy of psychotherapy. It should be noted that there were many weaknesses in the CR survey. First, it relied solely on the report of the subjects who had been treated and not on objective data. Although Strupp (1996) held that the report of clients who had received therapy was one useful criterion in evaluating therapy outcomes, he also held that self-report measures were not sufficient. Evaluation of behavior change for treated clients compared with untreated clients was also necessary. In addition, Strupp held that some measure of structural personality change was also required to determine therapy effectiveness. Finally, the CR survey was not based on controlled studies.

The Framingham heart disease study (Dawber, 1980) suffers from some of these same criticisms. Yet lifestyle issues, as discovered or confirmed in the Framingham study, have certainly had a positive impact on the treatment of heart disease. It is hoped that the CR survey will have a similar impact on the psychosocial treatment of disturbed people.

Despite all of the difficulties involved in attempting to develop a reliable and valid evaluation of the efficacy of psychotherapy or any type of psychosocial intervention, one may conclude from the literature that psychotherapy works. However, whether traditional or directive psychotherapy or other psychosocial strategies work in some global sense is not the critical question of this text. Rather, our primary question is what works and with whom.

Psychosocial Intervention

It is inaccurate to propose any technique of psychotherapy or counseling as the intervention method that will "cure" all troubled people. It is also inappropriate to omit psychosocial intervention methods other than psychotherapy and counseling from consideration with respect to effective modes of treatment. Perhaps it is our society's fragmentation of disciplines into noninteracting groups that has led to some incredible blunders in the treatment of the mentally ill.

Some very severely disturbed individuals (people suffering from psychoses, various personality disorders, problems of substance abuse, or a combination of these) require not only psychotherapy or counseling or both, but also inpatient treatment. It may be that only when inpatient treatment is comprehensive that the dreaded institution can become part of an effective treatment milieu. Jones in the early 1950s (Rapoport, 1960) suggested a general structure for engineering a structured milieu in which the inpatient treatment facility would become a major part of effective treatment for severely disturbed individuals. Bettelheim (1974) in his book *Home for the Heart* further fleshed out these notions for working with troubled children. Paul and Lentz (1977) framed a institutional approach based on behavioral techniques (principally the behavioral methods of Lindsley, 1956; Ayllon, 1963; Ayllon & Azrian, 1968) and tested its effectiveness in a controlled study. They compared their operant procedures (behavior program) with a standard milieu approach and a standard custodial institutional program and found that over 90% of the patients in the behavior program were able to return to the community.

Within this context we suggest that the concept of treatment be extended to include any psychosocial intervention intended to facilitate changes in the patterns of thought, feeling, and actions of troubled people that might lead toward the development of a fully functional person. The psychosocial environment is important, as is medication or psychotherapy (counseling), in the treatment of severely disturbed individuals (Karon, 1987).

Psychosocial Intervention and the Medical Model: Teaching and Facilitating versus Treating

Perhaps the most important issue facing therapists is the assumption that people who are distressed suffer from brain disease and require medication.

Even if such an assumption were true, medication alone does not help a person learn to cope with demands of daily living. In fact, the literature has demonstrated that psychosocial intervention strategies were more effective in producing socially effective behaviors than medication alone (Beck, 1967; Karon, 1987).

It is therefore essential that troubled people are treated psychosocially as well as medically. Such treatments include but are not limited to individual psychotherapy, group psychotherapy, family therapy, couples therapy, and active-milieu therapy (see Chapters 10 and 11) approaches. Attempts have been made to cut health costs and often these cuts have focused on reducing or eliminating psychosocial interventions. Truncations of effective treatment should not go unchallenged.

Instead of viewing the client or patient as a sick person to be treated one could view that person as an individual capable of learning more effective ways of coping with personal distress. Instead of *treating*, therapists would focus on either *teaching* (behavioral approaches and cognitive approaches) or *facilitating* (humanistic approaches) in their work with troubled people.

The teaching we refer to is a special kind of teaching. All people, but particularly troubled people need to learn certain basic social and psychological skills to function effectively. First, a person must be able to monitor his or her behavior and to tell which behaviors elicit positive responses, and which behaviors elicit negative responses from others. Second, a person must be able to consciously experience both positive and negative emotional reactions to environmental stimulation (particularly in reaction to other people) and to monitor whether his or her response is appropriate to the social-environmental circumstances. Third, a person must be able to learn new responses to self-defeating behaviors and dysfunctional emotional reactions. Finally, a person must be able to learn effective self-talk to maintain these new responses in environments that unfortunately may seem indifferent or hostile.

The facilitating we call for is also a special kind. It requires the development of a therapeutic relationship, characterized by the client's perception of the therapist as consistent, caring, and knowledgeable. The creation of such an interpersonal environment is intended to encourage self-exploration and emotional growth. Approaches that focus on relationship issues are often less structured and directive than behavioral and cognitive approaches.

Conclusion

The study of the effects of psychotherapy, counseling, or any type of psychosocial intervention should be similar in methodology and experimental analysis to the study of the effects of any other treatment of the "mentally ill." In actual practice it is extremely difficult to achieve such precision. The various psychosocial approaches do not lend themselves readily to analysis and evaluation. In addition, many practicing therapists have viewed any criticism of their therapeutic approach as a personal attack (Eysenck, 1960a). Although there is an obvious need for research, psychologists are not unanimous in condoning or supporting research activities.

Many therapists feel that if traditional techniques are shown to be of limited effectiveness, then the therapists themselves are at fault. As a result, emotional resistance limits the acceptance and utilization of research findings. One solution (Anthony, 1969) would be for the therapist to assume two roles, those of researcher and clinician. Anthony argued that if all clinicians accepted his position it would aid in the development of collegial cooperation and the discovery of what works and with whom. However, his suggestion does not answer questions of how research on psychotherapy and counseling is to be conducted nor how therapists' objectivity is to be obtained.

Our approach is to focus on empirically defined therapies (Chambless & Hollon, 1998). We have also included older therapeutic approaches whose effectiveness is less well demonstrated, because a premature rejection of older techniques and theories may lead to serious omissions. Similarly, many novel approaches are often excluded before the insights gained from them can be incorporated into the field. Therefore, we have included some of these approaches, as well as many other therapies that are often ignored.

Our approach is consistent with that of Truax and Mitchell (1971), who argued that only through the efforts of the practicing therapist will change take place in the understanding and process of psychotherapy and counseling. For this to happen, the practicing therapist and therapist-in-training require answers to the question, "What are effective therapists doing right, and how are they doing it?" The time has come for the development of a unified approach that can suggest some answers.

NOTES

1. Treatment here means any psychosocial intervention intended to produce change in a client's/patient's thoughts, feelings, or actions.

2 A Unifying Approach

Most of the literature on psychotherapy has focused upon narrow problems involving a specific technique, presented an eclectic overview of therapeutic techniques, or presented one system or treatment approach as all-inclusive. What is lacking is an approach that evaluates therapeutic techniques and systems within a theory designating precisely which psychotherapeutic techniques work. Or as Paul (1969) stated, "What treatment, by whom, is most effective for this individual with that specific problem under which set of circumstances and how does it come about?" (p. 44). Our purpose is to develop an approach that will allow us to sort out from the current literature which techniques may work and with whom. The qualifying "may" is a muted response to the argument of Patterson and Watkins (1996) that this type of integration was probably not possible. They argued that to attempt an empirical synthesis required specification of the taxonomies of disorders, techniques, therapist variables, environments, or circumstances in which therapy was provided and principles or rules for matching these variables. We agree that a purely empirical approach in the absence of theory would be unwieldy, if not impossible. However, our approach is to craft a developmentally based organization as the first step in a theoretical integration of what works and with whom. The elements of our theory focus on the intrapsychic structure of individuals, interpersonal issues, and an overview of how one can determine the content of psychotherapy and counseling.

Before developing our theoretical structure it is necessary to distinguish between theory and technique with respect to psychosocial interventions. Throughout the text, when reviewing a particular approach our focus is on what is actually done by proponents of different theoretical orientations. Further, we specify what type of client or patient is most often treated by therapists who claim success.

It is our contention that a therapy in which the technique cannot be at least partially specified is incomplete. We also hold that technique, no matter how clearly defined, cannot be mechanically employed if success is to be achieved. We hold that the development of a therapeutic relationship is critical for effective psychotherapy. Further, we contend that some techniques that spell out clearly what a therapist is to do lose their usefulness if applied as panaceas for all people who have problems in effective living. For example, A. Freud (1976) stated that psychoanalysis was not the treatment of choice for everyone who was psychologically disturbed. However, in the early euphoric days of psychoanalysis, many analysts claimed that everyone could benefit from it. This tendency to overgeneralize has been shared by advocates of virtually all schools of psychotherapy.

We also provide brief outlines of the theoretical basis of the techniques described, from the point of view of the therapists and their advocates. Our purpose in these presentations is to determine the extent of the correlation between the theories and the techniques that they propose.

London (1972) specified how to determine whether there was a fit between theory and technique. According to London, metaphoric description of treatment approaches involved analogous or—after the fact—word descriptions of what was done in treatment. There was no clear fit between the model or theory and what was actually done in the treatment of an individual, he claimed. A pragmatic description, on the other hand, stated explicitly what must be done with *this* client under a particular set of conditions. The outcome was predicted clearly from the model or theory. In this text we identify for each therapeutic approach the extent to which technique was specified and related to theory or whether the specific treatment was left to the therapist's own expertise.

Defining the Helping Relationship

Urban and Ford (1971) defined psychotherapy as a deliberate, planned pattern of intervention into the circumstances of a person in order to correct or modify psychological dysfunction. But what does it mean to help, correct, or modify someone's problem?

Two possibilities exist. First, one can help the client or patient learn patterns of behavior that allow that individual to cope more effectively with his or her surroundings, environment, or culture. Second, the therapist can try to aid the client or patient to reach his or her ultimate potential as a human being even if such a process will inevitably lead to conflicts with his or her surroundings, environment, or culture.

In order to effect the behavior change required for more effective coping strategies (the first possibility), one must identify a set of behaviors that allow for more effective coping in a particular situation or set of situations. Clearly, this is a difficult task.

One approach in identifying coping behavior involves dividing a person's overall behavior into much smaller pieces, or patterns, and then analyzing them. The whole of behavior modification—its approaches and techniques— could be viewed as simply attempts to clearly define these specific behavior patterns and to increase the occurrence of coping behaviors and decrease the occurrence of non-coping behaviors. In extreme cases such as autism, severe psychosis, and patterns of criminal deviance, both coping and noncoping behavior patterns may be readily identified (Burchard, 1967; Lloyd & Abel, 1970). Further, there is agreement that such negative behaviors ought to be modified. Problems occurred when behavioral techniques were applied to behaviors labeled by one cultural group as deviate and by another as effective coping behavior. For example, to be excessively deferential in the view of middle-class members of our society might be perceived as appropriate behavior by a second-generation Chinese American. Should one's behavior be modified so that one can fit in to a particular group?

Some psychologists (Walder, 1964) have argued that it was not their responsibility to determine which behaviors should be maintained or increased or reduced. Rather, they argue, these judgments should remain in the province of those whom the culture has designated as responsible for the care of any particular group of individuals. Parents, mental health professionals, teachers, and criminal justice personnel would then determine what behaviors were to be increased for their children, severely troubled clients, students, and criminals, respectively. Such a position implicitly assumed that any behavior and any means of producing it that a caretaker deemed necessary were appropriate and correct.

Some in the field, including the authors, are uncomfortable with any attempt to change a person when that person is viewed as an object and is not included as an active participant in the treatment process. The thrust of the arguments raised above is that to focus on adjusting an individual to his or her surroundings, either through behavior modification or more traditional approaches, without an analysis of the adequacy of those surroundings for maximizing human growth, misses an essential focal point of the process of helping.

The second possibility is that the task of the therapist is to aid the person to reach his or her ultimate potential as a human being. Such a task is more difficult than the identification of a specific set of coping behaviors. The therapist must analyze which of the client's or patient's needs have not been met. Further, an analysis of the cultural setting in which the therapist and patient operate is essential to determine whether the goal of reaching one's ultimate potential is possible.

An analysis of what needs are readily met within a particular culture and what needs are not must be specified. Finally, an analysis of what, if any, needs cannot be fulfilled in the culture at a particular time is required. Taken together, these requirements place the humanistically oriented psychologist in a tenuous position unless one can identify: (1) the client's needs and how to satisfy them; (2) what needs are readily met within the culture and its subcultures; and (3) what needs cannot be met within the given cultural milieu.

A complete cultural analysis would carry us far afield in our attempt to develop a practical model of psychotherapy, and we will leave that analysis to others. The speculative works of Skinner (1953, 1961, 1971) and Fromm (1941, 1947, 1955, 1956, 1973) are examples of attempts at cultural analysis that offered clues to the relationship between cultural adequacy and need satisfaction. We suggest that most cultural settings are neither so destructive nor so confining that human needs cannot be satisfied. However, the poor and disenfranchised individuals who exist in every culture cannot reach full human potential because their needs cannot be fulfilled.

The attempt to define human nature and to establish a complete set of human needs, instincts, drives, or motives is an extremely difficult if not impossible task. Our attempt is not to repeat Hall and Lindzey's (1970) catalog of personality theorists or their analysis of human needs, but rather to select a set of human needs that is fairly complete. We will use this set in our analysis to develop pragmatic models that can lead to our unified approach to psychotherapy and counseling.

Human Needs: Maslow and Fromm

We have chosen to focus on Abraham Maslow and Eric Fromm as theorists who developed comprehensive models that defined human needs or motives that control human behavior. Maslow (1970) posited five basic needs, which he argued are hierarchical in nature and comprehensive in scope. This well-known set is composed of *physiological, safety, love, self-esteem,* and *self-actualization* needs. Maslow argued that people must satisfy more basic needs before they can respond to higher-order needs. Fromm (1956) also posited five basic human needs: *relatedness*—the need to have emotional bonds between a person and significant others; *rootedness*—the need to be organically a part of a continuing cultural framework; *identity*—the need to be an individual; *transcendence*—the need to grow continually toward some distant goal; and *frame of orientation*—the need to have a consistent, internalized cognitive structure from which to view the world. We hold that these sets of human needs are very similar. Fromm did not deal with physiological needs and his system was, therefore, incomplete. However, one can consider safety needs as corresponding to need for relatedness, self-esteem needs as corresponding to identity needs, and self-actualization as being the synthesis of an individual's needs for a frame of orientation and transcendence.

If one accepts Maslow's analysis of needs, then the individual, as he or she develops, must be able to attain continuing satisfaction of these needs if that individual is to be considered a fully functioning human being. Any therapeutic approach that fails to recognize need satisfaction, within reality constraints, as a primary goal of the therapeutic process, is not necessarily wrong, merely incomplete.

The Intrapsychic Model

The basic notion of the intrapsychic model is that every child undergoes an orderly developmental process that moves from global and diffuse organization to clearly differentiated and adaptive patterns of thinking, feeling, and acting. Paralleling the child's psychological development is physiological development. This movement from global and diffuse to highly differentiated patterns, as a general principle, was proposed eloquently by Werner (1957). A second notion is that interruptions in the orderly sequence of development, whether produced by psychosocial stress or physiological disorders, impact negatively on later development. Finally, we would posit that severe psychological trauma can influence physiological development even as physiological damage influences psychosocial development.

The focal point for psychosocial development involves an analysis of need satisfaction, or more properly the failure of need satisfaction during the process of an individual's maturation and psychosocial development. The evolution in analytic thought beginning with S. Freud (1901, 1964), continued by Fenichel (1945), and more fully developed by Erikson (1963), allowed for our reformulation of this time-honored construct. Note well that Freud, Fenichel, and Erikson are joined in their notion of a coherent sequence of development by Piaget (1952) with respect to cognitive development, and Kohlberg (1963, 1981) with respect to "moral development."

Freud in his developmental model stated that there are five developmental stages—*oral, anal, phallic, latent,* and *genital.* He held that negative emotional experiences (*trauma*) caused the normal sequence of development to be blocked (*fixation*) and argued that fixations caused psychological dysfunction. Fenichel (1945) detailed and expanded Freud's ideas on the formation of psychopathology. One of his many important contributions was the idea that the development of feeling, thinking, and acting moves from concrete, undifferentiated, and egocentric modes to abstract, differentiated, and more universal modes. This notion was supported by Piaget (1952), Werner (1957), and Erikson (1963), who argued that a fully functional human being is capable of more abstract patterns of thinking and demonstrates a far more complex and accurate expression of feelings than is characteristic of young children. Further, Fenichel developed the analytic concept of fixation as functioning at a more concrete, undifferentiated, and egocentric level than the patient's age would suggest. To avoid obscuring what Fenichel achieved in conceptualization by referring the reader to his usage of analytic jargon, we will turn from Fenichel to Erikson for the particularization of the process of human development.

Erikson (1963) has posited a sequence of personality development that stretches from birth to the end of life. His eight-stage psychosocial model of personality development rivals Freud's five-stage model, in terms of both theoretical elegance and clinical significance. According to Erikson, each human being experiences developmental tasks characteristic of each of eight stages.

Erikson held that the task of the young infant is the formation of *basic trust*. Failure leads to *mistrust* or, in extreme cases, a profound withdrawal from others and from one's own experience. Bowlby (1969) offered a more detailed analysis of the first two years of a child's life, which we believe complements Erikson's analysis. Bowlby argued that there were four stages in the development of secure attachment. Phase one lasted from birth to age two months. During this phase the child simply responded to positive or negative stimulation, including emotional. Phase two lasted from age two months to seven months during which the infant developed preference for individuals who habitually responded to the infant's needs. In phase three the infant either did or did not form a secure attachment. When a secure attachment was formed the child's development essentially corresponded to Erikson's notion of the formation of basic trust. In phase four the solidification of secure attachment allowed the child to tolerate parental absences, and to turn to others to satisfy needs.

According to Erikson the task for the toddler is to achieve a sense of *autonomy*. Failure leads to a sense of *shame*, or in extreme cases, a sense that if one were noticed one would be the target of rejection or punishment. The task for the preschool child is to achieve a sense of *initiative*. Failure leads to a sense of *guilt* and in extreme cases to life patterns labeled neurotic by S. Freud (Coleman, Butcher, & Carson, 1984). The school-age child's task is to achieve a sense of *industry*. Failure leads to a sense of *inferiority* and in extreme cases could be the basis of lifelong attempts to compensate for feelings of weakness and vulnerability. The task in adolescence is to establish a sense of *identity*, with failure leading to a sense of an ill-defined or *diffuse self* and, in extreme cases, to a lifelong struggle with the issue of what one is good for or what defines one. The young adult's task is to establish the capacity for *intimacy*. Failure leads to *isolation*, and in extreme cases to the development of interpersonal alienation. The task of the mature adult is to bring one's life tasks to completion or, as Erikson defined it, to achieve *generativity*. Failure leads to *stagnation* and in extreme cases could lead to a profound sense of meaninglessness. Finally, the task of the old is to achieve *integrity*. Failure leads to *despair*, and in extreme cases leads to psychotic-like withdrawal and melancholia.

Although Erikson described this model as a psychosocial model, the traumatic developmental events which led to disruption (fixation) of this developmental process were emotional events as cited by Erikson. Cooper (1989) argued that in addition to the primary emotional fixation there could also be a secondary social and emotional fixation. That is, interpersonal and cognitive skills may not develop in lock step with emotional development. We explore this issue in greater depth in Chapters 7 and 14.

There are several other problems with Erikson's model. First, it is unclear how severe the emotional distress must be to interrupt development. Freud did not specify what constituted psychological trauma, nor did Fenichel. Erikson (1963), as opposed to Freud and Fenichel, was clear that no developmental task was ever finished and cumulative partial failures could lead to psychopathology. Second, controversy exists concerning the number of stages of personality development. And finally, it is questionable whether the psychological problems that emerge at different ages are consistent with those predicted by Erikson's theory.

Although little empirical evidence exists defining what constitutes trauma, it is reasonable to suggest that catastrophic stressors as defined in the DSM-IV are traumas. It is also clear that individuals may idiosyncratically experience events as traumatic that are less than catastrophic to others. It is essential that the psychotherapist or counselor try to discover how the client or patient experienced a particular stressor, if the extent of its severity is to be identified for that client or patient.

The second issue, concerning the number of stages, is also controversial. Levinson (1978) expanded the adult stages from three to five. Other theorists (Loevinger, 1966; Kohlberg, 1981; Fischer, 1983) posited different numbers of stages. Examination of their theories as well as Freud's five-stage theory showed more similarities than differences.

Valliant (1977) offered empirical evidence that supported both the existence of Erikson's three adult stages of development and the life tasks his theory predicted. Stipek and Hoffman (1980) found empirical evidence supporting Erikson's stage of *industry* versus *inferiority*. Orlofsky (1976) found that men who achieved *identity* in adolescence were able to achieve high levels of *intimacy*, a finding consistent with Erikson's theory. Van de Water and McAdams (1989) reported evidence relevant to and supportive of the notion that the task of *generativity* was important for adults in Erikson's seventh stage. Hannacheck (1990) defined behavioral criteria that can be used to assess the level of development for Erikson's last three stages. Ciaccio (1971) found that children achieved the first four stages as Erikson predicted; however, *autonomy* versus *shame* remained an important task for one-half of the five-year-olds in his study.

The third issue concerns whether problems emerging at a given age are consistent with Erikson's theory. For instance, schizophrenia is most frequently diagnosed in adolescence or young adulthood, not in childhood as Erikson's theory would predict. Arieti (1978) argued that he had never treated a schizophrenic who had normal childhood development. Walker, Newman, Baum, and Davis (1996) found that children who later became schizophrenic showed behavioral, emotional, and motor dysfunction when compared to normal children. We would argue that inadequate partial task resolution, as Erikson argued, could cumulatively lead to such profound later disturbance. Toder and Maria (1973) offered empirical evidence that supported Erikson's concept of identity as a major issue of adolescence. Valliant and Valliant (1990) gave evidence from their forty-seven-year longitudinal study that problems emerging in adolescence, young adulthood, and later adulthood reflect issues of identity, intimacy, and generativity, respectively. Greenwald (1967) argued that individuals who would be diagnosed as having antisocial personality disorders were abused as children and therefore viewed the world as a dangerous place. This too is consistent with Erikson's theory.

Although Erikson's model of human development and Maslow's model of human needs are not without critics, it seems to us that these two models taken together might well lead to the first step in discovering what therapeutic techniques work and with whom. Figure 2.1 presents Maslow's need hierarchy in juxtaposition to Erikson's stages of development. The model we propose states that when psychosocial development is blocked, the psychological problems that emerge correspond to the psychological problems as indicated in Figure 2.1. Further, we found that therapeutic approaches in which success was claimed or achieved tended to focus on particular disorders (see Figure 2.1). If correct, the therapist must fit his or her techniques to the client's problems and change techniques as the client's problems are resolved. When the client's pattern of thinking, feeling, or behavior changes from less fully developed to more fully developed, the therapist's technique must reflect these changes.

Our model predicts that for each of the major life stages a primary need exists that requires satisfaction if development is to continue without difficulty. However, need satisfaction overlaps stages and one is never free from more basic needs no matter how smoothly one's life has progressed.

It is nevertheless significant for our model that each age has its own preeminent need that must be satisfied if an individual is to be considered fully functional. For example, if an infant is to develop, his physiological needs must be met; indeed, as Erikson argued, the infant's trust in the world depends upon his hunger, thirst, and other needs being satisfied. The needs must not only be met, but also met as a function of the infant's demands. Contingent-need satisfaction and its importance was clearly demonstrated by Ferster and Demyer (1961) in their study of the interaction of parents with their autistic children. They noted that the autistic child's behavior produced no contingent responses in his or her parents' behavior.

As so well put by Sullivan (1948), human needs are met or not met by other human beings. If the infant's physiological needs to be fed when it is hungry and held when it cries are not met, the child has a great likelihood of developing severe problems. Perhaps he or she will eventually be labeled as suffering from early schizophrenia or some form of pervasive developmental disorder; at any rate the child will not be called normal.[1] Furthermore, when the child's needs for autonomy or exploration are denied either by a smothering or rejecting interpersonal environment, it is likely that the child will feel intense shame or guilt, and his or her world will not be experienced as safe.

If school-age children are taught to believe they are inferior, they will not perceive that they can, through their own efforts, achieve worthwhile accomplishments. Their world does not provide the prerequisites for self-love; that is, a feeling that through their industry they can accomplish a worthwhile objective or goal. Similarly, if adolescents cannot define their values and establish their own sense of identity following a successful adolescent rebellion, then they cannot share themselves with others and cannot have their needs for love met. Just as clearly, young adults cannot find achievement and gratification unless they have first formed an intense and intimate, sharing relationship with another human being. It is possible to accomplish great things without ever caring deeply for anyone; however, one may imagine that such accomplishments turn to dust and mean nothing to the individual achieving them without love. Assuming that young adults form an intimate relationship with another, their life work must itself be intrinsically valuable and important as they reach middle age, or once again, Erikson would argue, life loses its savor. Finally, as one reaches old age, one can become self-actualized and thus can continue to be a fully functional human being only if one has lived life well or has struggled to wrest meaning from existence in the face of tragedy.

It follows from a synthesis of the ideas of Maslow, Erikson, and Fenichel that if one's life tasks are not properly fulfilled, then one is impelled to seek need satisfaction consistent with the level of development at which the growth process was interrupted. Severely disturbed people whose problems appeared early in life, seek gratification related to physiological or safety needs. Very severely disturbed people may be identified as psychotic or suffering from a personality disorder while less disturbed people may be identified as neurotic or suffering from other disorders related to subjective distress.

In addition, there are many people who are dissatisfied but who do not demonstrate the behavioral problems of people who are severely disturbed or in extreme subjective distress. These people, after forming relationships and achieving some of their goals, find they do not like the person they have become. Their lives have no meaning; they do not feel fulfilled. They have failed to satisfy their need for self-actualization. We would identify such clients as having unresolved issues of identity, or of intimacy and generativity, or both.

It is possible that many people—the statistically average, "normal" people—do not often have their needs for self-actualization met. Perhaps Henry David Thoreau was right, and most people fail to become fulfilled. On the other hand, therapists rarely see people who are neither disturbed nor distressed. Humanistic psychologists, religious leaders, and such observers of

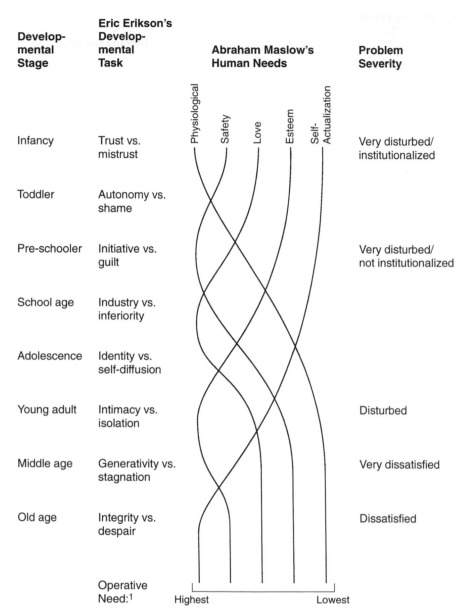

FIGURE 2.1 Intrapsychic Model.

[1]If sufficient needs satisfaction is not achieved at a particular level of development, then the individual is characterized by Erikson's negative stage-appropriate problem and is still primarily

culture and its effect on people as Reisman, Glazer, and Denney (1950) and Fromm (1941) all point to work undone for the common person. The end point of intrapsychic development in the model we posit is not the emergence

Hypothesized Problems Related to Needs-Development Task Failure	Therapeutic Approaches	Therapy Duration and Level of Control
Autism[2] Childhood schizophrenia Process or reactive schizophrenia Psychotic or other disorders requiring hospitalization	Bettelheim: Milileu Approach Ferster's Analysis of Simmons's Approach Ayllon & Azrin: Taken Economy and Operant Approaches Toward Management Taulbee & Folsom: Attitude Therapy	Duration and long-term level of control— highest
Psychotic disorders not requiring hospitalization Psychotic depression Character disorders	Glasser: Reality Therapy Fromm-Reichmann & J. N. Rosen: Direct Analysis Ellis: Rational Emotive Therapy Yablonsky-Synanon: Alcoholics Anonymous	Duration and long-term level of control— high
Neurotic depression Neurotic disorders Anxiety reaction Identity crisis	Freud: Classical Psychoanalysis Dollard & Miller: Stimulus Response Therapy Ellis: Rational Emotive Therapy Meichenbaum: Cognitive Behavior Modification Lazarus: Multimodal Therapy	Duration and long-term level of control— intermediate to low
Issues of intimacy Crisis in values	Rogers: Person-Centered Therapy May: Existential Analysis Perls: Gestalt Therapy	Duration and short-term level of control— moderate to low
Senile psychosis[2]	Jung: Analytic Psychology	Duration and short-term level of control— lowest

oriented toward stimuli configuration directly related to the corresponding need state described by Maslow. Indeed, at any stage of life, if one is deprived of basic needs, one will be motivated or controlled by stimuli that could satisfy these needs.

[2]Both autism and senile psychosis are thought to be partially, if not totally, produced by biological rather than behavioral factors.

of the common person but rather the emergence of the uncommon person. We have called such a person fully functional. Such a person would, in the usual course of activities, think beyond the real to the possible (Piaget, 1952) and sense with increasing accuracy the feelings of others (Rogers's empathy, Rogers, 1951). The main thrust of our intrapsychic model is that this end point is not an ideal state for the few but a real goal for all. Perhaps only by attaining this intrapsychic posture can the world of "peace and zest" that Alfred North Whitehead posited come to be.

In addition to specifying the end point for therapy, the intrapsychic model presented in Figure 2.1 juxtaposes techniques of therapy (in which success was claimed for different types of psychological problems) with unfulfilled needs and problem types. The reader will note that most therapists claiming success in dealing with severely troubled people defined the therapist role as active in structuring therapeutic sessions; and that their approaches required long-term therapeutic intervention. Such treatments are probably most effective (Bettelheim, 1950, 1974; Taulbee & Folsom, 1973) when the client's total environment is structured twenty-four hours a day, seven days a week. In addition to comprehensive treatment Bettelheim in particular maintained that severe childhood problems required long-term treatment. The general conclusion we draw from Figure 2.1 is that very disturbed individuals required therapists using techniques high in structure and long in duration. It seems that the severer the problem, the more the therapist must take an active role and engage the disturbed person, and the longer will that person need to be treated if the individual is to become fully functional.

Less severe problems, as can be seen from Figure 2.1, require less explicit structuring by the therapist and less time in treatment. Again, this generalization is consistent for therapists who have claimed success with dissatisfied people. Rogers (1961); Perls, Hefferline, and Goodman (1951); and May (1950, 1961, 1972) all maintain that it is the client or patient who must assume control of and responsibility for his or her life. Rogers (1961) in particular emphasized that client-centered therapy is often short-term. Still, the end point for therapy remains the same: a fully functional human being. But, one could ask, where do we begin; what techniques do we start with? The model presented in Figure 2.1 offers guidance to therapists about the entry level for effective therapy. By entry level, we mean that the therapist needs to fully assess the person's interrupted developmental task. The primary emotional fixation point is central to selecting therapeutic approaches and gives the therapist guidance on the probable duration of treatment for effective therapy.

There are a few cautions concerning an overly rigid adherence to the model presented in Figure 2.1. First, regardless of the "type" of problem or the severity of the initial behavior patterns, a therapist must modify his or her approach so that it corresponds to the client's or patient's behavior in a particular session. If the behavior in a specific session becomes chaotic, the therapist needs to provide more structure in that session. Second, the intrapsychic model presented in Figure 2.1 assumes that the individual's central nervous system is essentially intact. As noted in the figure, such an assumption is not correct for early infantile autism, senile psychosis, or dementia. These problems, along with chronic alcoholism, psychoses, and other central nervous system disorders, may not be fully resolved by any "talking cure" or other form of psychosocial intervention.

In partial support of the intrapsychic model, Gunderson (1975) has argued that in treating schizophrenics one's approach must change as the patient's needs change. As the patient's needs change, the treatment must change if continued improvement is to occur. However, Gunderson erred in assuming that his non-specific, non-individualized institutional treatments can improve the behaviors of schizophrenics or any person who is not fully functional. Bettelheim (1950) and Taulbee and Folsom (1973), far from postulating impersonal treatment for more severely disturbed institutionalized patients, argued that *because* of the lack of interpersonal contact shown by these patients, they must receive particularized and personalized treatment directed toward establishing realistic interpersonal contact. It seems that Gunderson all but ignored the interpersonal context of human need satisfaction. Indeed, we too have largely ignored the interpersonal context of psychotherapy issues of the psychotherapeutic relationship, until now. The purpose of the following section is to suggest a working model for the interpersonal operations of the therapeutic situation.

An Interpersonal Model for Psychotherapy and Counseling

H. S. Sullivan (1948) was among the first of the theorists–practitioners to emphasize the interpersonal component of the therapy situation. In addition he defined personality as the sum total of interpersonal roles which a person had enacted or observed during his or her lifetime. Therapy, for Sullivan, meant changing interpersonal roles. However, he failed to provide any concrete, technical instructions to inexperienced or, indeed, to experienced therapists about what needed to be done in the process of therapy, how to define maladaptive roles, and how to change maladaptive roles. Leary (1957), after acknowledging Sullivan's influence, developed his circumflex model of interpersonal behavior, which provided a working model for therapists that described both the interpersonal role of personality assumed by the client or patient and the suggested therapist role(s) on personalities to affect positive behavior change. The Leary model[2] is presented in Figure 2.2.

Leary summarized interpersonal behavior as a two-dimensional phenomenon. He stated that one's presentation of self to others varied in terms of power (dominance-submission) and affect (love-hate). Support for the two-dimensional model has been offered by Fox (1961), Schaefer (1959), and

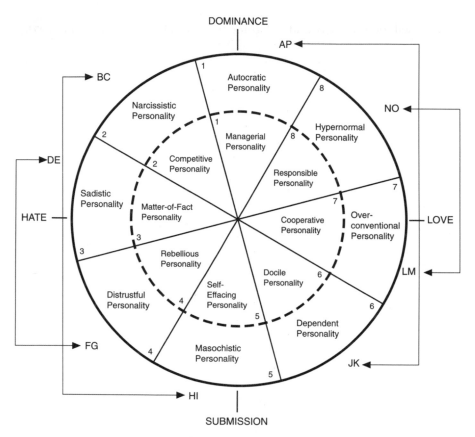

FIGURE 2.2 Interpersonal Model.
Adapted from Leary (1956) and Cooper, et al. (1975).

Gough (1957). By assessing a person's level of dominance and affect, patterns of self-presentation can be organized into eight interpersonal roles or personalities. The organization of these roles or personalities is best described by a circumflex model. In a circumflex model the adjacent roles are most similar and are organized into a circular presentation. The interpersonal roles are described at two levels, an adaptive level and a maladaptive level. The eight interpersonal roles are *AP* (**managerial–autocratic**), *NO* (**responsible–hypernormal**), *LM* (**cooperative–overconventional**), *JK* (**docile–dependent**), *HI* (**self-effacing–masochistic**), *FG* (**distrustful–rebellious**), *DE* (**matter-of-fact–sadistic**), and *BC* (**competitive–narcissistic**). The inner circle of Figure 2.2 is the appropriate level of self-presentation for a particular interpersonal role (personality) and the outer level is maladaptive. The role is expressed too intensely and according to Leary (1957) and Cooper (1975), will lead to interpersonal difficulties.

By the use of the Interpersonal Check List (see Appendix 1) a therapist can categorize client behavior into the eight interpersonal roles (adaptive or maladaptive level of intensity). Leary (1957) found that each interpersonal role produced a predictable response from the other person in a particular interaction. Given a maladaptive role intensity, the *AP* (**authoritarian**) role elicits the *JK* (**clinging vine**) role; the *NO* (**hypernormal**) role elicits the *LM* (**overconventional**) role; the *BC* (**competitive–narcissistic**) role elicits the *HI* (**complaining–whining**) role; and the *DE* (**sadistic**) role elicits the *FG* (**rebellious**) role. The reverse of the above interpersonal "reflex patterns" is also true, with the *JK* eliciting the *AP,* and so forth. Leary (1957) argued that whoever in an interpersonal dyad is most committed to his or her interpersonal role controls the interpersonal response of the other. Paradoxically, the severely disturbed or disturbed patient is often the one who is most firmly committed to an overly intense and inappropriately held role and elicits from the other a negative but predictable reciprocal interpersonal behavior pattern. This maintains the self-defeating patterns of behavior that produce many of the troubled person's difficulties.

Cooper, Adams, Dickinson, and York (1975) and Rice (1969) both demonstrated that inexperienced therapists could be taught interpersonal roles that were not, in Cooper's terminology, reciprocal to a disturbed patient's role—in other words, not the role usually drawn by the disturbed patient's behavior. According to Cooper, most people whom we would call severely disturbed and many people whom we would call disturbed portray themselves as weak and nasty or, in terms of role theory, as either *FG* (**skeptical–alienated**) or *HI* (**complaining–whining**).

Cooper's interpersonal strategy was to have the therapist assume a role that was reciprocal in terms of dominance but non-reciprocal in terms of affect. That is, if the patient were weak and nasty the therapist would be strong (reciprocal) and nice (non-reciprocal). Therefore, if a patient assumed an *HI* (**whining–complaining**) role, the therapist would assume a low-level *AP* (**managerial**) role ready to move to a low-level *NO* (**responsible**) role when the patient's interpersonal presentation was more positive. The low-level *AP* (**managerial**) role is predicted to shift the *HI* (**whining–complaining**) role to a *JK* (**docile**) role. The *NO* role then assumed by the therapist would lead the patient to assume the *LM* (**cooperative**) role. If a person assumes an *FG* (**skeptical–alienated**) role, the therapist would assume a very low-level *DE* (**matter-of-fact**) role to reduce the intensity of the client's or patient's alienation and rebellion. The therapist then would shift to a low-level *NO* or *LM* role (a somewhat warm role, more or less dominant as required). In turn, that role shift leads the client to shift to a warm and cooperative interpersonal role. There are other possibilities in terms of interpersonal strategies, but regardless of what specific role is chosen, the therapist must create an interpersonal climate that will allow the person to change from a negative and passive interpersonal posture to a less passive and more positive interpersonal role.

More concretely, if a therapist encountered a very passive, somewhat nasty person, the therapist would assume a strong but pleasant role rather than the strong and somewhat nasty role the person has come to expect from his or her caretakers (see Figure 2.2). No matter how whining, clinging, and nasty the client became, the therapist would act as though the client's demands were nicely put, though passive, requests for help. The client, according to Cooper, would maintain a somewhat passive role, but would slowly change from a negative to a positive emotional interpersonal posture. The therapist then would assume a more passive role, thus leading the client to assume a more dominant as well as a more positive interpersonal role.

The basic assumption is that when a client can relate to the therapist in a positive and appropriately dominant or submissive role, the emotional climate is established that allows for more effective problem solving and more effective therapeutic interactions. Essentially, Cooper's approach, following Leary's model, allows the initial contact between the therapist and client to be positive and trust-developing. Sullivan (1954) placed great emphasis on the initial interview as setting the stage for effective therapy. It seems to us that Cooper (1970b) and his colleagues (Cooper, Adams, & Cohen, 1965; Cooper, Adams, Dichinson, & York, 1975) have specified the why and how of the importance of the initial interview. Further, Cooper et al. (1975) demonstrated that by following his approach, one could establish the type of interpersonal environment that leads the patient to perceive a therapist as caring, consistent, and knowledgeable.

Some additional discussion is necessary with respect to the basic strategy presented for the therapist in choosing role patterns. Although most people who are disturbed to the extent that institutionalization is required frequently assume either an intense *FG* (**skeptical–alienated**) or an intense *HI* (**whining–complaining**) role, they may also assume other interpersonal roles. Other clients or patients not requiring institutionalization, those we have called disturbed or dissatisfied, often assume the interpersonal roles of *HI* (**whining–complaining**) or *JK* (**clinging vine**).

However, there are situations in which it is appropriate for people who are called "normal" to be distrustful (of almost any salesperson) or self-effacing (when one has made an error); fully functional people are quite able to assume these roles as the interpersonal situation dictates. On the other hand people who are very disturbed, disturbed, or even very dissatisfied often misperceive the interpersonal situation and cannot (we think because of their unsatisfied need states) assume the appropriate role. As Leary (1957) noted, any interpersonal role that is expressed too intensely, or expressed in the wrong situation, is self-defeating. One major part of the job of the therapist is to help the client or patient to assume all interpersonal roles at an appropriate level of intensity and at the proper time.

Such a task places a heavy burden upon the therapist. The therapist must not only correctly perceive the client's role but also must accurately judge whether it is likely to be self-defeating. Further, the therapist must find out if the client can assume, in appropriate situations, other interpersonal roles. By using role-playing approaches, the therapist may determine whether a client can assume an appropriate role, confront, express anger, show love, become passive, or show any other interpersonal behavior required to test the therapist's hypothesis about interpersonal role deficiencies. According to Leary, only when a person can assume all of the interpersonal roles in accordance with the reality situation, and at appropriate levels of intensity, can that person be said to be fully functional.

Nevertheless, if all a therapist is able to accomplish with the client is an interpersonal role change from a consistent expression of weakness, contempt, and distrust to an appropriate expression of warmth and interpersonal strength, the interpersonal part of the therapeutic encounter has been effective. To aid the therapist in determining what interpersonal role is being taken by the client, LaForge's (1977) version of the Interpersonal Check List (see Appendix 1) may be used. In addition to the role required, the Leary model also specifies the intensity level of that role. In general the therapist matches the client's intensity level to allow for a smooth interpersonal interaction.

An example of what may occur when interpersonal intensities are not matched arose during a therapy session conducted by the first author. When the author was working as an intern at a VA hospital, one of his early clients bolted out of the office after a session. The author intended his feedback to be clear, positive, and forcefully put; the client perceived it as intrusive and as a condemnation of him as a person. The intent of the author was "good" and the content of the message accurate and potentially useful to the client. However, the intensity of the therapist did not match the laid-back style of the client. Before one can deepen a relationship and produce the depth of emotional reactivity required for profound change one must first have or develop a therapeutic relationship that will allow for such intensity. One may not crash into a person's world; one must be invited in.

Content in Psychotherapy and Counseling: Issues to Be Explored

We have proposed that our intrapsychic model allow the therapist to determine the end point for and entry level of effective psychotherapy. Furthermore, we have stated that, for success, the client's or patient's problem must determine how directive or structuring therapists should be, and how long therapy is likely to last. Our interpersonal model gives some limited guidance to therapists in terms of the interpersonal role that will be most effective, at least initially, in particular therapy situations.

However, the practicing clinician wants to know more than the entry level and interpersonal style considerations for effective therapy. The clinician wants to know how to determine the specific content for therapy for a specific individual. One means of determining content is to refer to the person's history as an important tool for indicating specific problems. Also, one could use the presenting problem and questions relating to that problem as an aid in defining the content of therapy. In addition, the content of therapy is not only to be directed at what the client says but also how the client says it. Focusing on nonverbal behavior, personal mannerisms (particularly those that are offensive), and other process issues is essential to determining the content of psychotherapy. Finally, as therapists in training often are told, one could argue the content of therapy should be whatever the client wants to talk about.

In practice, a therapist will use all of these sources of data and others in attempting to aid a person to function more effectively and, indeed, to allow that person to realize self-actualization. The practicing therapist often is unclear about what parts of the history, presenting problems, or presenting behaviors should be part of therapy. Specific guidelines to aid the therapist in determining what thoughts, feelings, and actions should be discussed for a particular individual would be quite useful.

One possibility is that individuals go to therapists for help because of subtle, or not so subtle, violations of conventional or situationally defined, stated, or unstated social role expectations. It is our contention that people frequently get into repetitive patterns of violations of these expectations. Such behavior problems are not attributed in this text to undersocialization, as does Mowrer (1961), nor to oversocialization, as does S. Freud (1964), but rather to inadequate or incomplete socialization. The severer violations of social role expectations lead others to reject and punish the troubled person, often with such intensity that he or she will withdraw into fantasy or despair rather than face a world so hostile and rejecting. The subtler violations of social role expectations lead others to stop short of closeness or intimacy with the person (Haas, 1965). Specifically, Haas argues that neurotic behavior elicits covert hostility while psychotic behavior elicits overt hostility.

In extreme cases—psychosis, personality disorders, and severe neuroses—the troubled person does not find a safe world, one in which his or her needs will be met, and will not find safety and need satisfaction unless that person stops violating social expectations. For any individual who seeks help, the therapist can usefully focus on violations of specific social expectations that that person knowingly or unconsciously engages in. It can be argued that Horney's (1950) approach to neurotic disturbances in human relationships consists of cataloguing and bringing to consciousness specific violations of social role expectations. According to Horney, "Self-realization does not exclusively, or even primarily, aim at developing one's special gifts. The center of the process is the evolution of one's potentialities as a human being; hence, it involves—in a central place—the development of one's capacities for good human relations" (p. 308).

Haas (1965) developed a model of societal reactions to different levels of violations of social role expectations, which can serve as a guide to therapists concerning the impact of different classes of social role violations on their clients. As Haas saw it, people who are habitually quarrelsome, rude, and unstable tend to elicit rejection, either public or private, from other people. Those who habitually engage in compulsive patterns of behavior or other behaviors associated with the label of neurosis are often publicly rejected. Those who engage in psychotic behavior are isolated, avoided, and, in general, treated as non-people. If Haas is essentially correct, then the content of therapy for a particular person can be determined with some confidence. One would focus on the client's violations of legitimate social role expectations and allow those incidents to be a primary focus of the content of psychotherapy.

Drawing from personal history data, and presenting problems data and initial behavior patterns, the therapist can catalogue, as a first approximation, the violations of social role expectations that have led a particular person to seek help. The therapist should be cautioned that a particularized set of specific social expectation violations must be developed for *each client* and not for classes of clients. The particular social role expectation violations that cause trouble for a particular person will not necessarily be the same for another person. A psychotic person's specific psychotic behaviors may be different, usually will be different, from another psychotic person's specific psychotic behaviors; yet *both* people are violating the same category of social role expectations. Thus, both will be ostracized or committed to a mental institution unless their bizarre and peculiar behaviors can be modified.

Less disturbed individuals, whether they be called neurotic or suffer from an "identity crisis" or other lesser problems, are very likely engaging in social role expectation violations that lead to rejection and feelings of self-unworthiness. The task for the therapist, in terms of establishing the content of therapy, remains much the same as it was for psychotic or very disturbed individuals. First, the therapist must identify the social role expectation violations that are limiting effective coping and personal growth, and then create a climate that will allow the person to control or simply give up these self-defeating behaviors (self-defeating because they lead to rejection by others).

A second possibility, which Glasser (1975) seemed to overlook, as have we to this point, is that the individual may exist in an intolerable situation in which his or her legitimate needs or rights or both are violated. In such situations it is not the client's violation of others' legitimate rights, but rather that the client's rights are violated. In such situations to place the responsibility for the client's difficulties on the client as Glasser did, and we have to this point, is inappropriate. Child abuse, battered women, the homeless, the underclass, and others who exist in intolerable and often inescapable situations points to the vast and destructive violations of legitimate human expectations that our culture allows to occur. In these circumstances, and others such as prison and many hospital environments, it is virtually impossible to imagine that one's needs might be met or that one's rights would be respected.

Unless the brutalized person can find a minimally satisfactory environment, no psychosocial intervention is likely to be successful. In the main, an environment is required where the person, at the very least, has his or her physiological and safety needs met. Otherwise, all attempts at psychosocial intervention will be futile.

If the troubled person does not improve, the therapist might ask, "Have I identified the significant social role expectation violations or have I missed the boat?" If the client or patient is still engaging in the identified violations, then the therapist's approach is not working. Has the therapist misjudged the problem level? Is it more severe than suspected? Is the therapy sufficiently directive? Is the therapy too directive?

At least one other important issue remains with respect to the content of psychotherapy and counseling. It is essential that the therapist be aware that human beings think, feel, act, and address all human functions in therapy. Advocates of certain techniques (cognitive therapy) focus on the thought process, often neglecting feelings and behaviors. Advocates of psychoanalytic and many humanistic approaches focus on feelings to the exclusion of thoughts and actions. And certain approaches (the more radical behavioristic approaches) have denied the importance or even the reality of human thoughts and feelings. We hold that any therapeutic approach must, in one way or another, deal with thoughts, feelings, *and* actions of human beings.

Even if the therapist deals effectively with content issues, inescapable problems remain. Reality is such that we are often unable to move a person out of the destructive environment that encouraged the social role expectation violations causing the person to neither cope nor grow. Often the client's or patient's central nervous system is not intact or is in fact deteriorating. Often the length of treatment is inadequate because the client can no longer pay, the therapist goes to another job, or the client moves away. Just as often, other factors prevent the therapist from being able to carry a treatment through to conclusion. Perhaps we should ask ourselves how we manage as well as we do, given the limits of our profession.

Conclusion

We have presented two models and discussed therapy content to offer practical guidance to therapists. Taken together the models define our theory of psychosocial intervention strategies. The intrapsychic model is most useful in defining the entry level of psychotherapy and its hoped-for end point. Again, we are fully aware of the almost utopian nature of the end point that follows from the intrapsychic model. Although the fully functional human being is the hoped-for end point, we recognize two major problems that often prevent its realization.

The first problem is the necessity of assuming that the state of a client's or patient's central nervous system can allow that individual to become fully functional. We know that the assumption of central nervous system integrity is not true in senile psychosis or other brain trauma that produces "psychological" symptoms. We do not know the extent of brain dysfunction in autism, psychoses, personality disorders, and other mental disorders, but we do know that brain dysfunction exists in these conditions. The second problem is that environmental problems may be so disruptive that no psychosocial intervention will be effective. "War psychosis," other traumatic psychoses, and extreme stress-related problems may produce bizarre, acute psychotic symptoms. Usually, if the client is removed from the stressful situation and given kindly treatment, the symptoms clear and the individual is again able to function at pre-stress level. It would seem, though, that years of exposure to brutal and dehumanizing environments such as concentration camps, some, if not all, prisons, and some institutions for the retarded and "mentally ill" leave such deep scars upon the human psyche that removal from these settings is not enough. The therapist must start again at the bedrock of the individual and develop basic trust.

The interpersonal model is most useful for defining the therapist's role in the initial sessions—during which it is very helpful if the therapist can establish a relationship with the client or patient in which the therapist is perceived as different from and better (warmer and more loving) than the major role models (mother, father, or significant others) who have contributed to the client's present problem. There are several transitions in the interpersonal roles assumed by the therapist and the client in the process of effective therapy. First, after the therapist teaches the client to assume roles that are more positive and somewhat more dominant, it is more likely that the client's needs will be met. Second, if the client also assumes a more positive and dominant role outside the therapeutic setting, others will perceive him or her as a different person and will tend to treat that "new" person differently—in other words, more positively. Assuming that the therapist has established a good interpersonal contact with the client, and that the client now perceives the therapist as warm, consistent, and knowledgeable, then the therapist must deal concretely (Traux & Carkhuff, 1967) with the client's social role expectation violations. It is also clear that the therapist must deal concretely with society's violations of a client's legitimate expectations and needs.

   If negative behaviors are changed or the client moves into an environment where he or she is considered acceptable, then he or she is likely to engage in more socially positive behaviors, which will allow his or her needs to be met. As such individuals begin to have positive life experiences, they will restructure their world as a "good" world, one in which needs can be met. In this manner the process started in therapy gains its own impetus, leading eventually, it is hoped, to the emergence of a fully functional human being.

N O T E S

   1. It is likely that many severe childhood disorders involve physiological predetermining factors, although as Patterson and Hidork (1997) pointed out, psychological factors can also lead to severe childhood disorders.

   2. Marston (1928) may have been the first psychologist to offer an interpersonal model. Like Leary, Marston held that interpersonal roles could be adaptive or maladaptive. He also held that one's interpersonal role would produce a predictable response from the other. Finally, he anticipated the Leary dimensions of positive/negative affect and high and low interpersonal power.

CHAPTER

3 The Dissatisfied: Problems of Identity, Intimacy, and Meaning

Some Basic Issues of the Dissatisfied

Our starting point for developing a comprehensive approach to the psychosocial treatment of troubled people will be with those individuals whose level of subjective distress is barely severe enough to require treatment. However, the discomfort of subjectively distressed people certainly feels far worse than we have indicated. We have called them dissatisfied and suggested that this descriptive term best describes their experiential state. These individuals often show very few dysfunctional behaviors, or display dysfunctional behaviors that fall within normal limits such as appropriate grief, situationally determined sadness or anger, and so on. Still, their distress is sufficient to markedly reduce their capacity to achieve full potential as human beings. Without appropriate psychosocial intervention, they may slide slowly into a gray existence without experiencing either joy or fulfillment.

In this chapter we present psychosocial methods found to be successful with the dissatisfied; in subsequent chapters we will present other psychosocial methods found to be successful with other groups of troubled people. At the end of each chapter, discussions of how well these therapeutic approaches fit within our unified theory will be offered.

When distress emerges as "free-floating anxiety," such as concerns about identity, intimacy, and meaning, then approaches necessary to address more serious psychological problems are not appropriate. For people suffering from free-floating anxiety, overt behavioral change often is not required. Further, simply blunting feelings through medication is not appropriate and will not aid these individuals in reaching their full potential. We maintain that all human beings need to have a coherent sense of self, to love and to be loved, and to be able to wrest meaning from the experiences of life. It is with these issues, and how a particular person achieves them, that this chapter is concerned.

Issues of Identity

People whose primary complaint is diffuse anxiety without clear overt "symptoms" and who experience subjective distress resulting from a lack of a clearly defined self are precisely the types of individuals who constituted the primary client population for Rogers in his tenure as director of the counseling centers at Ohio State University, the University of Chicago, and the University of Wisconsin. Rogers proposed his person-centered approach as nondirective therapy in 1942. It seems to us that Rogers's approach was clearly focused on the problems of adolescence and young adulthood (Rogers, 1951, 1961). Subjective distress arising from diffuse anxiety or the lack of a clearly defined self, or both, may trouble human beings at any point in their lives. However, these issues most frequently come to the attention of counselors and psychotherapists when the client or patient is an adolescent or young adult.

We suggest that the struggle to develop an "authentic self" is the essential problem of adolescence and to some extent early adulthood. Rogers and Dymond (1954) did not clearly define what an authentic or genuine self was or how it was achieved. They were clear, however, that a coherent/congruent self was one in which the discrepancy between the "real self" and the "ideal self" was small. Rogers stated that when an individual received messages from significant others that were positive, a congruent self emerged. He called this process "unconditional positive regard" and stated that when a child received nothing but unconditional positive regard, that child had no psychological problems. Later when we discuss Rogers's therapeutic approach we will examine this notion more closely.

Issues of Intimacy

Young adults who have achieved a clear self-definition and are not consumed by anxiety face the task of forming a significant relationship with another human being. Forming a life bond with another at this stage has been one of the defining characteristics of Western European cultures. In many respects forming such a relationship is more difficult than in previous times in the United States. Extended families began to break apart as our economy changed from a rural economy to an urban, industrial one. And now the economy is changing again, from an industrial to an information and service economy. These changes make self-definition more difficult and therefore also compromise the formation of stable relationships leading to intimacy.

Even if a person develops a coherent self it is possible that he or she may choose a life partner who is not capable of forming an intimate bond. Failed marriages, stormy relationships, and any other attempts at intimacy that do not succeed cause psychological distress. When the trauma is extreme, people who are otherwise successful in life may need short-term psychotherapy or counseling to regain their balance. Such issues of intimacy were often the focus of the work of Perls and other Gestalt therapists (Wheeler & Backman, 1994). Their focus on the here and now and their insistence that individuals talk directly to each other all suggest that Gestalt approaches would be useful when issues of intimacy are paramount.

Issues of Meaning

At some point, young adulthood ends. Ideally one has found that other self with whom the formation of a significant and comfortable bond was possible. However, even if life's challenges have been met and well met up to this point, the "mature" adult must face the issues of middle age and the rapidly approaching end of one's career or at least one's attempt to prevail in that endeavor. These issues are often framed as existential issues. They involve the individual's concern with meaning and the reality that human existence is fraught with tragedy.

Levinson (1978) gave new definition to the issues of mid-life, and new meaning to the "mid-life crisis" (e.g., one's forties). He suggested that even if one has been "successful" it is difficult to deal with the fact of aging and with the losses that accompany it. According to Levinson, similar conflicts around these issues of life changes continue to occur until some new balance is achieved or the individual discovers one's own unique meaning. The general focus of therapy for such issues is existential, at least in the broader definition of existentialism offered by Yalom (1980).

Therapy and Issues of Identity

Rogers's Person-Centered Psychotherapy

Nondirective therapy, client-centered therapy, and person-centered therapy all represent the same approach and were introduced by Carl Rogers (1941). One example of clients Rogers frequently dealt with is described in Case History 3.1. Rogers was dissatisfied with the mechanical approaches of psychoanalysts and behaviorally oriented psychologists. He felt these approaches dehumanized human beings and turned them into automatons. One wonders what he would have thought of the current medical model that renders all human distress due to chemical or genetic defects or both. We may posit that he would still hold that human beings seek, on their own, to maximize their potential. We assume that he would have held that no psychoanalytic, behavioral, or physiological manipulation can supplant a person's self-discovery and active mastery of a complex internal and external environment.

CASE HISTORY   **3.1**

Issues of Identity—Richard Jaynes

Mr. Richard Jaynes was a nineteen-year-old white male college student. He was referred to the counseling center because he had expressed dissatisfaction with the university and was considering withdrawing. Since he was appropriately dressed and did not demonstrate any severely disruptive behavior, only limited psychological assessment was employed. In addition, he had no history of psychological problems and reported a normal developmental history. He was distressed and expressed extreme dissatisfaction with his current major, premed. The therapist decided to administer an MMPI and Strong-Campbell Interest Inventory to assess the client's current emotional status and interest patterns.

Psychological test data supported the initial impression of the clinician that Mr. Jaynes did not have serious psychological problems. There were indications from the MMPI that he was currently anxious and somewhat self-preoccupied. Interest Inventory data did not indicate that Mr. Jaynes shared interest patterns with successful physicians. Initial interview data supported these findings. During the second interview the client stated that his real dissatisfaction was with his major. He felt that his father would disown him if he did not pursue a medical career. The client was offered eight therapy sessions to address these problems. He was told that if concerns remained, he and the therapist would explore extended therapy.

The following is a short excerpt from the third counseling session.

CLIENT: I really can't stand my major.

THERAPIST: Um hum.

CLIENT: Yeah. I know now that I am not going to be a doctor but I still don't know how to tell Dad.

THERAPIST: You know what you want to do but you think your Dad would disapprove.

CLIENT: Yeah, he is a doctor and he always wanted me to be a doctor.

THERAPIST: What do you want to be?

CLIENT: I really like my English classes. I make As in them and—well, maybe I want to be a writer.

THERAPIST: A writer?

CLIENT: Yeah, but I don't know how I would pay my bills and I know Dad would cut me off emotionally and financially.

THERAPIST: You don't know what you would do for a day job and you think your Dad would cut you off.

CLIENT: Yeah, Dad would hate me.

THERAPIST: If you make a choice to major in English and perhaps become a writer you feel your Dad would cut you off.

CLIENT: Yeah.

THERAPIST: Have you ever checked that notion out, I mean have you ever discussed this with your Dad?

CLIENT: No.

THERAPIST: What is the worst thing that would happen if you discussed a major change with Dad?

CLIENT: He might cut me off.

THERAPIST: Could you survive on your own?

CLIENT: Maybe, I mean with student loans, a part-time job. I earned half my tuition this year from a summer job. It would be hard but I think I could.

THERAPIST: So if you, one way or another, get your English degree and write, what would you see as your day job?

CLIENT: I don't know, wait tables maybe.

THERAPIST: Have you ever considered graduate school?

CLIENT: No. I always thought I would go to med school.

THERAPIST: Well, what would you need to do to go to graduate school, since if I hear you right the last place on earth you wish to go to is med school?

CLIENT: Good grades, professor recommendations, I don't know what else.

THERAPIST: Does going to grad school and eventually becoming a college professor (for your day job) appeal to you?

CLIENT: Yeah, that's it! I could teach and write and live the lifestyle of the college professor. I think I would like that. I wonder what Dad would say about that!

THERAPIST: You really would like to know what your Dad would think about that?

Counseling ended after the fifth session. The initial focus on career choice and options changed. It became an exploration of the client's perception of his father as unbendingly focused on the client becoming a doctor. When the client finally discussed his feelings about his major choice and career direction with his father, his father, though disappointed, supported his son's choice. The client had the academic ability to do well and was able to complete his undergraduate degree and get into a good graduate program. No information exists about eventual outcome.

Rogers proposed that effective therapy required the therapist or counselor to take a phenomenological orientation toward the process of therapy. In essence the therapist or counselor must experience the world as his or her client experiences it. Specifically, Rogers argued (Rogers, 1957) that the necessary and sufficient conditions for effective therapy required that the therapist or counselor be perceived by the client as demonstrating unconditional positive regard, accurate empathy, and genuineness. If those conditions are met, the necessary therapeutic climate has been created to activate the person's self-actualizing tendencies. Self-actualization refers to the human need to be all that one can be or can become.

According to Rogers, the self-actualizing tendency is activated when the individual receives congruent as opposed to incongruent feedback from significant others. Positive regard by others was, according to Rogers, congruent with the self while negative regard was incongruent. Rogers argued (incorrectly we think) that if the child receives only unconditional positive regard, a congruent self, a fully functional self, will emerge. We take that to mean that the individual experiences himself or herself as the self whom he or she wishes to be. Rogers argued that for such people there is little or no discrepancy between ideal self and real self. However, children do not often, if ever, receive total unconditional positive regard as they mature. Severe discrepancies are experienced between the real self and the ideal self. Such events are approximations of the identity crises as described by Erikson (1963) and are consistent with what the DSM-IV calls an identity disorder.

If Rogers is correct, the creation of a positive interpersonal climate, characterized by the necessary and sufficient conditions for therapy, will produce a consistent, coherent, or as Rogers says, congruent self. The therapist or counselor assumes a nondirective posture with clients in an attempt to create this positive interpersonal climate. Simply reflecting the important feelings of one's clients was originally thought to be enough to produce these results (Rogers, 1942). Ivey and Authier (1978), Ivey, Ivey, and Simek-Morgan (1997), and Comier and Hackney (1993) have offered techniques that can produce this therapeutic climate and, in addition, have argued that therapeutic techniques borrowed from cognitive, behavioral, and psychoanalytic approaches need to be added to the relationship approach.

It is important to emphasize that Rogers held that the therapist characteristics that produce effective therapy are utterly dependent on the perception of the individual (Rogers, 1957). The client must perceive the therapist as consistent (congruent and genuine), caring (displaying accurate empathy and unconditional positive regard), and knowledgeable (dealing concretely with problems of significance to the client). However, Lazarus (1981) and Ellis (1984) argued that unconditional positive regard and other person-centered requirements for therapy are significant but not necessary for effective therapy. Further, Lambert, Shapiro, and Bergin (1986) found that therapists judged to be warm, consistent, and caring often were not effective. Of course this study was flawed because the therapist or counselor was judged to be warm, consistent, and caring by observers, not by the client.

These authors (Lazarus, 1981; Ellis, 1984; Lambert, Shapiro, and Bergin, 1986) argued that focusing on the relationship was of less importance than technique. They missed Rogers's injunction that the therapeutic relationship is dependent upon the client's perception of the therapist and cannot be mechanically produced by some therapeutic manipulation. We suggest that although the person must perceive the therapist as caring, consistent, and knowledgeable, such a relationship in and of itself is not sufficient for effective therapy. We would argue that certain technical modifications are required to facilitate the necessary and sufficient conditions for effective therapy. Many of the techniques of cognitive and behavioral therapy are appropriate when a non-directive style fails to allow a client to make significant and novel self-verbalizations in the course of therapy. Further, the content of therapy must often be directed by the therapist when the client fails to address violations of social expectations. A further modification of technique is required to address crosscultural issues as discussed by Ivey, Ivey, and Simek-Morgan (1993).

Although techniques to establish an effective therapeutic relationship and techniques to deal with the content of therapy are helpful additions to Rogers's original client-centered approach, we must not forget that such techniques applied mechanically are not likely to be helpful. With this caution in mind we turned to Ivey and Authier (1978) for a particularization of relationship technique training.

One additional caution is required. Hall and Lindzey (1970) and Davidson and Neale (1994) stated that Rogers found his techniques did not work for severely disturbed people.

Microskills and Relationship Training

Ivey and Authier particularized specific procedures for developing relationship skills. They referred to this process as microcounseling. Microcounseling evolved as an approach for learning how to develop the particular skills necessary to establish a therapeutic relationship. According to Ivey and Authier (1978), "many of the new skills taught under the current microcounseling paradigm represent the behavioral components of the central therapeutic ingredients mentioned by Rogers, i.e., nonpossessive warmth, empathy, and genuineness" (p. 32). The specific microskills are divided into the following: (1) *attending skills* (which include closed and open questions, minimal encouragement, "uh-huh" comments, paraphrasing, reflection of feeling, and summarization); (2) *influencing skills* (which include giving direction and expressing content—such as giving advice and making suggestions); (3) *expression of feeling;* (4) *sharing affective states;* (5) *summarizing;* and (6) *interpretation.* Numbers 1, 4, and 5 are primarily relationship skills and are specifically appropriate to the development of an effective therapeutic relationship. Ivey et al. (1997) and Ivey and Authier (1978) provided specific guidelines and training exercises to develop these skills. Ivey, Ivey, and Simek-Morgan (1993) presented what they called the microskills hierarchy. It seemed to us that Ivey et al. (1993) implied that if one learned these skills and applied them sequentially, effective counseling would occur.

However, the essence of the therapeutic relationship and the employment of psychotherapeutic technique do not depend only on what the therapist or counselor does, but also on how the therapist or counselor is perceived by the client. Certainly changes in technique are required for people whose ethnic, cultural, racial, and gender backgrounds are different from those of the therapist. What Ivey and his associates missed (Ivey et al., 1993), or at least downplayed, is that the therapist needs to modify his or her technique to develop an effective therapeutic relationship. Changes in technique are determined by the level of disturbance that a client displays. We will argue that in working with severely disturbed people a very low-level-intensity interpersonal role is required (see Chapters 11 and 12) to develop the appropriate therapeutic relationship.

Nonetheless the skilled therapist or counselor should be familiar with the specific skills-training format developed by Ivey and co-authors. Appendices I–VII of Ivey and Authier (1978, pp. 423–572) provide an excellent summary of microcounseling training. Any therapist or counselor would profit from these training exercises and workshops on microskill training.

We argue that microskills approaches work best when used with people who suffer from diffuse anxiety, neurotic levels of depression, identity issues, intimacy issues, and issues related to meaning, isolation, death, and freedom. Ivey, it seems to us, gets lost in the forest because he attends to the trees (the microskills) and fails to experience the forest as a whole (the therapeutic relationship). For example, Gunderson (1978) found that emotionally composed therapists or counselors did best with *very* anxious subjects; active warmth was judged to be ineffective. The microskills approaches are not likely to be effective with severely troubled people. Whitehorn and Betz (1960) found that therapists who expressed active warmth often produced negative results in schizophrenics. Again, accurate empathy, unconditional positive regard, and genuineness are not defined by what the therapist does but rather how the client perceives what the therapist or counselor does.

Cormier and Hackney (1993) have offered another, more global, approach for achieving mastery of relationship skills as well as other therapeutic techniques. We hold that it is their approach to the mastery of relationship skills that is most useful to therapists. Cormier and Hackney also recognize that effective counseling and therapy require more than simply the establishment of what Rogers called the therapeutic relationship.

Cormier and Hackney's (1993) particularization of Rogers's emphasis on the therapeutic relationship is articulate, clear, and compelling. We argue that the focal point of their text is Chapter 3: "Rapport and Relationships." They stated, "As you are learning to be an effective helper, you may feel pressure to learn the strategies and techniques needed to facilitate client growth. However, the relationship you establish with your client is the beginning part, the foundation for all that will follow in the counseling process" (p. 43). Cormier and Hackney's required skills for the therapeutic relationship are identical to those of Rogers—empathy, genuineness, and positive regard.

According to Cormier and Hackney the skills associated with empathy are nonverbal—and verbal—attending behaviors, paraphrasing content of the person's communications, reflecting the person's feelings and implicit messages, and being in synchrony with the person's experience. We will now outline their means of obtaining these empathy skills.

Cormier and Hackney stated that "good" eye contact is an essential nonverbal behavior for the development of empathy skills. The eye contact is neither a fixed gaze nor "inadequate" eye contact. York, Burdick, Tyson, Sozewska, and Rabinowitz (1992) found that for college students a gaze of more than one second was threatening, which meant a therapist would need to break eye contact after one second, shifting eye focus to a near object and then back to the client. Smiling and head nods *as appropriate* tend to be useful nonverbal behaviors. According to Cormier and Hackney a therapist or counselor should initially have a relaxed body posture, which becomes more tense as the therapist focuses on a significant therapeutic event. Furthermore, the therapist should be situated between three and six feet away from the client.

Cormier and Hackney pointed out that the therapist must be sensitive to crosscultural differences in the client's expression of and reaction to nonverbal behaviors. The key is to be aware that such cultural differences exist. One way of dealing with them in nonverbal behavior is to match one's nonverbal behaviors with those of the client. It should be noted that York, Wilderman, and Hardy (1988) found no significant crosscultural differences in the ability to *perceive* nonverbal displays of affect and dominance. Perhaps with sensitivity and care many of the difficulties that Sue and Sue (1990) documented may be overcome.

Verbal attentiveness is achieved by what Cormier and Hackney (1993) call "verbal encouragers" such as "Go on," "I see," "Tell me more," "Uh-Hmm," and similar verbalization that encourages clients to keep talking. Further, the therapist must allow clients to complete their utterances. Cormier and Hackney refer to what Minuchin (1974) called *tracking*. The critical element that categorizes a therapist's responses as tracking is that the therapist focuses on the topics expressed by the client. One may also indicate verbal (in this example, vocal) attentiveness by mirroring the loudness of the client's voice.

Two additional empathy skills referred to by Cormier and Hackney are paraphrasing and reflecting client messages. Reflecting as they define it means closely feeding back what the person is saying. In 1942 Rogers held that in non-directive therapy, reflecting meant to repeat significant client messages, often word for word. Paraphrasing as defined by Cormier and Hackney means rephrasing the parts of a message that are emotionally important. The rephrasing must accurately capture what is important to the client. If the client responds to the therapist's reflected or paraphrased message by disclosing more information or by expressing more affect (usually positive), then the therapist has probably communicated that he or she is empathetic toward the client.

To facilitate the person's perception of the therapist as genuine, Cormier and Hackney suggested focusing on supporting nonverbal behaviors (already described in discussing empathy skills). In addition, the therapist needs to emphasize congruence skills ("your words, actions and feelings all match or are consistent," Cormier & Hackney, 1993, p. 57). Being open and therapist self-disclosure are also important. Finally, immediacy skills (focusing on the here and now) and some Gestalt skills described later in the chapter can be applied here.

At a global level the therapist must constantly struggle to be "real," not phony. Certain cautions are necessary. First, don't overdo expressing what you feel, as you feel it, to the client. If the therapist becomes enraged, or feels lust, or other intense emotions, simply expressing and owning those feelings will not facilitate an effective therapeutic relationship. Second, complete, extensive self-disclosure is not required of a therapist, and likewise may disrupt or even destroy the therapeutic relationship. A therapist must always assess whether or not the person is ready for this or that particular feedback. Inevitably, the key responses must rest on the judgment and good sense of the therapist.

Finally, Cormier and Hackney discussed several skills to convey positive regard. If a therapist is to be perceived as possessing positive regard for the client, then he or she must *feel* positive regard for that particular person. In all therapy, the therapist must intend to communicate warmth and concern. Nonverbal skills can facilitate this. These skills are the same as the encouraging nonverbal skills referred to earlier, with the addition of gestures that are open and welcoming, and discrete touching. Further, enhancing statements may facilitate the person's perception of the therapist as showing positive regard. Cormier and Hackney (1993) stated that enhancing statements focus on something positive about the client and include offering encouragement, and offered a specific set of examples of how to achieve these skills (pp. 69–75).

We feel the need to caution the reader that one cannot learn or employ these skills (or any other therapy skill) in a mechanical way. Genuineness cannot be faked nor can empathy or positive regard. If you can't stand your client, if you don't feel warmth or at least respect toward that person, it is unlikely that you will be able to conduct successful counseling or psychotherapy.

The Legacy of Rogers

Rogers maintained that the therapist–client relationship is central to effective psychotherapy and counseling. He (1957) stated that the client's perception of the therapist as genuine, possessing accurate empathy, and showing unconditional positive regard defined the therapeutic relationship and constituted the necessary and sufficient conditions of effective psychotherapy and counseling. We would argue that although the client's *perception* of the therapist as caring, consistent, and knowledgeable is necessary for effective psychotherapy and counseling, it is often not sufficient. Further, what a therapist does to produce such a perception very likely varies with the severity of the client's disorder. Much structure, coupled with a low-level-intensity interpersonal role, may be required for effective therapy with psychoses and other severe disorders.

For less disruptive emotional problems the therapeutic relationship as described by Rogers and augmented by Gestalt psychologists and existentially oriented psychotherapists may be sufficient. People who suffer from identity disorders or who have diffuse anxiety concerning life choices, intimacy, or meaning need to have a positive and warm interpersonal environment where they can be heard and where they can hear themselves.

If one is to work with people who have identity issues, therapists are advised to pay particular attention to those parts of Ivey et al. (1997) and Cormier and Hackney (1993) that focused on empathy skills and positive regard skills. If one does not become *skill driven,* these skills will serve the therapist well. When one knows the techniques so well that they have become *automatic,* then one can *forget* the skills and focus on the person—which is, after all, what therapy is about.

Rogers's legacy to us all is only transcended, if transcended at all, by the contributions of Sigmund Freud. His focus on the therapeutic relationship has made all practitioners aware that the therapist *as a person* impacts on the client. No longer can counselors or therapists view a client as an object to be manipulated. We must create the conditions for change that will lead to growth, and as Rogers said, to self-actualization.

Gestalt Therapy and Problems of Intimacy

Introduction to Gestalt Therapy

According to Patterson and Watkins (1996) the two basic principles of Gestalt therapy are that people form organized wholes from their experience of disorganized reality, and that those wholes emerge as a function of the dialectical principle of opposites. It is only when a person can simultaneously experience pain and joy that a whole can emerge from these opposites. Whole formation, according to Perls, Hefferline, and Goodman (1951) is the creative process by which well-functioning people satisfy their needs. As with Freud, Skinner, and just about every psychologist who has commented upon the issue, Perls et al. held that an activated (Perls would have said experienced) need state leads to goal-directed behavior. Goal attainment and personal satisfaction could occur, Perls argued, only when the person had the resources (or supports) to form a new Gestalt. When a new Gestalt (or pattern) emerges that leads to goal attainment, the organism returns to a state of balance. If a person is able to repeatedly and easily engage in this process, then growth and self-actualization occur.

If this process is interrupted, the individual becomes distressed or perhaps even disturbed. Perls et al. argued that when an individual is unable to satisfy his or her needs, the individual engages in patterns of thinking, acting, and feeling that are pathological (we could label these patterns "defensive operations"). Perls et al. held that these defensive operations are self-destructive or self-defeating levels of *introjection, projection, confluence,* and *retroflection.*

Introjection is the wholesale taking-in of inputs by a person. It is as though something were shoved whole into a person. Consider the situation in which a child takes in some parental "should" or "should not" not as a principle but as an absolute. When the child grows up he or she may respond to those absolutes as he or she would as a child ensuring that his or her needs will not be met. *Projection* as used in Gestalt therapy is similar to *projection* as defined by Freud. In the act of *projection* the person constructs boundaries so that unacceptable parts of the self become part of the external world and are most often attributed to other people. *Confluence* also involves boundary issues. When an individual loses his or her boundary or separation from one part of the world or, typically, from another person, then *confluence* has occurred. In many respects it is similar to Kaiser's description of his patients being unable to maintain a separate identity (Feirman, 1965). *Retroflection* means that the person turns back onto himself or herself feelings and reactions (usually negative) that are really targeted toward something (usually someone) external to that person.

According to Patterson and Watkins (1996), the primary function of the Gestalt therapist is to allow the client or patient to become aware of unmet needs. In classical psychoanalysis, the therapist's primary function is to get the client or patient to substitute the reality principle for the pleasure principle—in others words, for the person to be able to satisfy needs within the context of reality. It would seem that the therapeutic goals are similar for both Gestalt and psychoanalytic therapy. However, the focus of therapy is not on resolving intrapsychic conflicts but rather on dealing with unfinished business, events from the past that are currently operative in the client's or patient's life. Therapy focuses on the present, on what is happening now.

The actual practice of Gestalt therapy focuses on the here and now, and the *I* and *Thou*. Pedantic emphasis on the here and now roots the client or patient to his or her current, immediate experience. The Gestalt therapist insists that the client when relating to another person must treat that person as a *Thou* not an *it*, as another person not a thing. Part of therapy may involve Gestalt techniques (to be discussed shortly). Yontef (1995) held that the basic Gestalt principles must drive the technique, and technique independent of the principles cannot be successfully employed. He focused on boundaries (really self-definition), the *I* and *Thou* relation, and the state of being here and now as the guiding principles of Gestalt psychotherapy.

Techniques of Gestalt Therapy

During the period from about 1960 through 1973, Gestalt therapy was one of the most popular "new" approaches used to deal with troubled people. Many Gestalt techniques were introduced during this period. Levitsky and Perls (1970) gave a list of those techniques Perls called *games;* Patterson and Watkins (1996) presented that work in their text (p. 370).

According to Patterson and Watkins the games are mainly techniques used by therapists in groups. They are defined briefly as follows:

1. *Games of dialogue.* The patient takes the parts of aspects of the split personality and carries on a dialogue between them. These parts include the top dog (superego or shoulds) versus the underdog (passive resistant), aggressive versus passive, nice guy versus scoundrel, masculine versus feminine, and so forth. (Present authors' note: "so forth" would include what Perls called the empty chair technique, during which the client/patient addresses an empty chair in which the split-off part resides.)
2. *Making the rounds.* The patient extends a general statement or a theme (for example, "I can't stand anyone in this room") to each person individually, with additions pertinent to each.
3. *"I take responsibility."* The patient is asked to follow each statement about himself or herself or feelings with "and I take responsibility for it."
4. *"I have a secret."* Each person thinks of a personal secret involving guilt or shame and, without sharing it, imagines how he/she feels others would react to it.
5. *Playing the projection.* When a patient expresses a perception that is a projection, the patient is asked to play the role of the person involved in the projection to discover his/her conflict in this area.
6. *Reversals.* The patient is asked to play a role opposite to his/her overt or expressed behavior (for example, to be aggressive rather than passive) and to recognize and make contact with the submerged or latent aspect of himself/herself.

7. *The rhythm of contact and withdrawal.* The natural inclination toward withdrawal is recognized and accepted, and the patient is permitted to experience the security of withdrawing temporarily.
8. *Rehearsal.* Since much of thinking is rehearsal in preparation for playing a social role, group members share rehearsals with one another.
9. *Exaggeration.* Exaggeration is also a repetition game. When the patient makes an important statement in a casual way, indicating that he/she does not recognize its importance, the patient is required to repeat it again and again with increasing loudness and emphasis.
10. *"May I feed you a sentence?"* The therapist suggests a sentence for the patient to repeat that the therapist feels represents something significant to the patient, so that the patient can try it on for size. This often involves interpretation (Patterson and Watkins, 1996, p. 370).

Since many of these techniques are very seductive to therapists and counselors, the reader should note Yontef's (1995) admonition not to mechanically apply them. Failure to place Gestalt technique as secondary to the client's or patient's needs is not acceptable.

Gestalt Therapy Applied to Issues of Intimacy

The application of Gestalt therapy to people who are struggling with issues of intimacy is particularly appropriate (see Case History 3.2). If a person does not form an intimate bond with a significant other and feels no distress, therapy or counseling is not indicated. However, while a functioning person may settle for being alone it is unlikely that a person would choose to be isolated, disconnected, and solitary. Aloneness and isolation most frequently conjure up a need within the person for intimacy. Forming a relationship involves dealing with one's boundaries and the boundaries of another. Maintaining a relationship necessitates being present with the other in the here and now. At least some of that contact must be of the *I* and *Thou* variety, in which each partner contacts the other person as person not as thing. Perhaps it is only within this context that intimacy occurs. Certainly such issues are consistent with the approaches of Gestalt therapy.

Perls et al. (1951), Wheeler and Backman (1994), and Yontef (1995) point out that being aware and conscious of being here and now are essential to being alive. Wheeler and Backman also make it clear that being present in the moment, with the other, is essential for intimacy. However, being present, although necessary for intimacy, is not sufficient. In addition, two people must neither be enmeshed nor self-contained but, with boundaries intact, maintain psychological contact.

According to Yontef (1995) the extent to which a person is in the past (unfinished business), or in the future (catastrophizing), is the extent to which awareness and contact are compromised. Patterson and Watkins (1996)

Issues of Intimacy—Rohana and Herbert Crown

Mrs. Crown contacted the therapist because she was distressed with her marriage. She complained that she was isolated in the family setting and that her husband and their children held her to be the source of all the family's distress. She said all of this in a somewhat breathy and almost tearful way and with a great deal of dramatic affect. After a few individual sessions it seemed to the therapist that this was, at least, a couples' issue if not a family issue. The therapist encouraged Mrs. Crown to invite her husband to come to the next session in which the three of them would explore couples issues. It was evident in the following session that the Crowns were not really talking to each other and were experiencing a great deal of pain related to the lack of connection.

Both Mr. and Mrs. Crown were given an MMPI and a Rorschach test to assess the level of distress and the level of ego integrity. No other assessment instruments were used since both of them were quite socially skilled and doing well in terms of raising their children, paying their bills, and so on. MMPI data on Mrs. Crown suggested that she would respond to emotional stress in a dramatic, one might say hysterical, fashion. Mr. Crown's MMPI indicated that his primary concern was diffuse anxiety. Rorschach findings (Exner scoring and interpretation) supported these intrapsychic focal points.

As an example of therapy, an excerpt from the twelfth session is presented.

> THERAPIST: Mrs. Crown, you seem to feel that your husband doesn't listen to you.
>
> MRS. CROWN: Yes, that's it.
>
> THERAPIST: Don't tell me, tell him—tell *him* directly, clearly.
>
> MRS. CROWN: I wish you [looking at Mr. Crown] would pay attention to me.
>
> THERAPIST: Do you mean—I want you to pay attention to me?
>
> MRS. CROWN: Yes.
>
> THERAPIST: Why don't you tell him that?
>
> MRS. CROWN: [in a meek and feminine voice] I want you to pay attention to me.
>
> MR. CROWN: [to therapist, in a strong, somewhat overpowering voice] I always pay attention to her.
>
> THERAPIST: Tell her.

MR. CROWN: [in the same powerful voice, to Mrs. Crown] I always pay attention to you.

MRS. CROWN: [head down, silence]

THERAPIST: Say to your husband, the way he talks to you, **I want you to pay attention to me.**

MRS. CROWN: **I want you to pay attention to me.** [Therapist was chilled here; she sounded exactly like the overbearing self-presentation of the husband.]

MR. CROWN: [his mouth fell open and somewhat meekly he said] All right, what do you want to tell me?

MRS. CROWN: I want you to let me see our financial statement so I know where we stand.

At this point Mr. Crown hemmed and hawed and Mrs. Crown became more insistent. The demand to know about the finances was really a demand for equal power. When power and power sharing became the issue in therapy and when the couple began talking directly to each other and asking for what they wanted, they began to look at each other, occasionally and then not so occasionally would touch each other gently. Towards the end of therapy (lengthened by a serious personal crisis) they expressed an intimacy toward each other that they stated they had not felt since they were first married.

---

argued that most people who need or would profit from a Gestalt approach are those who display few if any overt "symptoms," but are inhibited, "overcontrolled" individuals. Interpersonally, many of these people often give the impression of being cold and distant. Such an interpersonal presentation would make intimacy difficult to achieve or sustain.

The emphasis of Gestalt therapy on the organism–environment field (rather than the individual as separate and distinct from the environment), and the differentiation of the field by boundaries, applies directly to the issue of intimacy. In order for a person to share himself or herself with another, not only must both people possess a self but also both must allow contact (must have somewhat permeable personal boundaries) between the *I* self and the *Thou* self. Certainly if the need for intimacy is unmet, subjective distress of sufficient intensity to require attention is likely.

Wheeler and Backman (1994) offer an excellent selection of articles supporting our contention that Gestalt therapy is essential in working with people whose distress revolves around unmet intimacy needs. Most of these articles deal with couples' issues. Each addresses different issues that lead couples to have difficulty in achieving intimacy.

Melnick and Nevis (1994) consider power as central with respect to intimacy. Intimacy cannot occur, they argue, unless each member of a couple has equal power in the relationship. It is the constant shifting between the poles of dominance and submission that, in part, creates the possibility of becoming intimate.

The second issue of intimacy is the notion of the *I–Thou* dialogue. When one partner treats the other like an object (*it*) and not a person (*thou*), intimacy is ruptured. Talking to one's partner in the second person, "you are just like that," turns the partner into an object. The Gestalt therapy insistence on using "I" language, and turning questions into statements, at least creates the foundation for intimacy to occur. Further, requiring both partners to talk to each other about what they are experiencing *right now* often allows for the couple to share an intimate experience, if only for a moment. Melnick and Nevis (1994) point out that an intimate moment is not necessarily intimacy; however, it may be the beginning or reawakening of intimacy.

Lee (1994) suggested another factor that inhibits intimacy and is uniquely suited to the Gestalt approach: shame. For Lee, shame represents a loss of voice and is a negative introject. The shame introject is an internalized negative belief related to the possibility of contact: "I am such an ugly duckling that nobody would want me." Once internalized, shame leads to shame attacks. An event, internal or external, triggers a shame reaction that leads the person to retreat or attack. In either case intimacy is foreclosed.

When both partners have a high degree of internalized shame, either partner's shame reaction will lead to a very powerful and negative interpersonal event. Lee argued that when shame is a partner's primary defensive reaction there is a profound need for emotional safety. For Gestalt therapists, emotional safety occurs when the person experiences adequate support. If the therapy can provide emotional safety or more accurately, create an emotionally safe climate, then couples can become aware of what triggers a shame reaction that leads to interpersonal and personal distress. If the triggers can be deactivated, then the couple will see each other differently and, ideally, more intimately.

Lee also argued that one corrective experience was rarely enough; this is a lesson that has to be learned over and over. Behind the self-destructive games lies a desire for connection. If the therapist can aid the couple to own their own shame and provide support for them, then perhaps the couple can begin to support each other. If the therapist can also help the couple to deal with the power imbalance, objectification of the other, and shame perhaps growth towards intimacy can resume.

> CASE HISTORY   **3.3**
>
> ## Issues of Meaning—Mark Stern

Mr. Stern was referred to the therapist because he had been loudly denying that he needed hospitalization and apparently had been threatening his physician, a diminutive woman. Mr. Stern was a large, well-kept, rawboned man who presented himself as competent and in command. He had been admitted to the hospital after a night of drinking during which he had raged at his wife. He had not engaged in physical violence nor had he broken furniture, however. When the therapist saw him he was well controlled, socially appropriate, but still somewhat overbearing. Since he was likely to be discharged the next day, the therapist decided to give him an interview and on the basis of what was revealed, use whatever evaluation instrument might be appropriate.

The following is a short excerpt from the initial interview.

CLIENT: I don't know why they referred me to a psychologist, there is nothing wrong with me.

THERAPIST: Well, since you are here let's explore a couple of issues, all right?

CLIENT: Well, I guess so.

THERAPIST: What led you to wind up here?

CLIENT: I was having a few drinks and reading some poetry and my wife came in and said no real man would read that stuff. Now poetry is pretty important to me and I really got mad. I screamed at her, don't remember exactly what I said.

THERAPIST: Mr. Stern, I sometimes write poetry. In fact I have a poem here in my desk. [The therapist got the poem out of the drawer and gave it to Mr. Stern. He read it and said—]

CLIENT: That's great [his eyes were somewhat misty]. Would you mind if I shared with you the *Rubaiyat of Omar Khayyam?*

THERAPIST: No, that's fine. [Mr. Stern then recited, from memory, from the *Rubaiyat.* It was the most moving poetry "reading" the therapist had ever heard. Towards the end this veritable mountain man had tears streaming down his face, as did the therapist. Perhaps this is what the existentialists meant by the encounter.]

CLIENT: Well, thank you. I think I will tell my wife how important poetry is to me and tell her to accept that part of me or, tragically, we will have to part. I think that's all I need.

THERAPIST: So do I. Let me know what happens when you get home and if you and your wife want to see me, let me know.

Two weeks later Mr. Stern called the therapist. He said that he had told his wife something like what he said in the office, and she said she was very sorry and that she loved him. He dropped the therapist a postcard some years later. He was the president of a large union and his marriage was fine.

Issues of Meaning and Generativity: The Existential Solution

Existentialism as a philosophy grew out of the angst of Europe, beginning around 1840 with Kierkegaard, and formalized by Jean Paul Sartre's, *L'être et neant* (*Being and Nothingess*, 1956). Sartre held that the existential problem was to wrest meaning out of nothingness, chaos, and absurdity. He referred to two kinds of being: being in itself and being for itself. Being in itself describes the existence of things. A thing's essence (basic nature) is determined by its existence, and so long as it exists, it is *this* thing. A rose is a rose (with apologies to Gertrude Stein); it doesn't suddenly become a buttercup.

Being for itself is, according to Sartre, characteristic of human beings. A human being's essence, he argued, is not determined by that person's existence. Rather, a human being's essence is determined by his or her choices. Sartre understood that forces external to the individual act upon every person, and argued that what one chooses to do with these realities is what makes the person who he or she "is."

External forces often contrive to make independent choice difficult. When one feels insecure, it often feels good to give up making choices and to let someone else make them for you. Fromm (1941) noted that often troubled people surrender freedom for promised security; he especially referred to the choice to become Nazis. In fact, Sartre argued that choosing is often so difficult and the choices so ambiguous that people desire to become thing-like. However, even choosing not to choose is to make a choice, and to deny responsibility for that choice is something for which one is responsible. The not choosing, the denial of responsibility for one's actions, can lead one to become a mindless automaton, can lead one to abandon one's humanity. Riesman, Glazer, and Denney (1950) captured the developing non-choice psyche of America with their concept of the marketing personality. The term referred to becoming whatever is required by others to get ahead. They pointed out many of the negative consequences of such a shallow self-definition.

It is with these issues—of being, meaning, tragedy, isolation, and free-dom—that existential therapists struggle. Each human being is ultimately alone with his or her choices and with the inevitability of his or her own non-being, death. It takes courage to continue to be human, to choose, and to take responsibility for those choices in the face of a world often gone mad. It takes courage to choose when it is unclear where a particular choice will lead. It is hard to continue to act, to choose in the face of personal loss and tragedy. We hold that Fromm was right when he said that conducting therapy was somewhat like sharing in a particular person's own epic poem. It is within this context that Case History 3.3 illustrates what a therapist might do with someone in the group of an existential crisis.

Many practitioners have placed themselves in the existential tradition and have suggested that their therapy orientation is "existential" (Frankl, 1963; May, 1961; and Yalom, 1980, to cite a few). However, there has often seemed to be confusion about what existential therapists do in their therapy and counseling. Some existentially oriented therapists (May is one example) claim they are not interested in doing something with the client or patient but rather in relating not with the client or patient in an *authentic way.* Exactly what this means is not clear.

If there were no guidelines about how one conveyed, or rather established, an *authentic relationship,* existential therapy would be philoso-phy, not psychology. Yalom (1980) was reasonably clear in stating that the authentic relationship is very similar to Rogers's therapeutic relation-ship. Yalom argued that the therapist establishes an egualitarian relation-ship, with the therapist serving as a guide or senior colleague to the client rather than a controller or manipulator. The therapist encourages the individ-ual to make choices. It seems to us that Yalom implicitly endorsed the Gestalt notion that change cannot take place unless the individual has enough support to act, to risk change. If the focus of therapy is on making choices, what are the choices, and how does one aid the person to make those choices?

Yalom's approach (1980) to existential therapy called for a focus on what he called the four ultimate concerns: death, freedom, isolation, and meaning-lessness. Yalom argued that an individual's choices in struggling with these issues is central in determining whether or not a person can live fully and well in this ambiguous world.

Yalom also held that death, in an existential sense, is the issue of *my* personal non-being, *my* own death. It is curious that conflicts about death are rarely the focal point for distress in the aged (see Chapter 4 in this text for a full discussion of this notion). Rather the aged fear abandonment and, as Erikson (1963) suggested, loss of integrity. It is middle-aged people who, in one way or another, first confront their own mortality (through the death of close friends, serious disease, loss of physical and sexual prowess, and so forth) and are therefore consumed and troubled by death. How one deals with concerns about one's own death plays an important part, Yalom argued, in how well one will live the rest of one's life.

The questions of meaning, freedom, and isolation also seem to gain prominence in middle age. Unresolved issues of intimacy lead to a growing feeling of isolation. A realization that one's life work and belief system does not provide really good answers to the larger question of meaning may lead to personal distress. How many people who gain awareness that what they are doing has no meaning have the courage and the freedom to act, to change where they are and what they are doing?

Yalom argued that Freud's notion of anxiety as the cause of distress is correct, but that Freud had it wrong in terms of what caused anxiety. Rather than intrapsychic conflicts related to childhood trauma, Yalom held that awareness of one's ultimate concerns caused anxiety. An existentially oriented therapist deals with these concerns to the extent that they constitute the issues causing anxiety. Yalom devoted his work to developing a general method for dealing with these basic concerns of death, meaninglessness, isolation, and freedom.

Yalom stated that confrontation with one's own death has a profound impact on a person. Yalom did not specify at what age that confrontation occurred, but certainly his example of his own confrontation with death is consistent with our contention that the issue of one's own death becomes paramount in mid-life. If dealt with, death awareness and the anxiety it produces can lead to growth and active engagement in life and living. He gives several examples of people with serious and terminal illnesses who, when faced with death, cease their neurotic preoccupations. One patient on discovering she had cancer lost all of her social phobic reactions. Yalom (1980) quotes that patient as saying that, "cancer cures psychoneurosis" (p. 160). Perhaps when faced with the reality of one's impending death one's neurotic concerns no longer hold power over the individual.

One of the specific techniques Yalom proposed is related to the ability to focus on what is important in the face of death. He called this process *disidentification,* and offered specific techniques to aid people in the resolution of death anxiety. One technique required the therapist to ask the clients or patients to give eight important answers to the question "Who am I?" The responses were to be arranged, in order, from most important to least important to each person's self-definition. The clients or patients were then asked to spend a short time imagining what it would be like to be without each attribute. As they dropped one after another of those attributes they held to be essential to their self-definition, many observed that after giving up all these attributes, they, as individuals, still remained. Those who were affected by this exercise experienced a sense of awareness that behind all their roles, all their accomplishments, there remains a core self able to choose and to act even without the accumulation of roles, attributes, and accomplishments that they had held to be so important.

Another technique was to ask the individual to draw a straight line. One end was to represent birth, the other death. The client or patient was asked to place a cross on the line to represent where they were on their *life line*. Each person was then told to meditate on this for five minutes.

Finally, Yalom offered an exercise that he referred to as *calling out*. Members in reasonably large groups were divided into groups of three and asked to discuss something of importance to themselves. At some point each person was asked to write his or her name on a card and place it face down in a common pile. One of the group members was asked to select a name from the common pile and call the name aloud. The group member identified turned his or her back on the group and was no longer attended to by the others. According to Yalom many group members experienced a sense of the fragility of their existence and the arbitrary nature of life experiences. Yalom suggested other death awareness techniques, but these few are sufficient to give the reader an idea of his work.

A less contrived way to bring death awareness into the consciousness of clients or patients is for them to interact with someone who is actually dying and to listen to what that person has to say about life and death. Yalom (1980) reported that he has had group members observe terminal cancer groups. He reported that this experience had profound effects on many of his patients. One patient had organized her life around her search for what Yalom called "an ultimate rescuer." When she observed the cancer group, she developed a fantasy that she needed to get cancer so she could be with Yalom until she died. Yalom countered this with the observation that no relationship is forever and that it was possible he would die before she did. After this gentle confrontation, Yalom stated, his patient began to deal with her rescuer fantasy through the reality that all relationships end and that one's meaning is not given by another but rather by oneself. Yalom gave other examples of how confrontation with real death and dying encouraged many of his patients to get on with the business of living. It seems to us that much of the effect that Yalom reported was due to Yalom, the person, rather than these techniques. Yet the techniques, if handled carefully, could be of use.

First, Yalom focused on the death issue and gradually explored how this concern affects a particular person, but gently and with a supportive style. Any of his techniques may be employed to increase a client's death awareness if this concern seems to be central in blocking effective functioning. Second, he separated issues of death into different components, and rationally attempted to reduce the fear associated with each component. In order for these attempts to be successful, the magnificent sensitivity of Yalom, or of any good therapist, must be present. Again, the therapeutic relationship, although not sufficient, is necessary for effective psychotherapy and counseling.

In addition to death, as noted earlier Yalom also focused on freedom, isolation, and meaninglessness. When the existential issue of freedom is dealt with, then a person can make choices, assume responsibility for his or her life, and confront meaninglessness and isolation. To not make choices is to remain paralyzed in some meaningless cycle. If isolation and meaninglessness are confronted, then one can establish authentic relationships and find meaning even in isolation and loss. It seems to us that Yalom had no specific technique for dealing with these issues other than to focus on them within the context of a therapeutic relationship. Perhaps if the therapist has dealt with his or her own existential concerns such an approach will facilitate the client's or patient's resolution of the ultimate life issues. We are in essential agreement with Patterson and Watkins (1996) that Yalom's approach is very similar to Rogers's person-centered focus with respect to the importance of the therapeutic relationship.

However, when the approach taken by Frankl (1960, 1963, 1965) is considered, a rather different view of existentially oriented psychotherapy and counseling emerges. Frankl was much more directive in his approach to therapy than Yalom or Rogers. Perhaps this was because he often worked with seriously disturbed people. Perhaps it was because of his own experience in life. One cannot, as Frankl did, survive a Nazi death camp without being marked. In any event, Frankl developed some very specific techniques to facilitate resolution of that profound sense of isolation and meaninglessness that, in part, characterizes people who are more seriously disturbed than those we have previously discussed.

Frankl held that the focus of therapy and counseling is to allow the person to find meaning in the face of the capriciousness and tragedy of life. He concluded that two techniques could aid the therapist in easing the client or patient into achieving a sense of spiritual meaning: *dereflection* and *paradoxical intention*. Spiritual meaning refers to the ability to face suffering and to make one's individual and unique response to that suffering. Frankl felt that only by achieving spiritual meaning could life be lived fully and well.

When a person is paralyzed by anxiety, paradoxical intention is a useful technique. If that person anticipates that failing, being found out a fraud, or what have you, he or she is likely to become enmeshed in a self-defeating pattern of avoiding acting, which reinforces the anticipatory anxiety. If an individual is incapable of giving a speech for fear of embarrassment, Frankl would encourage that person to imagine speaking and to try to become embarrassed. For example, the therapist might say, "Make yourself as embarrassed as you can; see if you can turn your toes red." Frankl argued that when the patient intentionally tries to elicit the feared reaction, the patient will stop fighting the fears (anxieties) and the vicious cycle will be broken.

When a person pays excessive attention to some personal issue or engages in unending self-examination of his or her distress (or "symptoms" or both) then the technique of dereflection may be useful. Dereflection means to turn attention away from; to ignore. This technique not only requires the therapist to direct the individual's attention away from self-preoccupying thoughts but also requires the therapist to turn that person's attention toward some positive goal or focus. When Frankl used dereflection he often used it in a very directive fashion.

With one patient who suffered from schizophrenia Frankl employed dereflection with great force. When his patient complained of hearing voices and how distressing that was, Frankl almost ordered her not to pay attention to the voices or what they were saying. To paraphrase, Frankl said, "Let the doctors take care of that, that's what they're for" (Frankl, 1963). He then asked the patient to focus on something she could do creatively. We assume that Frankl knew this person had specific artistic ability and therefore the redirected attention had someplace real to go.

These two techniques are often useful with very distressed and even disturbed patients. Curiously, they are also useful for people prone to excessive use of intellectualization. As such, these techniques, gently employed, could be of some use with the people we have described in this chapter. If life has lost its meaning because of anticipatory anxiety concerning loss or other problems of middle age, then paradoxical intention could be of use in allowing the person to face this conflict. If a middle-aged individual is brooding about age-relevant concerns, then the gentle use of dereflection may be appropriate.

Conclusion

All the examined therapies in this chapter, person-centered therapy, Gestalt therapy, and existential therapy, are humanistic and phenomenological in focus. They hold that to know a person one must be able to experience reality as that person experiences it. Some advocates of each of the humanistic approaches we have discussed have stated that theirs is the one and only approach. Often theorists have advocated changes in technique but have maintained that they are still adhering to a particular theoretical orientation. For example, Ivey et al. (1997) and Cormier and Hackney (1993) made it clear that substantive changes in person-centered techniques were required if the therapy was to be effective with the whole range of troubled people who seek counseling and psychotherapy. Yontef (1995) maintained that with modification in technique, Gestalt therapy was useful even for severely disturbed people. However if one modifies technique, then it is no longer the same therapy at all. Yontef probably imposed structure and was more active when he worked with severely disturbed individuals. Certainly he didn't encourage the patient to engage in Gestalt games, or if he did, he did so only when that person had made significant progress in therapy. If you do not do what Perls did, you are not doing Gestalt therapy; you are doing something else.

Yalom (1980) and May (1963) indicated that all therapy was existential therapy and in a sense they are right. In that same sense, all therapy is person-centered therapy and is Gestalt therapy. Insofar as one deals with existential issues, one's therapy is existential. Insofar as one deals with the here and now, boundary conditions, and *I–Thou* issues, one's therapy is

Gestalt. Yet a therapist must employ more than any or even all of these humanistic approaches to be of service to troubled people.

One focus of humanistically oriented approaches is the importance of the therapeutic relationship. Although necessary for successful therapy, this relationship is not likely to be sufficient except when all the person needs is to be able to listen to what he or she is saying to and about himself or herself. If a person is struggling with the issue of identity and little else, then person-centered therapy and the relationship skills indicated by Ivey et al. (1997) and Cormier and Hackney (1993) should be sufficient. We would argue that a consistent low-intensity warm (*LM*) role as described by Cooper, Adams, Dickinson, and York (1975) is likely to produce a perception by the client that the therapist is consistent and caring. If the therapist is capable of accurate empathy, the client probably will perceive the therapist as knowledgeable. Rogers (1957) argued that therapy should be short-term, and for identity issues this is likely to be the case.

When the individual is struggling with issues of intimacy, a Gestalt approach is suggested. The focus on the here and now, *I* and *Thou*, is tailored to work with people who are isolated or, for example, have lost the sense of intimacy. Again, if the therapist assumes the warm, empathetic *LM* role (more or less intense as the client's intensity increases or decreases), it is likely that the therapist will encourage the client to perceive the therapist as kind and consistent. Attention to the specific issues of the person's or couple's distress, and a reframing of those issues, can lead the client to perceive the therapist as knowledgeable. Again, therapy is likely to be short-term *if* the problem with intimacy has emerged in young adulthood and is not enmeshed with severer issues.

When problems of meaning and concerns about the significance of one's life emerge in middle age and cause distress, then an existential approach may be useful. Recognition by the therapist of the client's sense of existential distress is required. Case History 3.3 demonstrates that the therapist needs to focus clearly on the immediate existential distress of the individual.

The therapist must assume a warm but not dominant role (*LM* or *JK*) to establish a perception on the part of the client that the therapist is open and attentive to the client's concerns. For all of these approaches, the level of control or structure, or the level of activity of the therapist, needs to be relatively low. If more serious problems emerge in a particular session, or if more careful analysis shows the problem of the client to be more severe than initially judged, then more structure should be provided, and the therapist should be more active.

For all of these approaches, it is expected that the duration of therapy will be short. If the client is not able to resolve problems in a few weeks, then the therapist should consider the possibility that the person is more seriously disturbed. For example, the length of treatment for Case History 3.3 was one session. It was not that the therapist was brilliant but rather that the client needed only that one session to wrest meaning out of his life and to resolve what had been extremely distressing to that person.

The content of therapy for these approaches focuses on the self-imposed violations of the legitimate needs of the person. Therapy—both technique and content—involves getting one out of one's own way. Many people who are socially skilled need to stop bending over backward and stop blocking satisfaction of their own legitimate needs and goals. Once freed, these relatively competent people can continue the life task of being all that they can be or can become.

4 Issues of Older People: The Question of Integrity

While the issues of late adolescence and adulthood revolve around self-definition, intimacy, and generativity, such issues are not likely to be the center of distress for older people. People who had been successful in life may not necessarily continue to feel fulfilled or completed as they grow old. Older people face age-related problems that may erode earlier successes and reduce their sense of well-being. People who have suffered only minor psychological distress may, as they age, slip into despair over the inevitable losses that occur (Cath & Sadavoy, 1991).

When personal distress becomes too great and life is no longer valued, what can psychotherapy or psychosocial intervention offer to older people? The answer to this question is the subject of this chapter. There are two separate and distinct answers. One concerns older people who are neurologically intact; the other concerns older people who are not neurologically intact or whose physical problems do not allow them to function independently.

The level of disturbance or dissatisfaction determines what psychosocial strategy is appropriate. We would argue that some variant of a Jungian approach is necessary. For intact older people we would expect a rather close fit with the Jungian approach and that treatment would be intermittent and relatively low in structure as opposed to continuous and highly structured (Kastenbaum, 1978; Shows, 1977). If an older person is no longer able to communicate, or suffers from late-onset deafness that also compromises communication, different psychosocial strategies are required. However, even neurologically damaged older persons have had rich life experiences, and the therapist's continuing search for links to these life experiences, although frustrating, seems to us to offer a practical way of helping these people to maintain as much dignity and integrity as is possible.

Jung argued that to achieve integrity, a new self-realization must occur. Jung (1960) stated that this self-realization occurred in the second half of life. A person suffering from Alzheimer's disease or other forms of dementia cannot maintain or realize the Jungian self. We contend that any treatment approach for these people must struggle with the psychological consequences of this loss and its effect on the older person's loved ones.

Analytical Psychotherapy: Carl Jung

Jung and his followers presented his analytic psychology as an alternative to psychoanalysis. Many of Jung's followers held that his system was the last word, the final truth, in psychology. Certainly, none of the humanistic approaches we have discussed or any other approach would be required if Jung's disciples were correct. We have consistently challenged any approach to the treatment of disturbed or distressed human beings that advertises itself as the only approach. Jung's theory and methods do not escape this challenge.

What is it that merits Jung's work being included in a systematic approach to therapy? It seems to us that Jung's focus and therapy were targeted to problems of older individuals. For the great bulk of his career Jung worked with well-educated people who were in the second half of life. We suggest that many of these people could be described as suffering from a crisis of values and beliefs (Jung, 1960).

The fundamental question of encounters with aging and loss is not, what does it all mean (really an existential question) but rather what do *I* mean—in a universal nontrivial sense. The aged do not regard death as nonbeing but rather as a terrible mystery. Often people will flee to fundamental religious beliefs to resolve this primal terror. Fundamental Christianity, many cults, some of the most orthodox Jewish sects, many radical Muslim sects, and many other similar religious or quasi-religious groups offer such salvation. Yet an individual answer or, rather, resolution of the awful and universal mystery can neither occur in a crowd nor can be read from a book.

It is with this and similar issues that Jung struggled. It is those who sought to find their individual epiphany, their *self* (in Jung's terms), whom he primarily treated. In order to place his ideas into a framework that does justice to them and makes them accessible to a majority of readers who are not Jungian scholars, we will present an overview of Jung's personality theory. It is a theory so original, so bold, and so comprehensive that no theorist since or before him has offered so many novel and controversial ideas. Since we have maintained that theory should dictate therapy, we will present a sketch of Jung's theory and then show the linkage between the theory and therapy.

Basic Jungian Concepts

Structure of the Personality. Jung posited three basic structural personality components. They are the *ego*, the *personal unconscious*, and the *collective unconscious.* The ego is that part of the personality of which one is aware. The personal unconscious is that part of the personality of which one is unaware. The personal unconscious consists of memories that stem from one's experience. The collective unconscious is that part of the personality that contains the racial history not only of humanity but also of animal species.

The first two concepts offer few problems to many practicing psychotherapists. It is the third concept, the collective unconscious, which causes difficulty. We shall discuss the first two concepts in terms of their implications for therapy and then discuss more generally the third concept.

The ego (personal conscious), if defined as internal self-talk, can be changed by a variety of cognitive, behavioral, and humanistic therapeutic techniques. The problematic parts of the personal unconscious involved what Jung called *complexes*. Complexes are clusters of unconscious memories that have motivational force, are often disruptive, and are therefore the focus of therapeutic intervention. Psychoanalytic techniques as described by Freud focused on such problems. We shall argue that Hayes, Ellis, Meichenbaum, and Lazarus have given us a substantial set of techniques to allow individuals to become conscious of these complexes or to be able to talk to themselves about them.

More problematic for therapists and scientific thinkers in general is the notion of the collective unconscious. Jung argued that all human beings possess the same collective unconscious. If one were to take that to mean that all human beings possess the same instincts or species-specific behaviors, the notion of collective unconscious would cause no theoretical or practical problems.

It is clear that Jung meant the collective unconscious to mean more than instincts only. To paraphrase Jung, the collective unconscious is the repository of the wisdom of the human species in the form of potential remembrances. Such information, he argued, does not exist, as such, in an individual person's psyche but rather exists as potential or possible. It seems to us that such a notion would be sympathetic with Plato's theory that all learning is remembering. What is remembered and how it is remembered emerge as questions that require serious attention and serious answers or abrupt dismissal.

Jung suggested that religions, mythology, certain commonly shared subjective events, and other, similar processes all give reason to support the contention that shared universal meanings determine the content of what is remembered. For example, Jung (1960) argued that notions of God, justice, truth, beauty, and other monumental ideas exist in some form for all human beings in all times.

God, for instance, may or may not exist. That is, may or may not be real in a physical sense. However, Jung argued that each of us struggles with the concept or the experience of God. This *subjective struggle,* he argued, is universal. How one deals with such issues (God, truth, and so forth) is extraordinarily important in understanding a particular person's *psyche* (personality).

Jung argued that there are two kinds of facts. First, there are *physical facts:* if God exists, prove it (demonstrate his/her/its existence empirically, publicly, and with high levels of consensual validation). Second, there are *psychological facts:* universal experiences that occur subjectively for all people (again consensual validation is required; also required is truthfulness and an accurate description of the subjective state).

The Archetypes. Jung attempted to further specify the *what* of the collective unconscious with his notion of *archetypes.* Perhaps Jung meant archetypes to be equivalent to psychological facts. In any event, the most important archetype is the notion of the self. Jung did not refer to the existential self, the looker never seen, or the self of Rogers and person-centered therapists, or Freud's ego, or the object-relation theorist's pre-Oedipal self. According to Jung the self as archetype is the universal potential for a new center of the psyche that emerges in the second half of life.

The self as an accomplished event, in other words, *myself,* cannot occur unless the individual achieves balance between sets of opposites. Many of the oppositions within the self-system are archetypes. These opposites may be best considered real contradictions, because they are nonresolvable but necessary oppositions. They do not simultaneously exist physically, but rather must simultaneously exist psychically if we are to be complete as human beings. *I* cannot be both a man and woman, yet if *I* am all man, *I* am a brute, a taker. If *I* am all woman, *I* am too pliable and cannot take for *myself.* Many would argue that these characterizations are sexist and that if this is what Jung believed he was simply wrong. However, Jung would not have referred to man/woman but rather to *anima/animus*—the male and female principle, or archetypes, that exist in opposition within all of us. According to Jung there are many other archetypes and all of them are in opposition within the self-system. In order for the self to emerge, the oppositions must be surmounted through what Jung called the *transcendent function.* This new center of the psyche, the self, is part of all levels of consciousness and casts all archetypes into an individually achieved harmony.

The emergence of a fully realized self is the Holy Grail of Jungian psychology and may be just as elusive. However, if such contradictions are psychological realities then the notion that balance must be achieved across these contradictions seems reasonable. How such balance is to be achieved will be discussed as the focus of Jung's approach to therapy. First it is necessary to list the archetypes. Second, a somewhat more detailed discussion of the contradictions is necessary for a satisfactory analysis of how these issues are addressed in Jungian psychotherapy.

First we shall consider the archetype of the *persona.* The persona is the public personality. The specific content of one's public personality comes from culture and individual experiences. However, all people have some form of public mask, or persona. The need for one is a basic psychological fact. When a society demands a persona that destroys a person's individuality, that demand demonstrates how the persona can be destructive. On the other hand, to get rid of the persona leaves the person without a social identity. Hopche (1995) pointed out that having no social identity is as detrimental to the development of self-realization as having an overly developed one. To be socially skilled without being phony, to be an individual and yet capable of relating to collective humanity are to have a persona that is in balance with other parts of the psyche.

The persona is often in conflict with the ego (similar to Freud's ego) and the *shadow archetype* (the vital animal side of man's nature). When these three elements of the psyche are brought into balance, part of what is required for the emergence of the self has occurred. As an example an individual might say, "I'm a member of this culture but I'm not consumed by it. I have a sense of passion that does not overwhelm me but energizes my existence. This passion is not something I can consciously put on or take off. It is not part of my conscious self-definition but it and my self-definition exist with a sense of harmony."

Jung also argued that two other basic Jungian concepts, *attitudes* and *functions,* were in conflict. The attitudes of the psyche, according to Jung, are *extroversion* and *introversion.* The extroverted person is oriented toward people and the external world. The introverted person is oriented toward his or her subjective internal world. Jung stated that these orientations were in opposition. Eysenck (1952b) offered empirical evidence that supported Jung's notion that introversion and extroversion were basic dimensions of personality. To these functions in opposition Jung added thinking and feeling as well as sensing and intuiting. He argued that all of these oppositions needed to come into balance for the individual to become fully realized. It should be also noted that the Myers-Briggs Personality Inventory (Myers, 1962) uses the latter four functions, and that the Myers-Briggs inventory is often used in industrial settings in personnel selection (Maduro & Wheelwright, 1977).

Jungian Therapy

How does an individual reach this union of opposites, this personal epiphany? According to Jung, the analyst does not remain passive but amplifies or connects the person to either failures in maturation (the type of issues Freud dealt with), or to failures in connecting with aspects of the collective unconscious. Jung's primary focus in therapy is based on the notion that whenever one part of the collective unconscious is suppressed, that part will become manifest in a self-destructive fashion. For example, if an individual is always the outgoing, demonstrative extrovert, some day that individual will experience uncertainty in a public forum and may be reduced to feelings of panic and despair. Jung advocated a dialectical procedure as an essential part of facilitating self-realization.

CASE HISTORY   **4.1**

Issues of Integrity—Emma McIntire

Ms. Emma McIntire was referred to the therapist by another client. She was seventy-seven years old and stated that her major problem was a diffuse sense of being unconnected. The immediate crisis that led her to seek help was the ending of a brief affair between herself and a younger (fifty-seven-year-old) man. She reported that this relationship had not brought her the sense of "connectedness" that she was seeking, that she wanted something but really couldn't put her finger on what it was. During the initial interview, the client reported that she felt a lack of connection throughout her life. She was the only child of a wealthy couple and was raised by a series of nannies. She reported that she had experienced her mother and father as distant people with whom she had had a formal and rather cold relationship. In adolescence she discovered sexuality and then felt "connected" with others. She married a man somewhat older than she when she was twenty, and she was widowed when she was forty-six years old. She entered college at that time and received a degree in library science. She had been a librarian until her retirement at age seventy. She reported several affairs both before and after losing her husband.

The client was well oriented with respect to person, place, and time and showed no evidence of mental deterioration. Her appearance and dress were appropriate. To screen for severer psychopathology the Wechsler Adult Intelligence Scale and MMPI were administered. No evidence of dysfunction appeared on the WAIS and her intellectual level was high. Except for a slight peak on the depression scale there was no evidence of psychopathology on the MMPI. Because of her desire to resolve her sense that she was somehow not connected, a ten-session course of therapy was begun.

The following is a short excerpt from the seventh counseling session.

CLIENT: Doctor, I went to a Phoenix Club meeting last week and found that there are a lot of people who have the same needs I have; I mean they want to make sense out of "it."

THERAPIST: When you say "make sense out of it," I want to know what "it" is.

CLIENT: Well this group of people are all struggling with where they fit in a larger sense. I mean, I always thought religion was a bunch of baloney—believe in an old man with a gray beard and everything will be all right. But these people are talking about the human community and a larger purpose—I know that's not very clear.

THERAPIST: Seems to me your search for "connectedness" is tied up with this group search for larger meaning.

CLIENT: Yes, that's it! That feels right. It's not sex or "love" but human connectedness—a bunch of people just trying to make sense out of things.

The client later joined a religious group and was an active member until her death at age eighty-four. Perhaps her continued activity and her active search for "a larger purpose" contributed to the quality of life she enjoyed during her last few years.

Jung described the dialectical procedure as one in which the therapist took an active, engaged role, with the client treated like a colleague and the therapist serving as a mentor or guide. Jung (1960) suggested that the most useful way to facilitate connection with the collective psyche was through fantasy. Perhaps the dialogue in which the therapist and client engage concerns the client's fantasies. Such fantasies point to oppositions that have not yet been integrated into the self-system. According to Jung, "The symbol is not a sign that veils something that everybody knows. Such is not its significance; on the contrary, it represents an attempt to elucidate, by means of analogy, something that still belongs to the domain of the unknown or something that is yet to be. Imagination reveals to us, in the form of a more or less striking analogy, what is in the process of becoming" (Sahakian, 1976, p. 87). So it is through imagination and the careful analysis of the individual's struggles with his or her symbols that the process, the transcendent function, comes into being.

This ill-defined process seems to us to refer to an ongoing struggle to connect the person with subjective events that are rarely, if ever, conscious. Perhaps these subjective events are consistent with what Maslow (1970) called *peak experiences*. Peak experiences are those life events that enrich and free the individual. Such events are beyond insight and are more closely related to the notion of an epiphany or individual enlightenment. It seems to us that the occurrence of such an event is equivalent to the activation of Jung's transcendent function. Perhaps a continuing sense of fulfillment is necessary if the Jungian self is to emerge. We would suggest that with the emergence of a balanced, unified self there is a need to share that experience with others. Of course, that experience is the individual's and can only serve as a model for other individuals in discovering themselves.

It is this process of modeling or serving as a guide, a colleague in the quest, that characterizes the role of the Jungian therapist. The process of therapy takes the individual from problems of maturation through problems of being to the individual quest for fulfillment. Although both Jung's definition of the transcendent function and the means by which a therapist enables the patient to achieve it remain unclear, Jung was clear about the sequence of therapy and its stages.

Jung (1960) characterized therapy as consisting of four stages: *catharsis, elucidation, education,* and *transformation.* Catharsis refers to the spontaneous outflowing of emotions that occurs early in the therapeutic process. This emotional outflowing is triggered by remembered events of the patient's life, or events currently occurring in the patient's life. Jung stated that, while necessary, such outpouring was insufficient for successful therapy.

Elucidation refers to the understanding of and therefore insight into the sources of one's difficulties. Jung was clear that insight, although necessary for psychotherapy, was insufficient. Curiously enough he shared that awareness with many behaviorists who criticized psychoanalysis for failing to require behavioral change as well as insight before claiming success.

The third stage, education, is the process of learning how to solve life's problems, how to reinterpret life's defeats, and how to use one's abilities to anticipate difficulties in the future. We would note that many behavioral and cognitive approaches could apply here, although one might imagine Jung would not be at all happy with this suggestion.

What is different about his approach from all the others is his notion of transformation, the fourth step in Jungian psychotherapy. According to Jung, the personality of the therapist is the key element in the process of transformation. It is critical, Jung argued, that the therapist not only influence change in the individual but also must change himself or herself. In transformation the therapist transcends the doctor/patient relationship.

Jung was unclear how this process was to be achieved. We suggest that it is consistent with Jungian theory that the therapist achieve self-realization. Perhaps the therapist's achievement of his or her self is the aspect of the therapist's personality that impacts positively or negatively on the other person. In fact, Jung argued that therapy keyed toward self-realization is a dialectic process. He meant that the therapist and the patient engage in an unstructured search for the patient's new center of balance. Since neither the therapist nor the patient can rationally define what it is that the therapist must do to create a climate within which the patient's self can emerge, the therapist's specific tasks remain unclear.

Perhaps what Jung meant was the therapist must always be aware that both he or she and the patient are in the process of becoming. It is as though both were characters in an unfolding story for which the end has not yet been written. The first author of this text, in an encounter with Bruno Bettelheim, was told, "Michael, the therapist, you, the therapist, are the medium of change. Never mind the theory." Perhaps we therapists are not only the medium of change, but are also, or should be, subject to be changed by the medium.

It seems to us that a Jungian orientation is well suited to therapy with intact older individuals who are struggling with what we have called crises in values. To be confident that one's life has been and is part of a larger truth may be essential to the maintenance of integrity and dignity. People who can realize something like Jung's self are more than merely tranquil, as the stoics would have it. Such people can stare death in the face and not blink.

Psychosocial Intervention with the Elderly Who Have Difficulty in Communicating

Treatment Issues with the Frail Elderly

If an older person has significant neurological impairment, or any other physical problems that compromise communication, then unmodified Jungian analysis is not appropriate. Psychosocial interventions with older people, those Lazarus, Sadavoy, and Langsley (1991) called the frail elderly, need to be highly structured and focused only on short-term goals. As with the intact elderly, therapy with the frail elderly will inevitably deal with loss and the need to maintain integrity. In addition to psychotherapy, many other psychosocial interventions are required. Taulbee and Folsom's (1973) reality orientation, Feil's validation approach (1984), Hughes's self-enhancement approach (Hughes & Espinosa, 1990), any and all appropriate behavioral approaches, and what Hughes referred to as distraction, reassurance, restorative, supportive, and reminiscence techniques are specific treatment techniques that can be used with the frail elderly.

A word of caution is necessary here. No therapy approach or any other individual therapeutic technique is effective if used in a mechanical fashion. If a person is not responding to one's interventions, then something else must be tried.

In addition, the total environment of the treatment center, be it a day-care center or an individual's home, must meet the requirements of a therapeutic environment or *milieu*. By milieu we mean something like the environment described by Rappoport (1960) or suggested by Bettelheim (1974). Their basic ideas apply to the treatment environment required for effective psychosocial treatment of the elderly.

In essence, the environment should feel warm and noninstitutional. It should smell pleasant, neither like feces nor urine nor the aseptic smell of a hospital. The decor should not be spartan or institutional but rather comfortable and homelike. The setting should feel like a place in which one would like to be.

The elderly who suffer from psychiatric symptoms (depression, active hallucination, delusions, or who engage in other bizarre or peculiar feelings, thoughts, or actions) are almost always given psychoactive medication. Antipsychotic medications include the older phenothiazines, similar newer medication (Haldol and Prolixin are two in common use), newer antipsychotic drugs (clozapine and Reserpedol), and others. Some antipsychotic drugs sedate patients and all produce a variety of unwanted side effects.

Antidepressive medications include the tricyclics, MAO inhibitors, serotonin reuptake blockers (such as Prozac and Zoloft), and other antidepressive medications whose action is less well known. All antidepressive medications have side effects (see Appendix 2).

One important caution in prescribing tricyclic medications on an outpatient basis is their potential to exacerbate the suicidal potential for suicidal patients. MAO inhibitors have numerous very serious side effects. At present, the serotonin reuptake blockers are most frequently prescribed for depressed patients regardless of age. Such drugs also have undesirable side effects. Antianxiety medications, mood stabilizers, anticonvulsive medication (sometimes used for violent or agitated individuals), and a variety of other medications and somatic treatment including ECT (electroconvulsive therapy) and psychosurgery are also employed.

It is estimated that 60% of nursing home residents suffer from some form of dementia (Lazarus et al., 1991). Many of them suffer from Alzheimer's disease or from post-stroke damage. Since the side effects of antipsychotic medications compromise central nervous system function, it is clear that caution should be employed in the administration of these drugs to individuals suffering from documented brain damage. Lazarus et al. (1991) argued that nursing home residents are often overmedicated. They cite antipsychotic drugs as the drugs most overly prescribed. Often medications do little good for the patient but are useful for the nursing home staff because the medicated patient is much easier to "manage." Other categories of medications are also overused and have their own side-effect profile that is often very bad for the patient. For instance, the addictive potential for all benzodiazepines suggests that behavioral or psychological treatment of anxiety would be preferable to medications (again, see Appendix 2).

Finally, it needs to be said that ECT produces brain dysfunction (such as a seizure). Psychosurgery, by definition, destroys brain tissue. Certainly these treatments should be considered a last resort for people suffering from any form of dementia.

CASE HISTORY **4.2**

Issues of the Frail Elderly—Stephen Owens

Mr. Stephen Owens, a seventy-seven-year-old white widowed male, was admitted to an extended care facility by his family as a result of advanced symptoms of dementia, most probably Alzheimer's type. Prior to his admission, Mr. Owens's daughter, an exceptionally loving and emotionally supportive caregiver for the past five years, struggled with the concept of "institutionalizing" her father. She finally resigned herself to the fact that she could no longer care for him at home, based on her own schedule and her father's increasing disorientation and tendency to wander, which clearly compromised his safety and well-being.

The client's daughter reported that as recently as ten years ago Mr. Owens was a bright, intelligent, vital individual. The transition from his high-powered life as an executive at a major manufacturing company to a retiring, leisurely existence was difficult for the client. He did not possess many interests other than his work, except for spectator sports when time permitted. He took enormous pride in his work and was dedicated to his company and staff for nearly forty years. Although he was viewed as a caring father and husband by his daughter, Mr. Owens's work was the focal point of his life.

The initial interview was conducted in the dementia unit. The client presented as alert and intermittently oriented to person, place, and time. His affect was flattened and he experienced periods of forgetfulness and confusion. He was able to recall events from twenty and thirty years ago but his recent memory was extremely poor. Although he was able to ambulate independently, he appeared apprehensive and vulnerable in his new environment.

After several weeks of placement, the client appeared to be experiencing a significant cognitive decline as evidenced by a decreased attention span, increased difficulty in following previously understood directions, and a decline in his ability to participate in toileting, bathing and dressing, and other activities of daily living. In addition, staff observations indicated he exhibited increased irritability and restlessness. Staff members requested social service consultation with the patient as a result of his persistent, agitated outbursts.

The following is a short excerpt from the third session.

THERAPIST: Good morning, Mr. Owens. You appear to be somewhat upset.

PATIENT: Well, yes, I am upset.

THERAPIST: Can you tell me what is upsetting you?

PATIENT: I have to get out of here now. Right now! Nobody is helping me to get out. They say I have to stay here.

THERAPIST: Why do you have to leave right now?

PATIENT: I have to get to work. I'm already late for the corporate meeting. Where is my car?

THERAPIST: This meeting sounds very important to you.

PATIENT: It is. Can I leave now?

THERAPIST: Mr. Owens, can you tell me some more about this meeting?

PATIENT: We have these meetings once a week. I have to let them know about the manufacturing contracts. I take care of all the contracts, you know.

THERAPIST: Mr. Owens, I'd like to take you over to the window for a moment. Is that all right with you?

PATIENT: Yeah.

THERAPIST: It is a very cold January day. The weather forecaster predicts snow as well. It appears to me the weather may be quite difficult for you to drive in to your meeting.

PATIENT: Well, I don't know.

THERAPIST: Do you think you may be more comfortable staying in today out of the cold, icy weather and driving conditions?

PATIENT: Well, maybe.

THERAPIST: I'd like to know more about your work and the corporate meetings. If you'd like to talk about it with me, we can go to the dining room. It's warm and cozy in there and we can have a cup of tea together.

PATIENT: That sounds all right with me.

The interaction between the client and the therapist was illustrative of the validation technique application. To employ reality orientation, that is to say, to remind Mr. Owens that he is retired, hasn't worked in ten years, hasn't driven for five years, and is a permanent resident at the facility, predictably would have escalated his level of agitation. The therapist needed to be at the same place and time with the client for the technique to be effective, and to be sensitive to his need to possibly reenact or role play his corporate position in the company in the dining room setting. The client exhibited more relaxed, controlled behavior and appeared empowered as he shared his experiences with the therapist about what was nearest and dearest to him now as it was throughout his lifetime—his work. This successful technique was shared with staff for future application.

Psychotherapy and Counseling with the Frail Elderly

Individual or group psychotherapy with the frail elderly requires that the candidate for therapy have adequate communication skills to allow meaningful interpersonal interactions to occur. Specifically, the frail elderly person must be able to recognize the therapist and, in a group setting, other group members, and must be able to process information, albeit in simplified fashion. In addition, the frail elderly person must be able to retain enough information relative to his or her difficulties to allow some continuity from therapeutic session to session. Again, the level of retention need not be as complete as would be the case with the intact elderly.

Given that these minimal requirements are met, what does the therapist then do? What therapeutic interventions does the therapist employ? And what is the content for effective therapeutic interaction? These are the primary questions with which this text is concerned. In this chapter we begin to answer them with regard to older people.

It is important to note that the major approaches to psychotherapy— psychoanalytical, cognitive–behavioral, and humanistic—largely neglected the elderly. One exception to that general pattern was Jung, whose practice, as we noted earlier, included many patients in the second half of life. Often, therapy in a generic sense is prescribed for the frail elderly. It is our contention that there is no generic therapy for everyone or for all disorders. What we hope to do is to focus on the therapists who have claimed success with the frail elderly and to find out what they did. Only recently, as our population has continued to age, are caretakers becoming aware that more frail elderly individuals require treatment. These people are going to be seeking and deserve to receive more effective psychosocial treatment, psychotherapy, and counseling.

It has long been held that even for the intact elderly, individual psycho- therapy is inappropriate. Freud (1964) held that individual psychotherapy is strictly contraindicated for the elderly (defined as age fifty or older). Kasten- baum (1978) and Shows (1977) have argued that Jungian therapy can be successful with some older patients. Brink (1979), Sherman (1981), Karpf (1977), and Burnside and Haight (1994) also supported the contention that various forms of psychotherapy can be effective in working with the elderly, even the frail elderly.

In general counselors and therapists who are successful in treating the frail elderly all seem to have the following common elements. They:

1. Deal with loss.
2. Focus on the individual patient's own life history to reestablish connec- tions between the patient's past and present realities.
3. Take an active role, not patronizing or condescending, but rather are present and ask questions, seek clarification, and offer guidance and direction. The therapist must not become the absent analyst so typical of traditional psychoanalysis, nor mechanically use the reflection tech- nique.
4. Establish behavioral patterns to prevent patient frustration leading to aggression, screaming, or other regressive behaviors.
5. Provide increased structure according to how dysfunctional the pa- tient is.

Note that the therapy is serially short-term. That is, psychotherapy must be presented as a short-term endeavor to the patient but with the option to resume at any time. The therapist must assume that there will be more than one short-term intervention with the frail elderly (Lazarus et al., 1991).

The issue of loss is one of the inevitable problems of the elderly. All older people have lost loved ones, friends, associates, and if they live long enough, just about everyone except younger family members. Older people lose physical strength, often lose financial resources, and in general lose their sense of empowerment and sense of personal control. If deprived of possibilities for sharing wisdom and receiving respect, it is likely that the older person will slip into feelings of despair, hopelessness, and helplessness.

Many frail elderly would be diagnosed as depressed. Most of these depressed older people receive antidepressive medications to "treat" their depression. Of course medication alone will not restore the losses or empower the individual to deal effectively with the ending of life. Lazarus et al. (1991) found that cognitive therapy (Beck's 1967 version) was as effective as medication in controlling "symptoms" of depression in the frail elderly. (See Chapter 10 for a more complete discussion of Beck's cognitive therapy.)

To deal more directly with loss, first the therapist must identify the significant losses for a particular individual. In the case of the frail elderly this task is often difficult. Such patients often have trouble with verbalizing or identifying their particular losses. If a patient seems depressed or withdrawn it is often useful to try to identify the particular loss with which this person may be struggling.

The first author happened to observe an elderly patient in a VA hospital who seemed to be depressed, judging by his nonverbal self-presentation. York decided to talk to the patient to find out if he was indeed depressed and if so what was producing this depression. He approached the patient with non-intrusive warmth and expressed concern that he seemed to be feeling blue. York asked the patient if he would like to talk about it. He began weeping and thanked York for his concern. He said that it was his birthday and that his son had not come to visit him as he had promised. The patient said that because of this he had made a decision to end his life that night. But, he said, now he had changed his mind because somebody seemed to care, and again thanked York.

Discovering losses triggering despair, which leads to the loss of integrity, is rarely so dramatic. Often the older person will need to search through his or her life experiences to be able to verbalize those losses that have produced the experiences of defeat, hopelessness, and helplessness. In a nursing home the first author was conducting an "orientation" interview with a patient. The answers suggested some problems in orientation with respect to person, place, and time. As York was jotting down notes, he began to muse on going fishing. The patient brightened noticeably and asked, "How are you going to fish the Mill?" (a river close to the therapist's home). York replied, "I was going to fly-fish using a Hendrickson fly, and work the pools." The patient said, "Oh no, not this time of the year. You should use a stone fly imitation." The elderly man then launched into a discussion of how to fish the Mill at different times of the year, how to tie the flies, and so forth. York tried to do what the patient suggested, and unlike his usual fishing expeditions he actually caught a couple of trout.

In a later encounter with this patient York asked him what he missed most. He answered, fishing with his son and showing him how to tie flies. Anyone who has ever been smitten with the fishing bug can experience the poignancy of his loss. York suggested that he share his expertise with a local Boy Scout troop. It was amazing how much of the patient's "dementia" cleared and how many depressive symptoms evaporated as he interacted with these youngsters.

The discovery of the significant losses for a particular individual rarely happens by accident. Perhaps the history of the patient reveals a loss that he or she has not discussed and seems to avoid discussing. The exploration of this event or events may produce the key to a frail elderly person's present distress. Recognizing loss may reflect opportunities to make restitution for past personal failures with significant others that remain unresolved. Often in the frail elderly such remembrances are experienced as occurring now, like a current crisis requiring immediate attention. A colleague of the authors reported that one of her clients was having a panic reaction because he thought he "had to go to work." Not going to work was the immediate crisis that led the client to become agitated. The therapist dealt with the agitation using distraction. She said to the client, "Mr. Smith, do you know it is Saturday?" He said, "No." She said, "You don't work on Saturday, do you?" He said, "I guess I don't work on Saturday." She said, "Besides, it's raining outside and you wouldn't want to go out in the rain, would you?" The client calmed down and seemed relieved that he didn't have to go to work.

The main point here is that the discovery of significant loss (in this case of being an employed person) often flows from the particular remembrances or reminiscences of that individual. The second common thread is that one uses reminiscence or life review or both in working with the frail elderly. These remembrances usually do not take the form of recovery of repressed material but rather are a categorizing of those personal history events that are of significance to the frail elderly person. To be able to share with an empathetic listener the events that define this elderly individual seems to have therapeutic effects in and of itself (Feil, 1984).

The therapist needs to feel as though he or she is sharing a patient's life saga. Within this context the therapist may discover significant losses and learn how the individual has coped with them. The discovery of the individual's past coping styles and a comparison with current coping styles is often helpful in working with the frail elderly. Reactivation of earlier successful coping styles may be beneficial. It is essential that the therapist take an active role with the frail elderly. Feil (1984) suggested that it is often useful to sit close to the frail elderly when one interacts with them. If appropriate, it may be useful to occasionally touch them. This active physical closeness, if toler-ated, is an example of the active nonverbal therapist behaviors that can be useful in creating and maintaining a working relationship with the frail elderly. In essence, the therapist must create an effective linkage in which the shifting patterns of leading (dominance) and following (receptive/passive) occur between the therapist and the patient. Again, it is essential that the patient perceive the therapist as caring, knowledgeable, and consistent. Attempts by the therapist to discern how he or she is perceived are critical for effective psychotherapy.

More General Psychosocial Intervention Strategies with the Frail Elderly

When the frail elderly can no longer profit from some sort of "formal" psychotherapy or counseling, a variety of staff "management" (staff caregiving and staff dignity-maintenance) techniques are useful. According to Hughes and Espinosa (1990) these psychosocial approaches are behavior modification and modeling, the validation approach, reality orientation, distraction and redirection, and self-esteem enhancement. Hughes and Espinosa also suggest that caregivers focus on what the frail elderly can do, and show them in myriad ways that they are valued and cared for. Positive nonverbal commu-nication, reassurance, and support and involving the frail elderly in activities to the extent they can participate are examples of the general psychosocial focus that Hughes and Espinosa have described.

According to Hughes and Espinosa the behavioral methods most useful in working with the frail elderly are behavior modification and modeling. *Behavior modification* involves reinforcing desired responses and not attending to undesirable responses. First the therapist should identify behavior to be changed. Second, the therapist should do a functional analysis of the patient's behavior patterns: when, where, or around whom does the undesirable behavior occur and how frequently? Third, the therapist should identify possible reinforcers and then reinforce desired behaviors, in particular those that compete with undesirable behaviors. For instance, when the patient who typically yells talks softly instead, he or she is reinforced by taking the patient on a walk or doing something that the patient likes. Talking softly is a behavior that competes with yelling.

All of this sounds easy to do; it is not. One caution that Hughes and Espinosa clearly underscored is that negative responses to the patient must be low in frequency. They stated that if negative responses to clients occurred more than 25% of the time, effective behavior control cannot occur. Also, one must be very clear about what behaviors are desired and show great restraint in not responding to negative behaviors.

Modeling refers to showing the patient what you want him or her to do. Modeling in this aspect is similar to role playing. A more important aspect of modeling requires the staff to interact with the patient the way they want the patient to interact with them. If a staff person models warm concern and is in control even in the face of chaos then the desired behavior has been modeled in a significant way.

Hughes and Espinosa (1990) suggested that the validation method of Feil (1984) could serve to aid frail elderly in maintaining integrity. Feil (1992) intended her method to be applied to the "old-old" frail elderly. Specifically, she stated that her approach is most useful with late-onset Alzheimer's disease. Age, as Feil pointed out, is a relative term. Some people are not "old-old" at age ninety, and some people are "old-old" at sixty. Feil's validation approach is keyed to people who have some physical loss of function and who have orientation difficulties. The frail elderly who can profit from validation should not have a history of mental illness or mental retardation.

Feil (1992) maintained that "validation workers" (VW) must be capable of accepting strong emotions or they cannot work with the "old-old." Feil argued that a successful VW is a person who can empathize with a disoriented old person and can communicate with that person on a deep emotional (often nonverbal) level.

According to Feil (1992) the basic structure of the validation approach requires the therapist or staff person to understand that the frail elderly person has lost his or her controls, has lost the will to control, and can no longer use defenses to deny feelings. Feil held that this outpouring of feelings serves the purpose of allowing, provided validation is given, the frail elderly to resolve unfinished life tasks. She felt that if there was a person—the validation worker—who could empathetically listen to the patient's or client's expression of those feelings and did not challenge them, then the feelings would subside. Feil held that the caregiver must neither analyze the frail elderly's feelings nor encourage the expression of feelings not voiced. In essence a good VW is one who can experience a frail elderly person's world and if asked, enter it and endorse its legitimacy.

Feil (1992) argued that earlier learned events (remote memories) are maintained better than recent memories. Further, for the old-old not only can an event in the present trigger an earlier memory, but also that recalled memory can seem to the old person to be occurring *now*. Feil claimed that there are different tasks relevant to each stage of life. She didn't specify what those tasks might be, but we have done so in Chapter 2. She argued, correctly, we think, that if a life task is not resolved, the person will keep trying to resolve it until death. Her notion that life tasks are rarely resolved may be overstated, but the idea that people will continue to be bedeviled by unresolved or unfinished life tasks remains sound. She also argued that people who reach very old age go through a last stage—*resolution* (a completion of life tasks) *versus vegetation*.

Feil held that there are four substages in the deterioration of the old-old frail elderly who are not validated. Stage one is *malorientation*, characterized by relative intactness but because feelings are denied there is a tendency to blame others for losses. Stage two is *time confusion*, characterized by time and reality disorder, and rather fluid and uncontrolled expression of emotions. Stage three is *repetitive motion*, characterized by unintelligible speech and repetitive sounds, often accompanied by body rocking. Stage four is *vegetation*, characterized by complete withdrawal. Feil argued that validation could prevent this ominous regression.

It seems to us that these "stages" are really another twist on Erikson's integrity versus despair stage. If one can maintain integrity in the face of loss then one can continue to resolve unfinished business rather withdraw into a vegetative state. However, as Frankl (1963) pointed out in his observation of victims of the Nazi concentration camps, loss of integrity leads quickly to despair, and to withdrawal into a vegetative state that precedes death. It seems to us that Frankl's observation supports Erikson's stage theory. In addition Feil didn't seem to give much credence to the fact that patients with progressive central nervous system disease can only function at a vegetative level or stage, regardless of the staff's attention, care, and competence.

Still, Feil's (1992) insistence that ignored feelings are a source, or eventually will become a source, of personal distress, seems to us to be sound. If such feelings are expressed and accepted as valid by caregivers, then distress will be lessened and perhaps overcome. According to Feil (1992) the primary thrust of the validation approach requires the caregiver to "listen exquisitely with empathy." If one ignores, placates, minimizes, or attacks a frail elderly person's emotions, he or she will get worse. Finally, Feil argued that "If no one listens to them their behavior worsens, or they withdraw to vegetation" (p. 45).

The reader is encouraged if possible to attend any workshop Feil offers. Some of the skills and much of the force of validation as a technique become evident when one sees Feil at work. Validation is not for all of the frail elderly; certainly not every part of every interaction should be focused on validating the person. Yet each patient in a nursing home needs something like validation as part of total treatment. One cannot observe Feil at work and fail to draw this conclusion.

A technique that is often presented as in opposition to validation is that of *reality orientation*. Taulbee and Folsom (1973) developed a general approach to the treatment of severely disturbed individuals called attitude therapy within which the "attitude" of reality orientation was first detailed. Taulbee and Folsom noted that many older psychiatric patients in a VA hospital often were confused and disoriented. They felt that if these patients could be supported by giving them a sense of who they were and where they were, and by making them aware of the current date and day of the week, their distress and confusion might be reduced. Taulbee and Folsom recommended that caregivers uniformly employ reality orientation for older people who were disoriented. The caregiver might say to a particular patient, "Good morning Mr. _____, how are you this Tuesday in October? How do you like being in _____ Hospital (nursing home)?"

Taulbee and Folsom (1973) cautioned their readers not to mechanically employ this "attitude." Further, the reality orientation was to occur within the context of the attitude of *active warmth*. If an older person became agitated or began to grow agitated, the caretaker was to assume the attitude of *no demand* and to attempt to reduce the emotional arousal by not challenging or confronting the distressed person. In addition they were to encourage their elderly patients to engage in whatever activities they could, and to encourage staff to interact frequently, again using the attitude of active warmth, with their patients. A more complete discussion of attitude therapy is presented in Chapter 11.

Another approach that Hughes and Espinosa (1990) recommended for working with the frail elderly is called *self-esteem enhancement*. In essence, the caregivers attempt to encourage older people to feel worthwhile and aid them in feeling and, to the extent it is possible, being independent. The methods offered to increase self-esteem are sensible and of practical utility. It is necessary for caregivers to accept patient values, express concern and active warmth, and to encourage and support independence and self-care. It seems to us that esteem enhancement is similar to the active warmth attitude of Taulbee and Folsom with some of the elements of validation included. However, in this approach, as with all others, no mechanical compliment or expression of support or positive affect will be effective.

We shall consider two approaches cited by Hughes and Espinosa (1990) that fit together and are particularly useful in working with frail elderly who often become agitated or upset. The first approach is *distraction*. Earlier in this chapter we offered an example of distraction with a patient who was distressed. According to Hughes and Espinosa, when a patient is fixated on a troublesome event, person, or situation, a change in focus produced by the caregiver can be of benefit. Indeed, effective distractions can prevent a patient from becoming agitated, or if agitated, can reduce or control his or her distress. It seems to us that *redirection* is essentially the same as distraction. It may be that Hughes and Espinosa intend for redirection to require the caregiver to be more directive in changing focus. We suggest that when an older person becomes agitated, great care should be taken not to "put him or her in a corner" or otherwise escalate the situation.

Hughes and Espinosa (1990) also described what they referred to as restorative techniques, listening, and anticipation of needs. Each of these approaches offers concrete guidance to caregivers. However, much of what they provide is well handled by approaches already discussed.

Conclusion

As our population continues to age, therapists must gain expertise in working with older people. Beyond the obvious fact that older people have amassed a vast storehouse of memories and experiences, we need to be reminded that older people are still in process, are still becoming. Even if Feil (1992) is correct and life tasks are never finished until death, each human being deserves to die with dignity. If, as Feil stated, the last stage of life is resolution versus vegetation, then we maintain that the preservation of integrity and the struggle to avoid despair are the central issues of the elderly.

When one's central nervous system is intact, then despair is likely if the person does not develop and maintain the psychic structure Jung called the self. To share wisdom (the positive stage-appropriate behavior according to Erikson, 1963), one must not only possess the necessary information but also those intangibles that turn the information into a larger meaning. This part of wisdom—the unconscious, nonrational, emotional part—springs not from the recollection of facts but from the deeper structures of the psyche that Jung described.

The therapist working with an older person who is disconnected from some larger purpose or who does not or cannot share his or her wisdom is well advised to take a Jungian approach with that person. One may expect therapy to be short-term, as would be predicted by our model. The therapist needs to take an active but not dominant role in the therapy process. An interpersonal role of low-level warmth and active engagement is consistent with our model. Content of therapy focuses on issues related to integrity and explores the person's subtle failures to satisfy his or her legitimate need for self-realization.

It is another matter to discuss therapy for the frail elderly. When a person's central nervous system is no longer intact, as is the case with dementia, then Jungian therapy, as such, is not appropriate. Validation and other psychosocial intervention strategies focus on maintaining as much of the old person's self-system as is possible. However, all of these approaches are highly structured and are, one way or another, long-term. Although the content of therapy focuses on violations of legitimate social expectations, it must also address the older person's need for integrity and must, to the full extent possible, find room for the expression of wisdom and give the older person a meaningful way to complete his or her life story. All of these considerations are consistent with our notion that the severer the disorder, the more structure the therapist must provide and the longer the treatment must be. The specific structure and content of therapy also seem to be consistent with our model. Certainly there are many issues that are age-relevant for these seriously troubled people. To ignore the frail elderly's specific needs within a set of standard prescriptions for "illness" is to miss the point of effective psychosocial treatment.

5 Chronic Disease, Psychosomatic Disorders, and Health Psychology

The DSM-III, DSM-III-R, and DSM-IV omitted any specific reference to psychosomatic disorders. Prior to the DSM-III, psychosomatic disorders were often held to be caused (or in part caused) by internal psychological events (Alexander, 1950). It has become fashionable to refer to psychosomatic disorders as psychophysiological disorders. We prefer the older term because it captures the "mind–body" orientation toward these diseases. Among those diseases *identified* (DSM-II) as psychosomatic disorders were peptic ulcers, high blood pressure, coronary heart disease, asthma, hay fever, hives and some other skin disorders, and headaches. No responsible and knowledgeable physician or psychotherapist would now claim that these disorders are caused solely by one's mental state or personality. Yet to deny that the mind influences the body in significant ways is equally implausible. Folks and Kinney (1992) in an extensive review argued that the DSM-III-R erred in omitting reference to psychosomatic disorders (specifically gastrointestinal disorders), and urged the framers of the DSM-IV to include this category in their manual. Their recommendations were not followed. In Chapter 14 we propose another way to deal with these disorders. We suggested that they could be considered illnesses to be treated medically but that they also have characteristic psychological dysfunctions that require attention. In addition, chronic diseases often require psychological treatment as well as medical treatment. In fact, a new field, psychoimmunology, has emerged due to the growing body of data that shows that state of mind is important in the survival rate of people who suffer from chronic and often terminal diseases such as cancer or AIDS (Maier, Watkins, & Fleshner, 1994).

Rosenhan and Seligman (1995) proposed a diathesis stress model as the mechanism by which mental events and environmental stress stimuli could lead to tissue or organ damage or both. *Diathesis,* in this model, referred to physiological, largely genetic, factors related to specific patterns of organ susceptibility. *Stress* referred to stimuli from the environment or generated by the internal processes of the affected individual. We will expand on their model in Chapter 14.

The Concept of Psychosomatic Disorders

Evidence suggests that genetic factors, infectious disease, and physical trauma are all factors that produce organ weakness. Infectious diseases and physical trauma can be substantially controlled or treated by standard medical procedures. The genetic factors leading to organ susceptibility are only now beginning to be understood. We would suggest that for coronary heart disease, peptic ulcers, asthma, and some of the severer types of headaches (migraine and cluster headaches), there is good reason to infer specific genetic organ weakness.

However, we also suggest that there is considerable evidence that psychological factors play an important part in many disorders. Psychological input into various disorders may be conceived of as consistent and recurrent patterns of negative self-talk, consistent and recurrent disruptive lifestyle behaviors, and destructive interpersonal interactions. Such self-talk as "I must succeed," "I must become president of my company," and "I must be loved" are self-generated stress stimuli. When such self-talk doesn't lead to neurotic difficulties, it may lead to heroic behavior (and therefore is a continuing source of stress stimuli). In addition, interpersonal interactions and environmental stressors can contribute to an individual's level of stress.

Health Psychology

Health psychology is a growing field in which the primary premise is that psychologists can assist physicians and medical personnel. The primary focus of health psychologists is to aid patients in changing destructive health habits. For both chronic disease and for disorders formerly called psychosomatic changes in destructive health habits are critical. Some of the negative health habits that require change are diet, exercise, smoking, drinking, substance use (abuse), and general "health" habits. For many chronically ill people, psychological treatment is required to get the individual to cease engaging in negative behaviors, even when such behaviors are literally killing the person (Becker & Rosenstock, 1984). At present, the general response of many practitioners in the health care community is that the sick person is at *fault* for the negative behaviors and therefore responsible for his or her distress.

We could hope that telling human beings they are responsible for their own problems would be enough. We humans are not that rational. Group psychotherapy was "discovered" by Pratt (1905) precisely because tuberculosis patients simply wouldn't follow sensible health habits. They felt that they were alone and were going to die anyway, so why do anything to prolong the inevitable? How many times have we heard a patient say, "Well, if I have to give up smoking [or whatever], I might as well be dead." A rational or a guilt-eliciting appeal to that person is not likely to change his or her patterns of behavior.

Health psychology is an emerging area in psychology that explicitly endorses the importance of mental factors as contributors to physiological well-being. Convincing the resistant patient to change lifestyle patterns clearly is part of what a psychotherapist can do. In addition, major changes in the personalities of ill patients may be required if they are to survive.

There are many negative patterns of thinking, feeling, and acting—negative self-talk, dysfunctional interpersonal interactions, destructive and irrational lifestyle choices, and failure to take medications as prescribed—that must be changed if one is to maintain or regain one's health. There are a variety of techniques, general life strategies, and other ways to dramatically change one's total orientation toward life and living that promise success. In our attempt to particularize methods of psychosocial intervention, we will explore general psychosocial approaches used with people who suffer from illnesses once called psychosomatic or chronic disease or both.

Treatment of People Suffering from Psychosomatic Disorders

Norman Cousins (1989) chronicled his own struggle with various serious diseases, including what he called a massive heart attack. He had survived this and other diseases far longer than anyone had expected. What was his "secret"? According to Cousins, "Don't deny the diagnosis, try to defy the verdict." In essence, he suggested that what was required was an optimistic philosophy of life geared to more than survival; in fact, one geared to fulfillment and bliss.

Cousins's advice may be particularly useful for people who suffer from chronic heart disease, asthma, and several gastrointestinal disorders. Consideration of psychosocial factors must be part of the treatment approach. If there is an important, if not causal, psychological element in the disease process, then it would seem that a psychological component should be included as part of the treatment process. There are several ways in which psychological intervention could be useful. First, support groups for patients with chronic diseases including those formerly called psychosomatic should be offered to deal with the psychological fallout caused by physical suffering. Second, these same support groups can provide support to the patient as he or she begins and maintains a healthy lifestyle, provide information about medications and advances in treatments, and finally, involve and empower family members in the treatment and maintenance of the ill person. Third, as catalogued by Lazarus (1981) and referred to in Chapter 6 (see pp. 125–129), there are a number of methods to control or neutralize stress stimuli that could be usefully employed in short-term individual intervention approaches (relaxation approaches). Finally, many individuals suffering from what were formerly called psychosomatic disorders usually do not distort reality by irrational self-talk or more dysfunctional means (such as delusions or hallucinations); in fact they may not distort reality at all. However they may engage in heroic behaviors such as competing, striving, and "asking not what have I done but what can I do now." Such driven activity often characterizes the psychologically nonsymptomatic individual who develops psychosomatic disorders. A change in world-view is often required in addition to more focused changes.

Changes in life goals are often required if sufferers of chronic disease are to live or be able to enjoy life. When working with an individual who was hypertensive and had been told by his physician that he was at risk for a heart attack, the first author adopted a strategy in therapy of exploring life goals as part of the individual's treatment. As a result the patient had an epiphany and returned to his childhood religious belief system, now framed in a much more mature way. This dramatic change enabled him to overcome some serious reversals in life without losing either hope or a sense of larger meaning.

Sahakian (1976) proposed an approach to psychotherapy that could be useful for working with people who suffer from chronic disease. He suggested that if one could assume a stoic attitude then one would not be consumed by anxiety, propelled by an insatiable desire to be liked or loved by everyone, or driven to achieve, whatever the personal cost. That is, if one could subjectively accept the stoic belief that it is not events that cause distress, but rather our interpretation of those events, then their stress component would be markedly reduced.

Sahakian was not clear about how a therapist produces this change in basic outlook for an oversocialized, highly successful American executive (or even for the Walter Mitty type who only daydreams of such achievements). He suggested a dialectical procedure in which meanings attached to highly emotionally charged events were explored and diffused. Perhaps a therapeutic atmosphere in which the crisis world-view of the driven person is eliminated, and a more tranquil and accepting demeanor established, constitutes the goal of Sahakian's intervention. However, it is extremely difficult to convince someone that any past, present, or future event in which great emotion is invested is not all that important.

If the patient can accept the therapist as a colleague or equal, then the initial condition for an effective intervention has been established. Second, a therapeutic relationship must have been achieved that allows the patient to entertain notions markedly contrary to those he or she usually holds. Finally, the patient must experience the attitude of "indifference" *without* experiencing it as a catastrophe. In our work with chronic heart disease, hypertension, chronic headaches, asthma, ulcers, and certain skin diseases, emphasis on our patients assuming a stoic attitude has been useful, as have frontal attacks on catastrophe-driven/obsessed thinking.

In addition to encouraging a reduction in the patient's emotional investment in significant life events, the therapist must enlist the cooperation of significant others in the patient's life. It is clear that social support must be provided not only in support groups but also in the patient's daily life. In fact, Uchino, Cacioppo, and Kiecolt-Glaser (1996) held that social support is one of the critical factors in sustaining health. Both limited couples therapy and short-term family therapy offer psychosocial means to achieve an increase in social support systems.

CASE HISTORY **5.1**

Psychosomatic Issues of Coronary Heart Disease— Richard Wright

Mr. Richard Wright was referred to the therapist following a myocardial infarction. Mr. Wright was somewhat overweight, but other than an inherited cholesterol problem (partially controlled by medication) had no other major predisposing health factors that correlated with myocardial infarctions. His cardiologist noted that Mr. Wright seemed time-driven and was "unduly" competitive. The cardiologist guessed that short-term psychotherapy focused on stress reduction might reduce the probability of a future heart attack.

The client appeared at the therapist's office precisely on time. He expressed some doubt about whether a "shrink" could have any positive effect on his "condition." The therapist suggested that since he was there, they might as well explore some of his psychological characteristics to see if there might be something useful to accomplish together. The therapist suggested the client take an MMPI to rule out any significant psychological problems and gave Mr. Wright a type A/type B questionnaire to fill out. Since he denied any psychological problems, was successful by cultural standards, and had never been in treatment for such problems, the therapist guessed that no further assessment would be necessary. The MMPI did not reveal any significant psychological problems. However, the other questionnaire concluded that the client was a "Type A." Type A behavior and thinking patterns are often correlated with both high blood pressure and heart attacks. In addition, data from the therapist's interview revealed that the client was under a great deal of stress (much of it self-produced) and got angry very easily ("I have a short fuse"). Ten sessions of therapy were agreed upon, with a focus on stress reduction and anger control.

The following is a short excerpt from the sixth session.

THERAPIST: If I heard you right, you see almost every block to your accomplishing your goal as a major conflict requiring you to mobilize your energy, often to defeat an "enemy."

CLIENT: I don't know if I would put it that strongly, but in my line of work people don't ask, what have you done in the past? They ask, what are you doing about *the problem* today?

THERAPIST: How do you feel about that?

CLIENT: I love the challenge. That's what makes life worthwhile—winning, reaching your goal.

THERAPIST: And then you can prop up your feet for a while and enjoy it.

CLIENT: No way—you have to look for the next challenge and forge ahead.

THERAPIST: I want to examine what you are saying to yourself. Is it always good for you to plunge into a problem situation with both guns blazing?

CLIENT: Well, sometimes other people get angry, but usually it's because I caught them.

THERAPIST: After you "catch them" are they sure to cooperate next time?

CLIENT: If they don't I'll fire them.

THERAPIST: How do you feel right now?

CLIENT: Angry, churned up.

THERAPIST: That's dangerous for you.

CLIENT: I guess it is.

THERAPIST: What about reframing the crisis issue? How about saying "this is a *small* problem that I need to address *with* my colleagues"?

CLIENT: That helps a little.

THERAPIST: Also remember that when you get stressed, get angry, you often, as we said before, have taken a small problem and recast it into a catastrophe.

CLIENT: Yeah, I guess I have.

THERAPIST: Tonight when you go home I hope you will stick to your tai chi and relaxation exercises, and jot down the number of times you made mountains out of molehills and *unnecessarily* got yourself angry.

Homework assignments, including performing the moving meditation (tai chi), developing a more stoic outlook, noting angry reactions, and catastrophizing, were continued until therapy concluded on the tenth session. The client returned for a few "tutoring" sessions, as he called them, over the next two years. He was symptom-free during that time but reported he still had a great deal of difficulty in "tolerating fools gladly." In addition, his wife was called in for a few sessions as a consultant to aid him in continuing his homework assignments and to lower his overall stress level.

Coronary Heart Disease and Essential Hypertension

The treatment of coronary heart disease and essential hypertension begins with medication or diet or both, but does not end there. If the arteriosclerotic disease process has progressed to the point that coronary arteries are severely occluded, then surgery or angioplastic procedures are required. However, after all the medical procedures are done and the diet has been "prescribed," other significant changes are required if the quality of the patient's life is to improve and the patient's life expectancy to increase.

Freidman (1969), Rosenman, Brand, Jenkins, Friedman, Straus, and Wurm (1975), Price (1982), Williams, Suarez, Kuhn, Zimmerman, and Schanberg (1991), and Williams, Davison, Nezami, and DeQuatro (1992) found personality characteristics often correlated with death due to a heart attack. Those people most at risk were Type A patients who maintained a high level of hostility either expressed or felt (Weinstein, Davison, DeQuatro, & Allen, 1986) when other factors implicated in heart disease such as diet, sex (male), smoking habit, cholesterol level, and exercise were held constant. Further, Jenkins (1976) stated that 50% of the deaths due to heart attack were not accounted for by diet and other risk factors, but rather were related to psychological and social factors.

Ornish (1982), a cardiologist, reported that, in addition to smoking and diet changes, meditation and support groups (very much like Pratt's groups for tubercular patients) are required. Ornish has had good results with his approach. It is interesting that one of Ornish's patients, who subsequently died, was involved in a failing marriage and that no resolution of that interpersonal conflict occurred in or out of the patient's support group. One wonders if he might be said to have died of a broken heart.

An essential factor in Ornish's support groups was that patients and their wives were in the same group. Couples shared recipes and discussed the major lifestyle changes that the diet and other parts of Ornish's treatment approach required. Ornish and his colleagues attempted to empower the couples in their management of the sick patient. Issues of depression were handled primarily by the empathetic attention of the depressed patient's partner's to the patient's feelings. Also, the therapist's focus was directed to the fact that the patient was not alone nor did he have to carry the burden of fear by himself (all of Ornish's patients in this study were male).

Ornish's emphasis on meditation as part of the total change in lifestyle is of interest. The Benson relaxation technique and all other stress management techniques (see Chapter 6) are intended to serve the same purpose as Ornish's focus on meditation. That is, they break the stress–arousal cycle. Ornish made meditation an almost religious, certainly a "West Coast" practice, which may have put some people off. However, if one believes in the value of meditation and goes through the procedure daily, one's stress level routinely will go down. When one employs relaxation/stress management techniques and finds time to exercise regularly, then it is unlikely that the driven lifestyle (with its attendant dietary and other problems) will continue. Ornish advocated *a total life change* that focused on three parts: diet, relaxation techniques, and increased social support and self-awareness.

A total life change with a renewed interest in one's family, some means of breaking competitive and angry striving, and an enlightened and informed self-interest in diet and exercise requires a rather substantial change in the individual. A change in one's internal world must, we suggest, go beyond Sahakian's modern (1976) stoicism (as discussed in this chapter). Being able to minimize the emotional impact of negative (or positive) experiences, although necessary, is not enough. One has to have a reason beyond expediency to change one's patterns of living.

To convince a bright, competent human being to verbally agree to change his or her lifestyle because it is rational to do so is relatively easy. The trick is to find compelling and emotionally powerful reasons why that person *must* change his or her lifestyle and then get him or her to do it. The basic question may be one of meaning or, rather, one's vision of one's place in the world. The question seems to be what must *I* be and do in order to be worthy?

If *I* cannot be or do "it" (fill in the blank for "it"), then *my* life has no meaning, *I* cannot go on. If *I* cannot do or be this or that, then *my* heart will be broken. What, for this person, are these self-defining needs? They could center on food: *I* must have *my* roast beef or life is not worth living. They could center on self-image: *I* must be active and competitive or *I* don't care whether *I* live or die. They could center on relationships: *I* must have my wife's (or any other significant person's) love or *I* cannot go on. Such self-referents resemble the kind of irrational thinking that Ellis (1967) and Beck (1967) have so clearly referred to, yet many people who suffer from congestive heart disease when confronted are clearly aware of the irrationality. Why then is Ellis's (1967) rational emotive therapy (see Chapter 6) or Sahakian's "philosophical" psychotherapy (1976) insufficient?

Many people tend to overvalue their importance and power in their daily lives and they attribute irrational meaning and importance to their conflicts. All issues then become major battles in which the total energy of that person must be mobilized to deal with the problem. Adversaries (often perceived as enemies) must be defeated. The therapist needs to enable the patient to change this pattern of attributing irrational meaning to conflict situations if the individual is to effectively change his or her life pattern. Thoresen, Friedman, Powell, Gill, and Ulmer (1985) reported that behavioral approaches have shown some success in changing lifestyles. In addition, the therapist must defuse the attendant hostility and cynicism of congestive heart disease patients (Weinstein et al., 1986). Gidron and Davidson (1996) have used behavioral treatment to reduce hostility in people who suffer from the disease. In addition, cognitive restructuring (Ellis, 1967; Beck, 1967) can be effectively used to defeat irrational beliefs that increase stress levels (see Chapter 6). We would suggest that reducing irrational thoughts (particularly those keyed to hostility and cynicism) would be the primary focus for cognitive restructuring for patients suffering from congestive heart disease. Assertiveness training (see Chapter 6) is particularly useful when keyed to ways to reduce stressful encounters from which anger, often unexpressed, is the result. Essentially, one learns how to clearly ask for what one wants and to frame the request in ways that respect the other. Teaching the person how to recognize what causes stress and how one might reduce one's reaction to stress is often useful. Finally, as is consistent with many of these disorders, one means of getting the competitive self under control is through social support.

Asthma

Respiratory disorders are often discussed within the general framework of what were formerly called psychosomatic disorders. It is plausible that emotional distress of sufficient intensity to activate the autonomic nervous system would also affect the respiratory system. For example, Stone, Reed, and Neale (1987) found that negative daily events were linked to episodes of physical symptoms, including respiratory symptoms. A relationship between stressful daily events and respiratory reactions was also reported by Davidson and Neale (1994). Evans and Edgerton (1990) conducted a study with similar results.

The respiratory disorder known as asthma is often linked to psychological factors. Asthma is a disorder in which air passages in general, and the bronchiole in particular, narrow, causing severe problems in breathing. Specifically, exhaling is extremely difficult and wheezing occurs. Further, during an asthma attack the mucus that lubricates the lining of the air passages thickens, and may plug the air passages. Also, the lining of the bronchial tubes swells and becomes inflamed.

As is the case with congestive heart disease, there are many nonpsychosocial factors related to asthma that may be classified as risk factors or causal factors or both. Among these factors are elevated blood levels of immunoglobulin E (antibodies associated with allergies), viral infections, exposure to highly allergenic substances, and genetic predisposition (Mrazek, 1993).

Mrazek has categorically stated that there are no consistent personality characteristics related to either asthma or asthmatic attacks and that studies purporting to show those relationships are badly flawed. He holds that stress, presumably produced either by daily events or the psychological characteristics of the individual, produces asthmatic symptoms.

Rees (1964) among others (Alexander, 1950) has offered findings in opposition to Mrazek (1993). Rees reported that 30% of the asthmatics he studied had asthmatic attacks related to emotionally stressful events. Further, Rees said that for asthma sufferers aged sixteen to thirty-five psychological factors were of less importance than they were for children aged six to sixteen, but that psychological factors again became significant after age thirty-five. Hyland (1990) also found psychological factors (mood ratings) related to asthmatic attacks for approximately one-third of the asthma sufferers he studied.

While Mrazek (1993) may be right that any stressor will trigger the asthmatic attack, it does not follow that all psychosocial stress stimuli will produce the same emotional reactions because phenomenologically the stress stimuli are not the same. A particular psychological stress stimulus may lead a congestive heart disease patient to become angry while that same stress stimulus may lead an asthmatic to become fearful. Of course, from the phenomenological point of view the stress stimuli in the two cases aren't the same at all. It is possible that the individual's personality traits determine the specific emotional reaction that, in turn, determines the pathological physiological reaction. This conclusion is speculative and a great deal of research will be required to determine if it is correct or not.

We have often found that our asthmatic patients feel powerless and fearful. Focusing on systematic cognitive restructuring that emphasizes their abilities to effect changes in their life situations has been part of effective therapy. Essentially, the therapist attempts to empower the asthmatic individual and to offer support in the face of the unfairness and the gratuitous pains that life often forces us to experience.

Rational approaches to nonpsychological factors that precipitate asthma attacks are another essential part of therapy. Does the patient smoke or engage in other lifestyle behaviors that are problematical? If so, the empowerment must include strategies to encourage the person to change these lifestyle problems. Is the patient knowledgeable about the relevant nonpsychological risk factors? A determination of that awareness or lack of awareness is essential for effective treatment.

Further, there are several interpersonal issues that are important in the psychological treatment of the asthmatic patient. Does the patient recognize those interpersonal situations that are stressful? Can they be avoided? Can the patient's reaction to those situations be reframed in such a way that the meaning of those encounters is changed? This type of cognitive restructuring fits nicely with explorations of how effectively the patient deals with the nonpsychological factors that exacerbate or cause asthmatic attacks. Increasing awareness of nonpsychological factors *and* empowering the individual to have more control over his or her life situation is essential in dealing with asthma.

In addition, several specific techniques are useful in helping people who suffer from asthma. First, assertiveness training is useful as part of the general empowerment process (see Chapter 6). Second, relaxation approaches, whether those of Benson, Jacobson, or others (see Chapter 6), are also useful. And third, cognitive/behavioral interventions could be useful to defuse potentially stressful interpersonal interaction (see Chapter 6).

CASE HISTORY **5.2**

Psychosomatic Issues of Peptic Ulcers— Herbert Spencer

Mr. Herbert Spencer was a self-referral who sought help because of his concern for his eldest daughter. During the interview he reported that he needed his daughter to get some help or her life was going to be destroyed. Nineteen years old, she was acting out sexually and using marijuana. He said that he was really stressed about her and, almost as an aside, remarked that his ulcer was flaring up. The therapist agreed to see his daughter and to explore therapy with her, but also suggested that a few sessions of stress management might be useful for Mr. Spencer. He had denied any significant psychological problems other than his concern for his daughter but was willing to see if stress management would help his ulcer.

During the first interview the client reported that his ulcer had begun when he was the co-owner of a small beef packing company in northern Florida. At that time it looked as though unproductive and very cheap land could be used for grazing cattle, and a lot of cattle were brought into that part of Florida. The meat packing business seemed a sure thing given the availability of cheap beef and a good rail and highway system for transportation. However, a disastrous cattle disease temporarily reduced supply and regardless of the client's and his partner's efforts, their business was doomed. They declared bankruptcy and the partner walked away leaving many unpaid debts. Mr. Spencer developed a bleeding ulcer at this time, which was life-threatening. After he recovered, he vowed to pay back his debts, and took the responsibility on himself to "make things right."

The therapist thought that if the client could somehow learn to "let go" and stop needing to make everything "come out right," he would be less at risk for a repeat of a bleeding ulcer and would lead an even more productive life.

The following is a short excerpt from the ninth therapy session.

CLIENT: You know, that Benson thing (breathing exercises) you taught me actually helps a little.

THERAPIST: How about the mantra I suggested?

CLIENT: Oh, you mean, to tell myself over and over again that this is not my responsibility—that some things are beyond my control? That's really hard for me.

THERAPIST: Hard?

CLIENT: Yeah. I mean when Jenny [his daughter] comes home late, I wonder what she was doing, what I did that was wrong.

THERAPIST: Somehow you hold yourself responsible for what your daughter does.

CLIENT: Yeah.

THERAPIST: Is that reasonable?

CLIENT: Well, I am the parent and it's my job to place limits on my children and to ensure that they grow up right.

THERAPIST: You mean that if your daughter lights up a marijuana cigarette, you are responsible?

CLIENT: Yes.

THERAPIST: You held the match?

CLIENT: Come on, you know what I'm talking about.

THERAPIST: No, I don't. It seems to me your nineteen-year-old daughter is responsible. Now you could say, "Young lady, if I catch you smoking you are out of here."

CLIENT: No, I couldn't—how could you suggest that?

THERAPIST: Do you feel that if you said something like that you would be brutal and unfeeling?

CLIENT: Yes.

THERAPIST: So you're trapped—you can't hold her responsible for her behavior and you can't admit to yourself that what she does is ultimately out of your control.

CLIENT: Yeah, I guess that's it. What do you want me to do? Reject my daughter?

THERAPIST: What I want you to do is to look at what you are doing to yourself. If you continue the belief that you can do something to make everything all right then you are going to continue to be under this horrible stress.

CLIENT: Maybe. Well, how do I let go?

THERAPIST: Yeah. That's the question, isn't it?

The client and his daughter were also seen together and the therapist modeled "letting go" and "gee you are responsible for your life" behaviors as examples for Mr. Spencer. As he gradually reduced his attempts to "control" his daughter and instead placed responsibility on her for both her actions and their consequences, his ulcer symptoms became less marked and his need for ulcer medication was reduced.

Peptic Ulcers and Other Gastrointestinal Diseases

Duodenal and peptic ulcers and other gastrointestinal disorders (particularly irritable bowel syndrome) have historically been attributed, at least in part, to stress. According to Whitehead (1993), physiological factors are much more important than psychosocial factors in causing ulcers, and drug treatments that block gastric acid secretion will lead to rapid healing of most ulcers. Recent work indicates that antibiotic treatment for the bacteria *Heliocobacter pylori* (*H. pylori*) is required when a patient tests positive for its presence. Further, it is now clear that *H. pylori* is one of the most common human pathogens infecting the gastric mucosa of almost all persons, particularly those raised in an "unclean" environment (Dubois, 1995). Ninety percent of duodenal ulcer patients and 80% of peptic ulcer patients are infected with *H. pylori*.

Although most people are infected with this bacteria, many do not develop ulcers. Clearly *H. pylori* is closely associated with ulcer formation; however, there is no simple causal relationship. Further, although *H. pylori* is a contributing cause, as is excess stomach acid, note that Weiss (cited in Sarafino, 1994) found that some ulcer patients had low levels of gastric acid. If excess gastric acid, either in combination with *H. pylori* or by itself, fails to cause ulcers in all patients, then a simple physiological mechanism to account for ulcers has not been found. Clearly *H. pylori* infection in combination with excess gastric acid causes ulcers in many clients and patients. However, ulcers can also be produced by relatively low levels of acid if the mucous lining of the stomach or duodenum is inadequate. But it is excess stomach acid that accounts for 90% of ulcers. This acid environment encourages the growth of *H. pylori*. Such an infection, plus excess acid, can overwhelm the body's protection and lead to ulcer formation.

The question remains, why does excess acid exist in the first place? Perhaps an individual produces excess acid because of a genetic defect. There is little evidence for this proposition, however. Or perhaps environmental stress produces the excess. Sarafino (1994) stated that stress of all kinds is related to ulcer rates that are higher than those occurring in the general population.

If one perceives oneself to be or is in fact under extreme stress (serious environmental stress or other kinds), then ulcers may form. There are data that indicate that a person under perceived stress will excrete excess stomach acid. According to Wolf and Wolff (1947), when a subject was stressed and as a result felt anxious and hostile (but did not express that hostility), stomach acid production markedly increased. Similar results were reported by Engel, Reichsman, and Segal (1956).

Alexander (1950) suggested that the wish to remain in a dependent infantile situation, to be cared for, is in conflict with the adult ego's pride and aspiration for independence, accomplishment, and self-sufficiency. He suggested that the repressed longing for love, security, and unconditional approval is the unconscious psychological process that may lead to ulceration (and perhaps other gastrointestinal problems). More recently, and less psychoanalytically, Lewin and Lewis (1995) have suggested that similar internal processes could, by some unknown route, result in an increase in acid-pepsin secretion or a decrease in tissue resistance to autodigestion (possibly by means of a reduction of the mucous lining), thus producing ulceration. Harper, Kane, and Stroehlein (1994) reported that patients suffering from peptic ulcers or irritable bowel syndrome, ulcerative colitis, and regional enteritis have higher rates of generalized anxiety, depression, and panic than do normal control subjects. York, Bradberry, Karis, Burdick, and Menore (1996) found that college students who reported symptoms of gastrointestinal distress were significantly more depressed on both the Beck Depression Inventory and the MMPI-D scale than those who did not complain of these symptoms. Further, the students reporting symptoms were more anxious than nonsymptomatic students on both Beck's measure of anxiety and the Taylor Manifest Anxiety Scale. Walker, Luther, Sahloff, and Feldman (1988) found that patients who suffer from peptic ulcers showed chronic levels of depression and anxiety. In addition they reported that such patients were unable, or more often so than normal people, to express anger and hostility in an adaptive manner.

There is evidence that psychological stress factors and internal psychological processes are related to gastrointestinal distress. Reduction of stress and changes in personal behavior would then be part of a total treatment approach for sufferers of ulcers or other gastrointestinal diseases. Meditation and relaxation techniques could be useful. So could cognitive restructuring, particularly around issues related to irrational beliefs that one must be liked by and please everyone. In addition, humanistic techniques (particularly client-centered) focused on reducing the discrepancy between the *real self* and the *ideal self*, and on producing what the existentialists call an *authentic self* could be of use.

Psychosocial Intervention and the Chronically or Terminally Ill

In dealing with people suffering from chronic physical disease, particularly if such disease causes substantial suffering or is a prelude to death, the primary issue (beyond sheer survival) is the quality of the suffering person's life. It is in improving the quality of life that psychologists can be of immense help. There is evidence (Kamen-Seigel, Rodin, Seligman, & Dwyer, 1991) that when people who are seriously ill are positive and optimistic, and are involved with other people and take effective and realistic care of themselves, the severity of the disease may be lessened and the survivability of the patients increased. However, the types of psychosocial interventions useful in chronic diseases often do not have a neat representation in traditional modes of psychotherapy. We hold that intervention strategies need to focus on practical reality-oriented interventions and warm concern for the patient as a person. These psychosocial approaches should be part of standard medical treatment, but usually are not.

For example, patients are told they must take their medication. They are told when to take their medication, how much to take, and perhaps some of the side effects. They are *not* told how to deal with the feelings that are evoked when they must orient their lives (at least in part) around taking their medication. Often patients feel burdened by medication regimens, but more often they feel subtly distressed because the taking of the medicine reminds them that they are ill, that they are at risk. It is essential that medical personnel deal with patients' feelings about taking medication and their dependence upon that medication. To help patients comply with prescribed medication, such support is critical (Becker & Rosenstock, 1984).

In addition, people who suffer from chronic illnesses have disease-related limitations imposed on them. For instance, someone who suffers from multiple sclerosis will often feel tired—a common problem of many chronic illnesses—and will not be able to do all that he or she could do before becoming ill. Often such patients or clients will feel depressed and inadequate, and will blame themselves for being weak or lazy or some other negative quality when, in fact, they are unable to do more. Sometimes family members will join in and blame the ill person for not trying or for being a "crybaby." A reality-based psychosocial intervention would be extremely useful in removing the person's self-blame and educating the family and significant others about the limitations imposed by the disease.

Further, the removal of illness-caused depression and pessimism could be related to improving the patient's physical condition (Kamen-Seigel et al., 1991). Finally, the more traditionally based psychotherapeutic approaches to be used would, in part, be based on the patient's psychological state. Chronically ill people who display patterns of psychotic thinking, feeling, and acting, should be approached as we discuss in Chapters 10 and 11.

To not deal with the psychological issues of chronically ill patients denies the reality of their psychological distress. To not tend to their psychological issues could contribute to a marked reduction in the quality of their lives. To deny that psychological suffering needs attention may condemn the chronically ill person not only to a more miserable life but also a shorter one, if current findings on the relationship between one's state of mind and the progress of serious illnesses are correct.

Conclusion

We hold that disorders formerly called psychosomatic are not simply caused by some characteristic personality structure or by environmental stress. That is to say, heart disease, high blood pressure, asthma (and certain other respiratory disorders), ulcers (and certain other gastrointestinal disorders), headaches, and other types of organ damage formerly called psychosomatic do not each have some simple and direct psychological cause. However, the hypothesis that personality is related to physical well-being and can even contribute to organ damage still has utility.

Treatment for people who suffer from chronic heart disease, asthma, and ulcers, as well as many other chronic diseases, can profit from supportive, nondirective, and more focused psychological approaches. The severer the psychological difficulties, the more structured should the treatment process be. Usually, overt psychological symptoms are few and the treatment is not highly structured. Most successful intervention strategies involve reasonably short (twenty sessions or fewer) and relatively nondirective emotion-engaging approaches, precisely as advocated by Ornish (1982). Initially, the consultation is with the patient and significant others involved in his or her treatment. Individual or couples therapy followed by supportive group sessions are useful. Followup sessions and some kind of relaxation training or meditation or both can also be included. It seems to us that this corresponds reasonably well with our intrapsychic model.

In approaching people who have developed heart disease, ulcers, asthma, or any other debilitating condition, a warm, somewhat strong but rather "laid-back" approach is recommended. The person who is suffering from a disease is understandably weak and complaining about his or her lot.

The interpersonal approach that we advocate for such problems—a warm, assertive role (low-level *NO*, see Figure 2.2, page 30), should move the patient toward a more positive role. If the physician can lower his or her interpersonal power position (become less dominant), the patient is likely to become an active partner in treatment. The importance of this liaison cannot be overstated. If the patient does not follow an appropriate diet, take medication on time, or slips into a state of hopelessness, the person's health will be compromised. In those cases where the patient is more severely distressed, a more intensely positive role (high-level *NO*) is often helpful. The interpersonal role to be taken in working with chronically ill people is also consistent with our interpersonal model.

The content of psychosocial intervention with patients who are psychosomatic or chronically ill or both revolves around reality issues associated with the particular disease and the patient's reaction to it. In addition, treatment focuses on a particular class of violations of social expectations. Often psychosomatic patients deny their disease and continue to engage in lifestyle patterns that are dangerous to them. Such issues as smoking, eating habits, and so forth constitute part of the content of therapy. Again, this is a reasonable fit with our model.

6 Neuroses

In this chapter we will discuss psychosocial treatment approaches for disorders once called *neuroses*. Although not our major focus, we will also refer to the use of drugs with neuroses (see Appendix 2).

Since the dramatic theoretical change in the psychiatric classification systems in 1981 with the publication of the DSM-III, it has become necessary to justify the term *neurosis*. The general category of neuroses (which would include anxiety disorders, somatic disorders, and dissociative disorders) was omitted from the DSM-III and from all subsequent APA (American Psychiatric Association) classification systems. Neurosis was called a theoretical term and therefore dismissed.

Neuroses

While the category of neuroses was dropped from the DSM-III and continued to be omitted from subsequent editions, including the current DSM-IV, we are in agreement with Rosenhan and Seligman (1995) that as a general category the term *neuroses* is at least as useful as the term *psychoses*. The most obvious characteristic of DSM-IV disorders formerly called neuroses (anxiety disorders, somatic disorders, and dissociative disorders) is that people who suffer from them experience extreme subjective distress. Although not all people exhibiting such distress would fit Freud's model of anxiety or irrational fear as the proximate cause of neuroses, many of these disorders could be described in that way.

In addition to extreme subjective distress, many of these disorders have easily identified behavioral or cognitive components that contribute to—if not cause part of—the person's subjective distress. Many of these "symptoms" are the same ones Freud identified in his specification of neuroses. Finally, all of these disorders involve, as Freud argued, a nonpsychotic level of reality distortion.

The rationale given for omitting neuroses from DSM-III and subsequent editions was that the concept was a theoretical one (psychoanalytic) and that the DSM-III was to be atheoretical. It is inconceivable to us that any classification system could be considered atheoretical since any attempt to classify anything must define the domain of interest and the criteria on which classifications are made. The domain of interest in the DSM-IV, for example, is mental illness and the criteria for classification are its behavioral indicators. This is the old medical model in a new guise. The DSM systems are modern versions of the nineteenth-century Kraepelinian system, which explicitly endorsed the medical model. Although the DSM system is mute on causes of mental illness, its principal framers are not. For example, Reid (1989) argued that mental illness is real, is a disease, and that the current focus on drug treatment is not only appropriate but also required. Reid suggested that medication was the treatment of choice for disorders formerly grouped under the neuroses category. Behavior modification (assumedly including cognitive approaches) is given some credence and so-called traditional psychotherapy is given tepid endorsement for disorders with less clearly defined "symptoms."

If one hypothesizes that neurosis as a general classification category has as much utility as psychosis, then what are the implications of that proposition? First, that there exists a set of disorders (neuroses) that are all related to subjective distress and anxiety as part of the causal chain that produces dysfunctional but not psychotic behavior patterns. Second, that effective treatment of people suffering from neuroses requires intervention targeted at changing self-talk and modifying self-defeating patterns of behavior *and* long-term learned patterns of inadequate, self-defeating thought patterns.

The position taken above does not rule out drug treatment. For the most "symptomatic" of the prototypes designated in the DSM-IV as agoraphobia, obsessive compulsive disorders (OCD), and severe neurotic depressions (dysthymic disorder), drug treatment is often useful (see Appendix 2). For example, Baxter, Schwartz, Bergman, Szuba, Minford, & Phelps (1992) found that people "diagnosed" as having OCD who took Prozac showed changes in glucose metabolism in their "caudates." However, a matched group of OCD patients receiving only behavior therapy using the desensitization technique showed similar physiological changes. It should be noted that response prevention and exposure therapy also have been empirically shown to be effective psychological treatments of OCD (see Chapter 7). We discuss desensitization later in this chapter and analyze response prevention and exposure techniques in Chapter 7. In addition, Beck (1967) found that people with so-called diagnosis of depression, even psychotic levels of depression, required only short-term drug treatment. He also found that many patients responded well to cognitive therapy alone. It is likely that targeted psychosocial treatment approaches may also show similar gains in other severer forms of neuroses. For people receiving DSM-IV diagnoses of simple phobias, generalized anxiety disorders (without panic attacks), and many of the somatic disorders, drug treatment may not be the treatment of first choice—if appropriate at all.

As is our strategy throughout this text, we will not offer "traditional psychotherapy" or "psychosocial intervention" as an adequate specification of what is to be done for these troubled people. Rather, we will focus on those theories and methods that have been influential and emphasize approaches empirically shown to succeed.

CASE HISTORY **6.1**

Issues of Anxiety and Asymptomatic Neurosis— Louis Ferrino

Mr. Louis Ferrino contacted the therapist because a friend suggested that therapy might be helpful. Mr. Ferrino was 63 years of age and reported that his physical health was good. He denied delusions, hallucinations, suicidal ideation, and any significant psychological problems except a pervasive sense of anxiety. Mr. Ferrino appeared competent, self-assured, and in command. He was dressed appropriately and reported that he was successful and had accumulated assets of over $1 million. In spite of his success in life, he reported that he was often bedeviled by an overwhelming fear "that the other shoe might drop."

In the initial interview Mr. Ferrino stated that he first became preoccupied with impending doom during his experiences in World War II. He was in the second wave of the invasion of Normandy and many of his buddies were killed. After the initial battle, he went to the rear lines as other combat units took over. Upon arriving at his barrack he found a letter from his wife of one year stating that she was filing for divorce. In addition, he received a letter informing him that his father had died. Shattered, Mr. Ferrino sought the counsel of his pastor, who unfortunately was drunk at that time. Following these disclosures, Mr. Ferrino was given an MMPI to screen for more serious difficulties. No significant results were found on this test. Further psychological assessment was not considered necessary. After the initial interview, he agreed to an open-ended number of psychotherapy sessions. The therapist felt that the client would need thirty or forty sessions to untangle what seemed to be a life pattern organized around anticipating impending disaster.

The following is a short excerpt from the seventeeth session.

> **THERAPIST:** The last time I saw you, your concern was that you weren't sure whether your [current] wife might leave you. You mentioned this at the end of our session and I didn't have the opportunity to ask you what your wife had done to cause you to fear her leaving you.

CLIENT: Well, she doesn't want to have anything to do with me sexually and she seems withdrawn from me.

THERAPIST: Can you talk to her about these things?

CLIENT: I don't know.

THERAPIST: What do you need to do to find out what is happening inside her?

CLIENT: I asked her to tell me what's going on and that just seemed to upset her.

THERAPIST: How did you ask her?

CLIENT: Pretty much the way I just said.

THERAPIST: You mean, you are the boss and you just want "the facts, ma'am."

CLIENT: I guess you could say that.

THERAPIST: Then she closed off?

CLIENT: Yeah.

THERAPIST: Could it be that you need to expose yourself somewhat— that you need to say to her that she seems closed off to you and it hurts?

CLIENT: I am not comfortable with that.

THERAPIST: Is it true that her closing off hurts you?

CLIENT: Yes.

THERAPIST: But to tell her that would make you vulnerable?

CLIENT: Yes, and I could get hurt.

THERAPIST: But you're being hurt now by not being vulnerable, or rather by not *admitting* that you are hurt and are vulnerable.

CLIENT: Oh God! My standard role of "executive" doesn't work here and what I am doing causes my wife to retreat.

THERAPIST: Sounds right to me.

The client and his wife were able to resolve their conflict. Both became able to express their needs to be in emotional contact with each other. The client was also able to contact and resolve his feelings of loss and fear of abandonment. However, in an attempt to increase his financial holdings to a point where he and his wife could maintain their current lifestyle, he lost his fortune. He was still in therapy at that time and was able to see this reversal as yet another event produced by his actions, which were intended to prevent the very thing they produced. He and his wife relocated and he was able to engage in a new business. He reported that his marriage was much more satisfying than before.

Freud and Dollard and Miller

Freud: Classical Psychoanalysis.   Freud (1901, 1961) argued that neurotic disorders were caused by early emotional distress (trauma) that produced fixations. Freud's focus was primarily on those fixations that occurred during the preschool developmental period (called by Freud the phallic stage characterized by the Oedipal conflict). He argued that negative experiences (trauma) produced changes in the structure of personality. This structure, according to Freud, included the *id,* the instinctual and irrational part of the personality; the *ego,* the learned and rational part of the personality; and the *superego,* roughly similar to the conscience. When the individual could not solve reality problems then that individual would become anxious. The anxiety (we would now say irrational learned fear) led to the use of specific unconscious defensive reactions (or, which Freud called *defense mechanisms*), which served to get rid of the anxiety but did not resolve the underlying conflict that had produced it. Further, similar situations would trigger anxiety again and the troubled person would engage in automatic and self-defeating behaviors or thoughts to get rid of that anxiety rather than solve the underlying distortions.

Common defense mechanisms include *repression,* the mechanism through which one unconsciously forgets threatening material and thus prevents oneself from experiencing the anxiety associated with that memory. Another defense mechanism called *rationalization* is characterized by unconscious, false self-justification. The defense mechanism known as *denial* is the blatant and unconscious ignoring of reality. There are many other defense mechanisms that can be found in any abnormal psychology textbook. According to Freud, much of the neurotic's life involves using these defense mechanisms to ward off unpleasant subjective experiences rather than more efficiently solving life's challenges.

For Freud, therapy consisted of bringing into awareness material of which the individual was unaware. That material would, Freud argued, consist ultimately of a collection of childhood traumas that had not been resolved and continued to control much of the thoughts, feelings, and actions of the troubled person. He felt that if the unconscious material became conscious, then a corrective emotional experience would occur and the neuroses would be defeated. Freud offered case history data to support his contention that psychoanalysis was an effective treatment. Although he stated that psychoanalysis was the treatment of choice for neurotics, it was not suitable for psychoses, personality disorders, and disorders caused by substance abuse.

The *how* of bringing unconscious material to consciousness is one major point of controversy for psychoanalysis. The technique requires proper patient selection—in other words, patients who have capacity for insight, ego cooperation, secondary process thinking, and high verbal intelligence, according to A. Freud (1976). Golderson (1970) stated that, "According to [S.] Freud, psychoanalysis is most effective between the ages of fifteen and fifty. . . . It is usually inadvisable to analyze patients whose life situation is too oppressive, who are in an acute dangerous state, or who lack the ability to reason by virtue of psychosis, mental deficiency, mental confusion or retarded depression . . ." (p. 1046). According to Fenichel (1945) the following disorders require increasing modification in technique, in the order listed: character disorders, depressions, perversions, addictions, impulse disorders, and psychoses.

Patient selection, or rather patient deselection, is only part of the problem of psychoanalytic therapy. Many neurotics can meet the selection criterion but people with character disorders, substance abusers, and psychotics must then be eliminated. Further, the costly process of therapy three or so times a week for years rules out all potential patients but the wealthy with a lot of time on their hands. In addition, the technique itself is open to question.

Technique for classical psychoanalysis requires that the client lie on a couch and the therapist sit behind him or her. The individual is instructed to say whatever comes to mind and to not censor anything. The therapist is required to remain quiet and only to intervene to (1) interpret transference issues, (2) interpret defenses, (3) interpret dreams and slips of the tongue, and (4) point out resistances. The therapist must also remain nonjudgmental and permissive.

Many people are not comfortable with this approach, even if they meet the stated and unstated (social class, money, and time) criteria, and therefore do not remain in therapy. For these reasons most analytically trained therapists have modified the classical technique. Still, the general agreement among psychoanalytic therapists is that unconscious conflicts are central to the problems of these troubled people and that structural change in the personality is required for the person to be free of his or her neurosis.

Freidman (1997) offered his synopsis of which aspects of Freud's psychoanalytic approach are still useful. He stated that Freud's emphasis on boundless curiosity about the patient and the patient's problems, the importance of the therapeutic relationship, and the absence of therapist value judgments, and his emphasis that the patient ultimately face the truth remain essential therapeutic orientations. In essence, it may be that psychoanalytic technique is not as useful as the psychoanalytic attitude or orientation toward treatment as described by Freidman.

Dollard and Miller: The First Behavioral Translation of Psychoanalysis.
Dollard and Miller (1950) attempted to translate Freud's insights into what was then the current learning theory of academic psychology, known as the *Hullian learning theory* or *drive theory*. Their attempt was a notable one. According to Dollard and Miller all dysfunctional patterns of behavior (neu-

roses) are learned. They are learned in the same manner that all other behaviors (and thoughts and feelings) are learned. Negative learned behavior patterns are therefore to be extinguished.

Following this general overview Dollard and Miller (1950) stated that in psychosocial treatment one must create a benign and nonthreatening environment within which the feared memories and metaphors for learned self-defeating orientations could occur without being reinforced. Eventually self-defeating patterns of thinking, feeling, and acting would be extinguished. In addition Dollard and Miller encourage the employment of "higher mental processes" to solve psychological difficulties. Since higher mental processes are synonymous with cognitive function, we would credit Dollard and Miller as being the first explicit cognitive therapists. But of even greater importance, Dollard and Miller suggested that the permissive environment could allow the individual to discover novel verbalizations, or self-talk. Such self-talk involves labeling those thoughts that are not part of the person's higher mental processes. We argue that this is another way of saying that one must make conscious that which was unconscious. Much of what is now called cognitive/behavior modification is focused on (1) changing behavior, (2) changing self-talk, and (3) allowing the troubled person to label and verbalize formerly inaccessible parts of the individual's personality, specifically those parts that are causing trouble. Dollard and Miller also used other techniques, now fashionable, such as modeling and labeling behaviors, thoughts, and feelings that were obvious to the therapist but not to the individual. However, neither Freud nor Dollard and Miller were either aware of or made use of the wide array of techniques that are now routinely employed by therapists.

CASE HISTORY **6.2**

Issues of Anxiety, Obsessive Compulsive Disorder, and Phobias—Melvin Leibowitz

Mr. Melvin Leibowitz, a college student, was referred to the therapist because he continuously fell asleep in his classes. His academic performance was adequate in spite of this, but one of his professors felt that "something was wrong" and asked him to talk to the therapist. Initially, Mr. Leibowitz appeared anxious, and was reluctant to disclose personal information. He was dressed in a somber fashion and could be described as "strange."

Because his behavior was peculiar and because he did express extreme distress (he reported feeling depressed and that he was getting little sleep), the MMPI and Rorschach were administered. In addition the WAIS was given to provide information about his academic ability. The MMPI revealed that Mr. Leibowitz was engaging in obsessive thinking patterns and was clinically depressed. The Rorschach indicated obsessive compulsive tendencies, as well as depression. Suicide indices were negative. Mr. Leibowitz's full-scale IQ was 132, indicating that he was extraordinarily bright. When this information was shared with Mr. Leibowitz, he agreed to begin weekly psychotherapy sessions with the therapist.

During the second session the client disclosed that the only way he could get to sleep was to read sixty separate passages from the Torah, or more accurately, from one of the sixty Torahs he had hidden in his bedroom. Each passage had to be read in sequence and from the "right" Torah. Almost every night the client would read a passage out of order or from the wrong Torah and then he would have to start all over. The therapist asked him why he had to read these passages and he replied because if he didn't, something horrible would happen to him. Of course, his Torah "reading" would often last through the night. Although deprived of sleep, the client had not been murdered during the night. The next night the ritual would begin again, and so on and so forth. He also disclosed fear of death, and anything associated with dying such as funerals, funeral homes, and cemeteries. He would go to great lengths to avoid being exposed to anything associated with death.

The following is a short excerpt from the twenty-third session.

THERAPIST: Mr. Leibowitz, today we are going to *approach* a cemetery. What I want you to do is to tell me when you are getting anxious and we will stop. All right?

CLIENT: Yes.

THERAPIST: [Heads to office doorway.] OK. Now we are going to start out of the office—how do you feel?

CLIENT: Fine, I am OK. [They leave the building for the parking lot.]

THERAPIST: Hop in the car and tell me how you feel.

CLIENT: Well, I am getting a little anxious—I mean I know I am going to a cemetery.

THERAPIST: Right now you just got in the car and it's just a first step. Do you remember the Benson relaxation exercise we worked on?

CLIENT: Yes.

THERAPIST: OK. Now, do it for four minutes—I will tell you when the time is up. OK, how do you feel?

CLIENT: Good. I am relaxed.

THERAPIST: [Starts the car engine, and they proceed out of the lot.] Now we are driving out of the University. How do you feel?

As can be seen from the above, this process was an *in vivo* desensitization approach to a specific phobia. The client reported less fear of cemeteries after this but his problems were far from over. In a later session he reported that his fear stemmed from a horrible experience that he had in Israel when he was an exchange student. He and a friend were to go to the Wailing Wall but he begged off because he had to study. His friend was killed in a terrorist attack and Mr. Leibowitz had been required to identify the body. The rituals and repetitive fears of attack and murder stemmed from this event. When he was able to absolve himself of guilt related to his friend's death, much of the client's distress, although not all, was reduced.

Steven C. Hayes: Behavior Therapy

Although Dollard and Miller (1950) attempted to integrate psychoanalytic thought with what was then the dominant learning theory in psychology (Hullian learning theory), there are probably few if any psychologists who now advocate their position. Today behavior therapists identify *classical conditioning* and *operant conditioning* as the two animal-based learning theories that lead to specific therapeutic interventions. Modern behavior therapists owe much to the work of Pavlov (1927), Watson (1925), and Skinner (1953), all of whom championed the application of laboratory-based learning as the only scientific means of influencing human conduct. In addition, Mowrer (1960) offered an animal-derived model (in his two-factor theory), which Hayes, Follette, and Follette (1995) used to account for the behavioral treatment of some types of human avoidance behaviors (we will discuss this later in this chapter).

From the 1950s through the 1960s many applications of classical and operant conditioning occurred. Salter (1949) in his book, *Conditioned Reflex Therapy,* and Wolpe (1958), in his book, *Psychotherapy By Reciprocal Inhibition,* maintained that they were applying classical conditioning theory to aid troubled human beings. Lindsley (1956), Ayllon (1963), and Ayllon and Azrin (1965) applied operant principles in the treatment of profoundly disturbed individuals (mostly back-ward chronic psychotics). Freedheim (1992) held that by the late 1960s the application of behavioral principles to clinical practice was accelerating and was no longer restricted to back-ward psychotics or to people who suffered from mental retardation.

According to Hayes, Follette, and Follette (1995), in the 1970s behavior therapists began once again to accept internal "mental processes" (thoughts). Homme (1965) anticipated this trend when he introduced the notion of *coverants,* which he defined as the operants of the mind. Hayes et al. stated that such sloppy thinking needed correction and that behavior therapy ought to return to its behavioral roots if precision in the therapeutic treatment of troubled individuals was to be retained.

Hayes et al. (1995) introduced the term *contextualistic behaviorism* and stated that adherence to this theory would serve to correct some of the errors introduced by the rush to "cognitive therapy." They defined contextualistic behaviorism as the analysis of behavior, including thoughts and feelings, in its context. In fact Hayes and his associates might best be called behavior analysts. They called for events to be described at the observational level at which they occur, and for theoretical terms to be justified only on the basis of usefulness. They also held that "causality is viewed as a useful way of speaking about one's scientific goals . . ." (p. 132). They stated that the goals of their approach were to develop an "organized system of verbal rules that permit the description, prediction, influence, and interpretation of interactive activity" (p. 133). All behavioral relationships were to be analyzed within the context in which they occur.

Hayes et al. (1995) stated that a functional analysis of behavior, particularly problematic behaviors, and the context in which those behaviors occurred, was the first step in effective behavior therapy. The definition of functional analysis is critical in comprehending the implementation of any behavioral approach. *Functional analysis* means the identification of a person's essential behaviors as well as the functions they serve for that individual. The therapist's skill and openness to revision of initial analysis is essential in this process. Behavior therapy requires that the therapist continually revise his or her analysis of the behaviors that require attention. Failure to identify the essential behaviors in their context will lead to treatment failure. Hayes et al. offered several specific methods to ensure a complete functional analysis (see pp. 142–147).

Once this analysis has been completed, the therapist implements treatment based on operant or classical conditioning principles. First the therapist attends to those behaviors that are controlled by directly observable *stimulus–response contingencies.* Such behaviors can be modified by the application of operant conditioning principles including the technique of successive approximation. Gradually the desired behavior is produced by reinforcing other behaviors that more and more closely approximate the desired behavior. Token economies and other operant procedures are also used (see Chapter 12 for detailed specification of these procedures). Phobic and other behavior patterns characteristic of conditioned emotional responses respond to approaches derived from classical conditioning procedures (such as extinction and exposure).

Hayes et al. (1995) stated that not all behavior is controlled by *direct contingencies* (overt reinforcement). Many behaviors are controlled by *indirect contingencies* (covert reinforcement). According to Hayes et al., "These principles—which are essentially the contextual reply to cognitive psychology—are little known outside of behavior analysis . . ." (p. 134). Basically, indirect contingency analysis requires an understanding of the relationship among written names, objects, and oral names. Hayes et al. held that all verbal processes could be understood in terms of these relationships.

Once a child has learned that a written word stands for a particular object, the child can reverse that process without further learning. The same applies to oral names and their relationship to objects, as well as the relationship between written and oral names. Thus if the child learns that the spoken word "dog" stands for the object dog, the child without further training will point to the object dog and say "dog." This analysis is used to account for the verbal processes of reading with understanding, writing, hearing with understanding, reading aloud, and dictation. We note that reading with understanding and hearing with understanding necessarily include internal responses that are not directly observable. However, as any behavior therapist would argue, the consequences of those processes are observable and therefore can be modified by behavioral techniques.

In order to modify indirect contingencies Hayes et al. (1995) held that the concept of *derived stimulus relations* was necessary. These stimulus relations constitute a new form of behavioral regulation called rule governance. According to Hayes et al., "Rule governance involves the transference of antecedent psychological functions among these relational networks" (p. 135). Skinner (1966) is credited with the derivation of this construct. These relational networks are the relations cited above between the written and spoken word and objects. The example Hayes et al. gave of how one of these concepts can be applied was the analysis of a woman who avoids dating. According to Hayes et al., "The woman may have constructed a response-consequence relation based on a verbal history (e.g., 'if I get too involved I will feel cornered and that will make me unhappy'). In fact, this contingent relation may never have been experienced and might be incorrect if it were tested. The rule may have been acquired in various ways (e.g., she may have heard similar rules from her mother who may have felt cornered and unhappy in her marriage" (p. 135).

Space limitations require that we omit much of the additional theoretical analysis in this article. However, Hayes et al. (1995) extended behavioral analysis to include issues of how one could deal with such questions as: what is personality, what characterizes healthy development, and how do psychological problems develop? The last issue requires some attention, from our perspective. How do Hayes et al. account for the emergence of psychological problems from a behavioral point of view?

Guidelines for the identification of the emergence of psychopathology focused on the specification of the unit of analysis. Hayes et al. (1995) stated:

The unit of analysis is a situated action: In a given context (composed of historical, motivational, and verbal features; a behavioral repertoire; direct and indirect stimulus functions; and other features), an organism with a current structure engages in an interaction with the world and the world is thereby changed in some way. By applying principles of operant conditioning, classical conditioning, and verbal control, myriad specific possible problems emerge. (p. 140)

Hayes et al. (1995) grouped psychological problems into the categories of inappropriate behavior regulation and problems related to what they called specific response forms. Examples of inappropriate behavior regulation are responses that are appropriate in some settings but not in the ones in which they have occurred, regressed behaviors that block the occurrence of potential reinforcers (for example, social approval), and so forth. Examples of response form difficulties are inadequate social behaviors and learned inappropriate social behaviors. Further, historical factors and current factors must be considered to understand the development of a psychological problem.

Once the therapist determines that a problem exists, he or she completes a functional analysis and selects treatment approaches. For practical reasons a DSM-IV classification is also included. Once the functional analysis and other appropriate evaluation is completed, the therapist begins behavioral treatment. Hayes et al. (1995) provided a general overview for problem identification and treatment (see their Table 5.2, pp. 150–151). Although extensive, the authors stated that their list of problems and techniques was not exhaustive. Hayes and his associates used many techniques not often associated with behavior therapy, such as *paradoxical intention* (a technique initially proposed by an early proponent of behaviorism, Knight Dunlop, in 1929) and the Gestalt *empty chair* technique (see Chapter 3, p. 107). These approaches were described in behavioral terms.

We have chosen to focus on the two approaches developed by Hayes and his associates that have broadened the application of behavior therapy to issues of "thoughts" and "feelings." These approaches are *functional analytic psychotherapy* (FAP) and *acceptance and commitment therapy* (ACT). FAP is the behavioral answer to Rogers's concept of the therapeutic relationship. The essence of this approach is that the therapist recognize *critically relevant behaviors* (behaviors that are effective and necessary for the person to function well). When the person displays such a behavior during the therapy session, the therapist must recognize that behavior and take appropriate action to reinforce it. In addition, the therapist must recognize the occurrence of functional behaviors that were not present earlier in therapy. Finally, the therapist and client must agree on how to label these important behaviors.

The basic concept of ACT was defined by Hayes et al. (1995) as, "That relationship between private events such as thoughts (or other private events) and overt behavior that is contextually established and maintained" (p. 156).

Hayes et al. held that therapists should not try to get rid of negative thoughts and feelings but rather should try to disentangle them from the context that related them to overt behavior. They argued that successful behavior therapy involved defeating the confusion of words with the associated described events (*literality*). For example, a person who has the thought "I am bad" may perceive himself or herself to be in a situation of being bad rather than being in the situation of having the thought of being bad. Repeating a word over and over again until it loses the power to conjure up negative reactions is offered as one of the many methods to deal with this problem.

ACT also addressed problems referred to by Hayes et al. (1995) as *reason giving* and *control of private events*. Reason giving referred to the dysfunctional tendency to give private antecedents (thoughts or feelings) as explanations of overt behavior. To quote Hayes et al., "For example, feelings are said to explain overt actions 'I was too anxious to go.') when from an ACT perspective there is no linkage between these described emotions and action ('I felt anxious and I went.')" (p. 156). According to Hayes et al., the attempt to control—to suppress or avoid—private events is self-defeating. In fact, Hayes and his associates held that "ACT shares common ground with experiential therapies in that experiencing and feeling are to be accepted and valued not controlled out of existence" (p. 158). Furthermore, once the client accepts his or her fear of a particular situation, then direct action can be taken to reduce that fear. The client is encouraged to commit to facing the feelings that have, in the past, led to avoidance behaviors. If the person can then tolerate the negative feelings and not make the avoidance behavior, then the fear will be extinguished.

The behavioral explanation of this effect, according to Hayes et al., is consistent with Mowrer's two-factor theory of avoidance learning. For two-factor theory, classically conditioned fear precedes operant avoidance behavior, which avoids the experience of the learned fear. Presumably if one can prevent the avoidance behavior without aversive events occurring, then the conditioned fear and the avoidance behavior will be extinguished. However, human beings do not only act, they think and feel as well. Meichenbaum (1977) argued that no simple S-R theory is sufficient to account for human learning; a self-talk or cognitive process is also required. We will discuss his arguments later in this chapter.

There is a great deal more to Hayes et al. (1995) than we can include here. If one wishes to employ these approaches in a systematic way it will be necessary to do an internship or postgraduate work with someone skilled in them. However, if one can maintain a behavioral focus, one can increase precision in treatment. Hayes and his colleagues also emphasized that behavioral techniques cannot be applied mechanically and that great interpersonal skill, awareness, and commitment are required if one is to be an effective behavioral therapist.

The Cognitive and Behavioral Approaches of Ellis, Meichenbaum, and Lazarus

We have chosen Ellis, Meichenbaum, and Lazarus as examples of psychotherapists in the cognitive–behavioral tradition whose client population was primarily nonpsychotic, and for whom technique was central to the treatment process. Among these practitioners, Lazarus (1981) was clearest about the importance of the therapeutic relationship in treating clients. According to Lazarus:

> Certainly, it is essential for the therapist to be respected by his or her clients, to establish sufficient trust for them to confide personal material, and to create an atmosphere whereby clients can freely disclose embarrassing, or anxiety-provoking information. (p. 133)

All of these therapists focus primarily on technique. Only Lazarus, however, gives us explicit guidelines about technique to establish a therapeutic relationship and states that it is necessary for the therapist to establish hope. The most cognitive of the cognitive therapists is Albert Ellis, and it is with his approach that we will begin our analysis of explicit approaches for these distressed individuals.

Ellis: Rational Emotive Therapy. Ellis (1962) argued that human beings suffer distress and act dysfunctionally because of their illogical patterns of thinking. He held that human beings are uniquely cognitive animals and that, alas, they are also inclined by their heredity to think irrationally and illogically. Furthermore, negative experiences in life make irrational thinking more likely, and the result of such thinking is misery and suffering. Therefore, if troubled people are to function more effectively, the therapist must change, or allow clients to change their irrational and illogical patterns of thinking. We should note that Ellis was not unaware of the importance of the therapeutic relationship. According to Ellis (1967) the individual, "must just be approached in a cautious, supportive, permissive and warm manner. . . ." However, "the rational therapist does not delude himself that these relationship-building and expressive-emotive methods are likely to really get to the core of the patient's illogical thinking . . ." (p. 95).

The primary technique of *rational emotive therapy* (RET) is what Ellis referred to as the ABC approach to the treatment of troubled people. Actually, this approach is an A, B, C, D, and E approach. A = *a*ntecedent causes of present irrational behavior. B = the irrational *b*eliefs generated by the individual's conceptualization of those antecedent causes. C = the irrational view of what the *c*onsequences of a particular event will be. An example of irrational thinking that leads to dysfunctional behavior might be as follows.

A person is rejected by a significant other (antecedent cause—A). That person believes (irrational belief—B) that the rejection occurred because he or she is totally unlovable. The consequence (C) of such irrational thought is that the individual views himself or herself as eternally unlovable and in fact incapable of ever being loved by anybody.

The therapist's role is to dispute (D) these irrational beliefs and to produce both cognitive and behavioral effects (E). An example of the disputation follows: The therapist might say, "Prove to me that you are utterly unlovable. Surely somebody must have loved you." If the client says, "No, nobody ever loved me," then the therapist might say something like, "How does that prove that you are utterly unlovable?" This process can go on for quite a while, but it is the therapist's job to dispute the irrational beliefs until the client accepts and understands that they are irrational.

Once this step is accomplished the therapist will also challenge the consequences produced by the weakened or, ideally, defeated irrational belief. For example, the therapist might say, "Just because Suzy rejected you, prove to me that all women will always reject you." This process may also be protracted and difficult, but the goal is to change the client's expectation of consequences based on irrational beliefs to expectations based on rational beliefs. Our example might resolve itself if the client agreed that Suzy's rejection didn't prove he was worthless and unlovable and that all women would reject him. Therefore, maybe other or at least *one* other woman *might* love him. What might he change in his pattern of behavior that could promise more success with women?

Ellis is by no means restricted in his approach to the rational emotive process described above. In addition, he often requires his clients to do homework (in other words, to change their behavior or to more concretely explore their irrational thinking process). Further, he advocates a variety of behavioral techniques where appropriate. These techniques are intended to produce cognitive or behavioral changes or effects. He includes stress management techniques, modeling, assertiveness training, and many other behavioral approaches. We will turn to Meichenbaum and Lazarus for our particularization of these techniques.

Meichenbaum: Cognitive Behavior Modification.   Meichenbaum (1977) has emphasized the necessity of changing self-talk if an individual is to accomplish behavior control. It seems that when desired behaviors are accomplished that explicit self-talk is not required, but when the individual engages in behaviors that are destructive and cause subjective distress, or engages in automatic self-talk that produces such behaviors, new patterns of explicit self-talk must be achieved. External control—either in terms of the control of antecedent and consequent circumstances (defined as operant and other procedures) or by using Ellis's rational emotive therapy—may not, probably will not, be sufficient to produce the patient's discovery of novel verbalizations, or more accurately to facilitate cognitive (conscious) awareness of automatic self-defeating sequences (either cognitive or behavioral). Although Meichenbaum might not agree, we suggest that he is one of the most important behavioral therapists to focus on the importance of making conscious that which was unconscious.

Meichenbaum (1977) pointed out that behavior modification attempts to handle all therapy changes by an appeal to "traditional" learning theory explanations (such as operant and classical conditioning) have not been convincing. He stated that the treatment effects produced by anxiety-relief conditioning, systematic desensitization, covert sensitization, and perhaps all other "behavioral" approaches, could not be accounted for by current learning theories.

As an example of a behavioral technique whose results cannot be accounted for by current learning theories, Meichenbaum discussed *anxiety-relief conditioning*. This procedure consists of pairing shock (aversive stimulus) with verbal behavior that produces relief ("relax, I can handle this"). The therapist then turns off the shock. This sequence is preceded by another sequence in which the phobic client is instructed to respond to the therapist's identification of the phobic object (for example, snake) by saying "It's ugly." Then the procedure is employed as indicated above. Reported fear of the phobic object is reduced as a function of this procedure. For a counter conditioning "explanation" to hold true, the above sequences ("snake"—"ugly," then shock—"I can handle it," then shock termination) must occur in order. Reverse the order and, according to conditioning theory, no counter conditioning should occur. Yet when the order of presentation was reversed, behavior change occurred, and occurred to the same degree as it had when the "proper" sequence of stimuli presentation was employed (Meichenbaum, 1977).

In addition, Meichenbaum challenged the adequacy of "learning theory" explanations of the effects of *systematic desensitization* or *covert sensitization*. Systematic desensitization is a procedure in which an anxiety hierarchy is constructed and then stimuli are presented from the least threatening to the most threatening, with instructions to the client to stop the sequence when he or she feels anxiety. Eventually the person can be exposed to all formerly threatening stimuli without reporting anxiety. Also, in systematic desensitization, the stimuli in the hierarchy that produced anxiety are coupled with the *Jacobsonian relaxation procedure*. In this procedure the client is asked to focus on the difference between tight and relaxed muscle groups. Covert sensitization is a procedure in which the client imagines aversive consequences related to a desired but negative behavior pattern, for example, imagine you are smoking, and then imagine the last time you threw up.

Meichenbaum suggested that the "Imagined Component" (1977, p. 120) was the key element in "explaining" the effects of systematic desensitization as well as covert sensitization on behavior and subjective process change. Meichenbaum seemed to be arguing that by explicitly changing self-talk, through training in *coping imagery,* changes in the client's cognitive structure would be produced that are essential for the effectiveness of *any* behavior modification approach. Meichenbaum concluded that all of the results above cannot be accounted for by any simple associative S-R learning model; we are in agreement. If one views all of the above approaches as aids to the client in discovering new and novel ways to self-talk, then Meichenbaum's cognitive focus becomes somewhat clearer.

The balance of cognitive behavior modification (Meichenbaum, 1977) is focused on the specifics of Meichenbaum's approach to integrating behavioral and cognitive strategies in the treatment of troubled people. The key to his approach is *stress-inoculation training,* in which the client is given a set of cognitive schema that allow him or her to reframe or understand current difficulties and to learn new-change responses to stressful events. The client is taught a set of coping techniques and then tries out these new skills in dealing with stressful situations in the "real world."

According to Meichenbaum (1977), coping skill programs include these components:

1. teaching the client the role of cognition in contributing to the presenting problem;
2. training in the discrimination and systematic observation of self-statements and images and in self-monitoring of maladaptive behaviors;
3. training in the fundamentals of problem solving (for example, problem definition, anticipation of consequences, evaluating feedback);
4. modeling self-statements and images associated both with overt and cognitive skills;
5. modeling, rehearsal, and encouragement of positive self-evaluation and of coping and attentional focusing skills;
6. the use of various behavior therapy procedures, such as relaxation training, coping imagery training, and behavioral rehearsal; and
7. *in vivo* behavioral assignments that become increasingly demanding (Meichenbaum, 1977, p. 147).

The first of the requirements for coping skills programs is most interesting. Before a client can appreciate the "role of cognition in contributing to the current problem," the client must identify the *specific cognitions* that are contributing to the problem. Meichenbaum, in his otherwise excellent overview of the approach, omitted this most important step. Insofar as the client is aware of his or her troublesome cognitions, behavior, or feelings, then all of the other steps outlined by Meichenbaum apply. But that first step is absolutely necessary if other interventions are to be meaningful, and it must also be applied to all behavioral and cognitive interventions.

One may at least in part consider Meichenbaum's (1977) cognitive restructuring techniques as a somewhat muted response to the fact that many of our clients are unaware of those events that trigger subjective distress, and also are unaware of the automatic thinking chain that deepens the subjective distress and may even contribute to problematic behavior patterns. Meichenbaum suggested that once nonfunctional self-talk is discovered, cognitive restructuring could deactivate self-talk and change noncoping behavior patterns to coping ones.

Meichenbaum suggested that if a therapist focused on identifying the presence of maladaptive self-statements and the absence of specific- and adaptive-cognitive skills, problematic cognition and behaviors would be discovered. Once discovered, some form of cognitive therapy (Ellis or Beck or some hybrid form of both) would be employed to facilitate cognitive change. Meichenbaum would include all of the other techniques as part of a total treatment focused on changing negative self-statements and discovering adaptive cognitive skills.

In an attempt to offer guidance to the therapist on how to organize therapy around something like a theory, Meichenbaum offered what he calls a "Cognitive Theory of Behavior Change." He suggested there are three components in such a "theory."

1. *Self-observation.* A troubled person often (always?) has a poorly defined and incompletely articulated internal dialogue about his or her maladaptive behaviors. The first step in therapy is to identify and clearly specify those elements of the internal dialogue that are maladaptive. This process leads to "increased self-awareness" (Meichenbaum, 1977, p. 220).
2. *Incompatible thoughts and behaviors.* Essential for effective therapy is the recognition by the client of maladaptive behavior. It seems that such recognition triggers internal dialogues; those dialogues must change and the client or patient must imagine outcomes that in turn initiate new behavioral patterns.
3. *Production of new behaviors.* "The third phase of cognitive theory of behavior change is concerned with the process of the client's production of new behaviors in his everyday world and how he assesses (or what he says to himself about) the behavioral outcomes" (Meichenbaum, 1977, p. 225).

It is clear that Meichenbaum has made, as did Dollard and Miller before him, a heroic attempt to bridge behavior modification with therapies focused on internal processes. Although Meichenbaum focused on cognitive therapies and not psychoanalytically oriented approaches (as did Dollard and Miller), he too sees narrow S-R behavior modification as inadequate to account for permanent change. The cognitive and behavior therapists discussed so far seem to emphasize the client or patient making conscious that which was unconscious, and employing secondary thinking or rational problem solving as opposed to self-defeating thoughts (in other words, neurotic thinking). These therapists emphasize behavior change as necessary for effective treatment outcomes.

CASE HISTORY **6.3**

Issues of Anxiety/Agoraphobia—Emily Train

Ms. Emily Train was a self-referral. She had been a student of the therapist and felt she could "talk" to him. She stated that she was having a great deal of trouble in getting out of her house and that she often "lost it" when standing on a large expanse of asphalt, in long halls with vinyl tiles, and in large department stores and malls. When asked what she meant by "lost it" she said that she felt like she was going out of her mind, that her body would seem to grow and shrink, and that she felt incredible panic. In fact, she could only leave her home with the support of one of her friends.

Ms. Train was given an MMPI and a Rorschach to determine suicidal risk and rule out severer psychopathology. Ms. Train was moderately depressed on the MMPI but Rorschach indices did not indicate suicide potential or psychotic levels of depression. No evidence of psychosis was found. However, indications of denial and extensive repression were evident.

The therapist felt that Ms. Train could profit from long-term therapy and should be evaluated for medication. While Ms. Train agreed to therapy, she refused to be evaluated for medication. The therapist pointed out that often the appropriate medication was very helpful for people who have her condition. Ms. Train still refused to follow up on the therapist's suggestion.

The following is a short excerpt from the seventeenth session.

> **THERAPIST:** During the last session you began to talk about being all alone and bedridden. You were very upset but unfortunately it was at the end of the hour. Would you like to start there now?
>
> **CLIENT:** Yes, remember I told you that my stepfather grabbed me from the rear and pulled me to him and I felt his hard penis against my buttocks.
>
> **THERAPIST:** Yes.
>
> **CLIENT:** Well, shortly after that I got a urinary tract infection and was bedridden. At that time my mother left my stepfather and left me all alone with him.

THERAPIST: Your real father, where was he during all of this?

CLIENT: He had called me after Mom contacted him and said he wanted to help me but couldn't.

THERAPIST: How did you feel about that?

CLIENT: I was disappointed.

THERAPIST: Disappointed, not angry? I feel anger toward your father for abandoning you; I wonder why you don't?

CLIENT: He couldn't help himself.

THERAPIST: Well, could you symbolically express anger toward Dad? I mean, pretend this book is Dad (throwing a book on the floor). Can you think about what Dad did to you? What would you like to do to Dad?

CLIENT: No, I couldn't do anything—don't make me [said with considerable emotion].

THERAPIST: Well, let me pretend that it is *my* Dad [at this point the therapist gets up and gleefully jumps up and down on the book. Ms. Train began laughing and then clapped her hands over her mouth in obvious embarrassment.] It's OK to laugh when *I* jump up and down on my Dad?

CLIENT: No.

THERAPIST: But it's really not my Dad—it is just me contacting my anger, perhaps my unresolved anger at Dad. When I first jumped up and down on "Dad," what did it feel like?

CLIENT: It felt freeing and I felt like maybe it would be all right for me to be angry at Dad for not being there for me.

The client continued psychotherapy for about two years. During that time she revealed a series of traumatic incidents around hospitals and hospital procedures that made sense out of her fears of expanses of asphalt and long halls with vinyl tiles (which evoked, from her memories, parking lots around clinics and the long halls in clinics and hospitals). She reported that she could now go out of her home and that all men were not like her father and stepfather. The client has since married and now has three children. At one point her primary care physician suggested amitriptyline for her depression and she reported that the medication helped her residual phobic tendencies. She still has difficulty with panic reactions in shopping malls, the only place in which her phobic reaction occurred, which was not fully explored in therapy. However, overall the client reported that she is doing well and is living a productive and normal life.

Lazarus: Multimodal Therapy.   One of the most comprehensive behavioral and cognitive approaches is that proposed by Arnold Lazarus (1981). Although Lazarus explicitly denies that his approach is a theory we hold that he is a theorist and a great one. Theory means an explanatory system that makes predictions, and in psychotherapy a theory is an explicit framework that specifies what works, with whom, and under what circumstances. Lazarus's multimodal therapy with its BASIC I.D. system and his comprehensive catalogue of techniques keyed to that system are consistent with our definition of a theory.

Lazarus argued that one must take any client as he or she is—a unique and complex human being. He stated that each client must be viewed, without qualification, as equal to the therapist and every other human being. For Lazarus this postulate must be entertained for successful intervention. We would argue that in some respects this way of viewing the client is very similar to Rogers's central requirement for successful therapy, unconditional positive regard. It is also similar to Fromm's notion that each client should be treated as the hero or heroine of his or her own epic poem. Further, the unique individual and his or her own problems must determine what the therapist does and the therapist must, as Lazarus put it, "fit [the] therapy to the requirements of the client" (1981, p. 14).

Lazarus reported success with his approach, but only limited success. He stated that he was very successful with "simple cases" but not so successful with "complex cases." In simple cases there were relatively few areas of distress (similar to asymptomatic neuroses). Complex cases involved "extended interpersonal (systems) problems; when cognitive restructuring called for more than the correction of misconceptions or the straightforward alteration of negative self-talk; when intrusive images conjured up a gloomy future; and when affective reactions were characterized by extremes . . ." (Lazarus, 1981, p. 9).

We would argue that Lazarus has had success with roughly the same group of clients that Freud targeted for psychoanalysis. It would also appear that many of the clients with whom Lazarus reported difficulties are the same types of clients whom Freud argued would not be appropriate for analysis (such as psychotics, people with personality disorders, and people suffering from substance abuse). We have called these clients seriously disturbed. Even if our analysis is faulty, it is important to note at least that Lazarus did not propose his approach as a panacea and explicitly stated that many troubled clients might only be marginally helped by multimodal therapy.

Lazarus held that there were certain theoretical concepts upon which his approach rested. "Personality structure," or some similar concept, was for Lazarus a product of classical conditioning, operant conditioning, modeling, and vicarious processes. To further account for why people act, think, and feel as they do, he included private events (subjective events), nonconscious processes, and defensive reactions. He maintained that he did not let psycho-analytic concepts in by the back door, but we do not find his arguments convincing.

Defensive reactions may be operationalized, as serving the same purpose as defense mechanisms, by preventing the client from being aware of threatening or disturbing thoughts, feelings, or actions. *Nonconscious processes* are mental operations of which the client is unaware that cause difficulties in the client's thoughts, feelings, and actions. As an explanatory concept, nonconscious processes serve the same function as the unconscious and refer to thoughts, behavior, or emotions of which the client is unaware. In any case the nonconscious components whether cognitive, behavioral, or affective must become accessible to the client *and* remain consciously accessible if permanent and sustainable change is to be maintained.

For Lazarus, at least one other set of basic concepts was required. He included family systems and meta-communication as those events that often produce significant conflicts for the client. He used techniques in individual therapy that he stated he had borrowed from Minuchin and Haley. We suggest that conflict engendered from family systems could serve as a theoretical bridge between some concepts of family therapy and Freud's notion of internalized family conflicts as the focus of psychoanalysis.

Regardless of one's position on Lazarus and psychoanalysis, it is indisputable that he focused on identifying problems and then applying the appropriate techniques to aid the client in resolving these problems. The assessment of the client was based on interview data as well as his Multimodal Life History Questionnaire (Lazarus, 1981, Appendix 1, pp. 215–226).

This problem identification procedure follows Lazarus's BASIC I.D. format. "B" stands for *behavior* (what behaviors does the client or patient have that are maladaptive?). "A" stands for *affect* (what emotional reactions of the client or patient are too extreme?). "S" stands for *sensation* (the client or patient's unpleasant sensory events). Lazarus is not clear whether hallucinations would be included as sensory events, but there must be a place in his model for them. The first "I" is for *imagery* (what images does the client or patient have that are self-defeating or distressing?). "C" refers to *cognitions* (what patterns of self-talk are nonfunctional?). The second "I" is for *interpersonal* (what patterns of interpersonal behaviors are dysfunctional?). "D" refers to *drugs* and also to biology (what physiological problems compromise the client's functioning?).

Lazarus does not explicitly invoke the medical model but he is clearly aware that dysfunctional thinking and feeling are related to the lack of physiological integrity. In addition we would suggest that the sensation and interpersonal components of his model are subcategories of behavior, and that images may be considered as a subcategory of cognition. Of course, Lazarus is correct to emphasize that therapists must clearly identify the specific images, sensations, and interpersonal behaviors that characterize a particular individual.

Once the client's problem areas have been identified, the therapist employs techniques uniquely suited to solving that person's difficulties. These techniques are not to be employed mechanically. According to Lazarus there are two "don'ts" in therapy, "(1) Don't be rigid, and (2) Don't humiliate a person or strip away his or her dignity" (Lazarus, 1981, p. 129). In addition, hope must be instilled in the client and the therapist must be able to change his or her personal presentation to fit the client's modes of processing information.

It is necessary to expand the last points Lazarus made. He stated that Rogers's criterion for a successful relationship—that the therapist be genuine, empathetic, and show unconditional positive regard—is useful (although not always necessary) but not sufficient for effective therapy. Lazarus argued that the therapist might be directive or nondirective, warm or cold, depending on the client and always as determined by the client's expectancies. He also stated that the interpersonal style of the therapist needed to be compatible with that of the client. He had something different in mind from our interpersonal model. Compatibility for Lazarus meant a reasonable degree of similarity between the client's BASIC I.D. and the therapist's BASIC I.D. But consider also, "In case this is not self evident, [present authors' note, *it's not*] let me stress also the importance that *differences* play in promoting growth. Matching some fundamental similarities is usually necessary for a rapport, but outcome is as much a function of creative difference as a product of comforting agreement" (Lazarus, 1981, footnote, p. 142). With his last point Lazarus hints at something like our interpersonal model.

He also offered another orientation that he argued is necessary for forming and maintaining an effective therapeutic relationship. He credits Bandler and Grinder (1982) with arriving at a position in part similar to his, in that they too held that the therapist must match the client's modality if a successful therapeutic relationship is to occur.

In practice, Lazarus's approach requires attention to the client's dominant modes of representing reality to himself or herself. Lazarus stated that there are three basic reactor modes: imagery, cognitive, and sensory (the sensory mode is the only mode that Bandler and Grinder focused on). Does the client fantasize, imagine, deal with his or her world speculatively? If so, the therapist might say something like, "Can you imagine your life situation different and better than it is? How would it be better?" Does the client deal with reality cognitively, rationally? The therapist then relates to the client using a rational style. Is the client a sensory reactor? Perhaps the client is using kinesthetic, visual, auditory, gustatory, or olfactory sensory descriptions of his or her reality. The therapist would then match or mirror the client's sensory mode. Clearly one cannot use these methods in a mechanical fashion if one wants to be a multimodal therapist.

Given that the application or use of technique is not mechanical, it remains for us to (1) specify which techniques are used, (2) give some examples of how Lazarus selects techniques, and (3) indicate where the interested reader can find a more complete description of how Lazarus uses these techniques. As in his specification of the BASIC I.D. approach, Lazarus is clear and concise in his presentation of the therapeutic techniques and when they should be employed with a particular client.

Following the identification of specific problems that are then classified as problems of behavior—affect, sensation, images, cognition, or interpersonal or biological or both—Lazarus employs the variety of techniques listed in his Appendix 2 (Lazarus, 1981, pp. 229–242). We have organized these techniques in terms of the problem areas to which they apply:

Behavioral techniques
1. *Behavior rehearsal:* Identical to role-playing.
2. *Modeling:* The therapist demonstrates the appropriate behavior.
3. *Nonreinforcment:* Not reinforcing negative behavior.
4. *Positive reinforcement:* Reinforcing positive behavior, usually social in nature but not limited to social reinforcement.
5. *Recording and self-monitoring.* The client keeps a scrupulous record of behaviors that are significant (often used in weight control programs).
6. *Stimulus control:* Consists in the main of removing access to stimuli that produce undesirable behaviors.

Affect techniques
1. *Anger expression:* An attempt to encourage the client to express anger so that it "can be owned." Lazarus is clear that catharsis is not enough; anger must either be eliminated or channeled into appropriate expression. In this he is consistent with Freud, holding that abreaction of affect is required for problem (conflict) resolution.
2. *Anxiety management training:* Involves pretraining in relaxation, goal rehearsal, and coping imagery. Once anxiety management is achieved the client is told to generate anxiety and focus on the unpleasant sensory experiences, then to calm himself or herself by focusing on reducing negative sensations and on peaceful, calming thoughts.
3. *Feeling identification:* In our opinion, Lazarus has not laid out a specific technique for feeling identification. He reported that clients need to define what they mean when they express undergoing certain emotions: in other words, what does "I feel depressed" mean? Clients also need to explore feelings to determine which are troublesome and need to be "resolved." We interpret Lazarus to be saying that once we know what our clients mean when they say they are depressed (or other emotional state) and know in which concrete ways the depression (or

other emotion) is causing them to have difficulties, then we have identified feelings in such a way that they can be changed.

Sensory techniques

1. *Biofeedback:* Appropriate and specific physiological functions are monitored and their functioning is signaled to the client by auditory or visual feedback. The client is instructed to do whatever he or she can to reduce that signal. There are several variants of this procedure using different physiological signals related to physiological arousal; all are intended to allow the client to produce a state of low physiological arousal.

2. *Focusing:* A technique in which the client is asked (while relaxed) to examine spontaneous thoughts and feelings until a single feeling emerges. The patient focuses on that feeling for several moments and is asked to discover new sensations, images, and emotions. The therapist guides the client to focus on what sensations are related to particular thoughts and feelings. Lazarus stated that ". . . the client is often able to circumvent cognitive blocks with the result that important material may be brought to light" (Lazarus, 1981, p. 233).

3. *Hypnosis:* A method of *trance induction* (see Frankel & Zanansky, 1978; Dengrove, 1976, for further elaboration of technique and applications).

4. *Meditation:* A technique used to calm clients. Benson's relaxation technique is one of the clearest of these approaches and involves repeating something to oneself over and over again. For example, say "peace," focusing on that word and one's breathing, and ignoring distracting thoughts.

5. *Relaxation training:* A technique (Jacobson's relaxation technique) in which the client lies down on a couch and systematically tightens and relaxes each major muscle group, from forehead, eyes, jaw, throat, neck, shoulders, arms, hands, chest, upper back, abdomen, hips, buttocks, thighs, calf muscles, to toes. The client is enjoined to pay attention to differences between what it feels like for a muscle to be tense as opposed to relaxed. The therapist coaches the client throughout this process in a calm and relaxed fashion. This procedure often allows for general relaxation and often has a calming effect. It is used as part of the process of systematic desensitization mentioned earlier.

Techniques for working with clients with sexual problems

1. *Sensate focusing:* Tactile stimulation that is sensual not sexual, and intended to produce closeness and intimacy for a couple.

2. *Threshold training:* A technique for premature ejaculation. The female manually stimulates the man's penis. When he feels that he is about to ejaculate, he says "Stop." By this stop-start stimulation, ejaculation is postponed. These two examples give the reader a clear idea of the variety of sensory methods used by Lazarus.

Imagery techniques

1. *Associated imagery:* Similar to free association *except*, and very importantly, the associations are guided. "While experiencing an untoward emotion, they [the clients] are asked immediately to focus on any image that comes to mind, to see [present authors' note: perhaps another sensory mode might also be employed] as vividly as possible" (Lazarus, 1981, p. 238). In this way significant *novel* verbalizations may occur.

2. *Anti–future shock imagery:* A technique to prepare clients for possible negative, stressful events in their lives. The client is asked to imagine the worst thing that could happen and then to imagine surviving that event.

3. *Aversive imagery:* Identical to covert sensitization, a technique we have already described.

4. *Goal rehearsal or coping imagery:* A technique in which the person imagines every step in an upcoming event. The client is encouraged to visualize himself or herself successfully coping with the situation.

5. *Positive imagery:* A technique in which the client is encouraged to imagine a pleasant scene. Often a fantasy trip or experience can engender a pleasant subjective state and break a recurring negative cycle.

6. *The step-up technique:* An imaging technique in which the client is asked to imagine the worst thing that could happen to him or her in a particular situation and to imagine that he or she survives and prevails.

7. *Systematic exposure:* Similar to *in vivo desensitization.* In this technique the client is gradually exposed to the feared stimulus.

8. *Time projection:* A technique in which clients are asked to picture themselves going forward or backward in time. What could they have done to improve things? What can they do in the future that will aid in producing better outcomes?

9. *The empty chair technique:* Discussed in Chapter 3 under Gestalt techniques and presented as an awareness technique that uses imagery.

Cognitive techniques

1. *Bibliotherapy:* A technique in which the client is encouraged to read any one of several suggested self-help books. Lazarus asked the client to read such a book carefully and summarize the relevant points. The readings were then discussed during therapy.

2. *Corrective misconceptions:* Clients' mistaken notions about important issues are corrected; for example, one can't get pregnant by kissing.

3. Ellis's ABC paradigm, as discussed in this chapter..

4. *Problem solving:* Essentially teaching clients the use of logic and the scientific method as the best means of solving problems.

5. *Self-instruction training:* Changing what clients say to themselves from negative, self-defeating self-verbalizations to positive, problem solving self-verbalizations. Again, the key to this treatment is to discover the

automatic negative self-talk and then get the client to engage in positive self-talk. Lazarus doesn't state exactly how this is to be achieved, but the explicit focus on self-talk is critical.

6. *Thought-blocking:* A technique in which clients combat obsessive thought. When a bothersome thought occurs, the client says to himself or herself (one way or another), "Stop!"

Interpersonal techniques

1. *Communication training:* ". . . is composed of *sending skills* and *receiving skills.* When expressing ideas or conveying feelings, many people send messages that are vague, ambiguous, contradictory, and difficult to follow. To improve *sending skills,* the client learns about the importance of eye contact, voice projection, body posture, the use of simple, concrete terms, the avoidance of blaming and pejorative remarks, forthright rather than manipulative interest, and statements of empathy. Good *receiving skills* call for active listening, verification and acknowledgment, and rewarding the sender for communicating. *Role-playing* and *behavior-rehearsal* (q.v.) are especially suited for promoting the development of communication skill" (Lazarus, 1981, p. 232).

2. *Contingency contracting:* A technique in which the therapist negotiates a contract with the client with respect to attaining some goal. If the client does not fulfill the contract, there are negative consequences. We question why Lazarus included this technique under interpersonal issues since it is focused on explicit behavior change.

3. *Friendship training:* Similar to communication training and behavior, rehearsal of how one acts in a friendly way toward others is central to this technique.

4. *Graded sexual approaches:* "Men and women with sexual anxieties are advised to engage in sensual and sexual play only so long as and as far as pleasurable feelings predominate" (Lazarus, 1981, p. 234).

5. *Paradoxical strategies:* A technique in which the client is put into a "therapeutic double bind." The most common approach is symptom prescription, which entails telling the client to do more of whatever negative behavior he or she is engaging in. Another approach is to forbid a desired response. Lazarus uses the example of a man with erectile difficulty who is told to engage in foreplay but not to engage in sexual intercourse until he is given permission by his therapist.

6. *Social skills and assertiveness training:* There are actually two processes involved here, the more nebulous social skills training, which is very similar to communication training, and assertiveness training. The *broken record technique* is one specific technique of assertiveness training, in which clients are taught to repeat what they want over and over again. According to Lazarus (1981), ". . . assertive behavior can be

reduced to four specific response patterns: the ability to say 'no;' the ability to ask for or make requests; the ability to express positive and negative feelings; the ability to initiate and terminate conversations" (p. 238). There are several good books on assertiveness training that give specific techniques. One example is Fensterheim and Baer's *Don't say yes when you mean no* (1975).

Lazarus deals with biological issues in a straightforward fashion. He encourages good health habits and is quick to refer the client to a physician when physiological problems are suspected. He is also clear that for patterns of dysfunctional thoughts, feelings, and actions that are resistant to psychosocial intervention (such as psychotic behavior) chemotherapeutic intervention may be required.

Summary of Cognitive and Behavioral Approaches to Severely Dissatisfied Clients

Hayes, Ellis, Meichenbaum, and Lazarus give the reader a comprehensive overview of the varieties of theorizing and techniques employed by those therapists who represent themselves as cognitive or behavioral or both. Each day new approaches and refinements in technique and theory occur, and the developing cognitive–behavioral paradigm is not yet exhausted. There are, however, several problems with an exclusively cognitive–behavioral approach. First, it inadequately deals with the phenomenological viewpoint, a shortcoming shared by the psychoanalytic model. Second, it fails to grasp the importance of one's belief system, in toto, as a significant issue in psychotherapy. Getting rid of dysfunctional thoughts, feelings, and actions is not enough. Developing an effective pattern of self-talk to solve life's problems is not enough. Some of life's problems (such as death) cannot be solved. Also, when one stops doing negative things (whether thoughts, feelings, or actions), what does one do? When one can do everything "right," what makes one feel good or fulfilled? Third, although all of the cognitive and behavioral psychologists endorse the importance of the therapeutic relationship, they (with the exception of Lazarus and Hayes) place the importance of the relationship as secondary to "properly" employed technique.

We have entertained the notion that properly employed technique *is worthless* without the prior existence of an effective therapeutic relationship. The essence of such a relationship is that the client must *perceive* the therapist as consistent and genuine, caring (showing unconditional positive regard and accurate empathy), and knowledgeable (a concrete focus on the client's particular problems). It seems clear to us that to expand the psychosocial approach beyond remediation to fulfillment the therapist would have to look beyond the psychoanalytic and/or the behavioral/cognitive frameworks to those orientations one might include under the rubric of humanistic psychology.

Conclusion

There is a substantial array of intervention approaches for individuals suffering from neuroses for which success has been claimed, based either on empirical studies, or on case history reports or studies without control groups. Further, people who develop neurotic disorders (usually in late adolescence or early adulthood) have had troubled early childhoods (Fenichel, 1945). Such people are troubled by intense subjective distress that, in the severer cases, is accompanied by dysfunctional repetitive behavioral difficulties. Much of what leads to these problems stems from automatic self-defeating self-talk. Therapists who have claimed success in working with this group of troubled people, from Freud to Hayes and his associates, have tried to create a therapeutic relationship within which these automatic self-defeating patterns of self-talk can be brought under the control of the individual. These long-standing problems are sufficiently difficult that an intermediate level of structure and a duration of therapy of about one year (Lararus, 1981) are required. These requirements are consistent with our intrapsychic model.

Since neurotics often present themselves as weak and either helplessly nice or somewhat nasty, the maintenance of a low-level *NO* (strong and warm) interpersonal role is often the choice for the therapist. If the client can be encouraged to take a positive role, the therapist decreases dominance, allowing for a therapeutic climate within which issues long-denied conscious expression may be discovered. We would argue that our interpersonal model fits well with what successful therapists do to produce a working relationship with individuals who fit into the prototype neurotic as defined in the text.

There is a characteristic class of social expectation violations that are engaged in by people we have called neurotic. In the main these actions are exaggerations of expected behaviors (for example, compulsive house cleaning), distortions of other's actual behaviors (such as fears of abandonment), catastrophic reactions (such as panic at being in the middle of a parking lot), and other distortions related to subjective distress. These distortions are not at a psychotic level but are automatic and self-defeating. In addition, neurotics often stay in damaging interpersonal relationships in which their legitimate needs are not met.

Often the issues of concern for these clients involve sex and aggression. Such issues may be couched in a number of guises such as denial of feelings of anger when anger is appropriate, feelings of weakness and impotence to justify continuing in a damaging interpersonal context—or myriad other manifestations. In most cases the repetitive, automatic, negative self-talk will activate self-defeating behaviors and rejection by others. Such thoughts and behaviors will constitute the focus of psychotherapy for these clients.

All in all we suggest that there is a relatively good fit between our models and successful therapy with neurotics. Therapy is likely to be rather long-term with its structure determined by the severity of the client's problems. The interpersonal role of the therapist is both strong and positive (with brief excursions into other interpersonal roles as required), but is at a low level of intensity. Haley, Lazarus, Meichenbaum, and Ellis all employ methods consistent with this general approach. All deal actively with whatever interpersonal issues the client has—violations of legitimate expectations of others, or others' violations of the legitimate expectations of the client—and actively structure the therapy rather than passively reflecting the client's responses.

7 Nonpsychotic Childhood Disorders

The purpose of this chapter is to discuss issues relevant to the treatment of nonpsychotic children and to present some of the specific treatment approaches aimed at troubled children and adolescents. The young people we are targeting in this chapter are characterized by extreme subjective distress and by nonpsychotic levels of behavioral and cognitive dysfunction. Much more space should be allotted to the treatment of children than we can include in this text. Clinicians are faced with children who need attention, and awareness of childhood disorders is essential. Unless the clinician has been trained as a child clinician, he or she cannot do more than recognize that the child needs attention and make the appropriate referral. Even to be sufficiently informed to make an adequate referral requires supervised experience with children and considerably more technical information than we can provide in this text.

Attention deficit disorder (ADD), attention deficit disorder with hyperactivity (ADHD), oppositional defiant disorders (ODD), and conduct disorders (CD) are one class of disorders affecting children that we consider in this chapter. Such disorders belong to the *externalizing problem domain* (Kazdin & Weisz, 1998). We also address the treatment of children who suffer from anxiety disorders and depression, whom Kazdin and Weisz have classified as belonging to the *internalizing problem domain*. Finally, we examine some of the issues unique to children who have suffered severe abuse.

Many children could receive more than one DSM-IV diagnosis. Many of these disorders occur together and with regularity. ODD and CD often occur in homes where parental abuse is common (Kronenberger & Meyer, 1996). Children with ADD or ADHD often appear depressed and anxious (Hallowell & Ratey, 1995). Children suffering from obsessive-compulsive disorder (OCD), as well as those suffering from other anxiety disorders often report feeling depressed (Kronenberger & Meyer, 1996).

Our first caution is for the clinician not to be blinded by a DSM-IV "diagnosis." Second, children under the age of legal majority are not independent agents. When one treats the child one also treats or at least deals with that child's parent or parent surrogate. Third, as Kazdin and Weisz (1998) pointed out, many problems of troubled children are similar to the difficulties experienced by normal children. Fourth, the use of psychoactive medications with children requires awareness of the lack of good research on their effects. Fifth, one cannot export adult therapies to child applications without adjusting techniques to the developmental level of the child. Finally, the therapist must be aware that the child's initial presentation may not accurately reflect the severity of that child's dysfunction. A bright child who has been removed from a brutal environment may learn enough social and cognitive skills to mask a more profound emotional disorder.

Issues in the Treatment of Distressed/ Disturbed Children

Locus of Control

As noted above, when treating a child one must first be aware that the child is not a "free agent." The child cannot be legally held to be fully responsible for his or her actions. Further, the child does not possess the power to make major life choices independent of parents or parent surrogates. If an adult married person decides to leave his or her spouse, then that person may do so. No external agency may say he or she may not act in that way. Yet if a child, for good reason or not, runs away from home, that child may be forcibly placed in some other environment, typically a foster home or institution. For these and other reasons it is essential to involve the parents or caretakers of the child in the treatment process.

The lack of power and self-determination, which is part of childhood, impacts on the issue of confidentiality. Therapists are required to contact the proper authorities if the child gives some indication of physical or sexual abuse. If the child confides in the therapist that he or she has been sexually active, drinking, or taking drugs, should the therapist share this information with the child's parents? What impact will such disclosures have on the progress of therapy? These important questions have received entirely too little attention in the literature about the treatment of troubled children.

Identifying Children Who Require Treatment

According to Kazdin and Weisz (1998), it is often difficult to distinguish troubled children from normal children. Normal children are often oppositional, aggressive, hyperactive, and anxious. When is the child sufficiently distressed or disturbed for treatment to be required? As Kazdin and Weisz stated, "When symptoms are extreme, form a part of a larger constellation of behaviors, and do not attenuate with maturation, they *may* signal dysfunction" (p. 19). Focusing on age-inappropriate behaviors that are a source of distress or disruption should indicate to the clinician when action is required. Kazdin and Weisz pointed out that when behaviors are extremely disruptive, treatment is required regardless of the age of the child or whether or not that behavior will go away with age. These guidelines leave a great deal to the judgment of the clinician, and we think that a thorough psychological evaluation of the child client could remove much of the confusion (see Case History 7.1, p. 136).

Use of Medication with Children

Another important issue in the treatment of childhood disorders is the use of medication. Both Hallowell and Ratey (1995) and Kronenberger and Meyer (1996) recommend the use of virtually every medication prescribed for adult disorders for the treatment of childhood disorders. Hallowell and Ratey are clear that medications used in the treatment of children with ADD and ADHD should be carefully monitored. They hold that current knowledge of the effects of psychoactive medication on ADD and ADHD children requires physicians to "empirically" arrive at efficacious medication for these children. What that means in practice is that the physician tries one drug and then another or a combination of drugs until positive change occurs (or fails to occur). Hallowell and Ratey are not clear when the "experimentation" should be stopped. Kronenberger and Meyer stated that their references to medication for the treatment of childhood disorders were for information only and not to be used to guide practitioners in the use of medication. Nevertheless, they clearly indicated that medication is required for the treatment of many children.

Allen, Leonard, and Swedo (1995) are generally supportive of the use of drugs for the treatment of childhood anxiety disorders but pointed out that little controlled research has been done with children and that extreme caution should be employed when using drugs with them. Dujoiner, Barnard, and Rapoff (1995) and Tarnoski, Simonian, Beckley, and Park (1992) were more pessimistic with respect to the use of psychoactive drugs in childhood depression. They stated that no consistent positive effects of antidepressant medication have been shown in double-blind placebo-controlled trials with depressed children. Since all psychoactive drugs have significant side effects (see Appendix 2), we would caution mental health personnel to be conservative in their use of medication with children. We would beg mental health personnel to carefully monitor children if drugs have been used, and to find the lowest effective dosage level for that medication.

Technique Modification with Children

It is necessary to modify therapeutic approaches used with adults when working with children. The obvious steps are to simplify language, to present material in ways that are consistent with the child's developmental level, and, as far as is possible, to be on the child's level (by that we mean to get down to the child's eye level and to talk to the child as a young colleague rather than an inferior person). In addition, there are several specific modifications suggested by Kronenberger and Meyer (1996) that require attention. Specifically, the authors suggest that to effectively use cognitive techniques with younger children who have mood disorders, the therapist needs to act out the child's distortions by using puppets. The therapist has the puppet act out a distortion, then demonstrate to the child that the distortion is unrealistic. Kronenberger and Meyer grouped these and other modifications of cognitive and behavioral techniques under the heading of *psychoeducation,* and they credit Lewinsohn (1974) with this and other techniques. Bromfield (1995) also suggested the use of puppets with children, but emphasized their use to aid in the development of an effective therapeutic relationship. Kendall et al. (1992) have made many modifications in technique when working with children who suffer from anxiety (to be discussed later in this chapter). In addition, Kronenberger and Meyer suggested that Axlinian play therapy (also to be discussed) would be useful with children who suffered from anxiety.

Stevenson (1999) pointed out that for abused children with interpersonal and environmental stressors (broken families, poverty, and a history of abandonment), a more systematic and comprehensive approach and modification of adult therapeutic techniques was required. Explicit, thorough, gentle exploration of feelings about authority figures who have been abusive or have abandoned the child is an essential part of therapy. Often the child must be removed from a destructive environment before any effective treatment can be initiated. In addition to other therapists' roles, the therapist must be an advocate for the child. Stevenson pointed out that the course of treatment is not a smooth or easy one with these children. Regressions and disruptions in the course of treatment often occur. One major point in this chapter is the identification and formation of a treatment plan for such a child (see Case History 7.1 on page 176). Stevenson also recommended that abusive parents receive training in how to deal effectively with their children.

The Problem of Differential Fixation

Another issue concerns what may be called *differential fixation* and is of critical importance in treating a child like Noah (see Case History 7.1). Clinical work with children such as Noah has led the authors of this text to rethink some of the time-honored ways of viewing the child developmental process. Social

CASE HISTORY   7.1

Noah—An Oppositional-Defiant Disorder with Unusual Regressive Features: Diagnosis and Treatment Planning

The following case study follows a ten-year-old boy with an apparent ODD from referral through intensive evaluation, and discusses the development of an integrated treatment plan. We have used an extended case study format to illustrate the technical details of therapy as applied to organizing and carrying out an intensive evaluation. The critical personality assessment employs a refinement of the interpersonal diagnostic system that organizes data by levels—from overt behavior through self-description and finally to fantasy productions that tap into preconscious and unconscious personality functioning. This method allows the resulting information to be applied to both social learning and structural analytic treatments.

The client, Noah, had been taken from his negligent and abusive natural mother and placed in foster care. After several years, evidence of abuse required his removal from this household and he was placed with therapeutic foster parents for two years prior to his adoption by them. At the time of referral he was displaying increasingly oppositional and defiant behavior, threatening other children in the household, and soiling himself. An independent psychiatric evaluation raised the question of possible sexual abuse and severer underlying problems. An intensive, multilevel evaluation was undertaken to assess the extent and severity of the client's emotional and personality damage and determine if additional therapeutic intervention might be necessary.

The evaluation began with a review of relevant available histories, interviews with the adoptive parents with and without Noah, and interviews with Noah alone. Since extensive individual and family counseling had not provided a clear explanation for the client's increasing emotional and behavioral regression, multilevel testing was scheduled that included standardized checklists, inventories, and projective tests such as the Thematic Apperception Test and the Rorschach Ink Blot Test to assess both emergent preconscious and deep-seated unconscious material. Neuropsychological screening was added because Noah's mother was known to have had problems with chemical dependency. Inasmuch as Noah had talked freely of physical abuse but had made no mention of sexual abuse, the diagnostic plan also included interpretation of the client's dreams, guiding him in creative fantasy productions, encouraging artistic efforts, and analyzing the content of his Rorschach test results using both the Klopfer Rorschach Prognostic Rating Scale and the Phillips and Smith developmental scoring system. The final battery included eight tests: the Ammons and Ammons Picture Vocabulary Test, the Benton Test of Visual Retention, the Conflict Behavior Questionnaire, the Interpersonal Check List, Kinetic Family Drawings, Rorschach, Rotter Incomplete Sentences, and the Thematic Apperception Test.

Noah's adoptive parents were interviewed and provided both observational information and test data for analysis. They appeared caring, concerned, and puzzled by the reversal of Noah's former progress. In addition to the more general defiant and regressive behavior already referenced, they noted conflicts over going to bed and the client's unhealthy interest in his adoptive mother's discarded sanitary napkins.

Noah was animated, talkative, and cooperative. His experiences in therapy were evident as he launched into an account of the physical abuse he had survived. "You know my mother smashed me across the room? I was in eight foster homes. I don't see her much and they won't let my father see me 'cause I didn't really know him. Both my adoptive parents love me. In one foster home they tried to throw me down the stairs. I was really mad at them for doing that and burning my sister. I almost got me a bow and arrow."

Fortunately, at this point the client had to stop and draw breath, which allowed some gentle redirection. He then worked conscientiously on various tasks, commenting freely in a spontaneous and often humorous fashion. He had problems with sustained effort but was able to redirect and focus after lapses of concentration. He spoke about his adoptive parents with genuine affection and trust, but had reservations concerning other foster children in the household and at least one "enemy" at school. He admitted that he lies when he does things he's not supposed to do. He loved computer games and hated the nightmares that come to him when he tries to sleep.

After the initial interview and observations, the issue of possible cortical damage was addressed. The client worked with energy and enthusiasm on the I.Q. test. He achieved a mental age of sixteen years, placing him in the superior range of measured intelligence. He seemed to enjoy vocabulary games and word play. Although his handwriting was often an indecipherable scrawl, his Benton drawings were better organized, better controlled, and well above age expectation for bright to superior children in both the number of correct reproductions and number of errors.

His drawing of a man, in contrast with Benton drawings, showed a number of regressive features and was blackened and overworked until it looked like a burnt offering. This suggested body-image damage of the type often associated with neglect and abuse. The Goodenough-Harris scoring of his figure drawing yielded a mental age equivalent to nine years and six months, placing him in the low-average range of measured intelligence. The discrepancy of almost four standard deviations between the two measures of intelligence emphasized the gap between Noah's very high intellectual potential and his low current ability to apply his intellect to emotionally sensitive issues. A difference of this magnitude often accompanies severe emotional damage.

The therapist then employed a variety of inventories to explore the interpersonal impact of various persons on Noah's life both past and present. His adoptive parents also provided a detailed description of Noah. Noah's adoptive parents were essentially in agreement in their Interpersonal Check List ratings of his interpersonal traits. Both saw him as high in aggression and anger, very reluctant to show fear or weakness, but also capable of normal affection. His mother also felt he had a good potential to be helpful and caring. To the therapist Noah described himself as skeptical and angry. He rated himself very high in his need to give and receive love. He admitted to a strong need for care and direction that his tough, rebellious, and independent demeanor totally failed to communicate.

The client saw both adoptive parents as loving and responsible. He made a clear differentiation between them and the "Foster Parents from Hell." He identified both "Matt" and "Jenny" as selfish, punitive, and domineering. Neither was seen as capable of expressing love or acting responsibly. In his ideal self-ratings, the client indicated a wish to be much less angry and skeptical. He wanted to be much more caring, affectionate, and friendly.

The behavior ratings indicated that both adoptive parents saw moderately severe conflict at this time in their relationship with Noah. Noah, on the other hand, admitted to anger problems but denied any other source of conflict. His denial had become another factor contributing to the level of distress in the household.

In the initial interview, the client showed mild distractedness and restlessness but, unlike most children appearing with a secondary diagnosis of ADHD, he was able to respond well to encouragement and structure and to complete all tasks. His teacher's ratings on the ADHD scale were above the mean for a ten-year-old but showed only residual or borderline problems. Either the disorder was then present in a very attenuated form or the medication previously prescribed was working well to control symptoms.

Noah's sentence completions emphasized normal and healthy interests and experiences. He liked his adoptive parents, and enjoyed Nintendo and baseball as well as "SEGA and chess with my dad." He had firm ideas on family structure, stating that "most women are the second head in the family arrangement." He was willing to apologize to another child in the family whom he described as his best enemy. "I regret flinging a rubber band at Ralph."

By the second session he did admit to problems but also showed a good recovery potential and guarded optimism. "The future is pretty bleak until you get there." "I feel happy, sad, and mad at times." "I am best when I am on my medicine or my best behavior."

The Thematic Apperception Test was used to access preconscious material to reveal the client's problems and strengths that might not be directly seen or expressed in day-to-day behavior. Here again, the initial story showed mild problems allowing cautious hope for a successful outcome. The TAT is a test that uses a sense of ambiguous interpersonal situations and requires the client to identify the hero, the antagonists, and the problem and outcome of the interpersonal event. The responses are indicated card by card; only the significant responses to specific cards are noted here. Card 2—"This boy has a violin for a present. He tries but he can't play it. He just needs to practice and maybe he'll get the hang of it."

After this card the stories became darker and more painful. The *heroes* had genuine and serious problems that they could not handle. *Others* were often cruel and uncaring. The following stories are representative. Card 3—"OK, people working on a farm. She's walking to school. He starts to hit the horse to get it moving. That's all I can think of. (Therapist asked, "Girl's feelings?") Man, I can't believe this. The woman's just gonna sit there smiling. If the horse don't move, it's off to the butchers. The girl feels pretty much like the horse—whipped by dad and forced to work." 3BM—"That's a gun. Maybe it's somebody who was depressed. Couldn't handle it. Shot himself. Probably thought the world was cruel and didn't care. He could have lived but in pain. He's so tired of it."

Noah's role as a strong survivor was congenial to him and often evident in his day-to-day behavior.

At the preconscious level of personality functioning, the depression under the surface of the defensive behavior was displayed with strong indications of prior abuse. His hurt and depression had been denied direct expression. He had learned to avoid revealing weakness and vulnerability and to depend on his own efforts to deal with cruelty and neglect. His behavior problems illustrate the way in which denial of depression and counterphobic defenses against anxiety distort the symptom picture.

Noah's projective family drawings were normal in content but had genuine problems in expressive style. He began with himself and his natural mother. He then drew his twin sister on a much smaller scale. He added his adoptive parents and seemed satisfied that the drawing was complete. He suddenly turned back to the paper and drew another figure, whom he identified as "Mindy."

Noah's strong identification with the natural mother is not unusual and he apparently had begun to incorporate his adoptive parents into his sense of "family." He had been very reluctant to share his parents with other foster children in the household. The addition of one of the foster children, Mindy, was a positive sign.

The qualitative aspects of the client's drawings amplified the sense of underlying damage. The figures were heavily blackened over with erratic detailing and a number of regressive features. The foster sister was especially primitive in rendering, perhaps because of the client's ambivalence regarding acceptance and sharing. The overall impression was rather chilling, reminiscent of horrifying still photos of forest firefighters trapped by a sudden shift of wind and burned beyond recognition.

There remained, at this stage of the evaluation, the issue of sexual abuse or more aggressive underlying pathology from stage-one development damage. To examine these possibilities the therapist administered the Rorschach test, which can tap into deep unconscious processes that are obscured by the usual operation of personality defenses. As such it offers an opportunity to examine in more detail the indications of possible severe, underlying emotional damage suggested in the projectives already discussed. The Rorschach provides useful data through the formal elements of task completion and unconscious data through content analysis. Incongruities between formal scoring and content provide insights into personality integration.

The formal response characteristics of the client's Rorschach results emphasized the assets that enabled Noah to survive neglect and abuse during his first four years of life. He produced a thirty-response Rorschach with good form level and creative elaborations. Five animal movement responses were balanced by three human movement and two human movement in animal figures—good indications that the capacity for empathy and the journey from childhood fantasy to adult imagination were progressing normally. Four color responses, slightly low for a record of this length, showed adequate emotional response. However, the color dominated by form responses was forced and arbitrary, suggesting that Noah was in touch with feelings he had trouble integrating into his cognitive activities. Four inanimate movement responses also emphasized a high level of internal tension with disruptive, painful, and ego-dystonic impulses threatening to break through personality defenses.

The dimension of response to soft texture also showed substantial damage. The warm and affectionate closeness found in children who were loved, cared for, and protected during critical years of development was missing or distorted into something far more ominous. Content analysis extended and reinforced the perception of affectional damage. The animal figure in Card 4 became a derealized monster. Instead of the hoped-for warm, fuzzy object, Card 6 produced two unusual responses. The top became "two immensely hot drills grinding against each other and throwing off sparks," after which the whole card was seen as "a red-hot jackhammer with big handles."

The symbolic content continued to develop in the same direction. Timid animal figures alternated with depersonalized aliens and imagery suggestive of rage and hurt; for example, Card 8 was "two blood-sucking chameleons." Such a response pattern could, if unchanged over time, be found in a young adult with disabling mental health problems. The Rorschach permits long-term prediction of personality development and the long view in Noah's case showed an individual with strong assets for recovery, but also the type of massive internal damage that could mature into an encapsulated paranoid schizophrenia.

At the time of agency referral this case appeared to involve an oppositional-defiant disorder with some unusual regressive features. On completion, the formal evaluation indicated that Noah suffered from severe
emotional damage of the sort that can only be inflicted by prolonged physical,
emotional, and sexual abuse. This damage was intensified by his conviction
that he had to protect his twin sister as well as himself. He seemed to have
borne the greater part of the abuse and to have regarded any attacks on his
sister as his fault, owing to his failure to defend. Although he could talk freely
about the physical abuse, the sexual abuse was still very painful and, obviously, capable of producing a short-lived psychotic episode. The four-year-old
Noah had done what he could to fight back during a period of sustained
victimization. The ten-year-old Noah put a bold front on things and, actually,
showed better than expected recovery supported by his formidable assets of
intellect and defenses in depth. The unresolved damage, however, was
capable of undoing the recovery to date.

Noah had begun to act out because he was in an environment where it
became safe to do so. The soiling, nightmares, and peculiar fascination with
sanitary napkins gave clues as to the type and intensity of underlying damage.
The resulting hypotheses were strongly confirmed by the psychological
testing. Without further treatment, the posttraumatic symptoms would be
expected to continue to break through from time to time and to accelerate
toward psychosis under the increased drive level and explicit sexualization of
puberty. It was, therefore, determined by the therapist and Noah's parents to
begin initial treatment without delay. Economic considerations limited the
number of sessions. Therefore the therapist would undertake the essential
structural and analytic work and transfer the social recovery and consolida-
tion counseling to the county social service facility, which had been involved
in earlier individual and family counseling with Noah and his parents.

---

and cognitive development usually proceeds at the same pace as emotional development, but not always. Classical theories of development, including Erikson (1963) and Bowlby (1969, 1973, 1980) focused on
developmental failures in terms of emotional distress. For example, Erikson
held that task failure at each developmental stage produced a unique kind
of emotional distress that often caused failure in later developmental
stages (see Chapter 2 in this text). Bowlby (1980) framed his analysis of
developmental failures around the concept of *attachment*. He held that the
need to be securely attached, first to parents and then to others, was required
throughout a person's life. According to Bowlby, failure to develop secure
attachment led to a disconnection between emotional responses and their
causes. For both Erikson and Bowlby failure to develop social skills would
be attributed to such emotional disruption. We define this most basic emo-

tional interruption of normal development as primary emotional fixation. Although Erikson did not make the distinction between cognitive development and *primary emotional fixation,* Bowlby did (1951, 1958, 1960, 1969). Drawing on the findings of Goldfarb (1945) and Spitz (1946) and the work of Harlow (1961), Bowlby reported that severely deprived and understimulated infants would not develop adequate social or cognitive skills, if they survived at all.

One does not often see children who are so severely disturbed in an outpatient setting. More frequently one sees children who have failed to develop a secure attachment but who may have compensated by developing adequate social and cognitive skills. Such children may appear normal until some precipitating event triggers the emergence of severe pathology. It may be that such children appear normal because the primary emotional fixation was not so disruptive that it caused the relatively complete emotional-cognitive social skills fixations described by Bowlby. In such cases difficulties in social and cognitive functioning would not become obvious until later in the developmental process, a state we call *secondary fixation.* Secondary fixation may be defined as the disruption of cognitive and social functioning due to underlying problems that were not resolved earlier which often appear in the fourth or fifth grade.

We suggest that it is entirely possible that both intellectual and social development, although usually paralleling emotional development, may proceed at either a faster or slower pace than emotional development. For example, a child may suffer early emotional damage but not be identified as severely disturbed because of that child's adequate, or more than adequate, intellectual and social functioning.

If our speculation is correct, the identification of children who have suffered severe early emotional trauma is an essential task for clinicians. Distortions in the ability of the child to form secure attachments or to develop the capacity for empathy will prevent the child from reaching normal adult status. Without skilled psychotherapeutic intervention it is likely that the lives of these children will be bleak.

Specific Treatment Approaches

Treatment of Childhood Anxiety

The focus for this section is on the treatment of general diffuse anxiety, separation anxiety, school phobias, and OCD. These disorders are conceptualized as childhood anxiety disorders and with the exception of OCD have responded well to short-term treatment (Kendall, 1994; Kendall et al., 1992; Barrett, Dadds, & Rapee, 1996). Kendall et al. modified cognitive behavior therapy so that it was appropriate for the age of the child. Barrett et al. added what they called *family management* to Kendall and colleagues' cognitive behavior therapy. We also address the treatment of children who have received a DSM-IV diagnosis of OCD. March and Mille (1996) and Kronenberger and Meyer (1996) have offered empirically based approaches to treat these children.

Kendall's cognitive behavior therapy (Kendall, 1994; Kendall et al., 1993) began with a comprehensive assessment that included interviewing the child, making behavior observations and anxiety ratings, administering self-report measures, assessing parent behaviors, and eliciting parent and teacher ratings of the child's behavior. If the child met the DSM-III-R criteria for one of the anxiety disorders, he or she was placed into a sixteen-to-twenty-session treatment program.

The program was divided into two eight-session segments. The initial segment targeted teaching the child to be aware of and to be able to identify somatic, cognitive, and behavioral indicators of anxiety. In the second segment, treatment consisted primarily of exposure (in vivo) to the child's anxieties and the implementation of the skills learned in the first segment.

Kendall and his colleagues used the acronym *FEAR* to characterize the initial phase of their intervention. *F* refers to feeling frightened. The child learns to recognize if he or she is afraid. Next the child is taught relaxation procedures and told they will help the child to conquer the fear. *E* refers to the child's expectations. Anxious children expect bad things to happen. *A* refers to actions (and attitudes) that help defeat fear. Once the child has mastered the skills of relaxing and disputing negative expectations and has learned specific coping skills, the last part of the program is implemented; that part of the program is *R*, which stands for rate and reward. The child judges the effectiveness of the coping plan and rewards himself or herself as appropriate.

The second phase of Kendall's therapy involved preparing and exposing the child to relevant real-world issues. The initial exposure was (consistent with Wolpe's [1958] reciprocal inhibition technique [see Chapter 6]) to imaginary situations in the therapist's office that were relatively less anxiety-producing than the more central issues troubling the child. Slowly the therapist aided the child in coping with increasingly real and more threatening events. Part of this treatment included homework assignments using what Kendall called the *show that I can tasks*. Completion of these tasks, recorded in the child's notebook, was rewarded with stickers. In addition, the therapist served as a model for the child when new coping skills were introduced.

Kendall (1990) used age-appropriate material, specifically *The Coping Cat Workbook*. Kendall et al. (1993) stated that the workbook would require the child to complete a number of tasks. For example, ". . . the child writes dialogue for the characters in the vignettes, draws pictures, and creates personal coping stories" (p. 28). In one example cartoon pictures depict situations that could be frightening. The child is asked to fill in the balloons about the cartoon characters pictured in these situations.

On the last therapy session in Kendall's approach, the child "makes a videotaped commercial describing the FEAR steps and their use in an anxiety provoking situation that was mastered during treatment. This is done to help the child (a) organize and crystallize his or her experience, (b) 'go public' with the new skills, (c) recognize the accomplishment, and (d) allow creative expression of his or her ideas. Each child receives a copy of the videotaped commercial to take home" (Kendall et al., 1997, p. 28). Kendall and his colleagues have offered a creative and novel approach for dealing with childhood anxiety; still, one question remains: how well can these children withstand future reality stressors without continued parental or other supports?

Barrett, Dadds, and Rapee (1996) used Kendall's (1994) approach augmented by their family management therapy. In this behavioral approach the parents were taught how to reward their child's courageous behavior and how to extinguish (by ignoring) behaviors that were identified as indicating excessive anxiety. Further, the parents' own anxiety issues were identified and they were taught how to model coping behaviors rather than behaviors indicating anxiety. Finally, the parents were taught communication and problem solving skills. Specifically, they were taught skills in conflict reduction and parental consistency, the importance of daily discussions, and the importance of weekly problem-solving sessions. While Barrett et al. (1996) have outlined a clearly defined set of intervention strategies, they were less clear about the importance of nonspecific factors in effective therapy involving the troubled child and that child's parents.

Axline (1969) applied the nondirective therapy approach of Rogers (1961) to her work with children. Kronenberger and Meyer (1996) recommended Axline's play therapy approach for children who suffered from problems of anxiety. Because Axline emphasized the nonspecific therapeutic factor, the therapeutic relationship, we will discuss in some detail how Axline established it.

The requirements for nondirective play therapy include specification of the materials required and a therapeutic orientation characterized by eight principles, listed below. The minimal materials included a doll family, a doll house with doll furniture, a baby bottle, toy soldiers, clay, watercolors, crayons, toy car, puppets, a rag baby doll, and a telephone. Optimal conditions for play therapy included many more materials. The eight basic principles were:

1. The therapist must develop a warm, friendly relationship with the child, in which good rapport is established as soon as possible.
2. The therapist accepts the child exactly as he is.

3. The therapist establishes a feeling of permissiveness in the relationship so that the child feels free to express his feelings completely.
4. The therapist is alert to recognize the feelings the child is expressing and reflects those feelings back to him in such a manner that he gains insight into his behavior.
5. The therapist maintains a deep respect for the child's ability to solve his own problems if given an opportunity to do so. The responsibility to make choices and to institute change is the child's.
6. The therapist does not attempt to direct the child's actions or conversation in any manner. The child leads the way; the therapist follows.
7. The therapist does not attempt to hurry the therapy along. It is a gradual process and is recognized as such by the therapist.
8. The therapist establishes only those limitations that are necessary to anchor the therapy to the world of reality and to make the child aware of his responsibility in the relationship (Axline, 1969, pp. 73–74).

Axline's focus on the therapeutic relationship and on emotions, emotional clarification, and the resolution of emotional conflicts is of paramount importance in her approach. Such explorations of emotional issues and the establishment of an effective therapeutic relationship are essential with children who have severer anxiety disorders, primarily OCD). Kronenberger and Meyer (1996) stated that the establishment of cooperation between the therapist and the child is essential for effective therapy with children who suffer from OCD. The child must trust the therapist or he or she will not reveal the troubling obsessions that are often the central feature in the disorder.

March and Mille (1996) emphasized the removal of compulsive behavior patterns and focused on technique, more specifically a cognitive behavioral approach. The technique of choice according to them is the combination of *exposure* and *response prevention.* In the exposure technique the child is exposed to the stimuli that elicit the compulsive behavior. In response prevention the child is prohibited from making the compulsive response. In the actual application of these procedures the child is gradually exposed to the feared stimuli. An essential part of the treatment is the blocking of the child's rituals or avoidance behaviors. In addition, these authors applied a variety of behavioral and cognitive techniques, including extinction procedures, relaxation training, operant techniques, modeling, and breathing control.

March and Mille (1996) begin treatment with an evaluation to uncover the child's compulsive behaviors and the stimuli that trigger them. The initial session in a series of sixteen is devoted to selling the medical model to the child and to the parents. We feel that this step is not only unnecessary but also may be detrimental in that it creates undue passivity in the child and the parents. In the second and third sessions the therapist instructs the child to give OCD a nasty name. By personalizing the disorder the child can be enlisted in fighting the enemy and will not be paralyzed by self-blame. In these sessions the child draws a circle and indicates how much of the OCD controls his or her life. Sessions four to sixteen focus on exposure, response prevention, and *anxiety management training.* Such training is a combination of relaxation training, deep breathing, and constructive self-talk. In general, exposure and response blocking are effective in the control of compulsive behaviors in children and adults. However, March and Mille were less convincing on the control of obsessive thoughts, which tend to be more difficult to address.

CASE HISTORY   **7.2**

Calvin—School Phobia and Speech Production Problem

Calvin was a twelve-year-old boy in his first year of middle school. Although he had seemed to enjoy his elementary school classes, both his attitude and grades had recently changed. He seemed subdued and unhappy as he began the new school year. He was never defiant or truant, but asked to be sent home on several occasions because he "was not feeling good." He made similar complaints in the morning before going to school. Since there appeared to be no medical basis for the complaints and he appeared tense, anxious, and unhappy, the evaluator recommended him for brief counseling. No unusual problems were uncovered in the sessions and Calvin ceased his complaints and seemed to settle into his classes. A few months later he began to stutter for the first time in his life. His hesitation, blocking, and initial consonant repetition worsened and he was treated by a speech therapist with little effect. On the advice of the speech therapist, he was referred for evaluation and treatment.

The client came from a supportive middle-class family with no history of physical or emotional abuse. His extended family was also free of substance abuse and there was no evidence that Calvin had experimented with alcohol or drugs. He had recently shown a normal interest in dating and reported no problems in his first experiences.

Calvin's father was a successful tax accountant. He had at one time hoped to finish law school and become a tax attorney but the need to provide for his family forced him to curtail his education. He had always shared his hopes and dreams with his son and was delighted that Calvin wanted to follow in his footsteps. Calvin's mother confirmed that Calvin had never been a problem at home or at school. Both were confused that the speech problem threatened their plans for their son's education and career choice.

Calvin was polite, compliant, cooperative, and unable to identify any problems in his home, school, or social life that might be upsetting him. He showed no self-consciousness or discomfort with his speech problem or with the relinquishment of his career plans. His bland indifference continued until the therapist remarked that he was handling his "disappointment" very well and wondered what Calvin might want to do with himself now that a career as a tax attorney was impossible through no fault of his own. He began to talk with enthusiasm of his work helping his uncle in his garage. He did not want to take classes with an academic emphasis. He knew his father would be disappointed but hoped he would understand that his son was making the best choice that circumstances beyond his control permitted.

After reviewing again the results of the speech assessment as well as the client's intelligence and aptitude scores and the vocational interest inventory, the therapist scheduled the parents for a session without their son. During this session the test results were reviewed and the therapist suggested that the speech disorder may have redirected Calvin from a career choice for which he was not well suited toward a career choice for which he had good aptitude and interest. Both parents agreed to assure Calvin that they would love him just as much if he became an auto mechanic instead of a fancy lawyer. His father agreed that he would respect an excellent mechanic more than a marginal attorney. A followup family session was scheduled in which both parents gave Calvin the assurances they had agreed to and rehearsed.

In his next session Calvin appeared cheerful and enthusiastic about his new shop program. He had been praised by his teacher for the skills he'd developed through his earlier work with his uncle. He was relieved that his parents did not seem to mind the abrupt change in their planning for his future. Over the next six months it was notable that the client's anxiety and reluctance concerning school never returned and his speech problem gradually abated completely.

Calvin's father asked for an individual appointment a few months after the completion of the school year. He began by saying that Calvin was doing very well with his shop work and receiving excellent grades. He then asked the therapist very directly, "Calvin really hated the idea of law school, didn't he?" The therapist replied, "At first Calvin had no idea what law school meant other than knowing talking about it made you happy. Then the strong pre-vocational preparation in middle school made it real enough that he realized he would hate it. His experience working with his favorite uncle also helped him recognize that he liked working as a mechanic. He didn't know how to tell you because he didn't want to disappoint you." Calvin's father smiled and said, "That's all I really want to ask." He paused for a moment and added, "And he didn't disappoint me."

Treatment of Childhood Depression

According to Kazdin and Weisz (1998), earlier theoreticians (mostly psycho-analytic) denied that children were capable of developing "true" depression. Kazdin and Weisz reported that sound empirical evidence indicates that there is such a thing as childhood depression and that it is increasing in frequency. They stated that there are several treatment approaches that have proved successful in treating childhood depression. They grouped most of these approaches under the heading of *coping skills training*, noting that the approaches share elements. They stated:

> Among the most common features are:
> (a) efforts to identify and modify depressogenic schemas and attributional biases; (b) skills training to enhance social interactions (e.g., how to start a conservation or make a friend), social problem solving (e.g., how to resolve conflict without alienating others); and other competencies relevant to self-esteem (e.g., setting performance goals and reaching them); (c) progressive relaxation training to reduce the tension that can undermine enjoyment; and engaging in mood enhancing activities to increase rates of positive reinforcement." (Kazdin & Weisz, 1998, p. 5)

These approaches are similar to the approaches of Kendall (1994). Since depressed children are often anxious and anxious children are often depressed, the isomorphism between these approaches is not surprising. In spite of the positive note set by Kazdin and Weisz, Holmes and Wagner (1992) noted that very little research had been done on childhood depression. Further, little direct attention has been paid to the emotional status of these children.

If Bowlby (1988) is correct, that a child needs to form a *secure attachment* before age two to not be vulnerable to depression or even more serious disorders, then attention to early estrangement is necessarily part of effective therapy with such children. According to Bretherton (1992), failure to form a secure attachment can lead the child to feel a sense of grief and loss. The task of the therapist in working with such a child is to allow for the development of a secure attachment to heal the profound wound that the child has suffered. To address this issue, we would recommend that the therapist pay close attention to the basic principles proposed by Axline and consider the establishment of the therapeutic relationship as an essential part of working with depressed children.

Treatment of Children with Attention Deficit Disorder

Children who have been diagnosed as suffering from attention deficit disorder or attention deficit disorder with hyperactivity are presumed to have a neurological disorder (Hinshaw, 1996; Hallowell & Ratey, 1994). Usually these children receive some sort of medication, often as their only treatment. Hinshaw stated that medication without psychological treatment provides only a partial solution. In addition, these medications have side effects and practitioners should be careful not to carelessly diagnose a normal inattentive child as having ADD or ADHD.

There are several ways to increase the accuracy of these diagnoses. If the child's measured intelligence is markedly higher than school achievement or grades suggest, then one suspects ADD. If there are consistent reports from the child's teacher and parents that the child cannot concentrate on anything for more than a few seconds, then one suspects ADD. If the child is so hyperactive that he or she is constantly in trouble, then one suspects ADD or ADHD. However, to confirm the diagnosis, a complete psychological evaluation is required.

Once a child is diagnosed as having ADD or ADHD, a comprehensive treatment program should be formulated that includes medication and targeted psychosocial treatments (Hallowell & Ratey, 1994; Hinshaw, 1996). Hinshaw's psychosocial intervention strategy was based on manuals developed over several years (Hinshaw, Alkus, Whalen, & Henker, 1979; Hinshaw, Henker, & Whalen, 1981). Hinshaw and his colleagues described their treatment process as self-instructional training, problem-solving therapy, and the explicit teaching of anger management skills. They made the significant discovery that anger management skills had to be learned in a group format. This was critical because individual approaches failed to promote children's practice of the new skills with peers, nor did individual attempts promote the emotional engagement required.

According to Hinshaw the two major components in effective self-management are *self-monitoring* and *self-evaluation*. First the child must be trained to observe his or her behavior. Second, the child must be able to accurately report how he or she is acting. In Hinshaw et al.'s process, the children meet in groups and discuss what behaviors are desirable; for example, cooperation and paying attention. Therapists then give the children specific examples of cooperative and uncooperative behaviors, and attending and non-attending behaviors.

In order to teach the children how to self-monitor and self-evaluate, the Match Game created by Hinshaw et al. is used. The child and the group leader compare their ratings of the child's behavior. When they match the child is given points. The child is also expected to comply with certain behavioral criteria, such as paying attention, cooperating, and so forth. Initially, the child gets points when he or she agrees with the leader's rating of his or her behaviors. After a few sessions the child must also meet the objective criteria or no points will be given in the Match Game.

The second part of Hinshaw's approach (1996) used what he called anger management training. ADHD children are often singled out for physical and verbal abuse by their peers. According to Hinshaw, in order to change the way their peers treated them, ADHD children needed to learn ways to manage their anger. The first step was to encourage these children in a supportive group to reveal names and phrases that caused them to become emotionally aroused. It is difficult for young children to identify the cues that trigger anger. Once the cues are identified, the child can be taught specific cognitive and behavioral strategies to employ when teased or stressed by others. Specific skills include ignoring provocation or distractions, engaging in calming self-talk, and using appropriate assertiveness behaviors. Finally, the child applies these skills in a group under realistic peer group provocation.

Another approach in which success has been demonstrated with these children focused on the training of the parents as opposed to treating the children directly (Analopoulos, Barkley, & Sheldon, 1996). The parents were taught the basic characteristics of ADHD as well as behavioral techniques, and were introduced to the four-factor model of parent-child conflict.

The four factors that Analopoulos et al. identified were child characteristics, parent characteristics, family stress, and situation consequences. For each family, the therapist identified the specific behaviors that caused stress in each of these factors. The parents were then taught specific behavioral techniques including positive attending, ignoring, how to set up a token economy which means reinforcement by tokens, response-cost techniques (for example, taking away points and calling for time outs). The parents also learned how to use these techniques in public, and how to involve the school in the process. The training process was to be completed in nine sessions and usually lasted three months. It should be noted that the parents would need to continue this program on their own for many years if gains are to be maintained. In fact, Hinshaw (1996) held that successful treatment for children with ADHD and ADD would need to be long-term.

Treatment Approaches with Children Suffering from Oppositional-Defiant Disorders and Conduct Disorders

Oppositional-defiant disorders and conduct disorders are difficult to treat. For the more serious disorder, CD, the untreated child is likely to develop an antisocial personality disorder according to Zoccoliollo, Pickles, Quinton, and Rutter (1992). In preadolescence and adolescence, many of these children become enmeshed in the criminal justice system (McCord & McCord, 1956; Finckenauer, 1984). Often children suffering from CD have been considered untreatable (Henggeler, 1989). However, many therapists and investigators have reported success with these children (Aichhorn, 1935; Redl, 1954; McCord & McCord; Wolf, Phillips, & Fixsen, 1975; Patterson, 1982; Borduin et al., 1995; Kazdin & Weisz, 1998). We will begin our review with the earlier residential treatment approaches.

CASE HISTORY **7.3**

Khalif—An Adolescent Conduct Disorder

Khalif was a sixteen-year-old black male prison inmate referred to the second author by a prison doctor for assessment and treatment recommendations. He had shown significant symptoms of depression during his initial intake screening. Given that he was facing a thirty-year sentence for murder committed with a handgun, the preliminary diagnosis was adjustment reaction with depression. Additional diagnoses established by the client's social and criminal justice history included conduct disorder and polydrug dependence.

In his initial interview with the therapist, Khalif was obviously distressed. He showed a very high level of agitation. He reported a pattern of sleep deprivation, that he felt sad, and that he was considering suicide. He was referred to the psychiatry unit for treatment recommendations, placed on observation for seventy-two hours, and scheduled for a followup interview to determine final disposition. During this interview, the client talked almost without pause, showing a strong need for support and some insight into his circumstances. He was returned to prison population with orders for a moderate outpatient dosage of Sinequan (widely used as an antianxiety agent) and scheduled for individual therapy on a weekly basis.

Khalif's history made it clear that his problems began well before his current—and first adult—offense. His father was incarcerated when Khalif was eighteen months old. His alcoholic mother made some attempt to care for him and his five siblings until she discovered crack cocaine. At age eight Khalif was placed alternately in group homes and temporary foster care until his maternal grandmother obtained custody after two years of negotiation with Social Services. Khalif showed a marked reduction in hyperactivity and anxiety during the next ten months until his mother, during a brief period of relative sobriety, attempted to regain custody. His symptoms returned, his school adjustment deteriorated, and he began using marijuana on a regular basis and spending as much time as possible with a group of young black males in late-middle childhood and early adolescence. Although his grandmother won the custody battle, the hyperactivity, learning problems, and emotional distress continued. When Khalif's mother became estranged from her mother, she also refused to have anything further to do with her son. When Khalif was thirteen, his father made a brief appearance and talked of taking his son to live with him—a plan that was rendered moot by his reincarceration. In the next three years, Khalif was arrested twice for possession of marijuana. He finally dropped out of school, and continued to live nominally with his grandmother but spent most of his time "hanging out." His drug problem worsened and he began dealing to keep himself in supplies. About a year ago he was accosted by a fifteen-year-old with a handgun who ordered him to surrender his drug money and supplies. During the struggle for the weapon, Khalif's assailant was shot and killed. Khalif was arrested, charged with first-degree murder, and convicted on a plea bargain arranged by the prosecutor and his court-appointed attorney.

Khalif responded well to the combined antidepressant regimen and individual therapy. He was able to bring out and to a considerable extent work through some genuinely terrifying memories from his childhood and early adolescence. He was then placed in an intensive drug and alcohol dependency treatment group where he began to relate strongly to several older inmates. He returned to individual treatment on an as needed basis to discuss what were essentially existential questions appropriate to adolescence. He completed his group treatment, obtained a General Education Diploma, and participated in several personal-growth groups offered by the Social Service Department of the prison. He began a reading program through the prison library, showed a preference for socializing with older residents, and worked conscientiously in various job assignments. During the three-year period after completing his primary treatment, he functioned without medication and was able to avoid any "tickets" for misconduct. He applied for a reduction in sentence but was summarily rejected. In spite of this, he retained a positive frame of mind and extended his interests to include classical music and jazz, making good use of the local music station. He bought a small television with the income from his institutional job assignments and began watching the local public television channel on a regular basis. He continues to self-refer from time to time to report progress. He remains free of depressive symptoms. He has had no known involvement with drugs. He has, interestingly enough, become an asset to younger inmates seeking to move from their earlier outside "street" associations toward rehabilitative programming. By his actions and associations, Khalif no longer meets the guidelines for either a conduct disorder or polydrug dependency. He is an asset to the prison community. Whether he can maintain his new values and conduct through the remaining years of his sentence is another question. Given the severity of his crime, parole is unlikely regardless of readiness and accomplishment.

Residential Treatment of ODD and CD Children

August Aichhorn.   Defined by the DSM-IV as conduct disorders and oppositional-defiant disorders cases of these childhood disorders are increasing in number. Historically children with CD or ODD have been referred to as childhood psychopaths and placed in residential treatment centers or prisons. At present, unless the child has been entangled in the criminal justice system, no residential treatment is likely and other treatment approaches are usually haphazard and ineffective.

In 1935 Aichhorn published a book called *Wayward Youth,* in which he described his psychoanalytically oriented approach to the treatment of the troubled children listed above. This early work of Aichhorn and others has been lost in the literature of treatment options for children who suffer from oppositional defiant disorders and conduct disorders. Aichhorn's main thesis was that these troubled children required, as the main thrust of their treatment, a milieu that could begin to satisfy their frustrated desires for love. McCord and McCord (1956) quote Aichhorn as stating that all of the boys in his program who could be diagnosed as psychopathic had been severely treated, having grown up under brutal circumstances without love or affection. According to Aichhorn (1935), "First we had to compensate for this great lack of love and then gradually and with great caution begin to make demands upon the children. Severity would have failed completely. Our treatment of this group could be characterized thus: a consistently friendly attitude, wholesome occupation, plenty of play to prevent aggression, and repeated talks with individual members" (p. 172).

Aichhorn stated that during the first contact in his treatment facility with the troubled young person, any staff member needed to communicate the message that this place was different from any place the child had known and its staff likewise different from the people that the child had known. The role of the staff member was to be what Taulbee and Folsom (1973) called matter-of-fact. It required the staff member to be neither too warm—lest he or she be perceived as weak—nor harsh, which could lead the child to perceive the staff member as an enemy. This approach is consistent with Glueck and Glueck's (1949) suggestion that such troubled youths require treatment by adults that is kind but firm. We would add that such treatment must be consistently employed by all caretakers who interact with the troubled children.

In Aichhorn's study limits placed on the children were restricted to the prevention of destructive acts. Those limits were imposed only when absolutely necessary, and then with a combination of a matter-of-fact role coupled with kind firmness. Aichhorn believed that as the troubled children tested the limits, this approach produced an emotional crisis characterized by "an increased feeling of their own power which found its expression in greater and more frequent acts of aggression; these later gave way to tears of rage, then to a period of sensitivity, and finally to acceptable behavior" (McCord & McCord, 1956, p. 130).

Once a relationship between a boy and a staff member had been established (what we call a therapeutic relationship and Aichhorn might have called rapport), limits were gradually employed with the staff requiring the boy to act in more and more appropriate ways. According to the McCords, "his aggressive boys acquired new tolerance for frustration and new consciences. All of his boys, he reported, subsequently became adjusted to society" (McCord & McCord, 1956, p. 132). Neither McCord and McCord nor

Aichhorn stated the average length of treatment required. We suspect that treatment was quite long-term.

Pioneer House.   Another analytically oriented residential treatment facility for severely troubled children, called Pioneer House, was founded by Redl in 1946 in Detroit. Redl felt that individual psychoanalysis would not work for his clients because they lacked the requirements for effective psychoanalytic treatment. For example, they could not form an adequate transference neurosis and did not have the ego strength necessary for insight. Redl's interpretation of these terms is useful: transference neurosis is in essence a therapeutic relationship, which leads to patient insight (meaning, awareness of one's own power, and responsibility for one's actions). According to McCord and McCord (1956), "Rather than employ the usual 'reformative' methods, Pioneer House attempted to establish an encompassing atmosphere, which, in its smallest detail aimed at the improvement of the youngsters. Every ball game, every meal, every temper tantrum was handled with an eye to the child's treatment" (p. 133).

Central to the restorative milieu of Pioneer House was the notion that children with these disorders have an early and debilitating inability to trust their feelings or the emotional reactions of significant others. Therefore, Redl focused upon affect gratification as the central feature in treatment. According to Redl (1954), "The children must get plenty of love and affection whether they deserve it or not; they must be assured the basic quota of happy recreational experiences whether they seem to 'have it coming' or not" (p. 174).

Unlike Aichhorn's well-documented approach, it is not clear what Redl and his staff actually did. But there are useful hints about what constitutes effective treatment of these children. One aspect of Redl's approach was to precipitate an emotional crisis; again, exactly how this was done is not clear. However, when the crisis occurred, an interpersonal interview with the child was conducted by the appropriate staff member, the purpose of which was to (1) bring out aspects of reality the child had ignored, (2) attempt to discover *or produce* feelings of guilt, (3) confront the young person's alibis and hostility, and (4) make the young person aware of his or her motives. It is interesting to note here the similarity of the confrontational elements of Redl's approach with similar confrontational approaches taken by Synanon-like substance abuse treatment centers and Glasser's reality therapy (see Chapters 8 and 9). However, McCord and McCord (1956) were correct in noting that empirical analyses of Aichhorn's and Redl's approaches, either in terms of a clear statement or operational definition of treatment approaches or specification of outcomes, were not presented. The McCord and McCord analysis of the Wiltwyck School is an example of a more empirical view of a milieu approach.

Wiltwyck School.   According to McCord and McCord (1956), an example of an institutional program organized to promote effective personal growth that addressed many of the objections to earlier attempts at treating these disturbed boys was offered at Wiltwyck School. First, Wiltwyck was adequately funded and staffed. Second, Papanek provided dynamic, consistent leadership. Third, the ratio of staff to troubled boys was about one to one. Finally, Papanek and his associates allowed the McCords to engage in systematic and extended evaluation of the actual treatment approach and detailed analysis of outcome effects.

Treatment at Wiltwyck focused on establishing an initial contact with the boys that "allowed [them] to express their pent-up antagonism as long as no irreparable damage is done." There were no disciplinary cottages, no punitive treatment, only constant attempts to impress upon the young people the consequences of their behavior. Once the child established a relationship with one of the adult counselors, limits were gradually imposed that focused on the development of impulse control. First treatment required the formation of a reasonably stable affective bond between the boy and a counselor; then and only then did they begin the development of a program of socialization.

Individual and group therapy as well as art therapy were offered to the children. Wiltwyck also provided the boys (aged eight to fourteen) an experience in a school that did not impose grades, taught by teachers skilled in the instruction of emotionally disturbed preadolescents and young adolescents. Further, remedial help in reading was provided for those who needed it. Regular staff meetings focused on individual boys having difficulty. These ensured that all staff members working with any particular child all cooperated to focus on that child and his particular issues.

The McCords (1956) summarized their outcome research on the Wiltwyck School, mainly focusing on two questions. First, was Wiltwyck, overall, superior to more traditional treatment modes? To answer, the McCords compared Wiltwyck with a school designated as the "New England" school, whose staff believed that hard work and discipline would "reform" their boys. The second question was, did the Wiltwyck approach work with "true" psychopaths—a small subpopulation of fifteen boys at Wiltwyck—as compared to other diagnostic categories (the ninety-two other boys)?

In answering both questions McCord and McCord (1956) focused on the boys' personality changes and changes in patterns of interaction as measured by a variety of instruments. In addition, McCord (1985) reported that five years after discharge, 9% of the Wiltwyck boys had been arrested for a major felony compared to 77% of the boys from the " New England" school (which was in fact Lyman School in Boston). According to McCord, these positive results went down until at the end of 1985 32% of the Wiltwyck boys (long since men) had been convicted of felonies while only an additional 8%

of the Lyman boys had been convicted of felonies. Overall, 41% of the Wiltwyck boys committed felony offenses following release as compared to 85% of the Lyman boys.

McCord (1985) argued that the racial and ethnic mix of the two groups was also a major factor in these results. The Wiltwyck group were primarily Black and Hispanic while the Lyman group were Irish and Italian. McCord presented speculation that employment opportunities existed for the primarily Irish ethnic groups in Boston that were unavailable to Blacks and Hispanics in New York City, where Wiltwyck was located. Essentially he argued that societal racism undid some of the positive work of the Wiltwyck School.

With respect to the second issue, the effect of the Wiltwyck milieu on "true" psychopaths, the results were even more convincing. According to McCord (1985), the Wiltwyck approach was most successful for the violent psychopathic group and least successful for the borderline-psychotic group. To the authors of this text these findings are not surprising. It is probably not a good idea to mix prepsychotic or psychotic youths with acting-out youths, since the tenuous grasp on reality of the prepsychotic and psychotic groups is likely to be escalated by such a population mix. In any event, those youths who met Cleckley's (1954) criteria and would be called "true" psychopaths in fact profited from Wiltwyck School. They should, according to Cleckley, have been untreatable. The data of McCord and McCord were sufficiently clear to refute such an overgeneralized and categorical statement at least for very young psychopaths.

Achievement House.   Montrose Wolf and his associates (1975) developed a behaviorally oriented treatment facility for working with young people from twelve to fifteen years of age. Wolf intended for Achievement House to be more like a home than an institution, with none of the trappings of a punitive institutional environment. The number of youngsters to be treated was kept low—no more than ten or so. These necessary preconditions for behavioral treatment are critical, because the very positive experiences of Achievement House have been used as an example of why behavior modification, as a technique, should be used in the "management" of young offenders and also older offenders throughout the criminal justice system. The best therapist cannot perform effective treatment in a battlefield, nor can the best treatment system work in a larger system that is primitive, inhumane, and brutal.

If the therapeutic environment has been established, then the techniques and theories of Wolf and his associates can be successfully employed in treating these children. In essence, troubled youngsters have behavioral problems because they are skill-deficient. These troubled youngsters will have to be taught the necessary behavioral skills to function effectively. Such skills can be taught by using any sound behavioral method. The primary method used by Wolf was a token economy system (see Chapter 11 in this text).

Wolf et al. (1975) used four main elements in their behavioral skills training program. They were:

[a] motivational system (token economy), a self-government system, a comprehensive behavioral skill training curriculum and the development of a reciprocally reinforcing relationship between the youths and the teaching parents. (Such a relationship enhances the reinforcing effects of the teaching-parent social interaction and allows them to fade the more artificial token reinforcement.) (p. 3)

The results of Wolf's approach were very effective, with far fewer of his youngsters coming into contact with the criminal justice system than did juvenile offenders either in a probation program or in a typical institution for juvenile offenders.

Other Behavioral Approaches.   Achievement House stands as an excellent example of how the humane application of behavior modification approaches can aid in the restoration of troubled people who have great problems with the control of their impulsive and irresponsible behaviors. Partial success for these methods has also been reported for such criminal justice institutions as the Robert F. Kennedy Center in West Virginia (personal communication, Gilbert Ingram, Chief of Psychology at the Robert F. Kennedy Center, 1971). In fact, behavioral approaches were widely introduced both in juvenile and adult correctional institutions in the 1960s and early 1970s (Finckenauer, 1984). Many of the inmates in these institutions would meet our criteria for inclusion in one or more of the categories of what we have called core personality disorders (see Chapter 9 in this text) or, for young offenders, CD or ODD.

However, the promise of behavior modification offered by such humane places as Achievement House has not been realized, according to Finckenauer (1984). He stated, "Unfortunately, as has been the case with so many fads and panaceas in this field, behavior modification has not been all that its supporters have hoped it would be. In addition, it has proved to be more subject to abuse and misuse than did psychotherapy" (p. 77).

What Finckenauer (1984) did not say was that the focus for all of these approaches was control of the inmates, not restoration of the person. All of these institutions were conceived as places to punish, even to deprive inmates of their freedom, not as places to provide opportunities to help prisoners learn to cope more effectively. In all cases their applications of behavior principles focused on controlling people. That orientation necessarily caused an intensification of the punitive climate of these institutions. Therefore, behavior modification could not work in such settings. Inhumane treatment is simply an ineffective means for facilitating effective coping behaviors, at least for coping in the larger environment that exists beyond hospital or prison walls.

Outpatient Approaches with Children Who Suffer from ODD and CD

Although thousands of children are incarcerated in prisons, virtually no milieu or behavior modification residential centers exist for them. Until these children become involved in the criminal justice system, they are likely to receive little treatment and what attention they receive is often sporadic and ineffectual. However, there are several established approaches that can effectively treat ODD and even CD, according to empirical evidence. We have selected G. R. Patterson and his colleagues (Patterson, 1982; Patterson, 1984; Patterson, Reid, & Dishion, 1992; Patterson, Dishion, & Chamberlain, 1993) and Henggeler and his colleagues (Henggeler, 1989; Mann, Borduin, Henggeler, Melton, & Blaske, 1990; Henggeler, Melton, & Smith, 1992; Borduin et al. 1995; Henggeler, 1994) as examples of therapists who have provided empirical evidence. Patterson and his colleagues focused on parent-child interactions as the main factor in CD and ODD. Henggeler and his colleagues, while noting the importance of the parent-child interaction, emphasized the importance of cross-generational coalitions as the primary factors associated with adolescent antisocial behavior.

Parent Training Therapy. Patterson stated that specific patterns of parent-child interactions accounted for much of the development and maintenance of aggressive and oppositional behavior (G. R. Patterson, 1982). He found that aggressive behaviors on the part of the parents led to aggressive behaviors on the part of the child. He observed that the child's aggressive behavior led to parental withdrawal, which negatively reinforced the child's aggressive behavior. As the child's aggressive behavior escalated the parents eventually responded in an aggressive manner, thus further escalating the child's aggressive behavior. Parent training in how to break this vicious cycle became the essential task for Patterson. It is clear from this analysis why Patterson held that parent training was essential for such children.

The first step in Patterson's approach was to discuss with the parents what is known about CD and ODD and to give them a sense of what children with these disorders are likely to be experiencing. The parents were then taught the basic principles of behavior modification. Specific techniques included specification of target behaviors, establishing baselines for these behaviors, and learning how to block or modify conduct problems. The parents were taught how to distract the child, how to attend to positive behaviors while not attending to negative behaviors, and the importance of ignoring irritating but not dangerous behaviors. Parents also were instructed to use *time-out* procedures in response to the child's hitting and other aggressive behaviors, and to remove privileges as another means of discipline. Time-out refers to removing the child from the situation and placing him or her in a gentle, secure, and nonreinforcing environment. Patterson had found that without some form of punishment, positive reinforcement and modeling of appropriate behaviors were insufficient to produce behavior change in these children.

Patterson et al. (1993) also developed a modification of their approach useful in working with children whom Patterson described as chronic delinquents. Rather than send these children back to families that could not control them, they were sent to foster families in the community who were skilled in working with children having such disorders. Once the child was placed in a foster home, the foster parents implemented Patterson's five-step program. The child received an individualized home program, a school program, individualized therapy, and monitoring of peer relationships, and the biological parents received parent training. The ultimate goal was to return the child to his or her original family.

Patterson and his colleagues also reviewed other approaches that they hoped could enhance the effects of their techniques. Kazdin and Weisz (1998) stated that cognitive skills training (an explicit method of developing problem-solving cognitive strategies for impulsive and aggressive children) had proved successful in working with these children. Patterson et al. (1993) did not find such approaches helpful. For readers interested in cognitive skills training programs, manuals exist (for example, Shure, 1992). Patterson suggested that Henggeler's multisystemic therapy might be a good adjunct to his approach. We feel that Henggeler's treatment methods merit more attention and that perhaps Patterson's approach might be considered an enhancement of Henggeler's approach rather than the other way around. It is to Henggeler's work that we now turn.

Multisystemic Therapy.   Henggeler (Borduin et al., 1995) held that in addition to inappropriate cross-generational collations that are formed between a parent and child other factors had to be considered, both in the study of the development of the disorder and in the treatment of the disturbed young person. They argued that antisocial behavior is not only due to family issues but also to problematic interactions with peers, the school system, and the larger community. In addition, the troubled child's personal characteristics either learned or inherited need to be considered.

Still, the universal component in multisystemic therapy is the use of family therapy; the approach Henggeler proposed was a combination of Minuchin's (1974) structural family therapy and Haley's (1976) strategic family therapy. (We will discuss these approaches in more detail in Chapter 13.) If one of the major problems in antisocial disorders is the existence of cross-generational collations within the family, then treatment needs to directly address this issue. One way to deal with such collations is to alter the structure of the family. The family therapists attempt to strengthen the mother-father bond and to weaken any inappropriate parent-child bond. When the mother-father dyad is strengthened, they can then act in a consistent and unified way towards their child. Thus the child's antisocial behavior will not inadvertently be reinforced by either parent.

In addition to the family therapy component, Henggeler and his colleagues used many other intervention techniques depending on the particular set of issues with which the child was struggling. The parent training approach of Patterson et al. (1992) could be used as could couples' therapy when the problems involved family dysfunctions. If, as is almost always the case, the child has inadequate control of his or her aggressive tendencies, Hinshaw's (1996) means of managing anger, already discussed in this chapter, could also be used. In addition, the child would engage in individual cognitive therapy if required. Peer interactions were closely monitored and school personnel were involved in the process. Clearly multisystemic therapy is a demanding approach. We expect the complete treatment not only would involve many people as active participants but also would be long-term.

The Complex Case

In reviewing the treatment of troubled children we have evaluated treatment approaches for children who are increasingly distressed or disturbed. It is clear that Henggeler et al. (1992) used far more structure and employed more varied treatments than did therapists dealing with less disturbed children. It is also clear that his treatment was intended to be long-term. When adolescents have become enmeshed with the criminal justice system, it is likely that their problems are severe; at least this is what Henggeler and many others have found. Some of the older residential treatment centers were places where treatment was in fact total; such facilities are now exceedingly difficult to find.

The case of Noah (Case History 7.1, pp. 136–141) is precisely the kind for which early (preadolescent) and comprehensive treatment is required. As is the case for so many severely disturbed children, Noah was physically and sexually abused as a young child. Although he originally was diagnosed as suffering from OD, as he moved into preadolescence his behavior regressed into very troubling patterns that required a more structured and focused intervention than he had been receiving.

More specifically, Noah's evaluation produced a picture of multiple fixations with early-stage emotional damage driving infantile regressive behavior. This was consistent with abandonment in the first year of his life and abusive foster care from ages two through four. Although Noah's social development was for the most part normal, some of his behavior and his fantasy life showed unresolved issues of depression and abandonment. He accepted his former therapist's assurance that he was a victim and was not to blame for his foster parents' abuse. However, he had not extended this waiver of responsibility to alleviate the guilt he experienced for failing to protect his twin sister from abuse. Although Noah was able to convert some of his internalized anger into defiant behavior, enough remained to produce feelings of depression and self-dislike.

The first step in the treatment of children like Noah is to encourage a shift in self-perception from "victim" to "survivor." This shift is essential to establish assertiveness and allow the child to build a positive self-image. In this particular case it was essential that Noah accept his inner strength without incurring increased remorse over the fact that this strength had not allowed him to better defend his sister against the foster parents' abuse. This acceptance was developed through a series of careful, realistic "then" and "now" comparisons. Noah gradually came to see that what a "mature" ten-year-old can do to resist two brutal adults is much more than a four-year-old child could have done (his age at the time in question). "He was one mean, big dude and you were built pretty close to the ground. But, hey, you kept him going after you instead of your sister. That makes you pretty brave." After additional role-playing and frequent reality checks, Noah came to see that doing all that is possible makes one a "hero" even though not doing as much as one wanted to do still makes one sad.

Projective data and some of the interview data indicated that the emotional damage to Noah had gone beyond that produced by physical abuse alone. There were indications that Noah's most deep-seated damage could produce a psychotic break if aggressively approached. This is one of the therapeutic conundrums—whether to pursue a covering approach and leave the buried material ticking away like a time bomb, or to help bring out the repressed material with the risk of making one's client worse. As Noah showed more self-confidence and greatly reduced self-blame, the therapist determined to neither actively uncover nor suppress. The topic of just how nasty "those crazy people" were developed naturally and the extent of the four-year-old Noah's protective efforts on behalf of his sister was defined. In this manner, Noah gradually approached dangerous territory.

After agreeing that it would have been nice if the visiting social worker had caught on to all the nastiness going on in the foster home and provided a little grownup help, Noah paused, and began to describe "Matt" and "Jenny's" night sex games—the pornographic videotapes that they played and the friends who would drop by to sexually abuse an older adolescent girl in the household. As he went on, he began to express a vivid fantasy in which he used an ax to defend himself and his sister. "Couldn't get through the floor so I chopped the door down. Hit him with my ax until he let my sister go. Didn't kill him but I hurt him." Noah then confided that he escaped long enough to tell the police and that "Matt" was arrested, convicted, and died in the electric chair. "Lit him up. Fried his eyeballs." Noah made it clear that these events actually happened. He did not, however, have any problem with the therapist treating the topic as another dramatic play exercise. As he became calmer, he agreed that the only good thing about the time with the "Foster Parents from Hell" was that it was over. Noah smiled a little and said, "You know what I did with my ax? I left it buried in the floor of 'Matt and Jenny's' living room." The examiner replied, "You buried the hatchet." Noah's smile broadened.

Noah had accepted his strengths without the penalty of increased guilt and then placed his genuinely protective actions in a realistic framework that allowed him to see himself as having fought "the good fight." He then brought out the extremely painful memories of sexual abuse and contained them in a framework of active resistance. This made him more than a passive victim and acknowledged that he had done all that he could to protect his sister. He could not match the former foster parents' talent for violence, but he and his sister had survived and were now both safe and loved.

Noah's adoptive parents were advised of the new information and coached in ways to help with the continued process of recovery. As agreed, they returned to a treatment and support relationship with their county facility. When last heard from, Noah was maintaining his progress and showing normal problems consistent with middle childhood. The extreme regressive behavior had abated.

Conclusion

In general, the length of treatment of nonpsychotic childhood disorders is consistent with our intrapsychic model. The results of empirically verified studies indicated that the severer the disorder the longer the treatment would need to be. Although many of the approaches that we have discussed focused on technique, they also stressed the importance of the therapeutic relationship. The focus on changing negative self-talk as well as modifying direct behavior to defeat anxiety and depression is consistent with approaches used to work with adults we have described as neurotic. Likewise, the more directive approaches used successfully with more severely disturbed children were consistent with treatment approaches found successful with more severely disturbed adults.

The two interpersonal approaches most effective with troubled children depend upon whether the child suffers from an *internalizing disorder* or an *externalizing disorder* (Kazdin & Weisz, 1998). If the child is anxious or depressed then a strong and warm interpersonal role is required (*NO*). If the child is overtly hostile, withdrawn, or suspicious, then a matter-of-fact role (low-level *DE*) is required with an immediate shift to a warm supportive role as the anger and suspicion lift. These interpersonal stances are consistent with those taken with adults who share similar difficulties.

With respect to the content of therapy, the technique and procedures discussed in this chapter are intended to reduce what we have called violations of legitimate interpersonal expectations. Aggressive behavior, social withdrawal, neurotic behaviors, and many other behaviors that will lead to sanctions or rejection are discussed in this chapter. However, children often have their rights violated and the therapist must be sensitive to the vulnerability. Frequently the therapist's role is to be an advocate for the child. After all, children require effective parenting if they are to become effective adults.

8 Impulse Control Disorders

There are people who cannot control their actions and reactions to environmental demands. As a result of this lack of control they may act out impulsively, placing themselves or others in danger. We have called people who habitually act in such impulsive ways people who suffer from disorders of impulse control. Such people frequently deny the extent of their destructive behaviors. Often their first reaction to stress is to act out impulsively (let's get a drink, go to the casino, and so forth). These people, although often manipulative, rarely engage in the characteristic defensive reactions of people classified as having personality disorders (splitting and projective identification). Splitting is a defensive reaction in which one part of the personality is split off and operates independently from the total personality, often leading the person to engage in destructive behaviors. Projective identification is a defensive reaction in which the person attributes a negative characteristic of himself or herself to another and then idolizes or vilifies that characteristic in the other. We consider severe substance abuse disorders, sexual disorders (particularly those characterized by destructive acting out), eating disorders, and severe compulsive gambling all to be examples of impulse control disorders. In these cases, the troubled person feels and acts as though he or she cannot control the self-destructive or other destructive behaviors that he or she engages in. Further, impulsive behavior, with or without reported anxiety, is that person's primary problem. Hatterer (1980) argued that many of what we have called disorders of impulse control could be described under the general heading of "pleasure addictions" or the "addictive process." However, throughout his book he focused not on physiological factors and treatment but rather on psychosocial methods to induce control of impulsive behavior.

The focus on impulse control and reducing destructive acting out accepts, at face value, the oft-expressed view of the troubled person, that he or she cannot maintain control over his or her "problem." It may be that the troubled person's internal chemical balance has become a part of the impetus leading to destructive acting out (almost certainly true with severe forms of substance abuse and anorexia nervosa) or it may be that the destructive acting out is a function of unknown factors (as is likely with compulsive gambling and compulsive sexual acting out). Such patterns of destructive acting out are often, if not always, triggered by psychosocial events. In fact, we suggest that any treatment approach that excludes complex etiology is likely to lead to treatment failure or inadequacy.

Some substance abusers recover, some anorexics recover, some people suffering from sexual disorders recover, and some compulsive gamblers cease their behavior without treatment. In almost all of these cases, some extraordinary serendipitous event has occurred in that person's life (G. A. Mann, 1979). However, most people who suffer from impulse control disorders do recover without help. What forms of intervention offer promise for people who suffer from serious disorders of impulse control? An exploration of that question is consistent with our attempt to reach a first approximation of what therapeutic approaches work, with whom do they work, and under what circumstances.

Theoretical Issues

The Concept of Addiction

The traditional view of addiction is that an individual acquires through the use of a substance a physiological need for that substance. What is implied in the definition is that once the individual becomes addicted, he or she must receive that particular (or a similar) substance—or an uncontrollable craving for that substance will occur. Also implied is that once the individual experiences an uncontrollable craving for a substance, then the craving will lead the individual to engage in any behavior to get that substance. In addition, the idea of an uncontrollable craving is linked with both drug tolerance, defined as the need for more and more of this substance to get the same psychological reaction, and withdrawal symptoms, which are caused by the removal or withholding of that substance. Hatterer (1980) applied this popular conception of addictive processes to all of the types of problems we have described as disorders of impulse control.

Currently, individuals suffering from these disorders have been labeled with some category of substance abuse disorder (according to DSM-IV) and are often described as having an "addictive personality" (Peele, 1989). Such people are seen as being dependent on a substance that is "mind altering." Further, the concept of addiction has been extended by some authors (according to Peele) to include all people who suffer from disorders of impulse control as well as those who have drug dependency disorders. Peele has challenged this notion, and has argued that the evidence for a unique physiological basis for people who abuse drugs is seriously flawed since most addicts are poly-substance abusers.

From Peele's 1989 position, it would seem that the present DSM-IV categorizing of people who abuse psychoactive drugs is not structurally distinct from the earlier notions of addiction. Considering drug abuse from the subjective perspective of the abuser is rarely part of either classification or treatment for medical model advocates. In fact, people who suffer from impulse control disorders have treatments applied to them not with them that is in forms of pharmacological treatment or the more technique driven cognitive and behavior therapies.

The focus on classification and treatment of these people as objects to be treated can only be part of the story. It is true that the cessation of some drugs—alcohol, tobacco, the opiates, phenobarbital, cocaine, and many oth-ers—causes severe or very uncomfortable withdrawal symptoms. It is also true that many of these same drugs lead to drug tolerance and increasing intake. However, it does not follow that dependence is solely physiological and that either physiologically based treatment or external manipulation are adequate treatments. If addicted people remain addicted even after detoxifi-cation, then there is no hope for them except to first remove them from society, to continue to "detox" them, and then to maintain them on some medication for life. The data show that many drug-dependent people will return to their drug or drugs of choice after detox even knowing that these substances may in fact kill them.

The notion that using addictive drugs will inevitably lead to physiologi-cally based addiction is not tenable given cultural differences in drug use. There are cultures in which the availability of cocaine (in the form of cocoa leaves) and opium do not inevitably lead to addiction. We hold that people turn to drugs or other impulsive acting out not for physiological reasons but rather for psychological reasons. Many people in our culture turn to drugs in a vain attempt to obliterate their experience of a world devoid of nurturance and support (Cooper, 1970). Consistent with our emphasis on the subjective experience of the troubled person, we will offer possible explanations of their behavior. Of course, such attempts are only temporary and in themselves ultimately create a world that is far worse than it was before they took the drug.

Our position does not rule out that some people may inherit a consti-tutional weakness (*diathesis*) that makes them vulnerable to drug addiction, or that specific cravings can be learned. It is interesting that Begleiter implicitly offered a diathesis stress model for addictions and eating disorders, as well as other disorders (Holden, 1991).

If the person has such a weakness and cannot control his or her behavior once a drug is consumed, then psychosocial treatment becomes more rather than less important. Alcoholics Anonymous (AA) and other self-help groups are intended to serve as lifelong support for such people. In many of the more effective drug treatment programs (i.e., the therapeutic communities beginning with Synanon and continuing with Phoenix House), DeLeon (1984) noted the importance of the group approach to aiding the addict to control his or her addiction.

But why would anyone, even a person who craved a substance, take a deadly poison? It seems clear to us that for whatever reason the person has lost control over his or her impulses. Perhaps that person, at that time, is willing to die rather than exist as he or she had been. If that analysis is correct, then a change in world-view, the development of survival skills, and a sense of hope must be part of any effective treatment for people suffering from addictions.

Psychosocial Treatment for Disorders of Impulse Control

The goal of treatment for all disorders of impulse control is to allow the troubled person to gain control over his or her impulses. The most prevalent of these disorders involves substance abuse. Often it is necessary to remove the drug-dependent person from his or her environment. Then, that person must become drug free through detoxification. Detoxification should occur in a medical setting to control toxic withdrawal effects and to use medications to block or reduce craving. Next a process of resocialization must occur. This stage is the most difficult. Often, the drug-dependent person must spend considerable time in a supportive environment to allow for resocialization. In addition, the environment must provide effective non-punitive controls during the first few months (perhaps years) of treatment. Both individual and group therapy (based on Glasser's reality therapy philosophy, 1975) are strongly recommended. In addition, all family members must be included in family therapy sessions. Finally, job retraining and vocational counseling and placement as well as an appropriate halfway house or other supportive residential milieu must be part of a total treatment program (Cooper, 1970). These general patterns of treatment with the exception of detoxification are the same as those used in treating other disorders of impulse control.

Drugs Used in Substance Abuse Treatment

It is clear that those substances whose abrupt cessation in extensive users produce unpleasant or even life-threatening physical effects require special attention. Such substances include alcohol, heroin, cocaine, and nicotine. Chlordiazepoxide hydrochloride (Librium) has been shown to block the severest symptoms of alcoholic withdrawal, delirium tremens (Schatzberg &

Cole, 1991, p. 287). Desipramine hydrochloride has similar effects in blocking the severe depression often reported by cocaine users following cessation (Schatzberg & Cole, 1991, p. 294). Some authors (Bjorkqvist, 1975; Gold, Redmond, & Kleber, 1978; Gold, Pottash, Sweeney, & Kleber, 1980; Glassman, Jackson, Walsh, & Rose, 1984) found clonidine to be an effective medication not only to reduce the withdrawal effects of alcohol but also for the withdrawal effects of opiates, cocaine, and nicotine.

It is clear that reducing the painful effects of drug cessation is not in itself sufficient for reducing drug dependency. The desire to use the drug to escape from reality is a more powerful factor in drug abuse than the fear of withdrawal. Some practitioners might argue that when a drug abuser suffers withdrawal, the experience itself serves to aid the abuser to cease drug use.

Many of the therapeutic communities founded on the Synanon model encourage "cold turkey" withdrawal accompanied by extensive social support, often twenty-four hours a day until the crisis is passed. Under such circumstances it is claimed that the severity of withdrawal is lessened. However, the high dropout rate in these programs is at least in part produced by the perception in many substance-dependent persons that these programs themselves are punitive. Both the cold turkey withdrawal process and some of the more aggressively confrontational approaches advocated by some of the Synanon-style therapeutic communities could lead to these high dropout rates.

As with other treatment approaches for troubled people, it is more likely that to force substance abusers to go cold turkey is, in the main, counterproductive to effective treatment, as is the case in all punitive treatments. It may be that a humane first step in the detoxification process could help reduce the high dropout rates in long-term treatment programs.

Drug Maintenance Approaches

The most common drug used to maintain substance abusers is methadone, which is prescribed for people who abuse opiates. The primary target group is heroin abusers who do not adjust to abstinence programs and are willing to regularly visit methadone maintenance clinics. Maintenance actually means substituting one drug, methadone, for another, heroin. Methadone is habit-forming and subsequent withdrawal from methadone is itself problematical. Newman and Cates (1977) reported that methadone users held jobs, committed no crimes, and in general functioned effectively in the larger society. However, as with all treatment approaches for severe substance abuse, methadone programs are only partially successful and cannot be considered a panacea. In fact, most opiate abusers who are maintained on methadone require psychosocial intervention.

At one time, Librium (chlordiazepoxide) was used as a maintenance approach for alcoholics. This drug was administered on an outpatient basis. It was found that people dependent on alcohol became dependent on Librium and would then abuse that drug. Because of Librium's tendency to itself produce drug abuse behavior, this drug is no longer used to maintain patients who abuse alcohol. In some respects this change is unfortunate. If Librium was given in a controlled setting (as is methadone) and used over a more protracted treatment period, it is possible that the substance could still have some limited utility. However, since alcohol is so readily available in our culture, it is clear that no simple extension of any maintenance program will be more than a small part of an effective treatment approach for people who are severe abusers of alcohol.

Disulfiram (Antabuse) is prescribed to produce a change in the body's chemistry that will lead anyone on a daily dose of that drug to become ill after drinking and cause them to vomit violently (Chic, Gough, Falkowski, & Kernshaw, 1992). More serious complications including death occasionally occur. These punitive aspects seem to fly in the face of the Hippocratic oath and its stipulation to *do no harm.* This treatment approach is of limited utility since the alcoholic who is not under supervision usually just stops taking the Antabuse.

Another drug treatment approach uses substances that will block the mind-altering effects of the abused drug. Naltrexone may be used to block the psychological effects of opiates (it is thought that this effect is produced physiologically through the blockage of opiate receptors). Apparently there are no aversive reactions, as there are in the case of disulfiram, save the failure of the abuser's opiate to produce its effect. It is to be hoped that similar chemical agents can be found that will block both the physiological and psychological effects of all drugs that produce dependency and abuse.

However, chemical approaches are not likely to produce a complete solution to drug dependency. Drug treatments simply do not address the psychological reasons for using addictive drugs. What are the psychological factors that lead to or contribute to substance abuse? Clearly, when some individuals suffer from failure, loss, or tragedy they are vulnerable to drugs. When an individual is subjectively distressed or filled with anguish and psychological pain drugs often look like a solution. Often the addict sees drugs as substances to relieve that suffering by adjusting his or her own chemistry, thus achieving so-called perfect psychological adjustment.

Freud's notion that the purpose of psychoanalysis is to trade neurotic suffering and misery for real suffering and misery certainly applies to treatment modalities for people who suffer from destructive patterns of drug abuse. Human beings who are capable of living productive, useful, and fulfilling lives are able to deal with misery and suffering. By employing higher mental processes people can learn to solve life's problems, or at least live with them and perhaps transcend them. Chemicals often block the full unfolding of human potential.

Alcoholism: General Issues

Our discussion of treatment approaches for specific problems of impulse control begins with people identified as alcoholics. According to Davidson and Neale (1990) lifetime prevalence rates for alcoholism as defined by DSM-IV criteria were over 20% for men and just under 5% for women. Davidson and Neale argued that alcoholism is implicated in one-half of all murders, one-third of all suicides, and much of child and spouse abuse. The National Institute on Alcohol Abuse and Alcoholism estimated that the overall cost of alcoholism (in 1983) was more than $116 billion. Finally, Davidson and Neale stated that 40% of patients in general hospitals are being admitted for alcohol-related disorders. By any standards, the issue of problem drinking is one of the severest of all mental health problems.

D. Goldstein (1983) held that alcoholism is a genetically produced disease that causes changes in neurotransmitters. One problem with these studies and others is that many different neurotransmitters and biological mechanisms were postulated. Wallace (cited in Wallace, 1989) argued that there may be many different types of alcoholism, such as hyperaroused alcoholism (the person has a high arousal level and seeks alcohol for its sedating effects), anhedonic alcoholism (the person has a low arousal level and drinks for excitement), depressed alcoholism (the person suffers from chronically low self-esteem and drinks to sedate himself or herself), and mixed-type alcoholism (which includes all of the above). Wallace argued that alcoholism is an illness and that a disease model of alcoholism is not only accurate but useful in treatment; he felt that alcoholics who adopted the concept of the medical model were more likely to recover. His notion was that the disease model allowed alcoholics to view their difficulties as caused by external factors, thus freeing the individual of destructive feelings of guilt.

However, Wallace (cited in Wallace, 1989) was also clear that alcoholism is a "multidimensional disease" with contributing factors such as learned patterns, cognitive processes, family systems, societal and cultural factors, as well as genetic and neurobiological factors. Begleiter (Holden, 1991) challenged the notion that there is a specific genetic basis for alcoholism, although that author reported that the issue was not resolved. In addition, he noted that it is harder and harder to find "pure" alcoholics (people who are abusers of alcohol only) anymore.

The DSM-IV defined alcoholism as a pattern of behavior consistent with Jellinek's early crucial period. Jellinek (1952) held that alcoholism has occurred when one can no longer control one's drinking and is suffering from psychological and physiological losses that will continue towards self-destruction unless one ceases this drinking behavior. We suggest that a person is an alcoholic if (1) that person feels and behaves as though he or she cannot control his or her drinking or (2) the person engages in a pattern of drinking that leads to loss of family, job, and friends and is damaging to physiological health, or (3) both.

CASE HISTORY **8.1**
Samuel Wells

Mr. Samuel Wells was referred to the therapist because he had a "drinking problem." Mr. Wells appeared somewhat "seedy," although his social skills and self-presentation were at variance with his recent history of chronic alcoholism. He was cooperative and gave a complete and elaborate history.

He reported that he came from a well-to-do family in Mississippi. He had been successful in his work with the local water company. When he was twenty-two years old he became vice president of that company and appeared to be on the road to a successful life. World War II broke out at about that point and Mr. Wells decided he wanted to become a fighter pilot. He was rejected because he was too tall and instead became a bomber pilot. He flew forty-nine missions over Germany before he was shot down. He crashed in France and was found by members of the French Resistance and hidden in a cellar. A somewhat inebriated German soldier, apparently on leave, wandered into the cellar and Mr. Wells was forced to stab him. It took the young German a few minutes to die. Mr. Wells stayed in the cellar with the dead German for several days.

Mr. Wells was able to get back to England just about the time the war was over. He returned home but did not return to his job at the water company. Instead, he got involved in a new and risky but exciting communication enterprise, television. He also got married. The stress of the new job and unresolved issues from the war led to excessive drinking. After several years, his wife divorced him and his whole life went downhill, until he now considered himself a skid-row alcoholic. He agreed to go into individual and group therapy although he did not think it would do any good.

An MMPI was given as a screening device. No evidence of psychosis existed nor were the results of the inventory particularly revealing. There was some evidence of antisocial tendencies. A WAIS (Wechsler Adult Intelligence Scale) and a Bender Gestalt (a screening test for brain damage) were used to screen for the possibility of brain damage. Full scale I.Q. was 131 and there was no evidence of brain damage on either instrument.

The following is an excerpt from the fifteenth session.

THERAPIST: Good afternoon Mr. Wells, what's going on?

CLIENT: You remember last time when I told you I had been shot down over France?

THERAPIST: Yes, was there more to tell?

CLIENT: When I was in the cellar a German soldier came in and we struggled and I killed him.

THERAPIST: Um hum.

CLIENT: It took several minutes for him to die and after he died I looked at him—just a boy. I searched his pockets and found a wallet with a picture of a young woman and a little boy, her son I guess. Dropping bombs was one thing but this really hit me hard.

THERAPIST: That was a horrible experience.

CLIENT: That's not the worst of it. I had to stay with the body for several days before I could be safely moved.

THERAPIST: I don't know what to say.

CLIENT: Well I finally got out, survived, but I don't think I ever completely got it.

THERAPIST: Got over it?

CLIENT: Yeah, I mean killing that boy and leaving a young widow and her son without a father.

THERAPIST: You are blaming yourself for the young man's death.

CLIENT: Yeah, I guess so.

THERAPIST: Mr. Wells, you are a hero. Forty-nine missions over Germany, shot down in enemy territory, and forced to survive any way you could. None of that was of your choosing.

CLIENT: I sure don't feel like a hero.

Therapy lasted for one and a half years. The client gained control over his drinking and began to make efforts to leave the VA. He did so, and returned to his home and was in the process of establishing a business that looked very promising when he was stricken with pneumonia and died.

Treatment Approaches with Alcoholics

Alcoholics Anonymous.   It is fair to say that the most widely known and used program for the treatment of alcoholics (and other chemically dependent people) is Alcoholics Anonymous (AA). AA has thousands of chapters in the United States and virtually every other country in the world.

The basic philosophy and approach of AA may be simply stated. Each chapter of AA has regular meetings. The first part of the meeting is usually open; anyone may attend. The second part of the meeting is closed and all participants are assumed to be self-admitted alcoholics. Newcomers are encouraged to admit, publicly, that they are alcoholics. This is the *First Step* in the Twelve Step program and is essential, according to AA, if the person is to gain control over his or her alcoholism.

After accepting one's alcoholism the new member is encouraged to complete the Twelve Steps (Davidson & Neale, 1990). Regular attendance at meetings is urged, as is the belief that one must engage in a lifelong struggle with one's illness. Significant others (often called enablers by AA) are encouraged to join appropriate AA-type groups (Al-Anon for the family and Alateen for children of alcoholics). AA maintains that alcoholics who stick with AA have a very good chance not only of becoming sober but also staying that way. AA emphasizes that the struggle to stay sober is lifelong and that lifelong support is likely to be necessary for maintenance of sobriety and restoration of the alcoholic to a useful and productive life.

There are some problems with AA. The major problem is that a large percentage of alcoholics will not complete the Twelve Steps; that is, they will drop out of the program. The question of what percentage of people drop out of AA is controversial, but Edwards, Hensman, Hawker, and Williams (1967) found in their sample that as many as 80% of the people who join AA drop out. Another problem is that many alcoholics cannot be induced to join AA in the first place. It is probable that many of these people have gotten into such a pattern of denial that they refuse treatment. It is hoped that the discovery of the factors that lead alcoholics to avoid treatment may be identified, since Step One—the admission that one has a debilitating and uncontrollable drinking problem—is a necessary first step for *any* effective treatment program.

St. Mary's Hospital.   Mann (1979), the director of the chemically dependent program at St. Mary's Hospital, described treatment of chemically dependent people as "the process that enables individuals to live a productive life without the use of mood-altering chemicals" (p. 86). He argued that an adequate treatment program must include inpatient, outpatient, and family therapy; aftercare or followup; and halfway house facilities. For seriously chemically dependent people, Mann required that patients spend four to five weeks in St. Mary's Hospital. Since many seriously chemically dependent people are ill, a complete physical examination was also required. At the same time that physical illnesses were attended to, the patient received treatment for symptomatology of detoxification. When physical symptoms subsided, the patient entered the outpatient program. St. Mary's treatment team set concrete goals for patients and gave them explicit information about chemical dependency and the St. Mary's treatment program.

After detoxification and orientation the patient was assigned a counselor and placed in a therapy group in the hospital that met five days a week. Mann (1979) did not specify a particular therapeutic orientation but described a primary focus for the therapy sessions, particularly for groups. According to Mann:

> The group becomes that "place" where individual behavior is analyzed. Defense systems are examined. (Here we assume that the primary focus is on denial, a defense very common with alcoholics as well as other substance abusers.) Patients will experience learning and growth in the ability to identify and respond to emotional states. They will have the opportunity to identify needed coping skills and to work for their development. Confrontation, caring, and development of intimate friendships are the dynamics present in the therapy group. (p. 88)

It would seem from Mann's account that therapy at St. Mary's is an informal combination of Glasser's reality therapy and the interpersonal focus taken by H. S. Sullivan and included some of the elements of the directive, nonpunitive confrontational style of Synanon, Elan, and Phoenix House.

In addition, the patient at St. Mary's Hospital attended lectures three times a day, which focused on five dimensions of human functions: emotional, intellectual, societal, spiritual, and physical. Lecture topics included the disease of alcoholism, other chemical addictions, the dynamics of recovery, relationship with family, the dynamics of forgiveness, the delusional memory system, the philosophy and lifestyle of AA, and the Twelve Steps of AA.

Individual counseling approaches were not well specified but were included as a necessary part of the treatment program. In addition, family counseling was instituted as well as specific programs that focused on spiritual growth.

The inpatient program lasted for five weeks. At the end of this period the patient graduated. Part of the graduation procedure required the patient to participate in the Fourth Step and Fifth Step work of AA. According to Mann (1979),

> The Fourth Step requires the patient to construct autobiographical statements that detail personal strengths and weaknesses and identify alcoholic behaviors to be eliminated. . . . The Fifth Step requires the patients to share the autobiographical material with at least one other person. . . . Through this process of analysis and making public their lives, patients have the opportunity to experience forgiveness and release from the past. (p. 92)

The hospital's outpatient program selected less seriously dependent patients. This program lasted five weeks and also involved group, individual, and family therapy as well as lectures. In order to be accepted in the outpatient program the patient had to (1) abstain from mood-altering substances, (2) continue employment, and (3) sustain home life and personal life. Patients met in groups five nights a week, in therapy groups of ten each. Significant others also met in therapy groups, and on Friday there was a couples group. Also provided on Friday nights was a psychoeducational group for everyone in the patient's family as well as family therapy. After five weeks, patients graduated when they had completed Fourth and Fifth Steps work. For both inpatient and outpatient treatment programs, the patients were strongly urged to join AA groups and family members to join appropriate AA-type groups.

All patients participated in the aftercare program. Patients and spouses were expected to attend this program two evenings per week for two years. In general the aftercare program employed a supportive approach. However, confrontation of a patient or significant others when denial was apparent was part of the long-term treatment. In addition, all members of an alcoholic's family were required to attend regular open AA meetings and appropriate AA-style groups.

Mann (1979) stated clearly that some chemically dependent patients must be removed from destructive environments for a period longer than the initial five-week treatment period. Halfway houses provide a protective environment for patients who were deemed appropriate for such placement. The general structure of the halfway house was similar to that of Rapoport (1960) and to the therapeutic community notions of Phoenix House (DeLeon, 1988).

Specific behavior charting was part of the halfway house treatment program, as were the explicit statements of personal goals and rules of the house. For example: time had to be accounted for, and patients had to work, remain chemical-free, and participate in regularly scheduled meetings.

A weakness of Mann's (1979) work at St. Mary's Hospital was that he did not specify dropout or restoration rates. However, the general program presented here was comprehensive, followed a clear overall treatment procedure, and made sense in terms of what is known about alcoholics and other chemically dependent individuals.

Behavioral Approaches with Alcoholics. Since the issue of noncompliance (measured by dropout rates) is of critical importance with chemically dependent patients, any method that reduces these rates should be useful in facilitating recovery. Nirenberg (1983) stated that the dropout rates ranged from 28% to 80% in his review of alcohol treatment. He recommended contingency contracting as a method to aid in reducing dropouts. The patient had to sign a contract to commit a sizable amount of money that was refundable only if the patient remained in treatment for a specified period of time. Nirenberg reported that followup letters and telephone calls were relatively effective in increasing compliance.

In addition to contingency contracting and followup as a treatment approach with alcoholics, Sobell and Sobell (1978) established the Individualized Behavioral Treatment (I.B.T.) program, which included:

1. functional analysis of the individual's drinking behavior;
2. videotaped examples of the individual's drunken behavior—which that individual then viewed and was confronted with;
3. problem-solving training;
4. assertiveness training;
5. aversive contingencies for abusive drinking (these are specific negative results in a patient's life as a function of abusive drinking, and must be individually generated; and
6. practice in non-problem drinking. Sobell and Sobell found that I.B.T. patients were functioning better than patients in the control group.

Nirenberg (1983) noted that certain behavioral techniques might not be effective with alcoholics. Specifically, techniques that focused on aversive procedures and those that attempted to modify problem drinking to socially acceptable patterns of drinking did not seem to promise success and might in fact exacerbate the problem. These findings are consistent with our skepticism about the utility of aversive means of behavior control and are consistent with AA's insistence on abstinence from drinking. Nirenberg was also fully aware that to simply modify a behavior or set of behaviors was not enough; such behavioral change must be maintained.

Targeted Problems in Alcoholism Recovery. Cooper (1996) held that any effective treatment of alcoholics must focus on the alcoholic person's specific content problems. He held that there are five primary problems that must be targeted in treatment:

1. *Alcohol effects.* Alcoholics begin alcohol usage because they like the effects. As alcoholics progress through the various stages of their disorder they eventually become driven primarily by the need to block the painful withdrawal symptoms. Alcohol's strong sedative effects relieve tension, inhibition, and anxiety. The accompanying loss of judgment and control is much more apparent to the observer than to the alcoholic. The enabling defenses and relationships operate such that after withdrawal the pleasurable effects are remembered and the pain of withdrawal repressed. Clients remain alcohol-free not because they hate their alcohol usage but because they have learned to love their sobriety.
2. *Habit strength.* Alcohol addiction involves the kind of habit training that does not weaken with time. Nonreinforced trials are not possible with a substance whose reinforcing qualities are built into the interaction between the substance and the user's body chemistry. The habit can be

put to sleep, but if the user wakes it up it comes back full-industrial strength. No amount of willpower can guarantee controlled usage.

3. *Personality defenses.* The primary defense is denial. Alcoholics also rely heavily on justifications and rationalizations. Criminal alcoholics often add projection of blame. Alcoholics must uncover and confront their own reality-distorting defenses and learn to see themselves and others clearly and undefensively.

4. *Abuse of relationships.* Alcoholics learn to put off or avoid people who care enough about them to confront them with their alcoholism. These healthy relationships are replaced with relationships that support the alcoholism and the alcohol-dependent lifestyle. As the alcoholism worsens, the alcoholic seeks out more dysfunctional groups whose level of dependency and inadequacy matches or exceeds the alcoholic's own. Maintaining sobriety requires cutting off dysfunctional associations and acquiring and maintaining functional associations.

5. *Lack of personal and social skills.* Every time an alcoholic solves a problem by drinking the opportunity to acquire and strengthen skills is lost. If the alcoholism begins at age fourteen, that individual's coping skills remain at that level or slowly deteriorate. For the alcoholic, age does not bring wisdom.

Opiate, Cocaine, and Polysubstance Abuse

We have grouped opiate, cocaine, and polysubstance abuse together because illegal drugs have been the basis of most of the societal focus on addiction. The number of heroin addicts in 1990 was approximately one-half million (Davidson & Neale, 1990). Cocaine use (including crack) dramatically increased during the 1980s. In 1985 it was estimated that 5.8 million people used cocaine in one of its forms (Kozel & Adams, 1986). Davidson and Neale (1990) commented that this number of users indicated a 260% increase in use over an eleven-year period. In the 1980s, cocaine abuse outstripped heroin as the most notorious of illegal addictive drugs. It is almost certain, unless there is a major change in the culture, that heroin, cocaine, and other illegal drugs will continue to be abused and that the pattern of usage will cycle as has been the case for the last one hundred years.

Since these drugs are illegal, that is, their possession, use, and sale are punishable under law, any user is by definition a criminal. With society's emphasis on punishment and the increasing thrust toward incarceration, including mandatory prison sentences, any user is at war with the larger society. It need not be said that if one is using drugs and fears entanglement with the legal system, one is likely to avoid any agents of the society who might be able to supply treatment for one's chemical dependency. At present, the society's inconsistency with respect to drugs leads many "offenders" to be "offered" treatment as opposed to doing hard time. One can scarcely imagine a worse situation for the successful establishment of effective treatment programs. Many, if not most, clients in drug treatment programs are court-referred. They are told that if treatment fails, they will be required to serve their time. The personnel of the treatment facility make decisions as to whether or not treatment is successful, and if their judgment is that treatment is unsuccessful then the client goes to jail.

It may be that such conditions create a punitive or aversive environment. An aversive environment is often made worse by the misuse of behavior modification, particularly the use of point systems constructed such that it is more likely that the offender will lose points (and hence be required to stay in treatment) rather than gain points and "graduate." In addition, often no provisions are made for the user to live in a drug-free and crime-free environment after discharge, nor are there provisions for job training and placement upon graduation. Some programs try in the face of these problems to make a successful intervention and to address these shortcomings. Many do not.

Treatment approaches for polysubstance, heroin, and cocaine abuse or other severe disorders of substance abuse suffer from the same problems as treatment approaches for alcoholics. That is, it is difficult to get substance abusers in treatment unless they become enmeshed in the criminal justice system, and once involved in treatment it is difficult to keep them in treatment. If such individuals seek treatment and remain in treatment, then successful outcomes are not only possible but likely (DeLeon, 1984).

DeLeon (1984) found that:

1. The pattern of dropout rates over time was remarkably stable for all major approaches for substance abusers (therapeutic communities, non-residential settings, methadone programs, and outpatient drug-free programs). The highest dropout rate occurred during the first fifteen days and leveled off to a low dropout rate after ninety days.
2. Length of stay in the program was the best predictor of successful treatment.
3. Retention rates for all treatment programs were low: 22% in methadone maintenance programs, 9% in drug-free ambulatory programs, and 7% in drug-free residential programs (Phoenix House fared somewhat better than most drug-free residential programs with a twelve-month retention rate that ranged from 9% to 15%).

Clearly, most people who are dependent on these dangerous and illegal drugs were not effectively treated by approaches currently used. Such a conclusion does not mean that treatments are ineffective. In fact many therapeutic communities for drug treatment have been established that not only promised success but delivered on that promise. We will examine several of these approaches.

An Overview

According to Davidson and Neale (1990, p. 301) most therapeutic communities (TCs) were modeled after Synanon, a therapeutic community of former drug addicts founded in 1958 by Charles Dederich in Santa Monica, California. These residences are designed to radically restructure the addict's outlook on life so that illicit drugs no longer have a place. Daytop Village, Phoenix House, Odyssey House, and many other drug rehabilitation centers share the following features:

1. A total environment in which drugs are not available and continuing support is offered to ease the transition from regular drug use to a drug-free existence.
2. The presence of often charismatic role models—generally former addicts who appear to be meeting life's challenges without drugs.
3. Direct, often brutal confrontation in group therapy, in which addicts are goaded into accepting responsibility for their problems and drug habits, and urged to take charge of their lives.
4. A setting in which every addict is respected as a human being rather than stigmatized as a failure or criminal.
5. Separation of the addict from previous social contacts, on the assumption that these relationships have been instrumental in fostering the addictive lifestyle.

Synanon. The first therapeutic community established for the restoration of drug abusers (primarily heroin addicts) was Synanon, founded by Charles Dederich, himself a recovering alcoholic. Its development was a rather haphazard one, at first evolving from a group of AA members whom Dederich knew. He became the group's leader and developed an intense confrontational style (later to be called a "Haircut"), which would come to characterize the group approaches used at other Synanons as well as at Daytop, Elan, and other similar TCs for drug addicts. According to Yablonsky (1965), the first self-admitted "incorrigible" heroin addict entered Synanon in August 1958. This addict stayed in Synanon for thirteen months during which he was drug-free. According to Yablonsky at the time he published his book, this addict had remained drug-free. Since this addict had been on probation, a number of probation officers visited Synanon and began to place drug addicts there. Synanon had already broken with AA and established a separate identity with some distinct philosophical differences. According to Dederich (Yablonsky, 1965, p. 50), "We were building something new and different. Although I will always be grateful to AA for helping me personally, Synanon has nothing to do with AA, anymore than a rowboat compares with an airplane. We have a live-in situation, with family characteristics. We emphasize self-reliance rather than dependence on a higher being."

Synanon was predicated on the notion that only a complete break with old ways of thinking and acting was sufficient to restore hard-core addicts to sobriety and socially appropriate behavior. That meant, in practice, that any addict must not only admit drug dependency but also commit to living in a Synanon setting for a protracted period of time. During that period Synanon reserved the right to restrict an addict's interpersonal contacts. In some cases Synanon groups became similar to communes with almost a cult-like character. However, this development was not part of the original approach, which was intended to prepare people to return, as functional members, to the larger community. All Synanons were to be open centers; that is, an addict was told upon entrance that he or she could break their commitment and leave at any time.

There were two firm rules in Synanon that could lead to an addict being required to leave involuntarily: (1) physical violence or assaultive behavior and (2) drug use, including alcohol. Each addict was informed of the rules upon entrance into the program. Drug abuse was always dealt with firmly upon its discovery and if such behavior recurred, that person was thrown out of Synanon. Violence simply was not tolerated and such behavior led to expulsion from the setting.

It became a custom in many Synanons to process and screen newcomers through a "Haircut" group interview. A Haircut session was extremely confrontational. Two or three (rarely more) Synanon members, who initially behaved and dressed as typical middle-class health care providers, started the "interview." When they encountered addictive behaviors (attempts to con, phony insights, outright lying, and so forth) the addict was confronted, often by being called a "baby," among other insults. Such encounters were so severe that the addict often broke down. In addition, entering addicts were charged with the sole responsibility for their behavior and told they would start at the bottom (dishwashing) and have to work their way up the ladder to receive higher status jobs and privileges.

Synanon was conceived of as a treatment approach that would be most effective when the addict began to perceive the Synanon community as family. To encourage the development of such closeness and openness, regular group meetings (called synanons—little s) occurred three times a week, along with house meetings in which the business of daily living and maintenance was discussed. Any time there was a crisis, group meetings were held so that the whole group participated in conflict resolution. No professionals were involved in this process; in fact, a basic belief of Synanon was that it takes one to know and to treat one.

Daytop Village. Another therapeutic community for drug addicts, modeled on Synanon, was Daytop, founded shortly after Synanon, which like Synanon claimed great success (Bassin, 1968). However, as was the case with Synanon, Daytop has been criticized as being overly punitive and requiring addicts to become and perhaps remain isolated from the larger community (Hawkins & Wacker, 1983). Unlike Synanon, however, Daytop programs responded to these criticisms and have become part of the national attempt to unify and evaluate outcome analysis of therapeutic communities in America (O'Brien & Biase, 1984).

The Daytop program itself was described by Bassin (1968). The core problem for addicts is that their primary defenses against life's pains are detachment and denial. We maintain that drugs are used by addicts as a means of removing pain, largely emotional pain. The purpose of Daytop treatment was (and still is) to enable the recovering addict to face his or her pain rather than to use drugs to mask that pain.

Only two things are required for an addict to be allowed to remain in Daytop: (1) no violence and (2) no chemicals or self-destructive deceptions. We would add a third requirement that the addict remain in the program until fully functional. That third point is the sticking point for most TCs and its importance cannot be overemphasized. Failure to leave any TC and return to normal living turns some TCs into commune-like entities.

In the initial phase of treatment at Daytop, as Basin described, the addict went through withdrawal without medication. It was held that the "cold turkey" withdrawal with continued support but without solicitous attention was the first and most important step in treatment. Basin did not say how many people left the program at this point, an important omission. After withdrawal, the addict engaged in street behavior, in other words, conning and other manipulation that was met initially with kind but firm limits. When these attempts at external control failed, then special types of confrontations were employed in an attempt to get the addict to confess his or her games and to change his or her behavior to comply with the rules of the house. There was a job status system at Daytop (and at most of the other TCs) and new members started at the bottom and worked their way up. If ex-addicts stayed at Daytop in treatment they were asked to "act as if"; that is, they were asked to act as if they knew what to do, as if they had the experience, as if they were mature, as if treatment was going to be successful, as if they were ready to grow up and get well, and as if they were already well and behaving like adults.

As with other TCs, peer pressure, confrontation, and stressful group encounters were a central part of the treatment at Daytop. Daytop treatment had an explicit reentry step in which the ex-addict gradually was reintegrated into the larger community. After reentry the ex-addict lived in the Daytop setting but had to work in the larger community. Finally, the ex-addict moved into the community to both work and live in it, and it was hoped, live in it drug-free.

According to O'Brien and Biase (1984), by the 1980s TCs (including Daytop) had become much more focused on objective analysis of outcome than was the case when Synanon and Daytop first began treatment. In addition, professionals have become a welcome part of these treatment programs. Finally, higher education programs and an explicit focus on the development of an improved self-concept have increased the awareness of Daytop—and through it, other TCs—of the necessity for effective reintegration of ex-addicts within the larger community.

Phoenix House.   One of the most thoroughly evaluated TCs is Phoenix House (DeLeon, 1984, 1988). It differed in significant ways from Synanon and Daytop. One difference was that prior to admission to Phoenix House, drug-dependent individuals were detoxified at a separate facility where they stayed for one to three months. Another difference was that Phoenix House residents had to agree to submit to random weekly urine analysis to demonstrate that they remained drug-free. Finally, Phoenix House facilities were located in neighborhoods in which substance abuse and crime rates were high. Drug abusers were not placed in a Phoenix House in their own neighborhoods, since part of the treatment program involved the removal of the drug-dependent person from old associations.

The program itself was similar to Synanon. Phoenix House viewed the development of a non-drug-using, non-criminal identity as critical to the restoration process. Central to this process was the notion that reformed addicts could serve as the most salient role models to facilitate others' establishing a new non-drug-using identity. Many of Synanon's confrontational approaches, intended to reinforce honesty and openness, were employed at Phoenix House. Group meetings occurred regularly and individual issues were dealt with within the context of an encounter in which the "target" person's "irresponsible" behaviors were attacked. It became difficult to maintain denial defenses, lying, or manipulation within this context.

All members of a Phoenix House community were given daily jobs, which were hierarchically organized. As a member improved, his or her status increased and he or she was given increasingly responsible jobs. Work activities were intended to increase the sense of community and also served to reduce operating costs for these facilities.

Odyssey House.   Densen-Gerber and Drossner (1974) described Odyssey House as a TC that was quite different from Synanon, both in philosophy and treatment approach. The main thrust for Odyssey House was to return the drug-dependent person to the larger community. Therefore the primary focus was on developing social-vocational skills that could facilitate the individual's effective functioning in the larger community. Densen-Gerber and Drossner placed great emphasis on education and basic accomplishments that served to bridge the gap between living in a TC and functioning in the larger community. Specifically, ex-addicts were not hired as staff members at Odyssey House unless they obtained a high school degree or a GED, a driver's license, and evidence of an offer of a job other than at Odyssey House. Further evidence of Odyssey House's effectiveness was that only about 40% of the graduates remained in the addiction field. Earlier TCs had been notorious for serving as places in which addicts recovered and then became counselors with other addicts. Often ex-addict counselors failed to maintain a therapeutic relationship with their clients either being too punitive or too permissive in their treatment of addicts.

Treatment at Odyssey House also differed from that of many other TCs. Not only was there a school at the facility but also each drug-dependent person received a full medical and psychological evaluation by appropriate professionals as part of the entrance process. Further, all activities were keyed to developing skills for effective functioning in the larger community. Central to the Odyssey House program was a workshop program in which these skills were taught. The workshop program and emphasis on education were supplemented by more standard TC approaches such as confrontation in groups, ex-addicts serving as role models, hierarchical structure, and house meetings. In addition, professional counseling was available.

Individual Approaches with Substance Abusers

Individual treatment approaches with substance abusers are not likely to lead to successful outcomes except when they are part of a more comprehensive treatment approach. In the main, individual therapy must follow similar strategies as those employed by Glasser (1975) and Greenwald (1967) in the treatment of antisocial personality disorders (see Chapter 9 in this text). As Greenwald noted, the establishment of a working relationship as a means of inducing self-directed control of impulsive behavior is required. Usually the client or patient will continue to attempt to defeat the therapist's efforts to produce effective behavior change. Similar strategies apply to other disorders of impulse including eating disorders and compulsive gambling.

Eating Disorders

It is difficult to overemphasize the extent to which our culture is preoccupied with body image. It is impossible to turn on the television or to read a popular magazine without reference to some weight loss or exercise program that claims to make people "beautiful" and therefore eternally happy. Such preoccupations, particularly in American culture, have led to an increasing number of patients who suffer from the eating disorders, anorexia nervosa and bulimia.

According to Andersen (1985), the primary shared component of anorexia nervosa and bulimia is a "morbid fear of fatness" (p. 4). In general, it is considered accurate to state that anorexic patients fear loss of control over eating while bulimic patients have lost control over eating and control their weight through induced vomiting and purging with laxatives. Andersen also commented that not all anorextic patients have actual loss of appetite, and cautioned care in inducing appetite stimulation approaches unless there is documented appetite suppression. It should be obvious that if someone is preoccupied with food and is starving himself or herself out of fear, then to goad him or her to eat would, from the point of view of that person, make the treatment team the enemy. Such treatment might produce bulimic behavior.

According to Andersen (1985) certain people have a pronounced hereditary bias toward developing an eating disorder (usually anorexia nervosa) even in the absence of social pressures for thinness. However, these individuals constitute only a small percentage of people who presently suffer from eating disorders. Andersen argued that people with obsessional-perfectionist personalities are likely to develop anorexia nervosa while histrionic-borderline personalities develop bulimia. It would seem that Andersen saw an underlying personality disorder as an important component in many people who suffer from anorexia nervosa and bulimia. However, he was quick to point out that many people who present problems with patterns of eating may have basically "normal" personalities and are in trouble because of their acquiescence to the considerable social pressures for thinness.

R. G. Meyer (1989) discussed anorexia nervosa and bulimia under disorders of impulse control. According to Meyer these disorders are seen primarily in the middle and upper socioeconomic classes. Meyer stated that they most often occur at puberty and that, "Sexuality may be channeled into the eating area" (p. 283). Further, Meyer stated that "Anorexics who also showed episodes of bulimia . . . in general are more disturbed than those who do not" (p. 283).

Anorexia Nervosa

Treatment with anorexics must begin with an intensive medical workup. The purpose of a thorough physical exam is to rule out physical causes of the eating disorder. If the patient is female, middle or upper class, and is 25% below normal body weight, the classification of that person as suffering from anorexia nervosa is reasonable, but only in the context of a complete medical exam that rules out Simond's disease, subcortical tumors that cause eating dysfunction, and other medical disorders that cause appetite loss.

If the above criteria are met, then the treatment of the patient must initially occur in an inpatient setting that specializes in treatment of eating disorders. External control of eating behavior must be imposed in anorexia nervosa. Again, Andersen (1985) specified, rather clearly, what must be done to address typical problem behaviors evidenced in such patients:

Patient Will Not Eat
This problem is met with firm insistence that the food is prescribed medicine and must be finished. This requirement, combined with understanding of the patient's fears and much encouragement, has resulted in our having no patient refuse food after the first few hours on the ward.

Patient Takes Too Long to Eat
If the patient takes more than one hour to eat, we move to a quiet room for full concentration on the nutritional work. This strategy is also adopted if the patient's behavior is disruptive.

Patient Hides Food
We assume that most patients will try to hide food out of a tremendous fear of fatness. Don't make the discovery of hidden food a game or a cause for scolding, explain that such behavior is unacceptable and that it arises out of a fear of fatness. Check pockets for food. Check also for butter smeared on the bottom of tables, partly chewed meat spit into milk containers raised to the lips, and food pressed under the table.

Excess Use of Condiments
One small, prepacked serving of pepper and/or lemon is sufficient for most meals. Foods should not be mixed in strange ways or made unpalatable with excess condiments.

Patient Vomits After Meals
If the patient vomits, ask in a non-punitive manner for her help in cleaning up. Estimate the amount lost and order that amount of food, usually as a milkshake, to be eaten as a replacement.

Weights on the Scale Seem Too High
Heavier than expected weigh-ins prompt us to check linings of clothing for weights, or the scale for tampering. Don't let patients drink large amounts of water before weigh-in. Check if large amounts of salt were ingested to produce edema.

Use of Laxatives or Diuretics
Be suspicious when serum potassium remains low or the patient has a history of abuse of diuretics or laxatives. Check blood levels of potassium and, if tests are available, for diuretics. Unexplained diarrhea should make staff think of hidden laxatives. . . .

Excess Talk of Food, Calories, Weight
Encourage the patient to talk about feelings, events, or other things but not food, weight or calories. Explain that these areas have been a source of unhappiness to the patient, and that in fact, she or he has lost control over them.

Excessive Exercise
Exercise should be prescribed like a medication. We feel that moderate exercise, proportional to physical health, is part of a comprehensive program. . . .

Staff Splitting
Patient may claim one staff member permitted them to do something that the person supervising that particular meal does not permit. Final judgment goes to the person supervising the meal, but the issue may be discussed in rounds. Patients are not allowed to talk *about* other staff—they are encouraged to talk to the person with whom they have a problem and to work on the problem directly. . . .

Countertransference
Staff members should always keep in mind that a particular patient may arouse within them feelings carried over from past experiences. Staff must take care that the patient does not become the current focus of prior unresolved conflicts. [Present authors' note: this way of viewing countertransference applies to virtually all modes of psychosocial treatment.] . . .

Patient Complains of Depression
When patients complain of depression, explain that it originates from a combination of starvation with effects of chronic illness. Depression will usually respond to nutritional rehabilitation: if it does not respond to improved weight, it will be treated by psychotherapy and/or medication. (p. 58)

Andersen (1985) suggested that psychotherapy of anorexics (as part of inpatient treatment) be viewed as a three-stage process. He recommended that stage one be supportive, by which he meant "non-specific encouragement, mobilizing the patient's remaining defenses, and helping the patient cope with the present situation" (p. 64). It would seem that the therapist should take an active role with the anorextic patient. Once weight gain is achieved and the psychological effects of starvation attenuated, then therapy moves to stage two.

In stage two, individual, group, and family therapy are essential. According to Andersen the therapies must be "*intensive, individualized and coordinated*" (Andersen, 1985, p. 68). Andersen provided specific guidelines about the structure of individual psychotherapy (pp. 68–74). We would note that his focus on "all or none" reasoning seems akin to splitting—"I must starve or I will become fat"—and "If I feel anything I will be destroyed." Special therapies for stage two are given (pp. 74–75). Group work focused on feelings, and relaxation techniques and assertiveness training were provided.

Stage three work was grouped under the unfortunate (in our view) heading of maintenance and focused on what the patient was to do following discharge to maintain gains. Much of the planning centered on maintaining weight gains rather than continuing psychological growth. We suggest that this is a significant weakness in an otherwise excellent treatment approach. Finally, Andersen referred to stage four followup. He stated that treatment often needed to continue for one to three years. We would argue that psychotherapy following discharge is almost always a necessity and should take place in order to facilitate the patient's reentry into the larger community.

In addition to Andersen's approaches, family therapy leading to the modification of the family structure is often required for effective treatment of anorectic clients. Minuchin (1974) suggested that the anorextic family member often feels powerless. Through their eating pattern, they gained some control of their immediate family environment. Minuchin gave a reasonably clear analysis of the family therapy approach useful in working with such families (see Chapter 13 for a more complete description of this approach). Andersen (1985) specified similar approaches to family therapy in his Chapter 10 (pp. 135–148).

Bulimia

Consistent with other DSM-IV classification approaches, bulimia is considered to be a disorder distinct from anorexia nervosa. Andersen (1985) suggested there were many different forms of bulimia (or at least different causes), each requiring somewhat different treatment. Further he argued that anorexia nervosa and bulimia may be related and that there was at least some overlap in the two disorders. In addition he found many normal-weight bulimics have characterological problems that increase the probability of such patients' engaging in drug-dependent behaviors, sexual acting out, other antisocial behaviors, and self-injurious behavior. This pattern of interaction is shown in Figure 12, page 112, in Andersen (1985).

According to Andersen (1985), outpatient treatment of bulimia was usually appropriate. In general, bulimic patients were older, had a more complex personality structure, and were characterized by binging and purging behaviors as well as preoccupation with food and weight and a pronounced inability to control their frequently excessive food intake. Treatment began by controlling or instituting control over the binging and purging behavior.

Behavior therapy focused on removing foods that trigger impulsive eating and on record keeping. The patient was encouraged to have meals with other people and to recognize urges to binge before they become uncontrollable impulses. Once recognized, the patient was encouraged to wait out the urge, often with a trusted friend. According to Andersen (1985), "The goal is not to fear the urge but to understand it, choose a different response to it, and ultimately to prevent it if possible by changing some of the contributing factors" (p. 124). Tolerance of urges was supplemented by relaxation therapy to reduce anxiety. The technique of thought-stopping was used to implement control over self-destructive thinking. Andersen also suggested paradoxical intention (that is, prescribing the symptom: "Go on, starve yourself to death") as a useful behavioral method to gain control over binging behavior. Note:

simply to employ these techniques in a mechanical fashion without a sound therapeutic relationship can make the patient worse.

Bruch (1978) argued that dependency issues, sexual issues, and the subtle (or not so subtle) selfishness and narcissism (or borderline patterns of them) that emerge in bulimic patients or clients require some of the intervention strategies used by Kohut and Kernberg with borderline and narcissistic patients (see Chapter 9 in this text). The extent to which a component of the bulimic's problem is characterological is the extent to which these and other techniques useful in the treatment of personality disorders might be employed. Perhaps Andersen's (1985) statement that the treatment modalities he employed were less effective with some bulimics than with anorextics may reflect a failure to deal explicitly with some characterological issues.

Obesity

According to Coleman, Butcher, and Carson (1984), hyper-obesity may be defined as a state in which an individual is 100 pounds over her or his ideal weight. This is a dangerous disorder requiring treatment both because of physiological hazards and because of the direct impact of obesity on positive self-evaluation. Coleman et al. (1994) considered that obesity shared many similarities with personality disorders. As with many of the disorders described in this chapter, current treatment approaches for obesity often fail. Many people who are extremely overweight have lost weight only to gain it back again, and even the most successful programs have a high relapse rate. The prudent clinician will suggest one of the more effective weight control programs such as Weight Watchers. In addition, we have found that it may be necessary for an individual to join a support group. Membership in such a support group may be necessary to maintain weight loss. The commitment is similar to that of an alcoholic who must remain a member in AA to successfully stay sober.

Destructive Patterns of Sexual Behavior

Overview of Sexual Impulsivity

Incest, rape, and child molestation are all forms of sexual abuse that carry with them legal consequences. Sexual promiscuity, whether male or female, heterosexual or homosexual, is a pattern of sexual behavior that is dangerous both to the individuals who engage in it and their sexual partners. These patterns of sexual behavior share the common thread of lack of control over sexual behavior and failure to consider "the other" or the possible consequences of one's behavior to oneself.

Incest, rape, and child molestation are all criminal acts in which "the other" is used only as an object. It is estimated that roughly 30% of all criminals are sexual offenders. Rape and, often, incest and child molestation are acts of violence against unwilling victims. In general, societal reaction to such offenders is to suggest castration (R. G. Meyer, 1989) and other forms of punitive treatment if treatment is considered at all. In fact, many of the treatment approaches dealing with sexual deviancy in the literature focus on the victims of these offenders rather than on what treatments could be employed to correct such behaviors. However, such abusers were often abused themselves and further punitive treatment is not likely to be successful (Davidson & Neale, 1990).

It may be that treating the victims, particularly of incest and child abuse, is the most effective means of preventing future child abuse and incest patterns, and perhaps even the more brutal forms of rape. Certainly our sensitivity to the frequency of these patterns of destructive sexual behavior has increased awareness that early treatment may reduce later problems.

However, once self-destructive or other destructive patterns of sexual behavior are established, they are extremely difficult to change. The tenacious character of these problems resists institutional placement, which usually fails, as is also true of most currently used treatment approaches. Our focus is on those therapists who have claimed success in working with this most difficult group of troubled people.

Treatment of the Victims of Rape, Incest, and Child Abuse

In cases of rape, the person who is raped is the object of a violent crime in which sexual intercourse is achieved by the use of force on the unwilling victim. Treatment, whatever its genesis, must focus both on that fact and the fact that the woman or man has a legitimate basis for anger. According to Meyer and Taylor (1986), many women blame themselves, irrationally, for somehow being responsible for "causing" the rape. Such self-blame is often associated with poor recovery. Activating legitimate anger within the context of the reality of the situation is a reasonable first step for guilt reduction. In addition, communicating that the victim's noncompliance is legitimate is a good first step in reducing feelings of responsibility.

According to Davidson and Neale (1990), long-term therapy is often required for a rape victim to deal with relationship issues. Often a husband or lover will adopt the culture's implicit viewpoint that the victim somehow "tempted" the rapist and is therefore responsible. We would argue that an even more important focus for therapy is to deal with the sense of violation the person who has been raped feels (and in fact has been subjected to). Support groups with rape survivors are often helpful. Recently some women have begun to confront the imprisoned rapist in a controlled situation, but whether this approach will be useful or not remains to be proven.

In cases of incest and child abuse, removal of the violated person from the family system or removal of the instigator of incestual child abuse behavior is often required. The power imbalance and the destructive acting out are often so ingrained that no effective psychosocial intervention exists. Often the abuser's spouse or lover is an enabler and has also been abused. Approaches similar to rape hot lines have been useful, particularly for abused wives and children. Once the abused members of a family are removed from the situation, family therapy is recommended. Their profound trauma and their sense of having been violated often require structured individual treatment approaches that include support and the use of gentle uncovering approaches, similar to those used with post-traumatic stress disorder victims. However, lifelong access to support group treatment may also be required—as is often the case in alcoholism, drug abuse, and other severe disorders—as well as family therapy.

Treatment of the Rapist and the Child Abuser

As noted earlier the treatment of rapists and child abusers is most often punitive or nonexistent. Specific approaches include castration, chemical castration, aversive conditioning approaches (such as shock to the penis coupled with the rapist viewing photographs of simulated rape or naked children), and combinations of these approaches. As is the case with other punitive measures, such approaches are not likely to be effective (R. G. Meyer, 1989). However, it is probable that approaches suggested for use with personality disorders may be useful (see Chapter 9 in this text).

The recidivism rate for sexual offenders is among the highest of all criminals. Efforts to treat these individuals are not working. Perhaps some of them should be locked up forever; perhaps some, particularly those who have also engaged in serial murders, should face capital punishment. However, permanent removal either through incarceration or death is not psychosocial treatment. Rather it is an admission either of our ignorance or our sense that these people are subhuman and therefore should be removed permanently from society. If one holds, implicitly or explicitly, that subjective position, one must not work with rapists or child abusers.

Sexually Acting Out: The Promiscuous Person

When either a male or female engages in impulsive, repetitious, extensive, and dangerous sexual acting out, we view that person as having a serious personal problem. Such patterns of self-destructive and disturbing behavior are frequently encountered in patients who have been diagnosed as having bipolar disorder (manic phase), bulimia, substance abuse disorders, and core personality disorders (primarily borderline, antisocial, and narcissistic personality disorders). Occasionally, one finds a person whose sexual behavior is impulsive but does not display one of the more serious disorders listed above. It is our contention that such people are rare and seldom seek treatment.

If the patient's or client's self-structure is characterized by the use of splitting defenses and narcissistic injury is discovered, then treatment proceeds as we have suggested (see Chapter 9). If an individual comes into treatment because someone else is concerned about the propriety of that person's sexual behavior, then treatment should focus on the real dangers of impulsive sexuality, such as AIDS, other sexually transmitted diseases, and unwanted pregnancies. At no time may a therapist offer moral guidance, even if sought by the client; the client should receive such guidance from parents or friends. For the therapist to take any moral position violates therapeutic neutrality and may prevent the possibility of establishing a working relationship with the client.

Conclusion

The first step in the treatment of disorders of impulse control is to prevent destructive acting out. In the more serious disorders an inpatient placement is required to interrupt destructive behavioral patterns. In the treatment of anorexia nervosa individuals must not be allowed to starve themselves to death. In the treatment of many forms of substance abuse, the individual must be removed from the larger community if that individual is to successfully cease taking drugs. However, in most cases of disorders of impulse control, initial blocking of impulsive acting out is insufficient to prevent resumption of negative patterns once the individual has left the inpatient setting, group home, or therapeutic community.

It is in the second stage of treatment of these troubled people that failure most often occurs: in the development of internal control, in other words, control by the individual over his or her destructive impulses. AA and other support groups either explicitly or implicitly replace institutional control with the support group itself. Many of the earlier therapeutic communities (particularly Synanon) substitute the TC for internal control.

However, in the most effective programs, an institutional or other type of external control is only a waystation en route to the individual gaining control over his or her impulsive behavior. Effective treatment may be claimed for these troubled people only in those programs that emphasize the individual achieving control of his or her own behavior within the context of the larger community.

Furthermore, effective treatment requires that therapists overcome two critical problems. First, people with disorders of impulse control can seem so normal when they are not "on" drugs or otherwise engaging in their preferred impulsive behavior. Second, they all use denial extensively, making it extraordinarily difficult to confront them with their contributions to their own problems. One must keep in mind that these clients and patients *are* troubled people and that their apparent normality may only be purchased by extensive denial. The denial must be defeated before self-control can be initiated.

In addition, the client suffering from an impulse control problem often lies. If the client is withholding important information or is actively distorting his or her actions, it is unlikely that any treatment approach will lead to a successful outcome. The essence of effective psychosocial treatment is the establishment of a working relationship between the troubled person and the therapist. No lying, no denying, a gradual increase in client self-control, and a realistic modification of the client's world-view is a useful definition of the rules for establishing a working relationship for disorders of impulse control.

The fit between our models and the treatment literature for these disorders is adequate. Such patterns of impulsive acting out are usually related to early severe trauma, as is indicated by our intrapsychic model. Treatment of such individuals must be highly structured. Lifelong support groups for alcoholics and substance abusers and similar groups for individuals with other disorders of impulse control seem useful. An "in-and-out" approach with one's therapist seems characteristic of both successful and unsuccessful treatment. That is, the patient will cycle up and out of active therapy but will continue to maintain intermittent contact with either an effective therapist or some other agent of our current mental health or criminal system. Taken together, these findings support the contention that treatment must be long-term.

The initial interpersonal style for all patterns of impulsive behavior is the matter-of-fact interpersonal role (*DE*). However, a rigid *DE* role does not do justice to interpersonal requirements. When the patient shows warmth, a gentle excursion to a low-level *LM* is required. If, as so often happens, the patient reverts to lying and manipulative behaviors, the therapist must shift back to the matter-of-fact role. If the person asks for help or admits weakness, an excursion to a low-level *NO* (strong and warm) interpersonal role is required. Again, if the person reverts to impulsive anger or manipulation, the therapist goes back to a low-level *DE* matter-of-fact role. In any event the therapist must not lose control.

In terms of therapy content, a simple listing of the person's violations of the legitimate expectations of others would not be effective. One must place those violations within the context of need satisfaction. As Glasser (1975) stated, human needs are satisfied by other human beings. When needs are satisfied in "responsible" ways, then the troubled person no longer need rely on impulsive acting out to find gratification. In addition, a careful exploration of significant others' violations of the client's legitimate needs is required. One must not identify with the patient's sense that the world is a jungle, but rather explore with the patient how to find realistic redress for his or her distress. Indeed, if no redress is possible, one must, as a good parent often must, own that the world is not always fair.

9 Personality or Character Disorders

The focus for this chapter is the classification and treatment of personality disorders. Wishnie (1977) and others (Horowitz, Rosenberg, & Bartholomew, 1993; Zvi, 1975) considered the primary deficiency in a number of disorders, including personality disorders, to be that of impulse control.[1] Wishnie proposed that a substantial number of people classified as suffering from personality disorders could be labeled as having *impulsive personality disorders,* and said such people seem to be living in a constant but stable state of chaos. We suggest that people who may be classified as having "core" personality disorders not only live in a state of stable chaos but also in a world that, owing to their actions, is in fact dangerous. Wishnie also characterized such people as living in the present and seeming neither to be able to learn from the past nor to anticipate the future. These characteristics seem to us to fit people suffering from core personality disorders.

Basic Issues of Personality Disorders

The DSM-IV and the Problem of Axis II

The DSM-IV is described as a multiaxial system consisting of five axes. Axis I refers to mental disorders. Axis II refers to personality disorders and mental retardation. Axis III refers to the patient's general medical condition. Axis IV refers to psychosocial and environmental problems and Axis V refers to global assessment of functioning. Insurance companies require diagnoses on Axes I, II, and III but do not require any reference to Axes IV and V.

Given its mathematical and scientific connotations the use of the term axis is confusing. It is common practice in psychological research to use the term axis interchangeably with the term dimension. The DSM-IV is not a dimensional or coordinate classification system but rather it is a category classification system, one of the three systems currently used in scientific classification. Widiger and Frances (1985) listed the three approaches as categorical, dimensional, and prototype systems. They noted there are advantages and disadvantages to all three classification systems (see Chapter 14 in this text).

There are two primary reasons given for the DSM-IV grouping of personality disorders on a separate axis. First, these Axis II disorders were considered by the framers of the DSM-IV to be of such importance that they needed to have attention called to them (Freedman, Brotman, Silverman, & Hutson, 1986). Second, these authors held that some disorders are characterized by personality traits that are inflexible, maladaptive, and occur in a wide array of circumstances and can cause subjective distress. They held that these disorders are different in kind, or are presumed to be different in kind, from Axis I disorders.

However, according to the DSM-IV *schizophrenia* (an Axis I disorder), is characterized by the personality traits of *anhedonia* (inability to find pleasure in any activity) and lack of affect (flattened or inappropriate affect) as well as other criteria. Following the reasoning used in the construction of the DSM-IV, there is no logical reason why schizophrenia should not be classified on Axis II given that the disorder is characterized by maladaptive traits that occur in a wide array of circumstances.

Millon and Davis (1996) offered an explanation for Axis II that would answer this objection. They stated that Axis II did not refer to personality disorders as such but rather to underlying and stable personality traits. They held that the interaction of maladaptive personality traits (Axis II) with psychological stressors (Axis IV) produced Axis I disorders. For example, if one had a schizotypal personality trait and was stressed severely (possibly by the stress of pubescence), then one would become schizophrenic.

Millon and Davis's analysis of the genesis of disorders is intriguing and requires continued attention (see Chapter 14). However, we hold that neither their explanation nor the other reasons given for a separate axis for personality disorders are defensible. There is neither a sufficiently compelling rational basis for a separate axis nor is there empirical evidence requiring it (Benjamin, 1994; Livesley, Schroeder, Jackson, & Jang, 1994).

Conceptually it makes little sense to introduce a major theoretical concept (Axis II) merely to call attention to a class of disorders. Further, all disorders are, by definition, characterized by patterns of thinking, feeling, and acting that are dysfunctional and occur in a significant number of contexts. In what concrete ways are personality disorders different in kind from Axis I disorders? We hold that no meaningful distinction can be made.

If Axis II can be collapsed into Axis I, could a theoretical analysis be made that would actually change the DSM-IV classification system into an axis or true dimensional system? One option is that disorders, including personality disorders, may be arranged in an ordered fashion from least severe to most severe, both in terms of the severity of and the number of symptoms. We argue that there are personality disorders different in kind from other disorders, and that they occupy an intermediate position between disorders of impulse control and psychoses. We have chosen to call these disorders core personality disorders. We suggest that our approach will get rid of the artificial notion of co-morbidity (many diagnoses for the same symptoms) (Frances, Widiger, & Fryer, 1990) and should reduce the problems of reliability and validity that have existed for Axis II "diagnoses" (Coleman, Butcher, & Carson, 1984; Francis, 1980).

Core Personality Disorders

We hold that a set of disorders exists that is different in kind from the prototypes of neuroses, disorders of impulse control, and psychoses. People who have these disorders may be characterized as impulsive, lacking empathy, and unable to form stable interpersonal relationships with others. In addition, such people are often manipulative and exploitive of others.

The DSM-IV classification system groups personality disorders into three clusters. Cluster A includes people characterized as eccentric, and classified as suffering from *schizoid, schizotypal,* and *paranoid personality disorders.* We would characterize these disorders as *psychotoform disorders,* disorders that are like psychoses. We hypothesize that the treatment of these individuals would be similar to that of outpatient psychotics (see Chapters 10 and 11).

Cluster C includes people characterized as eccentric and classified as *avoidant, dependent,* and having *obsessive-compulsive personality disorders.* In addition, we suggest that Cluster C could include *passive-aggressive* and *depressive personality disorders.* The *histrionic personality disorder,* with modifications in diagnostic criteria (extensive use of the defense mechanism of denial as the primary diagnostic criterion as opposed to the DSM-IV focus on dramatic behavioral displays), is similar to the old diagnosis of *hysterical neurosis.* It would be more descriptive if Cluster C disorders, and those disorders we have included with Cluster C, were classified as *neurotoform disorders,* similar to neurosis. We hypothesize that such people could profit from treatments useful for neurotic clients (see Chapter 6).

Those disorders included in Cluster B in the DSM-IV (with the exception of the histrionic personality disorder) we call core personality disorders. These, as noted previously, include the *narcissistic, antisocial,* and *borderline personality disorders.* Kernberg (1975) and Gunderson (1975, 1978, 1988) hold that there are several common features in the group core personality disorders. Kernberg held that these disorders shared a common personality structure and all vary in terms of severity from narcissistic to antisocial to borderline. Kernberg described the personality structure of people with these disorders as organized around an experience of the world as dangerous, in which only the strong survive and any feeling or expression of that feeling is extraordinarily dangerous. Kernberg (1975, 1976) argued that such people tend to act out impulsively and use the defenses of splitting and projective identification as their primary means of protecting themselves from the experience of such a world. Although we have briefly defined these terms earlier at this point more extensive definitions are required since the concepts are important to the understanding of what we have called core personality disorders.

Splitting is a primitive defensive reaction that leads individuals to react to the world in terms of absolutes; for example, a person or situation is all good or all bad. *Projective identification* is a primitive defense in which negative characteristics of an individual are projected onto another person, which leads to the individual's perception of that person as possessing godlike power and worthy of worship or so evil that overt hostility must be directed toward him or her.

In general, those people that we have characterized as suffering from core personality disorders are very difficult to relate to. Perhaps the way in which these people perceive their world is what makes it so difficult to empathize with them. Kernberg (1976) stated that "in borderline patients there is an excessive development of pregenital and, especially oral, aggression which tends to induce premature development of oedipal striving, and, as a consequence, there is a particular condensation of pregenital and genital aims under the over-riding influence of aggressive need" (p. 71). Although the content of Kernberg's analysis is somewhat unclear, we hold that he has portrayed the world as a dangerous place for people who could be labeled as suffering from the borderline personality disorder. Kernberg is clearer with respect to the world-view of those who are classified as suffering from the narcissistic personality disorder. He stated that, "The narcissistic character defenses protect the patient [from] . . . his frightening image of the world as being devoid of food, love, and his self concept of the hungry wolf out to eat, kill, and survive" (Kernberg, 1975, p. 71).

Greenwald (1967) described the world-view of psychopaths with even greater clarity. According to Greenwald:

> Now what does the psychopath really feel like? This is what puzzled me, and only when I reached an understanding of this inner feeling was I able to get some perception of the condition. Can you imagine yourself a Jew suddenly dropped into Nazi Germany and surrounded by SS men during the height of the Hitler terror against the Jews? What feelings of morality would you have? What kind of ability would you have to empathize with the people around you? What immediate gratification would you want to postpone? What would there be that you would not be willing to do? (p. 356)

Greenwald commented that until he was able to symbolically enter the psychopath's world he could not help such a client. We suggest that this process is required for all disorders, but especially for people we have designated as having core personality disorders.

Personality disorders, especially core personality disorders, are considered difficult to treat. According to Reid (1989), "The depth of pathology [for personality disorders] is such that any concept of 'cure' requires marked restructuring of very basic developmental characteristics" (p. 332). Kernberg (1975) also stated that people with these disorders are incredibly difficult to treat. Further, Carson, Butchner, and Mineka (1998) pointed out that these people rarely seek treatment on their own. Most frequently they are required to go into treatment by others.

Antisocial Personality Disorders: The Psychopath

The DSM-IV criteria for the classification of antisocial personality disorder are "A pervasive pattern of disregard for and the violation of the rights of others occurring since age 15 years, as indicated by 3 (or more) of the following": (1) engaging in illegal behaviors, (2) deceitfulness, (3) impulsivity, (4) irritability and aggressiveness, (5) reckless disregard for the safety of others, (6) consistent irresponsibility, and (7) lack of remorse. Nietzel, Speltz, McCauley, and Bernstein (1998) stated that the antisocial personality disorder as defined in the DSM-IV is not the same as what has been traditionally defined as the psychopathic disorder. They argued the psychopath possessed devious personality traits and interpersonal tendencies not represented in the DSM-IV "behavioral" criteria. Hare, Hart, and Harpur (1991) stated that there are two distinct disorders that are grouped under the rubric antisocial personality disorder. On the one hand are those people who act in accordance with the DSM-IV criteria and are diagnosed with antisocial personality disorders. On the other hand are those who may not display these behaviors but have no capacity for guilt, anxiety, loyalty, or remorse. They suffer from the classical psychopathic disorder. Hare et al. used the twenty-item Hare scale in their study to identify the latter group. This scale required that the person administering it know the subject well and know his or her history well.

The distinction between the "true" psychopath and the person who has antisocial personality disorder is of considerable clinical significance. Cleckley (1954) stated that there was no effective treatment for psychopaths other than removing them from society. Arieti (1978) agreed, painting a similar and discouraging picture with respect to intervention with and treatment of psychopaths. Underlying all of these conclusions is the notion that psychopathy is constitutional, meaning inherited or otherwise physiologically determined, and therefore represents a *type* of disorder that, at present, is incurable. Such a position is not new, and in fact Pritchard (1835) stated that psychopathy was both constitutional and incurable.

In spite of the general pessimism about the effectiveness of treating psychopaths, a number of therapists (Aichhorn, 1935; Redl & Wineman, 1954; Glasser, 1965; McCord & McCord, 1956; Greenwald, 1967; Wishnie, 1977; McCord, 1985) have claimed success. Unless these findings are dismissed as based on misdiagnosis, poorly controlled studies, or some other flawed process, one cannot hold that psychopathy is an incurable disorder. Perhaps the primary difficulty in treating those who suffer from it is that most caretakers, with a great deal of justification, take a moralistic and judgmental orientation towards people termed psychopaths.

Greenwald (1967), in a rare exception to the general case, stated that:

> It is amazing how little empathy is shown for psychopathy. Many authors writing about schizophrenia have tried to see it from the inside. In discussing neurotics, and even homosexuals, we are willing to admit that there is possibly some neurosis or homosexuality in ourselves. But in practically all the literature discussing the psychopath, there is a complete lack of the kind of empathic understanding that psychotherapists are supposed to have. I think that this inability to see the disorder from the "inside" may be one of the factors leading to our attitude of therapeutic nihilism and our belief that psychopaths cannot be treated. (pp. 364–365)

We will try to follow Greenwald's injunction "to see the disorder from the 'inside'" and will continue to avoid the trap of classifying any group of troubled people as untreatable. It is especially important to include in therapeutic efforts those people who do not seem to be able to control their impulses and who are capable of causing great distress, if not actual emotional and physical damage to others as well as to themselves.

CASE HISTORY   **9.1**
Tyrell Johnson

Mr. Tyrell Johnson was referred to a counselor in a residential center for drug abusers. This center was an alternative to incarceration for the use or sale of controlled substances. All clients were court-referred and accompanied by case histories compiled by their case workers.

Mr. Johnson was twenty-two years old and grew up in an innercity area of a major city in the East. He had dropped out of high school in the tenth grade and had a record of several arrests for sale and possession of controlled substances. Four of his siblings had also been arrested for drug sale and possession. He was one of six children in a single-parent family. There was no record of the identity of Mr. Johnson's father.

During the initial interview Mr. Johnson was neatly although somewhat flamboyantly dressed and seemed assured and confident. He denied drug use other than the recreational use of marijuana. He stated that his admission of drug use was more to get out of "hard time" than to seek treatment. The counselor stated that her purpose was to aid the young man in getting off the streets, more accurately confronting his drug use, and finding an alternative to dealing drugs. Her client was noncommittal and volunteered no further information. The counselor told Mr. Johnson that she would be his case manager and scheduled him for an appointment.

The following is an excerpt from the second interview.

THERAPIST: Tyrell, what are your plans for the future?

CLIENT: I don't know. I guess I'll go back to the streets and do what I know.

THERAPIST: What do you know?

CLIENT: Yeah, I'm gonna sell drugs.

THERAPIST: You understand that if you sell drugs you can wind up in jail or dead?

CLIENT: What do you want me to do? Work at Burger King?

THERAPIST: What would be wrong with that?

CLIENT: You fool. I ain't gonna work a minimum-wage job when I can make two or three thousand a week dealing.

THERAPIST: What about going back to school to get an education and then get a real job?

CLIENT: Hey man! I hate school. No way I am gonna sit around and listen to teachers that make thirty thou a year when I can have my Beamer and all the women I want.

Mr. Johnson attended sessions with the therapist only when initiated by the therapist or when required as a condition for remaining in the treatment program. He engaged in a major violation of the rules of the treatment center and was to be sent back to jail. He left the center illegally and no further information exists about him.

Treatment Approaches for Antisocial Personality Disorders

Glasser: Reality Therapy. William Glasser (1965, 1975), at least in part, developed his reality therapy treatment approach in working with young women whom the authors of this text would describe as suffering from antisocial personality disorders. His subjects, the young women in the Ventura

School, located in California, were not placed in that institution by choice. Ventura School was the last stop before the women were to be imprisoned.

The basic premise of the Ventura program, said Glasser (1975), was that these women "deny the reality of the world around them" (p. 6). We hold that Glasser has made a serious overgeneralization. While it is clear that psychotic patterns are clearly out of touch with reality, any definition of reality becomes increasingly difficult as the level of pathology (emotional and psychological disturbance) becomes less intense. Further, Glasser's assumption is also tenuous in implying that if one is fully in touch with reality then one will automatically meet one's needs. Although one must not identify with or applaud the schizophrenic's patterns of thinking, feeling, and acting nor endorse his or her socially dysfunctional behavior, it is necessary to see that the development of such patterns should not be simplistically attributed to the patient's lack of responsibility. Certainly, brutal treatment by others, which cannot be controlled by the person, can lead to the development of deeply disturbed thinking, feeling, and acting.

There are very few institutions or treatment programs that support the patient's attempts to responsibly satisfy personal needs. It is almost certainly true, as Glasser contended, that we satisfy our needs in interaction with other people. However, it seems obvious to us that the "other people" must create an environment in which responsible need satisfaction can occur. In all treatment approaches the responsibility for establishing this environment rests *solely* upon the treatment personnel, not upon the patients.

Another point to be made is that the treatment team must be fully in contact with reality themselves, not only the reality of the treatment culture but the larger reality of humanity and the smaller reality of the client's negative and destructive real-life experiences. These are not easy tasks. As we develop what Glasser reported undertaking at the Ventura School, it will become obvious that he constructed an environment uniquely suited to the psychological problems as well as the human needs of the Ventura residents.

According to Glasser (1975) there are two basic psychological needs: to love and be loved *and* to feel worthwhile to ourselves and to others. With what we have called personality or character disorders, the primary human need is to be safe, in particular safe from one's lack of control, which of course poisons all other human interactions and renders the world itself unsafe. Before one can love and be loved, one must be safe both from oneself and from others. It is our contention that Glasser's treatment program at Ventura, as he outlined it, accomplished this therapeutic goal. Parenthetically, patients more severely disturbed than those at Ventura (such as some of the VA hospital patients Glasser referred to) must have their needs taken care of in a humane way *and* be safe if they are to learn how to love and be loved in a responsible way.

Glasser (1975) was forceful in his emphasis on the here-and-now orientation as vital in the treatment of troubled people. He argued that the past history of a troubled person is of no consequence in the restoration of that person to effective functioning. Essentially Glasser saw references to bad past experiences as nothing more than convenient excuses rather than real explanations for the irresponsible behavior of troubled people. Of course he was, in part, correct with this analysis. However, it seems to us that inappropriate and irresponsible patterns of behavior learned in the past that recur in emotionally similar experiences in the present are grist for the therapy mill. Also, it seems to us that Glasser's examples of critical events that led to significant and positive emotional connections always focused on disclosures by the young women of problems of the past that were still active in the present (pp. 99, 103, 107).

The point is that past history of emotional problems per se is not often useful. However, discovering unresolved and still active emotional problems and how they relate to present behavior in a nonpunitive emotional climate may be the key element in the therapist's forming a significant and positive emotional relationship with a client.

In summation, we cannot accept Glasser's notion that one should use the word responsible as a synonym for mental health and irresponsible as a synonym for mental illness. In our view, the notion that one should abandon all labels and throw out psychoanalytic and medical and other orientations toward troubled people is part of Glasser's unfortunate tendency to overgeneralize. We can, however, applaud his major contribution, which was to offer hope to troubled people, even the severely disturbed. Psychoanalysis had in the 1950s often become an excuse for no treatment; in other words, if people—psychopaths in particular—were untreatable then why try to treat them? Glasser's challenge to the rigid traditional psychoanalytic methods employed in most psychiatric training remains important.

Glasser described the troubled women at Ventura School as youthful offenders who were one step from reaching the end of the line in the criminal justice system (incarceration in adult prisons). He stated that these young women:

> are characterized by their lack of deep feeling for themselves or anyone else and by their common history of usually taking what they thought to be the easy, irresponsible course when any choice was presented. Most have multiple self-inflicted tattoos on their arms, legs, and even their faces, pathetic attempts to gain attention from their peers. (1975, p. 82)

Most therapists, of whatever theoretical stripe, would agree with Glasser that these clients are as difficult to work with as any but the most profoundly disturbed psychotics and autistic children. Yet Glasser claimed that 80% of his young women who left the institution did not resume criminal activity, a remarkable outcome.

The treatment structure at Ventura required that its clients be informed that they were in a locked institution, that they were responsible for their behavior, and that they would be required to attend classes or work while at Ventura. Further, they were told that discharge from Ventura would depend on them. When they could convince the staff that they were able to act responsibly, then and only then would they be released.

The focus of treatment was to create a total environment in which the patients would experience what Glueck and Glueck (1950) called kind but firm interpersonal interactions. No excuses based on past experiences were to be allowed. The position of the staff was that neither staff nor patient could change what had occurred in the past—what could be changed and therefore what a person was responsible for changing is what one can do here and now.

It is important to point out that the emphasis on the Ventura client's responsibility for her actions and the unwillingness of the staff to accept irresponsible behavior had to occur within a nonpunitive environment if such treatment was to be effective. Further, *all* staff members had to be consistent in their treatment of their clients and the rules had to make sense. Glasser also stated that before treatment could be fully effective, someone (therapist, staff member, or even a volunteer) had to make an emotionally significant and positive connection with the client. It is clear from some of the letters from clients that Glasser received that many of his clients perceived him as caring, consistent, and knowledgeable, and that his input, and that of the environment of Ventura as a whole, was of great help to those troubled young women in changing their lives.

Attitude Therapy.   Taulbee and Folsom's (1973) specific behavioral approach with people they described as manipulative and impulsive was referred to as the matter-of-fact attitude. When a person was judged to need the matter-of-fact attitude, he or she was required to follow a pattern of activities designed to develop more socially adaptive patterns of behavior. The manipulative person had to wear a tag that stated he or she was to receive matter-of-fact treatment and listed the activities he or she was to engage in during the day. If the individual was not doing what the card said he or she should be doing, any employee of the organization was, in a matter-of-fact way, to see to it that this person began acting in ways consistent with the treatment program. This program would be applied to all people whose behavior was consistently manipulative and impulsive. Taulbee and Folsom stated clearly that all caretakers interacting with these people should conduct themselves in ways that would assume that manipulation, lying, and cheating would not be reinforced and that socially appropriate behaviors would be required. The other "attitudes" employed in attitude therapy are described in Chapter 11.

Outpatient Treatment of Antisocial Personality Disorders

Lindner (1944) was among the first therapists to claim success in working with individuals who might be classified as suffering from psychopathy. Lindner used hypnotherapy as part of his treatment approach. He felt that hypnotherapy facilitated the discovery of early trauma for those clients who could be hypnotized. He held this was particularly important in discovering trauma related to physical or sexual abuse or both. Such information would then be slowly introduced in therapy after a working relationship had been established between therapist and client. The purpose of the exploration of these early events was to allow the patient an opportunity to express, own, and dissipate the anger, rage, and hate that he or she had internalized as a result of the early trauma. Linder thought that the resolution of such conflicts would allow the client to form nonpathological relationships with others and to control his or her impulses. Precisely what was done in therapy to produce these changes was not clearly specified by Lindner.

Schmideberg (1945) also claimed extensive success in working with psychopaths. Schmideberg was a psychoanalyst and claimed to use traditional psychoanalytic methods in working with her patients. Since she claimed success, and other analysts have emphatically stated that psychopaths cannot be treated, she must have been doing something different from what they were doing. McCord and McCord (1956, pp. 110–111) noted that Schmideberg maintained that one must remain cool and not react to the manipulation and anger of the psychopath until the patient began to acquire a sense that he or she was cared for. In essence, one does not give up on a psychopath nor does one engage in covert or overt judgments of that person's moral character, or rather lack thereof.

Greenwald (1967) is another therapist who has claimed success in working with adult psychopaths. Greenwald endorsed Lindner's use of hypnotherapy and Schmideberg's injunction that one must not make moral pronouncements and that one must exercise great patience when working with a psychopath. In addition, Greenwald held that therapy must be highly structured. He also stated that in order for treatment to be effective one must be able to experience the world as the psychopath does, that is, as a very dangerous place in which one must kill or be killed.

Greenwald (1967) argued that one of the most difficult issues in the treatment of psychopaths was the formation of a working relationship. Colson et al. (1986) suggested that the therapeutic alliance (equivalent to what we have called the therapeutic relationship) would form as a result of the development of active patient collaboration with the therapist in treatment.

But what does the therapist do, with difficult patients like psychopaths, to develop such an alliance? What does one do to foster patient collaboration?

Again, it is Greenwald (1967) who offered some specific advice. In addition to agreeing with Schmideberg (1945) that one should not become moralistic and should bear with the psychopath, Greenwald introduced other specific guidelines. He cited several case histories in which the major vehicle for establishing a working relationship with his patients was to help them to manipulate more effectively to achieve their goals. In all these cases, what the patients wanted did not significantly violate the needs of others; one wonders what Greenwald would have done with a really vicious serial murderer.

Perhaps one could suggest a general principle—show the psychopath how to get what he or she wants without hurting other people and you have achieved one important component in establishing a therapeutic alliance with a psychopath. If Glasser was right (1975) and the focal point for severely disturbed people is their unresolved need to love and be loved in a responsible way, then perhaps what Greenwald was saying is that helping these troubled people to find more effective ways of satisfying their needs changes their world-view significantly. Perhaps, they might conclude, the world is not so dangerous after all.

Greenwald (1967) was equally clear, however, in stating that he would not allow certain manipulations to occur with respect to the interaction of the patient with the therapist. For instance, on the issue of the fee, Greenwald spent some time each session discussing the fee. He did not say whether or not he required a fee at the end of each session. It may be guessed that what he did on the issue of fee was determined by the particular patient. In general it may be a good policy to get payment after each session when working with psychopaths and many other impulsive patients. Ultimately, according to Greenwald, "you must work this issue of payment through or you cannot touch them in therapy" (p. 369).

The second issue of therapist control that Greenwald discussed was that of seduction. By seduction, Greenwald meant not only sexual seduction but also every other type of manipulation in which a "carrot" is dangled in front of the therapist. To accept these manipulations, according to Greenwald, was to become a victim in the mind of the psychopath, just like everybody else. A therapist must not allow himself or herself to be perceived by the psychopath as either a potential victim (one who can be seduced and manipulated) or as a police officer (one who stands in moral judgment).

What Greenwald attempted was to present himself as different from the punishing or stupid society of people whom the psychopath experiences; that is, to present himself as "not so different" from the psychopath (Greenwald, 1967, p. 371). For example, when challenged by one patient, "'Don't give me any bullshit that treatment won't be any good without money.' I [Greenwald] replied, 'No, the most important thing is that I like to get paid because I like money. While it also happens that treatment will not be effective without it, the most important reason for wanting the money is that I like to get paid'" (p. 371).

In addition to presenting himself as not so different from his psychopathic patient but a lot more effective at getting rewards from society, Greenwald was perfectly willing to join the psychopath in attacking our culture's hypocrisies. In this manner the psychopath's curiosity, according to Greenwald, was activated about how Greenwald managed to survive and succeed in this world.

According to Greenwald (1967):

> . . . at the point where they develop this curiosity I can begin to show them the self-destructiveness of their behavior. When they realize that the problem with their behavior is not that it is immoral or bad for society, but that it is self-destructive, it is an effective way of reaching them. After that, they will usually ask, 'What should I do?' And it is at this point that they are ready to listen to the hard lesson the therapist has to drive home, which is—*to learn control.* I do this in a variety of ways. For example, in sessions with this kind of patient I will insist on certain controls. I will ask them not to smoke. . . . (pp. 371–372)

The general principle here is to instill control in the therapy session, then to extend that sense of control through interpretation to self-control in general life situations. Precisely how Greenwald accomplished this is not clear, but the focus on establishment of control over impulsive behavior clearly is a central feature for any effective treatment of any kind of disorder of impulse control, particularly in working with psychopaths.

As noted earlier Greenwald endorsed the use of hypnotherapy as practiced by Lindner (1944) and also by Wolberg (personal communication between Wolberg and Greenwald, Greenwald, 1967, p. 874). Greenwald was consistent with our interpretation of how such an intervention procedure could be helpful. That is, the process of hypnotherapy may facilitate the uncovering of repressed dependency as well as the hostility and anger such dependency elicits when it threatens to erupt into consciousness.

M. E. Rice (1997) has also offered concrete suggestions about how therapy might be made more effective with psychopaths. He stated that given the background from which most psychopaths come (one of abuse and danger), their typical "cheating" strategies pay off. By "cheating" strategies, Rice meant that by being manipulative, deceitful, dishonest, and overtly charming, the client or patient in youth was likely to get the most he or she could from an alcoholic mother or brutal father. Once learned (coupled with the extinction of feeling) the psychopath then leads his or her life using these strategies. In order to treat psychopaths, the detection of the cheating strategies and the assurance that they will not pay off must be part of any effective therapy approach. Clearly, the level of therapeutic control would be high and the interpersonal role would be, as was the case for attitude therapy, matter of fact. Rice suggested that such an approach is not only likely to reduce impulsive behavior but also may be targeted to eliminate violent behavior. He was not, we think, sufficiently clear on how all of this was to be accomplished but his observations are of critical importance if his notions prove to be correct.

A note of caution is required when discussing the outpatient treatment of psychopaths and many other patients who suffer from disorders of impulse control. According to Baumeister, Smart, and Borden (1996), insight-oriented treatment programs designed to increase self-esteem actually increase aggression for psychopaths. Baumeister et al. stated that such treatments not only could cause psychopaths to become more violent but also could teach them to become more effective manipulators. They suggested that such training would only teach the psychopath how to appear caring and empathetic when in fact he or she feels nothing for others. If internalization of control does not occur and the patient is unable to experience some sense of emotional connection with other human beings, then institutionalization is required. Certainly, people who suffer from psychopathy and some of the severer disorders of impulse control require an amount of control most of us are not capable of providing without institutional support.

Other Personality Disorders

Narcissistic Disorders

In the main, patients diagnosed as suffering from a narcissistic personality disorder will be individually treated on an outpatient basis. Kernberg (1975) suggested that this population of patients required a different form of treatment than did other types of personality disorders (such as antisocial and borderline personality disorders). Specifically, Kernberg referred to more primitive narcissistic personality disorders as similar to borderline disorders in terms of personality organization but different with respect to narcissistic possession of a grandiose self. Although Kohut (1977) and Kernberg differed on a variety of issues, they seem to agree on the major point: that these patients required a specific change in techniques for effective treatment.

According to Patrick (1986) it was necessary to deal effectively with the rage reactions of these patients if therapists are to avoid early termination and therefore inadequate treatment. Patrick stated:

> I would like to suggest that in fact these patients can be treated more successfully, if we are willing to adopt an alternative stand to their expressions of narcissistic rage. If we insist upon viewing the phenomenon of rage reactions as a source of secondary gain, their origins to be interpreted through elaboration of the

negative transference, then as Kohut (1977) states, the therapy inevitably serves as a rage-inciting function. This is because the patient experiences the therapist's insistence on the presence of a primary envy-hostility complex in his archaic core as a repetition of the unempathetic approach of his parents in early life. Owing to severe deficits in these patients' self-structure, such an approach only serves to overwhelm their fragile defenses and drives them from treatment. I believe that more empathetic understanding of these patients' rage reactions is the key to a more successful treatment approach; I would like to suggest that in severe narcissistic personality disorders, rage reactions can serve several functions: These are (1) communication of self-object needs; (2) narcissistic repair; (3) revenge upon an unempathetic self-object; (4) restitution of self-object bonds; (5) creation of a more responsive self-object; (6) working through a re-evoked experience of loss and deprivation. (p. 152)

Self-object need may be defined as the need for a positive connection with the internalized representations of the person's parents. Presumably, although Patrick did not explicitly make this point in his paper, the therapist would use material disclosed in therapy to find out about self-object needs and then find ways to enable the patient to work through his or her primitive sense of weakness and worthlessness for which the patient's whole life has been an inadequate defense.

Glickauf-Hughes, Wells, and Genirberg (1987) were somewhat clearer about what the therapist does to facilitate repair of the profound infantile sense of inadequacy that forces such distorted demands for narcissistic gratification on a person suffering from a narcissistic disorder. Specifically, Glickauf-Hughes and colleagues stated that the effective therapist, "must help the individual to (1) learn to tolerate . . . despair, and share . . . ; (2) develop an integrated sense of self-identity; (3) gain a greater feeling of real self-acceptance; and (4) learn to develop pleasure in task mastery rather than exclusively from admiration by others." These therapeutic goals are to be accomplished primarily by using an "active client-centered approach" (p. 109) in which the therapist creates an environment that enables the patient to tolerate personal inadequacies without being devastated, so that the patient may appropriately desire relationships in which he or she is legitimately valued. In addition the therapist must aid the narcissistic person to set realistic goals and find pleasure in the acts of striving toward a goal as well as the joy in reaching the goal itself. Finally, the therapist must neither form a "mutual admiration society" (p. 112) nor retaliate against or knuckle under to the narcissistic patient's expressions of rage directed toward the therapist. What Glickhauf-Hughes et al. suggested was to interpret these negative reactions with the patient in terms of the interpersonal effects they might have on other people. With respect to this issue they were similar in technique to Fromm-Reichmann (1950) in her work with schizophrenic patients.

Borderline Disorders

Those persons diagnosed as having a borderline disorder are likely to require short-term hospitalization from time to time. However, for most of these individuals, treatment on an outpatient basis is recommended. *If*, and this is a big if, there is a stable working relationship between the patient and therapist, treatment will be long-term. As Colson (1982) noted, the bulk of the literature on the borderline condition, as described by Kohut, Kernberg, Masterson, and others, focused on the personality structure of and diagnostic issues concerning this condition. As is the case with the narcissistic disorder, we are at a very early stage in developing effective treatment approaches with these patients. Very likely this problem is directly related to the difficulty in understanding Kohut's and Kernberg's work.

One element which must be dealt with for the effective treatment of the borderline disorder is their difficulty in forming a close relationship with anyone. According to Colson, the borderline person resists the development of what we have called a therapeutic relationship. From the point of view of the borderline client, forming any significant relationship with another human being puts the client's survival at risk. These patients' subjective view of what is required for their survival depends on a complex system of internalized relationships. It seems to us that Colson was referring to the patient's internalized connections with significant others, particularly mother and father. Assuming that Kernberg (1975) is correct and the primary defining characteristics and defenses of the borderline disorder are splitting and projective identification, it may be that splitting in particular defeats the therapist's attempt to develop a working relationship.

If the internalized good object must be split off from the bad object (the aggressive tendencies towards mother–father or mother–father metaphors) to preserve or protect the valued (but unreal) good object, then any therapist's attempt to bring to patient awareness that which was split off will be met with extreme resistance. Colson (1982) argued that he discovered in the history of such patients that when they tried to separate from their parents they were met with the withdrawal or loss of the mother's or father's love. It seemed that the patients would rather disown their growth than to destroy their mother or father or lose their mother's or father's love. From this vantage point, and it is consistent with Kernberg (1975) and Kohut (1971), the thrust of therapy helps the patients to integrate their self-system. If the therapist was successful in creating a therapeutic relationship within which a patient feels safe, then the therapist is able to risk "the arousal of regressive needs and rage at the frustration of the patient's longing for both dependence and independence" (Colson, 1982, p. 315). According to Colson, "The patient invites the therapist to respond to the patient's moves towards independence with anxiety, anger, or withdrawal" (p. 315). Although Colson was not as clear as he might have been, he seems to require the therapist to assume a matter-of-fact role and persevere.

Colson is much clearer about what the therapist perseveres through. That is, the therapist must guide the patient through a series of identity crises and aid the patient to tolerate a sense of loss related to old internalized objects. The therapist must aid the patient in dealing with "profound narcissistic injury" (by which Colson seems to mean the loss of the patient's unreal sense of special importance). Often the therapist must deal with the patient's concerns about suicide or other self-destructive behaviors. Finally, the therapist must, over and over again, deal with the patient's fear of making constructive changes in his or her life.

That Colson (1982) could empathize with his borderline patients cannot be doubted when one looks at what he considered to be involved in reaching the end point in psychotherapy with borderline disorders:

> As these obstacles to the constructive use of psychotherapy are slowly and systematically worked through, the patient suffering from a borderline disorder gradually develops a more realistic sense of his potentials and limitations. Sadness and anger because of years of self-imposed sacrifice and deprivation and mourning for that which is lost will accompany the patient's increasing strength and pleasurable anticipation of the challenges and unknowns that lie ahead. (p. 319)

A treatment approach for borderline personality disorders that has received considerable attention is Linehan's dialectal behavior therapy (DBT). According to Linehan (1993), "In a nutshell, DBT is very simple. The therapist creates a context of validation rather than blaming the patient, and within that context the therapist blocks or extinguishes bad behaviors, drags good behaviors out of the patient and figures out a way to make the good behaviors so reinforcing that the patient continues the good ones and stops the bad ones" (p. 97). With the DBT approach, initially the therapist, in consultation with the patient, defined good and bad behavior. Precision here was very important. The therapist then reached an agreement with the patient on the goals and procedures to be used in the therapy process. The patient was informed of the importance of addressing the therapy goals in a specific sequence. Suicidal thoughts, feelings, and behaviors were addressed first and then other behaviors that undermine therapy, such as missing sessions, were dealt with. The therapist then focused on behaviors necessary to enhance the quality of life (reducing substance abuse and other escapist behaviors). Finally, the therapist addressed with the patient, in order, increasing skills required to regulate emotions, developing interpersonal skills, and developing the means to tolerate stress. Once these skills were developed, the therapist's task was to help the patient to apply them in the "real world."

Once a patient agreed to the requirements of DBT and entered the treatment program the therapist immediately needed to establish a therapeutic relationship. Relationship formation seemed to follow a client-centered format. The therapist attempted to create an atmosphere in which the patient would experience the therapist as genuine and caring. Linehan seemed to frame relational issues around what she called *validation*. She described two types of validation that she argued were essential to working with borderline patients. The first type dealt with issues of communication and acceptance of the patient's existing positive behavior patterns by the therapist. The second type required the therapist to communicate conviction that the patient has the ability to change their life and to resolve his or her misery.

Once a working relationship was established, DBT employed a wide array of behavioral and cognitive techniques to resolve difficulties. Linehan referred to this part of therapy as problem solving. The therapist performed a behavioral analysis, developed a solution analysis, and oriented and elicited commitment from the patient to the program.

Behavioral analysis focused on identifying the patient's critical target behaviors. The focus was on identifying problems in (1) defective self-system, (2) distress tolerance and emotional regulation, and (3) interpersonal effectiveness and self management (Linehan, 1993, p. 100). In addition, she stated that it must be determined if the problem was caused by reinforcement of maladaptive behaviors or nonreinforcement of adaptive behaviors or both. Does fear or guilt block the patient's use of existing positive behavior patterns? Does the patient use irrational thinking that blocks the use of existing adaptive behaviors? Each question suggested a specific intervention. It is likely that all three problem areas will be operative for most borderline personality disorders. According to Linehan, "A treatment program integrating skill training, contingency management, exposure strategies, and cognitive modification is likely to be required" (p. 100). She stated that the treatment of borderline personality disorders required weekly individual therapy, weekly group skills training, and additional therapy sessions and phone consultations during periods of crisis. She suggested that the skills training component be conducted by someone other than the patient's individual therapist. Further, Linehan described her approach in several manuals (Linehan, 1993). She pointed out that regardless of technique, the therapist must guard against subtly rejecting or overidentifying with his or her patients. However, she was also clear that part of the treatment was to teach the patient that tolerating the therapist's fallibility was just another part of the unceasing struggle of life.

Conclusion

Mahler, McDevitt, and Setflage (1971) argued that an early interruption of the individuation process was a central feature in the developmental fixation leading to the borderline condition. Kernberg (1975) placed borderline–antisocial–narcissistic personality disorders in a continuum in which the personality defenses of *projective identification, splitting, primitive idealization, denial, omnipotence,* and *devaluation* are characteristic. Such patterns are consistent with *preoedipal fixation*. Our intrapsychic model would suggest that therapy would necessarily be highly structured and long-term, a prediction consistent with the basic guidelines of Kernberg (1975) and also Colson (1982). Limit-setting must be done with as little intensity and frequency as concerns for the prevention of harm to the patient or others permit.

The appropriate interpersonal role for the therapist in working with patients who have character disorders seems to be a matter-of-fact role coupled with the capacity to not react to hostility. However, flashes of positive affect on the part of the patient should be reacted to with only low-level expressions of positive affect. Such interpersonal stoicism is no easy task but very probably is essential for effective treatment.

In dealing with character disorders one must avoid the trap of interpreting violations of legitimate social expectations as moral failings. The essential thrust must be to point out the functional utility of playing by "the rules." If the therapist is successful at this task then the patient is likely to become interested in what the therapist has to say. It is also very likely that such patients will point out, with incredible accuracy, the hypocrisies they experienced when they tried to follow "the rules of the game." At this point, the therapist's recognition of the real transgressions of the society and significant others with regard to the patient's legitimate rights is not only appropriate but also required (but without identifying with the patient). It is then likely that the patient will list grievances against the therapist. If the grievances are real, they must be owned; if not, one approach is to ask the patient if he or she sees that therapist as "just like the rest of them." Whatever the approach, it must focus on continuing elicitation of the patient's view of what the rules of the game are. Further, exploration of both legitimate and narcissistic patient claims is an essential part of exploring the patient's violations of society's legitimate expectations, as well as events in the patient's life when others violated the patient's legitimate expectations.

The fit between our intrapsychic model and our interpersonal model is an adequate one. The content of therapy for these patients must, of necessity, focus on the violations of the legitimate expectations of others. However, the need to abstain from sitting in judgment or subtly rejecting these patients cannot be overstated.

NOTES

1. It should be noted that what we will call primary personality disorder, psychopathic disorder, narcissistic disorder, and borderline disorder have in common a major problem: lack of impulse control. However, low impulse control is considered of secondary importance for people with personality disorders.

10 Depressive Disorders

The focus for this chapter is the psychosocial treatment of people who suffer from psychotic levels of either unipolar depression (continually depressed mood) or bipolar depression (a pattern of cycling between manic and depressed moods). We hold that the approaches that are effective in treating severe depressions are also effective in treating less serious depressive disorders. Effective treatment of depressive disorders is a critical concern for practitioners and the general public.

Robbins et al. (1984) estimated that one in ten U.S. citizens suffer a major depressive episode during their lifetimes. According to Robbins et al., the rate of increase in depressive disorders has grown dramatically in the last few decades. So rapid is this increase that it is appropriate to refer to the rising number of cases of depressive disorders as epidemic. Although extensive pharmacological treatment has occurred in response, similar emphasis on increasing the availability of psychosocial treatment has not. It is well documented that hospitalized patients treated with either medication or electroconvulsive therapy (ECT) suffer from a high recidivism rate. If a patient learns effective psychosocial strategies it is likely that his or her tendency to "relapse" would be reduced.

Once individuals are identified as suffering from a serious unipolar depressive disorder or bipolar disorder, they require treatment or may become a danger to themselves. If a person is psychotically depressed, the primary treatment focus will be on defeating the dysphoric (anxious, depressed, or restless) mood and increasing the individual's activity level. If a person is suffering from a bipolar disorder and is in the midst of a manic episode, then hospitalization is likely to be required. The patient will be medicated and maintained in a protective environment until the manic phase is controlled. At that point attention needs to shift to defeating the underlying depression.

Whenever a patient is admitted to a hospital for treatment that patient will interact with the treatment team. That interaction will be therapeutically positive or not. In spite of the fact that all depressed people will receive some kind of psychological treatment, the care and precision that effective treatment requires is often nonexistent. Several issues underscore the importance of well-defined and well-implemented psychosocial treatments of these troubled people, which we will examine in this chapter.

Issues in the Treatment of Depressive Disorders

Patients at Risk for Suicide

One of the most important issues faced by professionals is how to identify and treat people who are at risk for suicide. Farberow (1974), and Carson, Butcher, and Mineka (1998) have identified factors that predict suicidal behavior. First, if a person says he or she is considering suicide, that person is at risk. Second, if the person has a history of suicidal attempts or has made a suicidal attempt, that person is at risk. People who are recovering from a major depressive episode or a manic/hypermanic episode are also at risk.

To reduce the likelihood of a patient successfully committing suicide requires exquisite sensitivity on the part of clinicians. Of all of the many tasks of the clinician, none requires more sensitivity than that of determining just how extensive the risk of suicide is for *this* client or patient at *this* time. Knowledge of the many factors that place a patient at risk, although necessary, are insufficient without the clinician's ability to gain the confidence of the patient who is at risk.

If the patient's distress and behavior indicate that he or she is at risk for suicide, immediate intervention is required. That intervention often means that the patient needs to be hospitalized until the immediate danger of suicide is past. The tricky part of this intervention is determining when the immediate danger is past or, at least, when the risk of suicide can be judged to be low.

Farberow (1974) reported that 60 to 65% of the cases coming to the attention of suicide centers were people whose depression was not caused by some acute stress but rather who had lifelong histories of distress, despair, and repeated relapses of their depression. Such data underscore the danger involved in premature discharge and failure to follow-up on and continue to treat depressed patients. Clearly, such people require more than short-term hospitalization, medication, and crisis intervention if suicide is to be prevented in their future.

The immediate response to a patient who is judged to be suicidal is to hospitalize and medicate that patient (the physician will select the appropriate antidepressive medication—see Appendix 2). If a hospitalized patient responds well to medication (two to three weeks may be required to make that determination) then discharge and weekly outpatient treatment for two or three months should be an effective short-term means of preventing suicide. However, unless the depression is defeated and does not recur, continued long-term treatment (psychotherapy, drug therapy, or a combination of both) is required to prevent the recurrence of suicide risk.

If a hospitalized patient does not respond to medication and remains a suicide threat, then ECT may be required. ECT is most useful in immediately reducing depression and may be the method of choice if suicide is judged to be imminent (Carson et al., 1998).

Physiologically Based Treatments of Depression

There are two primary medical treatments for depression: antidepressive and mood-stabilizing medications, and ECT. The major classes of antidepressive medications may be grouped under the headings of tricyclics, MAO (Monoamine Oxidase) inhibitors, and second-generation antidepressive medications. Lithium salts and other mood-stabilizing medications are used to control elevated moods (see Appendix 2). Such drugs are now the most common treatment for people who suffer from major depression or bipolar disorders. In fact, not to medicate these troubled people would be considered inadequate treatment (Andreasen & Black, 1991; Conte & Karasu, 1992; Richelsen, 1993).

However, all drugs have side effects and far too often these serious problems are ignored or minimized by practitioners treating severely disturbed individuals. Tricyclics (Trofranl and Elavil are most commonly used) can cause weight gain, erectile failure, tiredness, and many other side effects. (One wonders whether impotence or other side effects might themselves contribute to feelings of depression.) Other antidepressive medications also have serious side effects: MAO inhibitors can cause fatal hypertension and require avoidance of certain foods; Prozac can cause nervousness and insomnia, among other side effects; and Wellbutin can cause seizures. Lithium also has many dangerous side effects (see Appendix 2).

Antonuccio and Danton (1995) have documented that although antidepressive medications are first-choice treatments for depression, alternate psychosocial treatments exist that are safer and as effective (or more effective) than drug treatments. They held that cognitive-behavioral therapy is an acceptable alternative to medication. They noted that unless patients who are medicated are closely monitored, they often do not take medications as directed or stop taking them. Further, the dropout rate of patients maintained on medication is quite high. Antonuccio and Danton reported that patients who were treated with Lewinsohn's behavior therapy, Beck's cognitive therapy, or Klerman's interpersonal therapy had lower dropout rates than patients maintained on medications and had treatment results that were as good as or superior to those of medication treatment. In addition they reported that for some patient populations, 60% of the patients (younger patients and older patients in particular) did not respond to any antidepressive medication. However Antonuccio and Danton did not address the issue of what to do with the acutely suicidal patient who did not respond to either medication or psychotherapy.

ECT is a somatic treatment approach that is once again considered an important treatment for some affective disorders. Abrams (1989) argued that ECT has been established as an effective treatment for people who suffer from serious depression. Avery and Wonokur (1978) reported that suicide attempts were somewhat less frequent for patients treated with ECT and medication than for patient groups who had received only medication (at that time Elavil was the medication of choice). No comparison was made concerning the rate of suicide attempts for those patients receiving psychotherapy alone or controlled with medication. However, relapse rates did not differ between the two groups. It should also be noted that modern ECT technology has markedly reduced negative side effects and many of the earlier objections to the technique have been answered (Carson et al., 1998). ECT may be useful for patients who are suicidal, are older and self-blaming, and whose depression does not respond to other treatments. The patient often fears ECT and will require careful psychological preparation to reduce the trauma. Practitioners often take sides as to whether ECT should be used. Often practitioners do not present a balanced evaluation of the technique. However, it is reasonable to restrict the use of ECT. It probably should not be the treatment of first choice. Further, the rate of relapse from ECT is high and therefore it should not be the only treatment for the depressed patient or client.

Residential Treatment of Depression

When a depressed person is unable to function outside of a protective environment, then hospitalization is required. Specifically, hospitalization is required when a person is at risk of suicide, is so severely depressed that he or she cannot care for themselves, or when the individual's behavior is so peculiar or bizarre that people close to that person (if any) cannot care for him or her. People who are suffering a major depressive or manic episode often fit these criteria. In addition, patients who have had prior hospitalizations for depressive disorders may relapse and may again require institutional treatment.

With the advent of managed care programs, hospitalization usually means treatment with antidepressive medication until the major symptoms clear and the patient is then discharged. During hospitalization the patient receives medication and may (or may not) receive some form of explicit psychosocial treatment (milieu, individual, or group psychotherapy).

Some general principles concerning what constitutes a therapeutic milieu can be drawn from the works of Rapoport (1960), Bettelheim (1974), Linn (1970), and Taulbee and Folsom (1973). The setting should be homelike as opposed to sterile or aseptic. Private areas should be provided for each patient who is neither in an acute state of distress nor placed under suicide watch. These areas need not be in private rooms but rather in a setting with a wardrobe, dresser, and some sort of privacy screen (not a curtain on a rod, as is so often used in hospitals) provided for each patient. Each patient is encouraged to personalize his or her area to some extent. The unit size includes no more than twenty beds and a low patient-to-staff ratio is maintained (not more than two or three patients to each on-duty staff member). Each patient should be known by name to all staff and frequent interactions between staff and patients should occur. There should be specific treatment goals for each patient and all staff should know them. Staff should also treat each patient consistently and review patient progress frequently.

Particular emphasis should be placed on keeping the patients active and on ensuring that their negative remarks and self-deprecating behavior is neither encouraged nor ignored. What should be encouraged is any activity, particularly those involving interpersonal interactions. The staff's job is to guide those interpersonal interactions toward positive outcomes for the patients and to note specific difficulties that might aid the patient's therapist. It is essential that patients be aware and agreeable to this sharing of information and that their wishes with respect to the issue of privacy be respected.

Individual Approaches to Depression

In addition to medication, other somatic treatments, and institutional treatment when required, there are several individual therapy approaches to the treatment of depression that offer guidance to clinicians. The work of Arieti (1978) has influenced countless therapists. Beck (1967, 1976, 1978); Lewinsohn (1974); Becker, Heimberg and Bellack (1987); Klerman and Weissman (1993); and Klerman, Weissman, Rounsaville, and Chevron (1984) have produced manual-driven research in which therapeutic technique is clearly defined. We will review the contributions of these authors and strive to clearly define what they were doing and to analyze their approaches to see where they are similar and where they appear to be dissimilar.

Arieti: The Psychoanalytic Approach to Depression

Silvano Arieti (1978) suggested there were two basic "types" of depression. The first is the *claiming* type in which the troubled individual seems to be saying something like, "You have the power to make things all better for me so you have to help me or I die." The second is the *self-blaming* type in which the individual seems to be saying something like, "I don't deserve help, I am worthless but please help me anyway." In both types, dysphoric affect (negative feelings) and acute subjective distress are the focus of treatment.

Arieti (1978) suggested that each of these models of depression require a separate and distinct approach if treatment is to be successful. In the claiming mode, according to Arieti, "The patient is guided to stop at the first stage of this sequence: 'I am not getting what I should.' Can he substitute this recurring idea with another one, for instance, 'What other ways, other than aggressive expectation and dependence, are at my disposal to get what I want'" (p. 222). In the self-blaming mode, the patient's tendency to attack the self for imagined wrongs—often caused by a significant other's "bad" treatment of the patient—must be challenged. Getting patients to accept their anger is often part of this process.

In addition to dealing with feelings in psychotherapy, Arieti (1978) argued that a cognitive approach was essential for effective treatment of depression. However, Arieti's main contribution was his focus on the concept of the dominant other (an internal representation of a significant other who failed to provide reliable gratification to the patient. When the patient can no longer depend on the dominant other (or any metaphor for the dominant other, mother, father and so forth) to satisfy needs for gratification, that person experiences a loss that, from their point of view, can never be overcome. No matter what life goals have been accomplished, no matter what ends achieved, the person remains sure that he or she is a failure and can never earn mother's (or any metaphor for mother's) love.

Arieti argued that this belief system must be successfully challenged by the therapist if the troubled person is to recover. Specifically Arieti (1978) argued that the first thing a therapist must do is to enter into the troubled person's life with a strong and significant impact (we would also add a *positive* impact). The therapist *must* assume an active role; if the therapist has been successful, the troubled person will accept the therapist as a *dominant third* (that is, a person of significance to the troubled person in addition to the self and the dominant other) who is a new and reliable love object. The therapeutic relationship must change from that of a "dominant third" into that of a significant other. According to Arieti, the essence of this transformation is that the patient becomes fully aware of his or her destructive thinking patterns and replaces them with new and effective cognitions in which he or she is neither a victim nor passive.

It is significant to point out that while we have cited Arieti's primary contribution in psychotherapy to be his extension and modification of psychoanalytic practice to work with depressed individuals, he began his interest in the "talking cure" through his experiences working with advanced process schizophrenics and has published a great deal of work concerning schizophrenia. He was extensively influenced by Frieda Fromm-Reichmann and focused on the notion of loss in schizophrenia as well as in depression. Arieti (1978) learned the most important lesson a therapist can learn in working with anyone, but one particularly important in working with severely disturbed individuals: that is how easy it is for someone to hurt a person who is severely disturbed.

Beck: Cognitive Therapy

We have noted that Aaron T. Beck's (1976) primary orientation in the treatment of depressed individuals was to focus on cognitive psychosocial interventions, often in preference to chemotherapy or electroconvulsive therapy. Perhaps Beck's primary focus on psychosocial treatment arose in part from his extensive review on biological studies of depression. Beck (1967) stated that the argument that physiological factors alone caused depression was not convincingly supported by research. He held that genetic and constitutional factors might not be critical causal factors in the manic-depressive (bipolar) disorder. More recent data led Beck (1991) to take a less psychological view of this disorder.

According to Beck (1967, 1976) the primary characteristics of depression are: (1) a negative view of the world, (2) a negative view of oneself, and (3) a negative view of one's future and the future in general. Such views arise, Beck (1976) argued, *not* from unconscious processes or from self-hate as psychoanalysts would postulate but rather from distortions in the individual's cognitive process arising from loss either real or imagined. Feeling sad could arise from real loss—loss of a tangible object, result of an insult, some kind of reversal, or perhaps a disappointment—or from what we would call "imagined" loss—expectation of future loss, hypothetical loss, or what Beck calls "pseudo loss." *However, depression, according to Beck, occurs only when there is a cognitive distortion of loss, regardless of its origin.* The essence of the distortion is that the individual views himself or herself as lacking an essential element required for personal happiness.

Beck pointed out that traumatic experiences predispose the person to overreact, in other words, become depressed through cognitive distortion of trauma metaphors. He argued that the first and essential stage in effective treatment of the depressive was to understand the meanings the individual attached to personal experiences. Beck concluded that only through a process of empathy would such an understanding occur.

Techniques in the Cognitive Treatment of Depressives.   Although Beck stated clearly that there are specific techniques that are essential in the treatment of depressives, he was equally clear that one must use these techniques in a humanistic rather than a mechanical fashion. According to Beck, the syndrome of depression must be separated into its component parts—*emotional, motivational, cognitive, behavioral,* or *physiological*—and each component must be specified as a possible focus for treatment. Beck argued that each component interacts with other components and therefore improvement in one is likely to lead to improvement in other areas.

Specifically, Beck (1976) held that the troubled person's problem can be identified at three levels: (1) abnormal behavior (particularly suicide threats, crying, or other displays of sadness and fatigability); (2) underlying motivational disturbances; and (3) cognitive belief system (self-defeating belief). According to Beck, a behavioral therapeutic approach is necessary for the therapist to deal with behavioral displays related to affective symptoms. By behavioral, Beck meant something as concrete as getting a passive patient to become active. However, just because the overt behavior of the troubled individual ceases to appear depressive does not, in Beck's view, mean that person is less depressed. Changes in thinking must also have occurred.

Underlying motivational disturbances (if any) and cognitive belief symptom distortions require a direct assault on the client's belief system, first by eliciting the client's reasons for being depressed and second by presenting evidence that the reasons are incorrect. It is necessary to add that since the troubled person engages in a substantial amount of self-talk (a series of automatic, unexamined, self-destructive, repetitive thoughts) it is often difficult to find out what the client's belief system is. That is why careful and empathetic questioning is required.

Sequence of Treatment.   Initially Beck attempted to get the depressed client or patient to become active. He suggested that one give the client an activity schedule. The initial approach was behavioral. The client was given a series of activities of increasing difficulty, each of which the client could *successfully* achieve or accomplish. The key feature here is to design this procedure so success is guaranteed. Also, the client was asked to keep a current account of mastery experiences and pleasurable experiences.

The therapist employs the technique of cognitive reappraisal either following or simultaneous with the client's collection of mastery and pleasurable experiences. Cognitive reappraisal consists of seven steps:

1. Identify processes between depressed thinking and feeling sad.
2. Identify avoidance wishes and suicidal impulses.
3. Explore depressive thinking.
4. After further examination, attempt to modify depressed thinking.
5. Identify overgeneralized, arbitrary, and dichotomous thinking.
6. Identify underlying assumptions.
7. Modify basic assumptions.

Once cognitive reappraisal has led to sufficient clarity, the client is required to offer explanations or alternatives different from those showing that person's customary negative bias. Second, the client is led to focus on the steps necessary to reach a goal. This leads the client to focus on specific obstacles (and therefore obstacles that can often be overcome). Third, the client is given homework assignments. These assignments may consist of, but are not limited to, carrying out specific activities, keeping a log of automatic thoughts, listing things to do, setting priorities, and checking off accomplished tasks. It seems to us that Beck's techniques constitute a flexible yet focused program for working with depressed clients. The reader is encouraged to refer to Beck's (1976) work, specifically pages 274–301 for examples of how he used an active cognitive approach with respect to specific targets for cognitive modification.

Lewinsohn and Becker: Behavioral Approaches to Individual Treatment of Depression

Ferster (1974) held that depression resulted from non-reinforcement of patterns of behavior that would lead to positive reinforcement. Lewinsohn (1974) expanded this notion and found that when depressed people received few positive reinforcements, their overall number of responses (response rate) was reduced. This lowered response rate further reduced the number of positive reinforcements that the person received and therefore deepened the depression. In addition, Meany (1998) stated that depressed people are stressed by their depression, and as a function of that stress not only psychological but also physiological changes occur. These physiological changes reduce activity level, that is, reduce response rate.

Getting seriously depressed people to become active has long been a goal for therapists working with these clients. Depressed people seem to be skilled in eliciting behaviors from others that exacerbate their depression. Early in the depressive reaction, the needy helplessness of the depressed patient is reinforced by significant others. Later in the depressive cycle, the depressed person places such demands on significant others that they no longer reinforce the passive and dependent behaviors of the depressed patient. Finally, depressed people usually live in rather negative psychosocial environments. Lewinsohn and his associates have framed their treatment approach around these concerns. First, the patient is encouraged to do things that he or she finds enjoyable. However, finding activities that depressed people regard as pleasurable is difficult. Practitioners often find such exploration difficult. Yet such exploration is useful, if only to distract the patients from their inertia. Second, active intervention into the patient's daily life circumstances may temper the patient's negative experiences. Often such changes are as simple and concrete as getting the depressed person's spouse to become less critical or withdrawn and cold. Finally, Lewinsohn and his associates focused on social skills training. The main goal was to teach the individual how to elicit positive reinforcement from others, thus creating an interpersonal pattern that would maintain a reasonably high level of positive interpersonal reinforcement.

Becker, Heimberg, and Bellack (1987), building on the work of Lewin-sohn, developed a manual that is primarily focused on the social skills acquisition component of the treatment of depressed patients. Becker et al. offered an overview of their method. Initially, the clinician confirms that the client is in fact depressed. Once the clinician determines that is the case, then the clinician (1) assesses the client's social skills, (2) engages in direct behavior training, (3) focuses on changing negative self-talk, (4) attempts to change the client's self-evaluation (one important pattern of self-talk), and (5) teaches the patient self-reinforcement procedures.

Becker et al. (1987) offered several ways to measure social skills. First, molecular responses are scored: voice loudness, response latency, duration of speech response, smiles, speech disturbances (defined as incidences of "ummmm," "oh," "er," and "ah"), affect (flat, moderate, or lively), and gaze (whether eye contact is 33% or less, 33–66%, or 66% or more). Second, behaviors related to social skills (positive assertion and negative assertion) are rated on a five-point Lickert scale. Third, "dynamic" stimuli are evaluated. Dynamic stimuli are not well defined by Becker et al., but include restate-ments of the others' message, "floor" shifts, and behaviors showing emotion or the acceptance of others' expression of emotion. Situational factors are also measured, such as who is troubling the patient and that person's age, sex, and power-role relationship; and whether the patient is troubled at work, home, or other locations.

In addition, Becker et al. (1987) specified that a clinical interview be used to gain information about a person's social skills that might be missed by objective approaches. They point out that specific behavioral responses, ratings of behavior patterns, and any other cataloguing of behavior might well miss the meaning of the particular behavior for the particular person. Becker et al. believed that the interview could provide information on situations, people, and behaviors causing the patient difficulty or through which the clinician could make a determination that the patient lacked social skills.

To aid in identifying social skills deficiency, the patient self-monitored his or her behavior. The therapist gave the client specific assignments in the form of keeping a written log. Patients were instructed to count the number of times they had had a conversation with someone. In the log they were to indicate the date, time, interaction partner, and topic of conversation. In addition, they were to record the number of times they had a disagreement with someone and to record the date, time of disagreement, partner, and topic. Patients also noted the setting of each event and their reaction to the partner's response. Finally, the practitioner administered one of eight assertiveness scales to the patients. Becker et al. (1987) suggested that in general the Ralthus Assertiveness Schedule would be most appropriate.

Once the data were gathered, the targets of treatment were determined for each patient and placed into a hierarchy of skill deficiencies. The least threatening skill deficiency targets were chosen for the initial intervention. Exactly how this was done is not fully specified in the manual. However, we assume that behaviors indicating vegetative dysfunction (sleep disturbance, loss of appetite, and so forth) would be among the most difficult of target behaviors to change. We would guess that behaviors related to assertiveness skills would be less difficult to change.

Once the target behaviors were identified and placed in hierarchical order, social skills training began, starting with direct behavior training. First the therapist explained to the patient what they were going to do. Essentially the therapist tried to convince the patient that interpersonal interactions were critical in both causing and maintaining the depressed state. Then the therapist explained the method that was going to be used to change what the client did in these situations so that the client could feel better. At this point the therapist explained the role-play procedure and defined the length of treatment (which was short-term, about five months). According to Becker et al. (1987), this process was usually sufficient to elicit the patient's cooperation.

One critical problem for both Lewinsohn and Becker was that they spent little or no time discussing how to form a therapeutic relationship. In fact, it seemed that they were either unaware of the importance of this relationship or considered it unimportant. In spite of this obvious weakness, Becker et al. were fairly clear on the use of techniques in their approach.

The first of those techniques was the *role-play technique.* Becker et al. (1987) stated that the therapist must ensure that each role-play performance met these five criteria:

1. Give the client specific instructions about what he or she was to do.
2. Demonstrate the desired performance to the client and follow this demonstration with questions to be certain that the client has attended to the aspects of the performance that are being trained.
3. Ask the client to carry out the role play he or she just witnessed.
4. Provide positive feedback to the client about good aspects of the performance and give new instructions and demonstrations for areas that need to be improved.
5. Give praise for following instructions and trying to carry out the role play and encouragement to continue with the next role play. (p. 74)

Becker et al. (1987) focused in the role play on a set of moral behavior sequences. The patient was to model the appropriate interpersonal behavior. Then that behavior was reinforced and the sequence was continued until the appropriate interpersonal behavior was consolidated during the therapy sessions.

The second technique Becker et al. (1987) called *flexibility training.* The patient was encouraged to apply what he or she had learned in therapy in as many real-life situations as possible. It is important to note that flexibility training should not occur prematurely. In addition, patients received homework assignments. They were required to keep a diary in which they recorded situations where conversations occurred, persons with whom these conversations occurred, and the topics of the conversations. If all went well, the therapist provided reinforcement in the form of positive feedback. If the patient did not comply with the homework assignment, what action the therapist was to take was not well defined. In fact, Becker et al. pointed out that one major limitation of social skills training was that no method was provided to deal with clients who would not follow the social skills procedures. Certainly the demands made of the patient by Becker's approach required considerable effort on the part of the patient. Many of our depressed patients could not comply with these demands.

Becker et al. (1987) then focused on a series of important, more complex, but still reasonably well-defined issues. Specifically, if a person is to respond positively to an interaction with the client, the client must note topic shifts, avoid drifting from topic to topic without giving the other person his or her turn, shift gently from one topic to another, and not stay on any topic too long. Further, if the client wishes another to respond positively to the client, then the client must seek to clarify the other person's communication. Another skill required to elicit reinforcement from another person is the ability to convince that person of the correctness of the client's position. It is also important to correctly perceive the other person's nonverbal behavior and moderate one's own so that he or she responds positively. For people to respond positively, one must be able to recognize unpleasant emotional states in the other person and use appropriate social skills to defuse or change the situation. Finally, to be liked one must not treat other people harshly; that is one must not punish others. Becker et al. used role-playing techniques to allow clients to learn and apply these skills.

If the client becomes sufficiently socially skilled to elicit reinforcement from others, one task remains for the formerly depressed person in order to maintain a nondepressed adaptation. This involves learning the skills of self-evaluation and self-reinforcement. People who are depressed, according to Becker et al. (1987), need to focus on four goals that not only will increase positive self-evaluation but also increase self-reinforcement. These goals are to:

1. Improve the client's ability to attend to important details and not overlook critical information.
2. Help the client base self evaluations on the technical adequacy of her or his behavior rather than others' responses to it.
3. Help the client develop more rational and lenient standards for self evaluation.
4. Increase the range of positive self reinforcers the client can use and increase the rate of application of these reinforcers. (p. 74)

The four goals were implemented by Becker et al. through role-playing exercises and homework assignments keyed in to them.

Interpersonal Psychotherapy

Interpersonal therapy begins with a detailed analysis of the patient's depression. The therapist reviews the patient's symptoms. Included in the review is a description of the patient's mood, exploration of feelings of guilt, determination of suicidal potential, and review of the patient's sleep patterns (early, middle, and late phases). In addition, the patient is asked whether he or she feels anxious or has experienced somatic symptoms indicative of anxiety. Other symptoms the therapist explores include general somatic symptoms (for example, does the patient tire easily?), sexual problems, weight loss, and gastrointestinal symptoms. The therapist notes whether the patient is psychomotor-retarded or agitated, and determines in what activities the patient can engage. We would also recommend that the therapist explore whether the patient has any sense of pleasure in daily life. Klerman, Weissman, Rounsaville, and Chevron (1984) also required the therapist to obtain information on times of day when the patient felt best and worst, and to gain information about behavior patterns, thoughts, or feelings indicative of depersonalization, paranoia, or obsessive-compulsive disorders.

Klerman et al. (1984) stated that part of IPT was allowing the patient to assume the "sick" role. The basic idea was that if the patient's problems are presented as driven by the depressive illness, then the patient will accept the sick role and treatment and perhaps will stop blaming himself or herself for his or her own suffering. Paradoxically, Klerman et al. held that by accepting the sick role, the patient will be able to cooperate with the therapist whose goal is to help the patient relinquish this role. Klerman, in advocating that the patient accept the sick role, is subtly endorsing the medical model. Implicit in that model is the notion that the patient is to be passive and to accept the doctor's authority. While the goal of reducing patient suffering is laudable, we hold that there are more effective psychosocial strategies to defeat patient guilt without further underlining the passivity of the depressed person.

In addition to prescribing the sick role to the patient, Klerman et al. (1984) focused on evaluating the depressed person for medication and held that the 1978 Research Diagnostic Criteria (RDC) of Spitzer, Endicott, and Robins should be used in making such decisions. Klerman held that a preponderance of vegetative symptoms and more severe symptoms called for medication use.

After the evaluation for medication, the therapist analyzes the patient's current interpersonal situation. How many significant-other relationships does he or she have? What are these peoples' expectations of the patient?

What are the good and bad aspects of each of these relationships and how might they be changed? From this analysis Klerman et al. (1984) held that the therapist could determine the interpersonal issues central to the patient's depression. Klerman et al. also held that the therapist should be able to define the "primary problem area" (p. 87). The authors seem to be saying that it is likely this primary problem area will be guilt, interpersonal disputes, role transitions, or interpersonal deficits.

Once the nature of the interpersonal problem is defined, a contract is established between the IPT therapist and the troubled person. The contract states the interpersonal focus of psychotherapy, treatment duration (twelve to sixteen sessions, once per week for one hour each), and specific problem areas. The therapist must inform the patient that the therapist will be less directive and active as therapy proceeds, emphasizing the patient's responsibility to bring in significant interpersonal difficulties that require attention in later therapy sessions. Our position is at some variance with Klerman. We argue that therapist structure and activity are not determined by the stage of therapy but rather by the patient's presentation in a particular session.

Next the IPT focus is on the primary interpersonal problem and its resolution. In addition the therapist addresses *any* issue that was causing the patient distress even if it was not connected with the primary interpersonal problem. Abnormal guilt was dealt with by reconstructing relationships with significant others that the patient had lost. For all other issues, the focus was on concrete interpersonal interactions with significant people in the patient's life. As noted above interpersonal deficits led the therapist to focus on insufficient interpersonal skills that prevented the patient from having satisfying interpersonal relationships. Some work on more traditional personal historical material related to the patient's unresolved conflicts was also included in the therapy. However, even here the focus was on concrete interpersonal interactions occurring in the here and now, and how they related to those unresolved issues.

Klerman et al. (1984) commented that many of the techniques used in IPT are common to dynamic psychotherapy (present authors' note: Klerman and his associates also used techniques borrowed from client-centered and behavior therapy). Klerman was clear, as we have been throughout this text, that these techniques could not be applied mechanically. He downplayed the importance of the therapeutic relationship although he discussed interpretation of transference, countertransference, and so forth. We would argue that the essence of a successful therapeutic relationship involves the perception by the patient that the therapist is caring, knowledgeable, and consistent. The essence of how one achieves such a relationship is discussed in Chapter 2. It is curious that this critical interpersonal aspect of therapy was not central to interpersonal psychotherapy.

CASE HISTORY **10.1**
David Chen

Mr. David Chen was referred to the therapist by his family physician. Mr. Chen was described by his doctor as depressed and possibly suicidal. He was a third-generation Chinese American who had lived in Connecticut for the last three years. At the time of the referral he was thirty-two years old, unmarried, and living alone.

During the initial interview Mr. Chen was clearly depressed and stated that he had no hope that his life would be worth living and that he felt hopeless and alone. He denied that he was considering suicide. He often stared at the floor and as he spoke, he verged upon tears, finally breaking into tears when he said that nobody really loved him. Mr. Chen was not currently on medication for depression even though his family doctor suggested a trial of antidepressive medication.

When asked how long he had been troubled, the client stated that his first memories of being severely depressed occurred when he was fifteen or sixteen years old. His family, particularly his father, praised his older sister for outstanding accomplishments in high school and college. Although Mr. Chen's academic work was very good, he was compared unfavorably with his sister. Mr. Chen went to college and received a degree in accounting and on his second try passed his CPA exam. Although he was now a successful accountant, he described his personal life as unsatisfactory. He was not currently dating anyone and he did not admit to having had a serious relationship. Psychotherapy was recommended, as was a referral for medication evaluation that the client refused.

The following is an excerpt from the sixteenth session.

THERAPIST: You feel your boss criticized you unfairly.

CLIENT: Yeah, just like my father, I could never do enough.

THERAPIST: Tell me, what did your boss do to remind you of your father?

CLIENT: Well, he said that Dan, another accountant in the firm, did more work than I did.

THERAPIST: Was that fair?

CLIENT: Well, he got two accounts finished and I was still working on one.

THERAPIST: Were the accounts equal in terms of complexity?

CLIENT: No, mine was much more complex.

THERAPIST: Did you confront your boss with that difference?

CLIENT: No.

THERAPIST: Why not?

CLIENT: He wouldn't listen.

THERAPIST: Did you ever confront your father?

CLIENT: Yes!

THERAPIST: Did he listen?

CLIENT: (Teary-eyed) No.

THERAPIST: But you really didn't check out whether your boss was unfair like your father?

CLIENT: No, I guess I sort of gave up.

THERAPIST: What would you like to say to your boss?

CLIENT: Look, George, the account I am working on is much more difficult than both of Dan's accounts combined.

THERAPIST: Could you have proved that if he challenged you?

CLIENT: Sure! No question, but he wouldn't give me a chance.

THERAPIST: How do you know? You never tested that guess.

Mr. Chen continued therapy and occasionally returned for what he called a "refresher session." He continued to contact the therapist every few months for three years. He gradually learned to become more assertive, that not all authority figures were like his father, and that none of them had his father's power over him. He also learned that he was a competent human being. He was encouraged to explore the development of relationships and formed a stable relationship with a supportive woman. He is now married and somewhat reconciled with his family. He also reported that although things are not perfect he feels able to "weather the storms."

Severe Depression: The Cyclic Disorders

The psychotherapeutic approaches of Beck, Arieti, and Lewinsohn, Becker, Klerman, and Arieti are appropriate during depressed phases of the cyclical types of depressive disorders. However, the evidence is compelling, from our point of view, that the manic phase must be dealt with other than by psychosocial means. Lithium or other appropriate medications for bipolar depression is essential. The bipolar disorder's manic phase leads to such a disordered and chaotic state that psychosocial intervention may be futile without medication.

Here the genetic evidence for a physiological imbalance in the central nervous system, primarily from homozygous twin studies (Gottesman &

Shields, 1972, among others) is too compelling to be ignored or minimized. Nevertheless, once the more dramatic of the manic symptoms are under control, problems remain (Beck, 1967) and psychosocial treatment is still required. We have outlined Beck's approach and would suggest that depression underlies the manic displays and must be treated by psychosocial means as well as any appropriate chemotherapeutic therapy.

Conclusion

Treatment of psychotic levels of depression may and often does require institutionalization. Such troubled individuals may and often do require medication, although as seen in Appendix 2, caution is required. Psychoactive medication is best used to alleviate symptoms that prevent interpersonal contact and to prevent destructive acting out rather than as the sole treatment mode. Further, such medications may best serve their purpose in the acute phase of the disorder and later be used only as a means of alleviating periods of severe relapses for difficult patients, and in as low a dosage as is possible to aid in long-term treatment.

In spite of the rush to short-term treatments for depression, we hold that successful treatment is likely to be long-term. By successful, we mean that the formerly depressed person is no longer depressed and remains that way. Many of the manual-based treatments, including those discussed in this chapter, argued that treatment of depressed patients is short-term. The high level of recidivism with depressed patients suggests that such short-term psychosocial treatment is a misguided economy. Perhaps one can view the treatment of depressed people as "intermittently" long-term. That means it is likely that the psychotically depressed person will cycle in and out of treatment over several years. It is also likely that the psychotically depressed person will have given evidence of a sad and lonely childhood, long before the diagnosis of depression was made.

Highly structured and active treatment approaches of those therapists who have claimed success working with psychotically depressed people are consistent with our intrapsychic model. We suggest that with the qualification listed above, the duration of treatment and the origin of the depressive disorder are also consistent with our model.

With depressed patients, the interpersonal role of the therapist is clearly specified in our interpersonal model. The client communicates an intense *HI* role (self-effacing and often self-punishing). The therapist must assume an interpersonal role that will change the patient's self-presentation, or no significant movement will occur. We have argued that the therapist needs to assume a *NO* role (a warm and strong role) that is reciprocal to the client's need for dominance, but nonreciprocal with respect to affect. The strong, positive role of the therapist will allow the patient to remain passive but will increase the probability that the patient will present himself or herself more positively. The therapist then lowers the level of dominance that encourages the client to become more dominant as indicated in Chapter 2 in the interpersonal model. In this fashion a workable therapeutic relationship is established. We hold that what the effective therapist does interpersonally in working with depressed patients is consistent with our interpersonal model.

Once one has established, or even while one is establishing an effective interpersonal climate, one deals with the content of psychotherapy (or the psychopathology itself). It seems to us that Arieti, Beck, Lewinsohn, and Klerman all deal explicitly with the client's violations of the legitimate role expectations of society, while also struggling with the client against those parts of the client's environment that are in fact violations of that client's expectations of a just or even tolerable world. Certainly Glasser (1965, 1975) framed his approach to dealing with troubled people precisely in this fashion, holding that people must satisfy their legitimate human needs in responsible ways or they will not be able to help themselves overcome their sufferings and defeats. However, one must not place total responsibility on the depressed client; to do so, in all instances, is to blame the victim. One must become an ally in fighting those circumstances in that client's life that are, in fact, destructive to his or her welfare. All in all, it seems that therapists who are successful with depressed people deal with many of the same issues in very similar ways.

11 The Severely Disturbed: Schizophrenia and Related Disorders

The focus of this chapter is the psychosocial treatment of severely disturbed adolescents and adults who would be classified as psychotic (except for those who suffer from psychotic levels of depression). We will examine specific treatment approaches claiming success. Such treatment approaches share the conclusion that many of these troubled people will require occasional intensive inpatient and long-term outpatient therapies and concurrent appropriate psychoactive medication.

For many severely disturbed individuals who are dangerous to themselves and others or who cannot function outside a protective environment, inpatient treatment of some kind is required. Even after hospitalization or halfway house placement is completed, many severely disturbed individuals continue to require long-term outpatient treatment. That treatment need not be continuous but should be available when required. It is again necessary to emphasize the need for intensive long-term care for schizophrenic patients as well as for other severely disturbed patients.

A major crisis in treating the emotionally disabled is the premature discharge into the community of vast numbers of these troubled human beings who are unable to care for themselves (Keith, Gunderson, Reifman, Buchsbaum, & Moser, 1976). In part, the crisis is a function of austerity budgets at the federal, state, and local levels. In part, the crisis is related to the abandonment of the mentally ill by HMOs. The problem is also related to the self-centered and self-serving orientation of our culture that ignores the needs of less fortunate people. Finally, the crisis is related to two significant and positive advances in mental health: chemotherapeutic treatment of the severely disturbed, and the community mental health movement.

Chemotherapy and Disorders of Thought

Chemotherapy is one advance in the treatment of severely disturbed individuals that has contributed to the deinstitutionalization process. With the advent of powerful psychoactive drugs (see Appendix 2), it seems that many of the most disabling symptoms of thought disorders and affective disorders can be controlled. However, these drugs do not, with the probable exception of Lithium for the manic form of the bipolar disorder, actually cure or even, as in the case of diabetes, fully control the symptoms of the disease. Instead, drugs control some of the symptoms related to emotional distress and disturbance. All of these drugs have serious side effects. In Appendix 2 the major psychoactive drugs in current use are listed and some of their significant side effects are described. It also needs to be noted, as Gronfein (1985) argued, that chemotherapeutic treatment does not remove the need for psychosocial treatment.

If nothing else works, extreme measures are justified and, for many severely disturbed individuals, there can be no question that such interventions are required. Yet psychosocial interventions, including psychotherapy, remain an important part of the total treatment of the profoundly disturbed. We would hope that some day advances in drug treatment will "cure" all severely disturbed people of their problems, and that the institutions to treat them and most of the mental health personnel now employed would no longer be needed. However, as Arieti argued (1978), medical treatment at present cannot promise such success and therefore psychosocial intervention is necessary.

The Community Mental Health Movement

Institutional treatment of severely disturbed individuals has often been a horrible misadventure for mental health personnel. With the exception of a few small institutions founded during the Moral Therapy Movement in the early 19th century (Grandjean & York, 1979), and others referred to in this chapter, most institutions were, and until the 1950s continued to be, little more than dead-end holding tanks for severely disturbed individuals.

The advent of effective psychoactive drugs (1950) and the focus on prevention (the early 1960s) and community mental health centers (the early 1960s) gave practitioners many excellent alternatives to long-term hospitalization. In the 1960 publication of *Action for Mental Health*, such options were proposed. New legislation encouraged treatment of disturbed people in their own communities in response to the negative consequences of institutionalization on institutionalized patients. The present emphasis on deinstitutionalization and short-term placement even when hospitalization is required stems from these worthwhile aims. The basic assumption nowadays seems to be that even severely disturbed people can be maintained with some kind of coordinated outpatient treatment, usually chemotherapy, and some kind of interaction with community mental health centers. It is unfortunate that this community-based, prevention-oriented approach, which is so well-intended, encourages the early release of many people who simply cannot function outside a protective environment (Mechanic, 1987).

In fact, the well-intended initial thrust to remove troubled people from inadequate institutions and treat them in the community has, along with the reduced funding, led to an intolerable situation and crisis in the treatment of the severely disturbed. Perhaps what is required is a clear statement of what makes a neuropsychiatric hospital therapeutic, and a clear specification of those psychosocial treatment approaches found useful in such environments. Much of the rest of this chapter is devoted to defining how to design and run an effective mental hospital.

The Decision to Institutionalize

Placement in an inpatient neuropsychiatric facility usually requires that the individual display patterns of behavior that are manifestly dangerous to self or others. In addition, the decision to hospitalize a person may be based on their lack of orientation (failure to know the date, who one is, where one is, and the like), and their verbal report of hallucinations or delusions, and/or suicidal or murderous threats or reported feelings.

Referral to a neuropsychiatric hospital is a very serious decision and is not to be entertained lightly. Some hospitals, usually large state hospitals for anyone who can't pay or whose insurance coverage has been exhausted, are often unsuitable. Many state hospitals, as well as some private hospitals for the "mentally ill," are simply human warehouses where the only treatment that exists is chemotherapy and custodial care. These institutions are often the same ones that the state uses for severely disturbed children and suffer the same limitations (see Chapter 12). Linn (1970) in his extensive analysis of hospital environments found that the least successful hospitals (defined in terms of reported discharge rate and claimed treatment success) were large, had few patients in therapy or even in defined treatment programs, had little staff and patient interaction, and left patients unattended and inactive.

Linn's work (1970) would lead one to conclude that the kind of hospital to be desired when institutionalization is required should be small, have a low patient to staff ratio, and have a well-defined, active treatment program focused on the behavioral patterns of the patients and their reported psychological state. Because such facilities are at a premium and are quite expensive, the decision to hospitalize is made with reluctance by most therapists. As a result, most therapists attempt to keep the severely disturbed person in the community and to treat that person on an outpatient basis. Day hospital programs, various support groups, psychoactive drugs, and short-term hospitalization during crises, as well as psychotherapy, often can be sufficient, even for profoundly psychotic patients, to prevent hospitalization.

The moral therapy movement was one of the first effective options to the horrible conditions in hospitals in the late 18th century. Phillippe Pinel (1945–1806) and William Tukes (an English Quaker who lived in the same time period) held that if mentally ill people were treated with kindness and taught ways to act appropriately in the culture of the time that such moral treatment could aid these people to be restored to society. After the demise of the moral therapy movement during the middle of the 19th century a rather long period of miserable institutional patterns of nontreatment began. The failure to treat was based in part on the notion of *social Darwinism,* which held that the insane were incurable because their "disease" was inherited and untreatable. With the combination of psychoactive drugs *and* the rise of humanism during the latter part of the 1950s and early 1960s, institutions again became more humanistic and the discharge rate (which had remained about 30–40% for almost 100 years) climbed to 60–70% (Grandjean & York, 1979).

Inpatient Treatment of Disorders of Thought

Milieu Therapy

The noted English psychiatrist Maxwell Jones and Harvard anthropologist Robert N. Rapoport developed the concept of milieu therapy in the early 1950s. Jones and Rapoport's conception of the *total institution* as constituting *the treatment* came to be called the third revolution in mental health treatment. It is, Jones and Rapoport (Rapoport, 1960) argued, necessary in the cases of severely disturbed clients who require hospitalization that the treatment be total, that is, twenty-four hours a day, seven days a week and extended to every part of the patient's life in the hospital. Further, the whole staff is to be involved in the treatment of any individual patient. Jones and Rapoport also argued that the patients as well as the staff must be involved in the treatment approach.

That much is clear; the treatment must be total, meaning that *everyone* is involved in the treatment, and *all* facets of the institution contribute in concrete ways to facilitation or lack of facilitation of patient progress. Exactly what everyone is to be involved in or even approximately what everyone is to do was only partially worked out by Jones and Rapoport.

According to Rapoport (1960), five elements must be considered in developing an adequate milieu program: (1) the formation of a treatment ideology, (2) the organization of staff roles, (3) the organization of patient roles, (4) the involvement of individuals external to the hospital treatment, and (5) the conceptualization of treatment and rehabilitation as goals.

Rapoport (1960) stated that the central characteristics of an effective treatment program ideology are: (1) a belief that the total environment may be structured in ways that lead to changing individual patterns of social behavior, (2) a belief that such an environment should be structured to be as democratic and as permissive as it can be, consistent with patient safety, and (3) a belief that the treatment program must, in many ways, resemble a family or, as Rapoport states, "a quasi family." In the remaining sections of his book Rapoport described, in general ways, how to organize the staff and patient roles and to involve individuals external to the hospital in the individual patient's treatment within the milieu.

It is not clear which patients are most likely to improve as a function of this treatment, except that patients with greater so-called ego-strength at the beginning of treatment are most improved at its completion. Other than so-called ego-strength, patients who stayed in treatment longer than six months, patients who showed improvement (regardless of the judged level of original psychopathology), and patients who accepted the values of the treatment with only moderate resistance, made the best posthospital adjustment. One caveat Rapoport noted was that the group focus tended to obscure individual treatment. Or, as he said, "Although the patients are *defined* as a mixed group, they are handled as a homogeneous group" (Sahakian, 1976, p. 547). Rapoport listed thirty primary "Postulates" to explain the milieu treatment approach that he and Jones developed. It is, however, not clear precisely what a therapist does to construct a psychological environment that is consistent with the basic philosophy of the milieu approach.

Alternatives to Hospitalization

The Lodge.   One of the therapeutic communities that challenged conventional wisdom and the medical model and continued the milieu approach to the treatment of severely disturbed patients was called the Lodge by Fairweather, Sanders, Cressler, and Maynard (1969). The home-like Lodge was intended as a bridge between the hospital and the community. Most of the residents (about thirty) in this treatment program carried a diagnosis of schizophrenia. In general, the approach of Fairweather and his associates was consistent with the milieu approach of Jones and Rapoport.

Several important differences existed between the original Jones and Rapoport hospital-based milieu treatment and the Lodge approach. First, the focus in the Lodge was to engage the former hospital patients in active work related to maintenance of the home. Second, after these patients were able to work productively at the Lodge, they took over control of running the program. Third, extensive efforts were made to reconnect these individuals to the larger society by helping them find employment. Once employed, the newly rehabilitated former mental patients formed a network to aid partially recovered Lodge residents to find employment. In comparison to hospital patients receiving standard treatment, 50% of the Lodge members were employed as compared to only 3% of the hospital patients. Furthermore 65% of the Lodge participants remained outside of a hospital while only 27% of similar hospital patients remained outside of a hospital.

Soteria House. Mosher (1974), Mosher, Menn, and Matthews (1975), and Hirschfeld, Matthews, Mosher, and Menn (1977) described another alternative for patient treatment, known as Soteria House, that employed many of the principles of milieu therapy. In addition, the Soteria House program focused on a process of resocialization that was predicated on the staff's faith that profound disturbance is often part of a potential growth process. As was the case for the Lodge the number of patients was small (nine or so) and the ratio of staff to patients was about nine to one. Many staff members were nonprofessionals who not only could tolerate madness but who could react to it without becoming threatened or threatening. In fact Mosher (1974) held that the staff must assume a therapeutic role that is analogous to that of LSD trip guides. This viewpoint means, in practice, that the staff would often spend hour after hour in close but nonthreatening, nonauthoritarian and nonintrusive contact with actively hallucinating patients. According to Mosher, after five weeks the patients' more blatant schizophrenic symptoms would clear, *without medication.* According to Mosher et al. (1975), 10% of the residents at Soteria did not respond and required medication (thorazine). However, the majority of patients (90%) were maintained as well or better without medication compared to hospital patients with similar diagnoses and pathology. Upon discharge 60% of the Soteria residents were able to live independently while only 4% of the hospital patients were able to live independently.

Certainly the Lodge and Soteria House offer alternatives to current practices of hospitalization and outpatient drug maintenance with severely disturbed patients. It is hoped that the earlier insights of moral therapy and the work of Jones and Rapoport as well as the insights of the Lodge and Soteria approaches, will not be lost in the current rush to medicate.

A Modern Therapeutic Community

According to Stern, Fromm, and Sacksteder (1986), their hospital is "a private, fully open, long term psychiatric hospital that accommodates approximately 45 patients" (p. 18). This hospital is still in operation and is expected to remain in operation. Stern et al. advocated having no locked wards or any other means to restrict the patient's freedom within the hospital or to create barriers between the hospital and the external world. This hospital accepts only voluntary admissions and only those patients who are judged to be able to tolerate the total lack of restrictions. According to Stern et al. the therapeutic process includes intensive psychoanalytic therapy (four times a week) and participation in the therapeutic community program (TCP).

The TCP they proposed is composed of:

1. The *community meeting* (CM). Held four times a week, this meeting is open to all patients, all members of the nursing staff, and other staff members who have a specific issue to raise with the community. The CM is chaired by a person elected from the patient community. A therapy staff member (Stern et al. [1996] did not specify the selection procedure) consults with the chair and also coordinates CM outcomes with the hospital.
2. *Resident groups.* In addition to the CM, groups meet in one of the four areas ("houses") where the patients live. These groups meet once a week and deal with issues that arise when people live communally.
3. *Other groups.* Additional groups are formed to deal with specific issues, often undertaking clear and narrowly focused tasks.

Patients could choose whether or not to participate in any or all of these groups. One wonders just how significant nonparticipation might become, at least as an issue in the individual therapy sessions. In the Stern et al. (1996) article no reference was made to group therapy or other interventions (such as art therapy), but one suspects that many of these treatments were also available to patients.

In this particular article patients' adjustment to the treatment environment was traced with care and clarity. What is of more importance in our view is that this program has been demonstrated to work for many of the seriously disturbed people who were admitted. The general milieu of this hospital meets Linn's criterion (1970) for success as well as that of Bettelheim (1974).

Attitude Therapy

One ingenious attempt to make more precise the concept of milieu treatment is the approach of Taulbee and Folsom (1973) or, as they called it, attitude therapy. Attitude therapy is defined as a systematic psychologically based intervention intended to produce behavioral changes. The hospital staff where Taulbee and Folsom implemented the program was to apply the appropriate "attitude." Taulbee and Folsom held that this would reinforce positive behavior and extinguish negative behavior. They stated that there are no hopeless cases nor should one use standard psychiatric categories in determining the specific treatment approaches. Instead, Taulbee and Folsom identified specific behavior patterns that then specified specific treatment approaches, called "attitudes."

Before developing any treatment approach, all members of the treatment team evaluate each patient with respect to these questions:

1. What is happening to the patient?
2. How did the patient get to be as he or she is?
3. How is his or her behavior to be interpreted?
4. What changes can be brought about by the treatment modalities at our disposal?

After the treatment team reaches consensus concerning each of these questions, a treatment approach is determined.

Any patient may receive any one of the treatment modalities available, which are described below. Often a patient will receive more than one although the general model is to focus on one modality as the primary treatment approach. Each patient wears a badge that identifies which treatment modalities apply to that patient. All staff members are to follow the basic approaches required by that treatment modality. The five basic approaches, or attitudes, are:

1. *Active friendliness.* When a person is judged to be regressive and apathetic (often having come from a back ward), the attitude of active friendliness is suggested. The caretakers, *all caretakers,* are to actively give attention in a positive, friendly way whether or not the patient is receptive to it.
2. *Passive friendliness.* When a person is judged to be distrustful and suspicious, the attitude of passive friendliness is suggested. All caretakers are to offer friendliness if the patient desires it but are not to "move in" on the patient. Available but not intrusive best describes the posture to be taken.
3. *Kind firmness.* It is unclear to the authors why Taulbee and Folsom call this approach kind firmness (Jurvick, 1973, Vol. 1). This particular approach is to be used with patients who are depressed and express feelings of being worthless. The technique involves "firmly" enforcing in a "kindly" way the requirement (for all depressed patients) that the patients continue to perform a monstrously boring task until they explode, at which point they are no longer depressed. However, Taulbee and Folsom are clear that once the patient explodes, that patient is to be put on the *no demand* schedule.
4. *No demand.* When a patient is judged to be violent, in a state of panic, and literally striking out, no demands are to be made of the patient. (There are four exceptions to the no demand attitude: the patient may not leave the treatment program, the patient may not engage in self-destructive behaviors, the patient may not endanger others, and the patient must take prescribed medications.

5. *Matter-of-fact.* When a patient is judged to be manipulative, all caretakers require that patient to follow his or her treatment program. Any attempt to avoid compliance is met with a matter-of-fact statement by a caretaker such as, "You are supposed to go to OT (Occupational Therapy). Go to OT." All caretakers follow exactly the same interpersonal strategy.

In addition to these five attitudes there are two special treatment programs. The first is the *antidepressive program* (which is always used with the attitude of kind firmness). Severely depressed patients are given a nonrewarding, boring task to do and are required to continue doing this task until they become very angry. At this point the patient is no longer depressed. Taulbee and Folsom advised that staff personnel immediately assume a no demand attitude with the now angry patient.

The second treatment approach is for patients with reality orientation difficulties. Using a combination of active friendliness, passive friendliness, or matter-of-fact attitudes, the treatment staff actively structures all aspects of patient current life. The patient is told who, what, when, and where, as well as concrete aspects of the patient's present or past life. The purpose of this treatment program is to structure reality so clearly that individuals who suffer from severe brain dysfunction may become sufficiently oriented to be able to leave the hospital. As stated in Chapter 4, reality orientation is not recommended for patients in the later stage of Alzheimer's disease or other demented patients who react negatively to this approach.

The claims made for the attitude therapy approach are considerable: a markedly increased discharge rate, reduction in drug usage, and a much higher turnover rate at the hospital. However, the specification of what to do and to whom in this approach is still far from being a clearly defined behavioral treatment program.

Behavioral Approaches with the Severely Disturbed

The specific techniques that could give greater clarity to the attitude therapy approach of Taulbee and Folsom (1973) have their roots in the work of B.F. Skinner (1953) and the early clinical applications of Lindsley (1956) and Ayllon (1963). Essentially, the now well-known format of behavior therapy developed by these men was to apply the principles of operant psychology to pathological behaviors. This behavior modification approach requires:

1. Identification of the target behaviors, those one wishes to increase and those one wishes to decrease.
2. Establishment of the baseline of the undesirable behaviors.
3. Reinforcement of the desired behaviors and *non*reinforcement of the undesired behaviors (not an easy task).

4. Changing behavior patterns slowly and in a series of small steps (the technique of successive approximations or shaping).

According to Lazarus (1971, 1977), behavior therapy was first used by Skinner, Solomon, Lindsley, and Richards in 1953. Lazarus (and Eysenck) independently used behavior therapy in 1959.

One of the best and earliest examples of the use of behavior therapy techniques and the modification of "psychotic" patterns of behavior was reported by Ayllon (1963). He used specific techniques to systematically modify the behaviors of one severely disturbed patient in an institutional setting. The patient was grossly overweight (250+ lbs.), stole food, hoarded towels, and wore excessive clothing—"e.g., a half dozen dresses, several pairs of stockings, sweater, and so on," Ayllon, p. 54). Each negative behavior was treated separately.

To modify the eating behavior the patient was allowed to eat only at a private table, only what was on her table, and only at regular, scheduled dining hours. Otherwise, she was removed and not allowed to eat. She soon learned that if she did not follow the procedure she would not be allowed to eat at all. The hoarding and stealing of food stopped; she ate a diet that had been judged appropriate and lost seventy pounds.

The hoarding of towels was controlled by a technique not yet discussed, known as *stimulus flooding*. The idea is to give so much of a particular stimulus to a subject that the formerly positive stimulus becomes aversive. In this case, the patient was given more and more towels until she finally wanted to get rid of them, and worked to remove the piles and piles of towels. It took thirteen weeks and the number of towels in the room reached 650 before aversion set in, but in twelve more weeks the number of towels was down to one or two, an acceptable and appropriate number.

Finally, the amount of excess clothing was controlled by pairing removal of unnecessary clothing with food reinforcement. Again, in a relatively short time the patient was normally dressed, and the standard technique of reinforcing desired responses was successful.

During the early 1960s many other behaviors were identified and many reinforcers (other than food) were tried with institutionalized patients with varying degrees of success. Any behavior that could be identified—and for which a baseline could be established—and that could be paired with a reinforcer was modified or controlled or at least the attempt was made during this period. Overall the main thrust of the behavior therapy movement with severely disturbed people was not to restore them to society but to aid in institutional management of these patients (Ayllon, 1963).

In the late 1960s the token economy approach began to offer a more readily and exportable technology to the mental health field. In this approach, a token would be given to the patient for the desirable behavior and the patient could exchange so many tokens for a desired object. Rather than food or other reinforcers, tokens became the general means of gaining behavioral control.

A major difficulty with the token system was that very severely disturbed patients wouldn't cooperate. Before very severely disturbed patients would work for tokens, the patients had to be given tokens on a noncontingent basis, *from the therapist's point of view,* and then encouraged to exchange the tokens for things they wanted (Atthowe & Krasner, 1968). Once the patient found the connection, then and only then could behavioral control be gained. Clearly the patient must have some trust in the world or learn to have trust before the secondary reinforcement effect of the token or any other social reinforcer will be effective.

A second and more general problem with many behavior modification approaches is that they focus on a narrow range of behaviors and fail to view the individual wholistically. The thrust of therapy is not to change this or that behavior or even to be able to control *all* behaviors; the thrust of therapy is to equip the individual to function effectively, often in aversive situations. How behavioral therapy leads to internalization of "the rules of the game" with severely disturbed individuals is not clear.

However, the demand of the behavioral therapist for concreteness—in other words, identify the behavior, measure what one is doing, and report one's findings—has served a very useful function. Such a corrective for the vagueness both of psychotherapy and other more general institutional treatment approaches was then and remains now an important contribution to the process of the treatment of troubled individuals.

Paul and Lentz: A Comparison of Milieu and Behavioral Approaches

Paul and Lentz (1977) compiled an impressive array of data during a longitudinal study in which they compared a standard state hospital approach (characterized by what they called an aide culture, in which the aides determined how patients were treated) with two different psychosocial intervention strategies: (1) the *milieu strategy* (Paul and Lentz, 1977, pp. 49–73) and (2) The *social learning strategy* (Paul and Lentz, 1977, pp. 74–101). The milieu program seemed to us to be more structured and institutional than was the Jones and Rapoport milieu approach (Rapoport, 1960) but since the milieu part of what one is doing is at best ambiguous it is hard to be sure. The social learning strategy as described by Paul and Lentz was a well-conceived token economy program.

It is clear from the data that both the milieu and the social learning strategies were beneficial to severely disturbed institutionalized patients. Paul and Lentz found the social learning program to be superior to the milieu approach both in terms of discharge rate and symptom reduction. Given their extensive record keeping and well-conceived experimental design, it seemed that even with long-term, severely regressed institutionalized patients active treatments proved vastly superior to doing nothing. It should also be noted that patients receiving treatment in the social learning program perceived their caretakers to be more caring and concerned than were those in either the milieu or aide culture programs. Since the relationship component of the milieu approach is central to effective treatment, perhaps it was the belief of the staff in the social learning program rather than the methods that accounted for the superior results.

Individual Approaches with the Severely Disturbed

The problem with many behavior modification approaches is that they are effective only in institutional or other controlled settings. Such approaches may not lead to either self-control or to the development of the ability to survive outside of a supportive environment. Perhaps a shift in focus from the group-oriented inpatient treatment modes of the milieu, attitude, and behavior modification approaches to individual therapy approaches would aid in discovering how more permanent change might be achieved and maintained. The focus of the therapists discussed in this chapter is not institutional but rather individual with the exception of Hogarty et al. (1996). We have selected Freida Fromm-Reichmann (1950), Rosen (1947, 1953), and Hogarty et al. (1995) as our examples for discussion.

Hogarty employed his approach as part of a total treatment program. Fromm-Reichmann and Rosen, although they worked in hospital settings, defined themselves as practitioners within the psychoanalytic tradition. However, both Fromm-Reichmann and Rosen felt that they were doing something dramatically different in terms of technique from classical psychoanalysis. The approach taken in this text will be to present Fromm-Reichmann's approach and Rosen's approach and to see what differences and similarities exist. Hogarty and his associates (1995) define their approach as personal therapy and do not adhere to any "school" of psychotherapy. Their emphasis is on using strategies that work with severely disturbed patients (primarily schizophrenics).

Glasser's reality therapy (1975) was also widely proposed as a method for treating severely disturbed individuals. We presented this approach in Chapter 9, because it is our contention that such a focus is more consistently applicable to people suffering from personality disorders. In addition, Glasser is even less clear about what he is doing or not doing than Fromm-Reichmann or Rosen; it may very well be that his effectiveness is due to Glasser the man, rather than to Glasser the reality therapist.

Freida Fromm-Reichmann

In *Principles of Intensive Psychotherapy* (1950) Fromm-Reichmann proposed her approach to working on an individual basis with severely disturbed patients. In this work she challenged much of what was then common knowledge; that is, that the psychoanalytic technique as Freud proposed it was not appropriate for work with "psychotic" or "character disorder" patients. In many significant ways she challenged classical psychoanalytic approaches and argued that to work with troubled people with any level of psychopathology, particularly severely disturbed individuals, certain important changes in technique were required. Although she did not challenge the basic intrapsychic theory of Freud (Fromm-Reichmann, 1950, pp. xiv), she defined the essence of psychotherapy not as an exploration of the intrapsychic state of the patient but rather as an analysis of the nature of that patient's interpersonal relationships.

For Fromm-Reichmann the essential feature in working with severely disturbed individuals (or anyone else) is effective listening. One must suspend judgment of the rightness or wrongness of a particular interaction and *somehow* hear what the person is really saying. We feel that in order to do this with severely disturbed individuals one must symbolically enter their representational system; this to us is the essence of effective listening—to put ourselves into their system or, as Fromm-Reichmann said, to be a participant observer. Entering the psychotic world may be extremely disturbing to the therapist. Yet if one does not experience the psychotic terror, it is unlikely that one can form a satisfactory therapeutic relationship. In essence, one must experience the psychopathology as does the patient, but one must not identify with that psychopathology.

In terms of technique, Fromm-Reichmann argued that the therapist should not focus on free association but rather on the patient's present interpersonal relationships. Of course past internalized interpersonal relationships as they relate to the here and now must also be attended to. In fact, Fromm-Reichmann (1950) stated that the patient's repetitive negative interactional patterns with the therapist were related to unresolved issues and often mirrored what the patient was doing with other people. She stated explicitly that to use free association with ". . . borderline patients and with outright psychotics . . . [could lead to] inducing and increasing disintegrated thinking. For this reason encouraging psychotic patients to freely associate *is strictly contraindicated*" (p. 72, our italics). She noted that the culture had changed, resistance to talking about embarrassing topics such as sex was no longer much of a problem, and therefore free association, as a technique, might no longer be needed even for neurotics. Fromm-Reichmann pointed out that by focusing largely on the technique of free association the therapist may miss or not hear about what is really going on in the patient's present life situation. Fromm-Reichmann argued that a gentle but directive analysis of the patient's current interpersonal patterns was much more useful as a technique. Specifically, to discover the patient's defensive and security operations, one must focus on the patient's interpersonal patterns or the central issues of the therapy will be missed.

However, it should be noted that Fromm-Reichmann (1950) suggested that the technique of free association is, ". . . especially recommended in cases in which either patient, therapist or both notice that they are at a loss in regard to the clarification of certain points under discussion or in regard to additional information needed for further understanding of unclarified difficulties, or if a patient's flow of thought runs dry and this situation cannot be remedied by direct questioning" (p. 76). It is our experience that in working with people we have called severely dissatisfied ("neurotics") that such additional information is often critical; it therefore is not surprising that Freud saw his approach as most useful with such people.

Fromm-Reichmann argued against highly symbolic analysis of marginal thoughts and psychical sensations on the basis that such interpretations might lead to further confusion for severely disturbed clients. Similarly, she argued against uninformed interpretations about slips and errors, daydreams, dreams, and hallucinations or delusions with severely disturbed patients because to interpret at a level so removed from consciousness might well elicit internal anxiety and lead to increased difficulties for the severely disturbed individual.

In general, then, Fromm-Reichmann suggested that the essence of individual therapy with severely disturbed clients involved the use of concrete and explicit elicitation and interpretation of present interpersonal difficulties. Specific focus was to be given to the patient's traumatic early life experiences in which disturbed interpersonal transactions were acquired.

John Rosen

John Rosen's (1953, 1962) approach, which he called direct psychoanalysis, offers a treatment model for working with severely disturbed individuals that seems rather different from the approach of Fromm-Reichmann. Rosen maintained that psychotic states were like an unending nightmare (C. T. Sullivan, 1967). A psychosis was, for Rosen, a regression to more primitive modes of functioning analogous to those of younger children. In this analysis Rosen differed little from H. S. Sullivan's concept of paradoxical or magical thinking, a thinking process characteristic of schizophrenia according to Sullivan (1948). It may be said that nightmare thinking, where cause and effect are the product of chaos rather than "reality" shares much with such "magical" thinking. To live in a world of chaos, even if one could begin to trust such a world, would not, could not, be safe or even lead to reestablishing a world that was predictable. Rosen more than any other therapist (except maybe Laing [1959], who seems to enjoy chaos) wades into the chaotic world of the psychotic and by main force wrests meaning and order out of that patient's particular nightmare world. (The notion of the mental process of schizophrenia as a living nightmare is also suggested by Jung, 1939, and Arieti, 1978).

Rosen (1962) gave a theoretical analysis of the various nightmare motifs that might be held by severely disturbed individuals. Rosen held that there is a hierarchy of disturbance for individuals who are seriously disturbed (whom he calls psychotic) and that each type has a characteristic nightmare motif. He argued that catatonic schizophrenia is the most severe, followed by hebephrenia (now designated in the DSM-IV as disorganized schizophrenia), followed by paranoid type, followed by what he called manic depressive reaction-manic type (now categorized as bipolar disorder–manic in DSM-IV) and finally by what he called manic depressive reaction depressive type.

The description of these motifs gives one pause and could lead "practical" people to reject Rosen out of hand because of the peculiar psychoanalytic metaphor he employed. We will invert Rosen's order of motifs going from the most severely disturbed (most psychotic) to the least severely disturbed (least psychotic) *phase* (as Rosen suggests) of the disorders (C. T. Sullivan, 1967).

1. "I am dreaming that I am frightened stiff because I must be dead to please mother."
   Compare to: schizophrenic reaction, catatonic type

2. "I am dreaming that I am terrified of mother and screaming for her because she is both indispensable and deadly."
   Compare to: schizophrenic reaction, catatonic type

3. "I am dreaming that I am almost frightened stiff because mother refuses to love me unless I die."
   Compare to: schizophrenic reaction, catatonic type

4. "I am dreaming that I am a silly baby, laughing and playing with my fingers and toes because I am trying to make-believe that I am the whole world."
   Compare to: schizophrenic reaction, hebephrenic type

5. "I am dreaming that I know what to do because I have figured out my special importance in the world."
   Compare to: schizophrenic reaction, paranoid type

6. "I am dreaming that I am being harmed, or threatened with harm; therefore my problem is external, not internal."
   Compare to: schizophrenic reaction, paranoid type

7. "I am dreaming that I am very much alive because I am making-believe that I am united with the penis, feces, and breast."
   Compare to: manic-depressive reaction, manic type

8. "I am dreaming that I am mourning because I have lost the penis, feces, and breast."
   Compare to: manic-depressive reaction, depressed type (p. 95)

According to C. T. Sullivan (1967):

> The first part of each motif attempts to characterize the outward appearance and behavior of the individual in that phase of psychosis, and to emphasize the dreamlike quality. Rosen often speaks of psychosis as being an interminable nightmare. The second part of each motif attempts to characterize the reasoning of the unconscious portion of the ego, in relation to the superego. (p. 96)

When one pushes beyond the psychoanalytically oriented jargon and metaphor and looks at what Rosen actually was doing, and how he used the nightmare metaphor, one finds that he honors Truax's (Truax and Cancuff, 1967) injunction for concreteness not in the breach but in action. Again, according to C. T. Sullivan (1967):

> When he addresses a psychotic, Rosen customarily uses the kind of language in which the motifs are expressed. For instance to a "depressed" psychotic, he might say, "You are sad because your mother [i.e., superego] has deserted you [i.e., ego]." He rarely uses psychiatric language—such as "hebephrenic"—or psychoanalytic language—such as "superego"—when talking to a psychotic. Even with a neurotic or with a neo-neurotic (i.e., a recovered psychotic), Rosen seems to prefer the simpler, more direct language of the motifs. (p. 98)

More specifically, what did Rosen do in his treatment of the severely disturbed? First he argued that it is necessary to become a foster parent to the psychotic. The therapist must, according to Rosen, accept the neoinfantile psychotic as a mother would accept a real infant. The therapist must become a good mother and reestablish basic trust. Second, each psychotic must be in a treatment situation in which the therapist is, *in fact*, in control. Rosen (1947) often used assistants both to protect the severely disturbed individual and to reinforce the notion that the therapist is in control. These two points are not in opposition. A good mother not only gives assurance but also controls the child's environment in such a way that the child is both safe and eventually able to safely begin to try things on his or her own.

The third part of Rosen's treatment involved a special way of viewing the transference relationship. Rosen argued that psychotic transference is qualitatively different from neurotic transference. When the linkage (transference) is formed the therapist assumes an almost godlike status for the patient (Wallerstein, 1963, has made similar points with respect to the nature of transference in psychoses). Interpretations within this context must clearly establish the therapist not only as "the good mother" but also as the "powerful" (perhaps even omnipotent) mother. For example, if an acute catatonic person in an excited state said (whether or not the statement referred to anyone present), "Please don't cut my balls off, Pa," C. T. Sullivan stated that

Rosen would say something like, "I'm your father, and I have no intention of punishing you. I give you permission to have those thoughts about Mother" (C. T. Sullivan, 1967, p 101).

After the psychosis has been defeated (often in a few months) then treatment must continue. According to Sullivan (1967) Rosen argued that under the psychosis is a "neo-neurosis." Treatment must continue until that problem is defeated. Rosen argued for more traditional psychoanalytic treatment at this point.

A Proposed Synthesis of the Methods of Fromm-Reichmann and Rosen

Both Fromm-Reichmann and Rosen clearly indicated that effective treatment of the profoundly disturbed requires the therapist to enter into the nightmare world of the disturbed individual. To establish contact one must accept the psychological fact that the troubled person experiences the world as he or she does, no matter how disturbed and nightmarish this world-view is. However, both Fromm-Reichmann and Rosen were equally clear that the therapist must not do anything that maintains that nightmare; rather the therapist must somehow lead the patient from the nightmare experiences and into reality. Both Rosen and Fromm-Reichmann held that the therapist taking a passive role and conducting standard free association elicitation and interpretation of defenses are strictly contraindicated.

Rosen is more explicit than Fromm-Reichmann concerning the necessity of the therapist not only communicating but also in fact having the power to protect the disturbed individual from his or her own self or other destructive forces. Yet according to one of Fromm-Reichmann's patients (personal comment to the first author of this book, 1978) Fromm-Reichmann was one of the most powerful people and most directive therapist one could imagine. In short, after contact is established, then the therapist and the therapeutic environment must provide the equivalent of the satisfaction of Maslow's need for safety.

In addition, it seems to us that to establish contact with the profoundly disturbed individual the therapist must often be able to enter that person's nightmare world nonverbally. Perhaps the best example of how one might do this appears in Erikson's chapter in Greenwald (1967):

> George had been a patient in a mental hospital for five years. His identity had never been established. He was simply a stranger around the age of 25 who had been picked up by the police for irrational behavior and committed to the state mental hospital. During those five years he had said, "My name is George," "Good morning," and "Good night," but these were his only rational utterances. He uttered otherwise a continuous word salad completely meaningless as far as could be determined. It was made up of sounds, syllables, words, and incomplete

phrases. For the next three years he sat on a bench at the front door of the ward and eagerly leaped up and poured forth his word salad most urgently to everyone who entered the ward. Otherwise, he merely sat quietly mumbling his word salad to himself. Innumerable patient efforts had been made by psychiatrists, psychologists, nurses, social service workers, other personnel, and even fellow patients to secure intelligible remarks from him, all in vain. George talked only one way, the word salad way. After approximately three years he continued to greet persons who entered the ward with an outburst of meaningless words, but in between times he sat silently on the bench, appearing mildly depressed but somewhat angrily uttering a few minutes of word salad when approached and questioned.

The author joined the hospital staff in the sixth year of George's stay. The available information about his ward behavior was secured. It was learned also that patients or ward personnel could sit on the bench beside him without eliciting his word salad so long as they did not speak to him. With this total of information a therapeutic plan was devised. A secretary recorded in shorthand the word salads with which he so urgently greeted those who entered the ward. These transcribed recordings were studied but no meaning could be discovered. These word salads were carefully paraphrased, using words that were least likely to be found in George's productions, and an extensive study was made of these until the author could improvise a word salad similar in pattern to George's, but utilizing a different vocabulary.

All entrances to the ward were changed to a side door some distance down the corridor from George. The author then began the practice of sitting silently on the bench beside George daily for increasing lengths of time until the span of an hour was reached. At the next sitting, the author, addressing the empty air, identified himself verbally. George made no response.

The next day the identification was addressed directly to George. He spat out an angry stretch of word salad to which the author replied, in tones of courtesy and responsiveness, with an equal amount of his own carefully contrived word salad. George appeared puzzled and, when the author finished, George uttered another contribution with an inquiring intonation. As if replying, the author verbalized still further word salad.

After a half-dozen interchanges, George lapsed into silence and the author promptly went about other matters.

The next morning appropriate greetings were exchanged, employing proper names by both. Then George launched into a long word salad speech to which the author courteously replied in kind. There followed brief interchanges of long and short utterances of word salad until George fell silent and the author went to other duties.

This continued for some time. Then George, after returning the morning greeting, made meaningless utterances without pause for four hours. It taxed the author greatly to miss lunch and to make a full reply in kind. George listened attentively and made a two-hour reply to which a weary two-hour response was made. (George was noted to watch the clock throughout the day.)

The next morning George returned the usual greeting properly but added about two sentences of nonsense to which the author replied with a similar length of nonsense. George replied, "Talk sense, Doctor." "Certainly, I'll be glad to. What is your last name?" "O'Donovan, and it's about time somebody who knows how to talk asked. Over five years in this lousy joint" . . . to which was added a sentence or two of word salad. The author replied, "I'm glad to get your name, George. Five years is too long a time" . . . and about two sentences of word salad were added.

The rest of the account is as might be expected. A complete history sprinkled with bits of word salad was obtained by inquiries judiciously salted with word salad. His clinical course, never completely free of word salad, which was eventually reduced to occasional unintelligible mumbles, was excellent. Within a year he had left the hospital, was gainfully employed, and at increasingly longer intervals returned to the hospital to report his continued and improving adjustment. Nevertheless, he invariably initiated his report or terminated it with a bit of word salad, always expecting the same from the author. Yet he could, as he frequently did on these visits, comment wryly, "Nothing like a little nonsense in life, is there, Doctor?" to which he obviously expected and received a sensible expression of agreement to which was added a brief utterance of nonsense. After he had been out of the hospital continuously for three years of fully satisfactory adjustment, contact was lost with him except for a cheerful postcard from another city. This bore a brief but satisfactory summary of his adjustments in a distant city. It was signed properly but following his name was a jumble of syllables. There was no return address. He was ending the relationship on his terms of adequate understanding. (Greenwald, 1967, pp. 316–318.)

Finally, both Fromm-Reichmann and Rosen are clear that one does not lie to an individual who is profoundly disturbed. The kind of lie they are referring to is what Gregory Bateson would call a double bind. One does not say one thing with the mouth and another thing with the body. If one is angry or sad or fearful with the client, one must express the anger or any other emotion clearly. For example, when a profoundly disturbed client said, "Yes in St. Ives I slit my throat," the first author said, "When you say things like that you scare the shit out of me." Whether the remark, in some ultimate sense, was therapeutic or not is not clear; however, following that statement, the client stopped acting in a psychotic fashion and began to talk about real concerns.

Hogarty and Associates: Personal Therapy

G. E. Hogarty et al. (1995) proposed an approach to the psychosocial treatment of schizophrenics that included individual psychotherapy. They have called their manual-driven approach *personal therapy* (PT). Hogarty et al. conducted experimental outcome research that indicated that PT is an effective psychosocial treatment for schizophrenia. However, their research showed that PT may be effectively employed only if certain preconditions are met. First schizophrenics need to be maintained on the lowest possible dosage of antipsychotic medication to allow for adequate cognitive functioning. The schizophrenic patient must be able to process verbal information if any "talking cure" is to be effective. Second, the antipsychotic medication dose must be sufficient to control the active symptoms of schizophrenia (particularly hallucinations and delusions). Third, psychoeducation and social role training need to be part of an effective psychosocial intervention (Hogarty, Anderson et al., 1986). Finally, the patient must be in a supportive and nonpunitive social environment.

PT is intended to aid the patient in developing the internal monitoring skills required for the control of affective dysregulation "defined as loss of control or regulation of mood" (Hogarty et al., 1995, p. 382). The focus is on employing techniques to enable the patient to learn strategies to control affect. According to Hogarty et al., "PT became an exercise in managing personal vulnerability through a process of guided recovery" (p. 323).

As discussed by Hogarty and associates, the PT approach focused on increasing the schizophrenic person's awareness of that person's subjective state. Specifically, the client or patient was led in therapy to become aware of emotional reactions that were disproportional to the actual events, and to develop means to control his or her reactions. The intent was to reduce a person's reactivity to any stress stimuli.

The specific techniques used by PT have been discussed elsewhere in this text (for example, modeling, rehearsal, specific feedback about behavioral displays, practice of behaviors modeled as effective, and homework assignments). The application of Hogarty's technique followed a specific set of phases.

Phase I emphasized the necessity of forming a therapeutic relationship (or "joining") and reducing the positive symptoms of schizophrenia to a manageable level. One means of facilitating the formation of a therapeutic relationship was the establishment of a formal therapy contract between the patient and the therapist. Patients had to agree to comply with medications, not to abuse drugs or alcohol, and to contact the therapist during any crisis. As part of establishing a therapeutic relationship the therapist told the patient that this approach had been helpful to many schizophrenics. In essence, the therapist attempted to instill hope. In addition, the therapist fully described the three phases of treatment. Psychoeducation (the process of imparting accurate information about the patient's disorder) was a central part of PTs total psychosocial intervention. Further, all patients attended four to six patient workshops in which schizophrenia and its causes were described. The therapist used supportive therapy (defined as offering appropriate reassurance, reinforcement of appropriate behaviors, empathy, and active listening) throughout the three phases of treatment. Finally, the therapist assumed the role of patient advocate.

The conclusion of Phase I was determined by the following criteria:

1. A therapeutic relationship.
2. The patient was relatively free of positive symptoms.
3. The patient had achieved a stable medication dose for two months.
4. The patient was able to tolerate a thirty-minute discussion of schizophrenia, medication, and social skills.
5. The patient understood schizophrenia is an illness sensitive to stress factors.
6. The patient regularly attended therapy sessions.
7. The patient had shown evidence of using positive comments and avoidance techniques. (Hogarty et al., 1995, p. 385)

The thrust of Phase II was to continue work to increase the patient's self-awareness of emotional states, cognitive states, and current behaviors that trigger emotional dysregulation. In addition, the therapist attempted to continue to increase the patient's personal control over emotional reactivity to stress. The primary techniques used in Phase II focused on decreasing sources of stress by withdrawal or some form of active distraction. Nonfunctional responses to stress (worry, anger, loss of control, and so forth) were noted and "internal coping exercises" were employed. These exercises included deep breathing, guided imagery, and social skills training (see Chapter 6 in this text). Patients were also taught to focus on how they were feeling in reaction to problematic interpersonal interactions (see social skills training as detailed in Chapter 10 of this text).

The criteria for mastering Phase II were:

1. The patient continued to meet Phase I criteria.
2. The patient maintained awareness of the relationship between stress and the internal reaction to stress (and possible decompensation).
3. The patient continued to identify and address social-behavioral deficits (for example, by complying with role-playing exercises and completing homework related to behavioral deficits).
4. The patient gave evidence of accurate social perception in the office and had shown limited generalization of these skills in interpersonal situations outside the office.
5. The patient had shown some awareness of the cues that trigger negative affective responses.
6. The patient had mastered deep breathing in stressful situations and exhibited a concomitant reduction in behavioral decompensation at a rate showing improvement over baseline responses.

Hogarty et al. (1995) stated that the Phase III focus was on relationship issues. The primary distinction between Phase III and Phase II was the transition from self-awareness training and affective dysregulation recognition to (in Phase III) management of internal emotional reactions in interactions with others, particularly significant others. They argued that there is a clear and predictable reciprocal response between how one acts and how the other person responds. Mastering interpersonal skills is critical to the patient's achieving resocialization and eventual vocational success. PT required that these skills be gradually acquired and mastered in structured situations to prevent failure. These individuals are still very vulnerable to interpersonal stress and the stressful demands of holding a job and living in the larger community and need support. In terms of technique, psychoeducation was coupled with Phase III's focus on mood, cognition, and neurovegetative fluctuations. Such fluctuations were discussed as predictable consequences of schizophrenia and not internal cues. As such, the patient must learn to compensate for these distressing events. Relaxation approaches were employed, often when fluctuations corresponded to interpersonal stress. Social and vocational interactions frequently caused the activation of subjective reactions that signal to an individual that his or her control is slipping. Relaxation approaches (see Chapter 6) were used to deactivate these cues and to truncate the escalating emotional arousal. Social skills training and stress inoculation techniques (see Chapters 10 and 6) were employed. Specifically, these techniques were used with respect to criticism and heated interpersonal exchanges, events which schizophrenics find difficult to deal with effectively. These stressful situations, so common in the real world, need to be carefully handled until the person develops necessary internal controls. Follow-up therapy sessions are required to work on unsuccessful encounters. As these skills are mastered, therapy sessions become less frequent.

The PT technique is relatively clear and provides the therapist with some structure. The interpersonal and intrapsychic treatments are graded, and each skill must be mastered before more demanding reality issues are confronted. The treatment is necessarily long-term and it is expected that people accurately diagnosed as suffering from schizophrenia will need to be maintained indefinitely on medication. During the first year of treatment the patient will be seen in therapy once a week or more if he or she needs it. In subsequent years greater spacing of therapy sessions would be expected; however, Hogarty suggested that more sessions could be offered as required.

In Phase III of PT, even more than in Phases I and II, the therapist must be a patient advocate as the client or patient attempts to assume normal social and vocational tasks. Schizophrenics who did not live with their parents or relatives had particular difficulties in Phase III. Specifically, the therapist had to spend time ensuring that the legitimate needs of the patient (food, shelter, and so forth) were met. In the face of these and other real-life obstacles, roughly 50% of the schizophrenics who participated in the Hogarty et al. study (1995) successfully completed Phase III. In other words, roughly half of these troubled people are now able to function independently.

Conclusion

Treatment of the severely disturbed may and often does require institution-alization. Such troubled individuals may and often do require medication, although as seen in Appendix 2, caution is required. Psychoactive medication is best used to alleviate symptoms that prevent interpersonal contact rather than as the sole treatment mode. Further, such medications may best serve their purpose in the acute phase of the disorder and, later on, only as means of alleviating periods of severe relapses or for difficult patients.

In addition it seems to us that recovered schizophrenics and those people recovering from severe affective disorders will require some sort of gradual reintroduction into the larger environment and continual long-term individ-ual or group psychotherapy, or both, to remain symptom-free. Some sort of well-structured, adequately funded halfway house system is an appropriate means of reintroduction into society. Psychotherapy of the general types examined in this chapter give practical guidance to therapists who work with severely disturbed patients.

The fit between our proposed models and the treatment of the severely disturbed is adequate. The majority of authors cited in this chapter suggested that there have been early and severe psychosocial stresses in the lives of severely disturbed people. As Arieti (1978) said, "Those authors, including myself, who have studied cases of schizophrenia intensely and psychody-namically have found not even a single case that did not come from a very disturbed environment and that did not present a very revealing psychody-namic history" (p. 5). It is reasonable to suspect that early and severe psychological stressors occurred before the oedipal period and are significant factors in the client's psychopathology.

Interpersonally, the therapists who have success with schizophrenics tend to assume a very low-level intensity *DE*, or matter-of-fact role, with their clients and change to a warm supporting role only after establishing some sort of trusting relationship with a client. Note well that the commitment to the matter-of-fact role must be consistent and clearly expressed. Rosen's (C. T. Sullivan, 1967) confrontational approach with some of his severely disturbed patients is more intense than we would recommend. However, Rosen's case history data suggest that his intensity followed or mirrored the patient's level of intensity.

If the major interpersonal problem of the schizophrenic is the commu-nication of intense distrust of the world about her or him, in fact denying reality, then a low-level *DE* (matter-of-fact) role should reduce the intensity of the *FG* (distrustful and suspicious) role of the schizophrenic. Once the skepticism and lack of trust of the client are defeated, the therapist may gently try positive affect. If the client responds with positive affect, then a workable interpersonal climate for psychotherapy has been established. Incidentally, work of British therapists with families of schizophrenics, which is only now being applied in some of the treatment facilities in the United States, focuses on a similar sort of interpersonal event as significant in the outcome of treatment with schizophrenics. Brown, Birley, and Wing (1972) found that the outcome of treatment was superior in families in which affect intensity was low, as opposed to families in which affect intensity was high.

Once one has established, or even while one is establishing an effective interpersonal climate, one may deal with the content of psychotherapy (or the psychopathology itself). Fromm-Reichmann, Rosen, Arieti, and Hogarty all deal explicitly with the client's violations of the legitimate expectations of society, while also struggling with the client against violations of a client's legitimate expectations of others with whom the client interacts. It is extremely important for therapists who work with schizophrenic patients and other severely disturbed people that they be prepared to be advocates for these people rather than detached experts.

12 Severely Disturbed Children

It is difficult for us to describe the treatment[1] of severely disturbed institutionalized children or children who require highly structured environments without first attempting to capture the feelings of a neophyte therapist or teacher first encountering old-style large treatment centers for such children. The feelings of despair and hopelessness that sweep over a new staff psychiatrist, teacher, psychologist, social worker, nurse, or aide when he or she first enters a large treatment center must be experienced to be understood. Even now, such centers tend to be dumping grounds for the culture's young who are labeled hopeless or autistic, or profoundly psychotic. One often finds these centers to be drab, smelling of urine, and wholly without a feeling of humanity. Unattended children crowd around every new person who enters their world; perhaps hoping for something new that will change that world. It is no wonder that alternatives to such treatment centers have been sought and have changed our whole approach to the treatment of severely disturbed children.

What is needed is not another impassioned cry that we treat severely disturbed children like the human beings they are, but rather some specific guidelines of how to shift the emphasis in these long-term treatment centers. It is clear that these treatment centers must not be either custodial maintenance centers or centers in which medication is the only treatment.

One approach that could improve treatment would be to develop a better classification system for severely disturbed children. It is hoped that precise identification of disorders would lead to the development of effective treatments. One early attempt was that of Kessler (1966), who classified children that we have called severely disturbed into four categories: (1) autistic, (2) atypical child, (3) symbiotic psychosis, and (4) early schizophrenia. More recently most of these disorders have been classified in the DSM-IV as either autism or some form of pervasive developmental disorder (PDD). Childhood schizophrenia has been removed from the DSM-IV leaving children who suffer from hallucinations or disruptive delusional systems or both essentially unclassified. Szatmari, Bremner, and Nagi (1989) suggested that there is a continuum of autistic disorders ranging from Kanner's early infantile autism to what is described in the DSM-IV as PDD. Szatmari et al. suggested that Asperger's syndrome might represent an intermediate position on this continuum. If one takes Kessler's classification seriously and agrees that there are such disorders as childhood schizophrenia, then one can speculate that there are two major patterns of severe childhood disorders: the autistic continuum and the childhood/early schizophrenia continuum.

However, Kessler (1966) among others (Lovaas, 1972; Bettelheim, 1974) point out that these categories may not be mutually exclusive and that in any event, differentiation between them is difficult. Another approach would be to consider the individual child and to develop a treatment approach based on that child's functioning regardless of what "disorder" the child "has."

The practitioner, as opposed to the theoretician, focuses on the all-encompassing nature of the treatment demands of severely disturbed children. Most of us would agree that there are unique requirements for effective treatment of some children, particularly those with marked central nervous system (CNS) dysfunction. In general, however, the nature of the treatment demands remain constant, regardless of the label that has been given to the child. An orderly, warm environment in which each child's needs are known and attended to describes the general treatment strategy that best responds to the child's needs.

The trap, which we are trying to avoid, is to place any child into the category of "hopeless" because of a label assigned to that child. For this reason and because of a general distrust of the adequacy of labels, our method will be to outline a treatment approach for all children whose behavior is primitive or regressed and often destructive (either directed toward individuals or objects). Specific techniques for addressing the more unique and relatively consistent maladaptive patterns of behavior evidenced by severely disturbed children will determine treatment choices. We are aware that some children will not become fully functional and will require lifelong attention. Yet small gains are real gains, and improvements in a child's quality of life must be the goal of intervention.

Another issue to be dealt with before developing a treatment approach is neurological dysfunction and its effect upon treatment per se. It is probable that early infantile autism, if not all disorders on the autistic continuum (Kanner, 1943, 1944; Kanner & Eisenberg, 1955; Rimland, 1964; Wing, 1966), simply do not occur in the absence of brain damage. Clearly, if brain damage causes the behavior dysfunction then the limiting factor for the progress of such children depends on the extent of the physical integrity of the child's brain. If the brain is markedly damaged, the end point used to define successful treatment will not be a fully functional human being but rather a human being who is at least capable of self-care or whatever level of function is appropriate.

However, we contend that even if neurological dysfunction is the primary causal factor for the child's dysfunctional behavior, the practitioner must remain realistically optimistic with respect to the treatment of that child. Here the problem of a label of CNS dysfunction and the larger problem of the effect of labels on treatment become paramount. Often the label of brain damage (as well as other labels attached to severely disturbed children) equals "untreatable" in the minds of their caretakers.

That notion often leads to no treatment or only reduced treatment. The reader should understand that a no-treatment approach can and usually does mean regression and the necessity for lifelong care for the child. Such labeling without adequate treatment may relieve guilt for treatment failure, but can hardly be defended as an effective treatment approach. Monahan (1977) showed that labels indicating severe psychosis led professional staff to judge patients they had *never seen* to be hopeless. Bettelheim (1974) reported that one of his "hopeless" children showed no major change for years and yet finally responded to treatment, becoming capable of independent living as an adult. Staff attitudes toward and expectations of a severely disturbed child cannot be underestimated in terms of a treatment approach's eventual success or the lack of it. Monahan's work and Bettelheim's observations taken together suggest that "hopelessness" may often stem from labels and staff expectations based on those labels, not on fact.

Treatment Approaches with Severely Disturbed Children

Let us put aside the tough issues that underscore any treatment approach with severely disturbed children. Our task is to review treatment approaches that were deemed successful and to attempt to find general patterns in these approaches. So long as a severely disturbed child remains alive, a just society must provide the best treatment available. Our primary focus is on children who have been diagnosed as autistic. We have selected four programs for the care of autistic children, which we think demonstrate effective treatment approaches applicable to a wide range of types of severely disturbed children.

These are four very different models in which success or at least partial success has been claimed. It is ironical that these four approaches often clash in an extreme fashion.

The four approaches are (1) Bettelheim's school, representing the psychoanalytic tradition; (2) Ferster and DeMyer (1961) and Lovaas (1973), McEachlen, Smith, and Lovaas (1993) representing the cognitive and behaviorist tradition; (3) Lettick (1970) and Wing (1966) representing the special education tradition with a strong humanistic thrust; and (4) home intervention using applied behavior analysis (Maurice, Green, & Luce, 1996). We suggest that these approaches, far from being mutually exclusive, are more similar than dissimilar; and that one should pay less attention to doctrinaire statements and more attention to what is actually done.

Bettelheim (1974) has a long history of treatment of severely disturbed individuals and has claimed a high rate of success (85%). By success, Bettelheim seemed to mean what we have called a fully functional human being. At the very least, for Bettelheim to claim success, the child (most often an adult by treatment's end) had to be able to get a job, display appropriate interpersonal skills, and not require psychiatric or psychological treatment. These are large claims and our task will be to specify what Bettelheim did and to determine whether or not one should accept his interpretations of the results of his work.

Bettelheim: The Milieu Approach

The key to Bruno Bettelheim's treatment approach, echoed over and over again in his works (for example, 1974, p. 274; 1967, p. 16), is that profoundly disturbed children (regardless of the diagnostic category to which they are assigned) must be treated in an environment in which their needs will be met. In *Love Is Not Enough* (1950), *The Empty Fortress* (1967), and *A Home for the Heart* (1974), Bettelheim described in detail (1) the type of physical setting in which effective treatment takes place, (2) the type of people he selects for treatment and how he selects them, and (3) the circumstances in which problems emerge, and how to allow the total environment to meet rather than deny need satisfaction.

However, before getting lost in a segmental description of Bettelheim's approach, it is necessary to underscore one very important point that he made unequivocally. According to Bettelheim, effective treatment of severely disturbed children requires that the treatment be total—twenty-four hours a day, seven days a week and fifty-two weeks a year. Often the length of treatment will need to be measured not in months but years. Bettelheim found no relationship between initial severity of the disturbance and eventual success, but he did find that the more severe the disorder the longer the treatment required.

By total treatment we understand Bettelheim to mean that not only must the therapist be concerned with treatment per se but also with all of the other factors that form the total Gestalt that the troubled child experiences. Each part of the environment communicates something to the child. Bettelheim called this communication "the silent message," which he held will either aid in or detract from the treatment of the child. Every encounter a child has with the therapist and staff is significant and carries with it its own silent message.

The Treatment Environment. One source of these silent messages, which is often ignored in describing the treatment of the severely disturbed, is the character of the treatment facility itself. Bettelheim (1973) pointed out that the disturbed child is very probably quite sensitive to the character of the institution into which that child is thrust. The physical characteristics, the size, the furnishings, the cleanliness, the "decor," and many other nuances of a treatment facility are important media for Bettelheim's concept of the "silent message."

The first physical characteristic of a treatment facility that we will consider is its size. Bettelheim held that the optimum size of a treatment center should allow for forty children and a like number of staff. This means that the center's buildings should be few in number and within hailing distance of one another. The state hospital and other very large institutions for the "treatment" of severely disturbed individuals force patients into large structures that are often stark and shabby, or into living facilities widely scattered over extensive grounds. Both settings separate administrative and treatment staff from the patients. In a smaller setting all participants in treatment could and indeed would be required to interact on a face-to-face basis. Bettelheim argued that the separation imposed by larger institutions reinforced the isolation and alienation that is central to the problems of severely disturbed children. The smaller center with only a few staff areas promotes the opposite message that is, "We are all part of the same place."

Equally important, the treatment center must convey in its design and furnishings a message different from that conveyed by most institutions. Attempts should be made in the architectural design of the buildings to construct a setting for people, not for "efficiency."

As Parr (1977) said:

> The application of minimalistic doctrines to modern architecture has increased the damage (to the human spirit) manifold. We do not have to look at paintings that do not give our souls a lift. But we cannot avoid the cityscapes we must work in and walk in whatever their impact may be.
>
> . . . The architectural brutalization of the cityscape does not encourage gentleness among its inhabitants. We must demand more than mere efficiency, comfort, diversion and relaxation from our surroundings. We also need inspiration.
>
> Beauty is never a luxury, and least of all, where our spirit needs it to support our confidence in the world we live in. We need more of the complex beauty that beckons our minds forward and upward to higher goals, and less of the monolithic walls that imprison body and soul in a state of helpless awe. . . . (p. 17)

If the architecture of the city needs to "support our confidence in the world we live in," how much more must the architecture of a treatment center matter in supporting the confidence of troubled children in the world in which they *cannot* or *do not* or *fear to* live? If "monolithic walls . . . imprison body and soul in a state of helpless awe" (Parr, 1977) in the case of city dwellers, how much more will monolithic walls imprison the bodies and souls of our profoundly disturbed children?

Clearly, the furnishings and decor as well as the overall architectural design convey their own silent messages. If we read Bettelheim right, he would plead that treatment centers not be Spartan, sterile, and functional; that is, not be furnished as institutions so often are. Instead, the furnishings and decor should offer comfort, color, and a sense of warmth. There should be little difference in either the quality or character of the furnishings and decor between the director's office and the children's living areas. Private areas should be provided, and each living area should allow the child occupying it to individualize that area. As we understand Bettelheim, the primary silent message to be given is that the child is an individual, not a thing. The private patient area and the possibility of making that area somehow unique clearly make the statement to the child that he or she is a person. Proper furnishings and decor contribute significantly to a silent message that says "You are important, you do count."

In addition to each child's living area, special attention needs be given to the dining facilities, classrooms, and the initial area of contact for the child with the treatment center. Bettelheim argued that cafeteria approaches should be avoided and dining areas should be relatively small and cheery. Classrooms should be inviting but orderly, not cluttered or distracting. Finally, Bettelheim felt that the area of initial contact with the treatment center was very important. This area must offer the child protection from the outside world and at the same time communicate (or at least explicitly seek to communicate) to the child the all-important message that it's O.K. here. Again the furnishings and the decor are the medium of communication. One may find in Bettelheim's book *A Home for the Heart* (1974, p. 178, Plate 3) the prototype of his design for the initial contact area. If all of these requirements are met the total physical Gestalt would be as Bettelheim titled this work—a home for the heart.

The Staff.   The second factor in Bettelheim's total treatment program was the selection and training of his staff. Although Bettelheim gave many case history examples of staff–child interactions and many descriptions of "good" staff members versus "bad" staff members, it is difficult to find a passage where Bettelheim clearly spelled out what was required, according to him, for a professional to work effectively with troubled children. There were, however, some hints about what one should be like and some clear admonitions about problems that prevented some people from being able to work with these children.

Since the people problems preventing a staff member from becoming an effective team member are more clearly spelled out, we will start with them. Over and over again Bettelheim argued that effective staff members are not concerned with objective results or methods, but rather with the children and that staff member's personal and professional relationship with that child. To be avoided are staff members who remain isolated from the child or other staff members, or who go to the other extreme and smother the child with affection. According to Bettelheim, technique-oriented staff members are also to be avoided. Bettelheim views any emphasis on technique as a way for a staff member to avoid working out unique means to meet each child's particular needs. Bettelheim felt that such needs are not readily apparent but rather must be discovered.

By negative inference it seems to us that Bettelheim regards the good staff member as possessing the objectivity to see each behavior's antecedents, which can be described as points in the child's life when the child's needs were blocked, or when the child learned to expect failure or rejection. In essence the effective staff member is able to enter the child's world, no matter how distorted, as a guide to lead the child away from emptiness and toward self-fulfillment. This is the tricky part, the objective-subjective vantage point. Each child's total existence must be acknowledged and concretized by the effective staff member. The child then must be aided to develop more socially appropriate or effective behaviors.

Therefore, in staff training Bettelheim focused on a person's awareness rather than on technique. The training of personnel attempted to develop an attitude of continuing and nondefensive evaluation of self as treater (used only in the broadest possible sense), in interaction with the troubled child.

In training sessions Bettelheim tried to get his personnel to examine their motives, their intrapsychic strengths and weaknesses, their fears, and their "blind spots." Often this was a difficult and painful experience, demanding that each staff member explore personal weaknesses that most of us try to avoid. Bettelheim assumed that the troubled child can sense the double messages that occur when one is unaware of one's blind spots. Such messages can well become part of the negative silent messages already discussed. However, Bettelheim's emphasis on self-awareness and his insistence that technique gets in the way is unfortunate. Perhaps one can be aware of one's "dark" parts *and* knowledgeable about cognitive and behavioral techniques.

The Treatment Program.   Bettelheim viewed treatment as a complex and total event in that unmet needs of children were met and their expectations of failure and rejection were replaced with experiences of success and feelings of self-worth. He noted that negative behaviors were most often expressed in areas where the child lacked necessary social and interpersonal skills. Such daily activities as toileting, sleeping, eating, keeping clean, and expressing hostility or any other intense emotion were situations where self-destructive, peculiar, or atypical behavior patterns were likely to emerge.

In the most severely disturbed children the primary task is to instill in the child a trust that his or her environment will meet his or her needs. Initially, need satisfaction must be contingent not on some socially desirable behavior but rather on the child's demand for need satisfaction. Therefore, regardless of the situation and the "appropriate" social patterns of behavior, the staff worker must first try to help the child to establish contact through need satisfaction.

Bettelheim's treatment program divided each child's day into three segments. The first dealt with the activities involved in "getting up" including toileting, getting dressed, and eating breakfast. The second segment involved school, "therapies," and lunch. The third segment consisted of all activities after school including dinner, bath time, and bedtime. Ideally, each staff member contacting each child during these three segments was required to communicate with other staff members working with the children. Thus all staff members would get to know the "whole" child, and then slowly lead the child step by step toward more socially appropriate patterns of behavior. Although Bettelheim gave many examples of how the process occurred, he did not spell out the techniques as clearly as one might desire. Perhaps that was because of his distrust of techniques that too frequently become masks for the therapists to hide behind. In any event we shall turn elsewhere for the development of a clearly defined treatment program for severely disturbed children.

Specific Techniques for Working with Severely Disturbed Children

The Behavior Modification Approach. Charles Ferster (1961) and Ivar Lovaas (1973) were perhaps the earliest and most articulate advocates of the application of learning theory to the treatment of severely disturbed children. Both endorsed an individualized analysis and treatment of behavior deficits. In addition, both placed heavy emphasis on early learning as well as organic factors in the production of dysfunctional patterns of thought, feeling, and action.

Ferster (1961) developed a model for the application of operant principles to structured residential treatment approaches with severely disturbed children. In 1962, with DeMyer, he applied these principles with good success. However, it was in 1967, with his observation of the therapist Jean Simons at work, that Ferster most clearly underscored the complexity of even "simple" interactions and the difficulty of applying operant approaches to the treatment of severely disturbed children.

The texture of Ferster's analysis of the interactions between Simons and an autistic child is sufficiently important to quote in some detail. Wrote Ferster (1967):

Jeanne Simons placed Karen on a rocking horse where she stayed without crying as long as Miss Simons rocked the horse for brief periods but kept on singing. She carefully sensed how long she could stop rocking the horse without losing control of Karen. The return to rocking always followed some behavior other than crying. In general Miss Simons stopped rocking the horse whenever she judged that Karen's behavior was strongly maintained by some current factor, such as playing with the handles of the rocking horse. Next, Miss Simons took the plastic doll from Karen's hands, set it on a nearby table, and quickly moved the table next to Karen who promptly picked up the doll. One would guess that under other circumstances taking the doll away from Karen would lead to screaming. Although Karen was without the doll for only a few seconds, this situation provided the basis for the reinforcement of a specific constructive piece of behavior—reaching for the doll. This was the first time that Miss Simons required some behavior of Karen.

Now Karen moved the rocking horse slightly, and Miss Simons' singing usually occurred contingent on the rocking. When Karen sat quietly, Miss Simons simply watched, smiled, and hummed gently. When Karen rocked, Miss Simons sang in rhythm to the movements of the horse. Then the episode with the doll was repeated, but this time the movements were a little slower and Karen was without her doll for a few seconds longer. When Karen returned to rocking, Miss Simons sang in rhythm. Soon Karen placed the doll on the table herself. This probably occurred because the behavior controlled by the rocking horse was becoming prepotent over that controlled by the doll. Also, it was difficult for Karen both to clutch the doll and to hold the handles of the rocking horse. Karen continued rocking without the doll for over a minute as Miss Simons sang along. The magnitude and rhythm of the rocking were quite vigorous.

Next Miss Simons kept silent for brief periods while Karen rocked. Technically this was intermittent reinforcement of the rocking. At this point Karen turned to the doll, possibly because she was less inclined to rock the horse when Miss Simons did not sing. But in picking up the doll Karen dropped it to the floor, perhaps accidentally, and for the first time during the episode, she began to cry. Miss Simons asked, "Do you want to pick up your doll? I'll help you," and extended her hands to Karen. When Karen touched Miss Simons' hand Miss Simons clasped Karen's hands and helped her from the rocking horse. When Karen did not lift her foot over the saddle, Miss Simons simply held her there until she made some movement. When Karen did not move, Miss Simons prompted the behavior by moving the foot partially over the saddle and allowed Karen to complete the final part of the action. Miss Simons then held Karen in the vicinity of the doll until Karen picked it up, and once more she offered her hands as she said, "Do you want to get up?" Karen lifted her hands and the gesture which many children characteristically use as a mand for being picked up, but Miss Simons simply continued to hold her hands out until Karen touched them.[2] Back on the horse, Karen now rocked without Miss Simons' singing. Once again, she dropped her doll and the same episode was repeated. This time Miss Simons supported the behavior slightly less than she had on the previous occasion.

Next Miss Simons placed the doll on a couch about fifteen feet away. Karen stopped rocking for a few seconds while she looked at the doll, but then began to rock again, and after about a minute Miss Simons picked up the doll, attracted Karen's attention by tapping it, and sang in rhythm to the tapping. Karen made some sounds and began rocking the horse in the same rhythm, possibly in response to the tapping. At this point Miss Simons returned the doll. Karen had been away from it for over a minute without crying. However, the next time Miss Simons took the doll away and placed it on the couch, Karen began crying even though she continued to rock. Miss Simons sang in rhythm to the rocking and the crying stopped. At this point Miss Simons herself took Karen off the horse, and they walked over to the sofa where Karen picked up the doll and sat on Miss Simons' lap. A minute later Karen indicated some disposition to get on the horse again by tugging on Miss Simons. Miss Simons did not take her to the horse, but instead picked her up and hummed to her as she carried her about. Several times Miss Simons picked up Karen, smiled, and sang to her, but she did not place her on the horse.

The whole interchange lasted about thirty minutes during which several hundred reinforcements altered Karen's repertoire substantially. In contrast to food reinforcement, in the usual animal experiment, very simply features of the child's environment were manipulated very skillfully and rapidly in a symphony of action. Even though these behavioral processes were the same ones that I knew from animal and human laboratory experience, I discovered many new ways to control and influence the behavior of these children as I observed this and similar episodes. Although I saw applications of every principle of behavior I know, there was a content here that could not come solely from laboratory experience. I could make a functional analysis of the interaction, but I could not have designed it. (pp. 145–147)

The principles of operant learning that Ferster witnessed are the techniques that most practitioners using a behavior modification approach would endorse. *First,* one must identify the desired behaviors and the undesired behaviors. *Second,* one must *not* reinforce the undesired behaviors and one must reinforce the desired behaviors. From the behavior modification literature it would seem that the slightest attention to negative, even self-destructive behaviors will maintain those behaviors, while it is quite difficult to reinforce positive behaviors. To reinforce positive behaviors with so-called psychotic (and, in our words, severely disturbed) children, Lovaas (1973) suggested the use of food reinforcers initially and then perhaps social reinforcers after some sort of contact was made with the child. *Third,* one must bring about changes in patterns of behavior slowly, in small steps. This process is called *successive approximation.* If the intent is to get a child to eat with a spoon rather than with the hands, one first reinforces the child for picking up the spoon, then for putting food in the spoon, then for putting a spoon with food on it in the mouth, and so forth, until the child learns to use a spoon properly. It is assumed that not attending to undesired behaviors will extinguish them and that one can, piecemeal, build a large and effective behavioral repertoire by following the above procedures.

Lovaas (1973) developed specific techniques that could follow from a *functional analysis* (see Chapter 6 for a discussion of functional analysis) of behavior such as that observed by Ferster. In addition, Lovaas specified behavioral methods for language training with severely disturbed children, as well as punishment techniques and fading techniques. Other behavior modification advocates have described additional techniques for working with psychotic children (again we prefer to avoid the label of autistic or psychotic and merely designate these children as severely disturbed).

Central to the more innovative and significant techniques developed by Lovaas (1973) are those designed to facilitate language development in children who are mute or who have very little language. According to Lovaas the first step in language acquisition is to increase the child's vocalizations. When the child makes a sound he or she is reinforced, usually with food. Second, the child is reinforced when he or she makes a sound in response to the therapist or teacher's voice. Then the child is reinforced only when the child's vocalization begins to match the therapist's or teacher's vocalization. After the child can imitate the therapist's or teacher's sound, new sounds are introduced and, if properly imitated, reinforced.

As soon as more complex sound imitation is established the therapist or teacher presents a set of common objects or one object only to the child. After the child fixates on the specified object the therapist or teacher says the name of that object (for example, chair) as a "prompt," and if the child then repeats that word, the child has been reinforced. The prompt is soon stopped and the child is only reinforced when he or she labels the object correctly. The teacher may occasionally have to prompt the child nonverbally by pointing to the object. This process continues until the child has a useful "labeling" vocabulary. After a labeling vocabulary is acquired the child is trained to use prepositions, pronouns, and increasingly abstract words. The first operation is the acquisition of proper prepositional usage. The child is prompted to nonverbally and appropriately respond to a particular preposition. The prompt is then removed and again the child is reinforced only if he or she can nonverbally demonstrate the preposition (by placing a penny on a rug or under a rug, for example). Pronoun training follows a similar pattern beginning with a nonverbal pronoun prompt and continuing the training until mastery of pronoun usage occurs. For more complete technique specification the reader is encouraged to read Lovaas's book, *Behavioral Treatment of Autistic Children* (1973).

The most controversial part of Lovaas's approach was his use of aversives, that is punishment to control self-destructive behaviors (behaviors that Ferster labeled atavistic). The first task was to establish a baseline of the self-destructive behaviors. When the child emitted a self-destructive behavior the child received a painful but harmless shock. The frequency of self-destructive behaviors then went down. However, there is another way to get rid of self-destructive behaviors, which is to physically restrain the child and prevent him or her from emitting the self-destructive behavior. As soon as the child emitted any positive behavior, the therapist would reinforce it. For example, if the child relaxed the therapist might give the child a desired toy. If the child played with the toy the therapist might give the child a food reinforcement. Each of these positive behaviors competes with the occurrence of negative behaviors, that is, reduces their frequency.

Punishment in animals has been shown to be a very inefficient means of controlling behavior, and indeed, such punishment often leads to blocking, unpredictable generalizations, and other negative side effects best avoided. Perhaps the use of punishment with human beings suffers from many of these problems and should be avoided unless there is no other alternative. Ferster (personal communication, 1976) went further and stated that the systematic use of punishment to control the behavior of severely disturbed children cannot be justified. Lovaas has moved away from this practice in his more recent work but probably would include "aversives" as a rarely used technique.

One of the more difficult problems a therapist or teacher encounters with a profoundly disturbed child, particularly those labeled autistic, is that of overselective attention. Lovaas (1973) developed a procedure for dealing with overselective attention. The technique has been labeled *fading* and is of considerable importance. There are three steps in fading. First, the therapist gradually presents (fades in) the stimulus that confuses the child (S–), say the color of a ball. Second, the therapist fades out size and position prompts to make sure the child can tell the difference between the stimulus that confuses the child (S–) (color) and the stimulus (S+) (ball) the therapist wishes the child to attend to, regardless of size and position of S– and S+. Finally, the therapist fades in the nonconfusing components in the larger stimulus display until the child can easily discriminate between the two stimulus displays. Refer to Lovaas (1973, page 14, Figure 7) for a pictorial display of this procedure.

Lovaas and his associates have continued to refine their treatment of autistic children (McEachlin, Smith, & Lovaas, 1993). In this article McEachlin et al. reported that early intervention with a vast array of behavioral techniques was required if success is to be hoped for. The thirty-eight children selected for the study were very young and had received a diagnosis of autism from a licensed clinical psychologist or psychiatrist. A complete description of these children may be found in Lovaas (1987). The children were divided into two groups of nineteen, a standard "no-treatment" (actually "standard" treatment) control group and an experimental group. The children in the experimental group received forty or more hours per week of "intensive intervention." Note well that the children in the experimental group were treated in their homes and that parents were required to become part of the treatment team. It seems to us that this approach satisfies the notion that effective intervention of severely disturbed children requires total treatment. Of the nineteen children in the experimental group, eight were found to be "normal" at age thirteen as compared to no children in the control group. McEachlin et al. commented that although gains occurred for almost all of the children in the experimental group, the majority of these children could not be said to be normal.

Another technique used by Lovaas (1973) is that of *imitation learning.* This technique focuses on the nonverbal aspects of profoundly disturbed children's behavior. Often such children have little or no nonverbal expressiveness—a problem of some importance since this flatness places them apart. First the child is prompted (the therapist or teacher smiles and moves the child's mouth into a smile) and then is reinforced. Then the child is reinforced only when he or she imitates a smile without prompting. An extensive repertoire of nonverbal imitative behaviors may be established in this fashion.

Foxx and Azrin (1973) have devised a technique called overcorrection to reduce or eliminate the occurrence of repetitive self-stimulating behaviors. The common forms of self-stimulation treated by the overcorrection approach were object mouthing, head weaving, and hand flapping.

The application of overcorrection for object mouthing was to say "No," brush the child's teeth and gums with mouthwash, and wipe the child's outer lips with a washcloth that had been dampened with the mouthwash. The child was then encouraged to spit. This procedure occurred every time the child mouthed something. The overcorrection method for head weaving was first to restrain the child's head. Then the child was instructed to move the head up, down, or straight. The child was then required to hold his or her head stationary for fifteen seconds. The application for hand flapping was similar. First, the child's hands were restrained. Then the child was asked to move his or her hands into one of five positions: above the head, straight out in front, into the child's pockets, together in front, or behind the back. When the child failed to follow instructions the therapist or teacher moved the hands to the designated position. Again the child was required to hold his or her hands stationary for fifteen seconds.

It is easy to see with such an impressive array of specific techniques—and we have by no means enumerated them all—why the behavior modification therapists have focused on behavior segments rather than the totality of the child's functioning. However, the end point of treatment is not, we think, the acquisition of this behavior or that behavior, but rather of a total behavioral repertoire, the development of self-referred feelings of worth, and cognitive skills necessary for effective coping outside an institutional setting. Lovaas's emphasis on the acquisition of language skills as the first and most important step toward cognitive integrity is one way to address this issue. However, the acquisition of language must occur within a broad context if these skills are to be most effectively used by troubled children.

The special education approach to the treatment of profoundly disturbed children, particularly when applied to children called autistic, focuses more clearly on the total cognitive functioning of these children than do the more narrow of the behavioral approaches. It is to this family of approaches that we now turn.

Special Education Approaches with Severely Disturbed Children

An important development in the treatment of severely disturbed children is the emergence of special education approaches which focus on the cognitive aspects of the child's problem including perceptual and motor dysfunctions. The clearest example of this more general trend may be seen in the special education treatment of autistic children or children whose behavior would lead us to describe them as profoundly cognitively disabled.

There are numerous schools in Europe and the United States that were founded to work with severely disturbed children. J. K. Wing (Wing, 1966) has published an important book that detailed many features of the educational approach toward such children in England. Most frequently these schools are not residential. They share common orienting hypotheses: educate the child rather than treat the child, and focus on social problems as learning problems caused by perceptual deficits rather than emotional problems produced by the parents. These schools often work with the children on an extended regular school schedule basis. In general, whether they call themselves schools for learning-disabled children, schools for autistic children, or something else these schools admit very severely disturbed children who cannot function in a normal classroom. Indeed, such children are often denied any other placement because of the severity of their dysfunctional patterns of thinking, feeling, or acting.

A Special School: Benhaven. We have chosen as a model a school that demonstrates the special education approach and has incorporated some of the behavioral approaches discussed earlier. The Benhaven School is located in East Haven, Connecticut. According to Lettick (1979), Benhaven has received recognition from Rimland, J. K. Wing and L. Wing as one of the best treatment facilities for autistic children in the United States. Although Benhaven is a day school, the children attend class six days a week year-round with only six holidays. In addition, Benhaven provides limited, though expanding, long-term living accommodations for children who, as they reach adolescence, can no longer live at home. For parents of younger children, for older children who are not living full-time in Benhaven's structured living accommodations, short-term placement at the structured living center is available.

According to Lettick (1979), when a child arrived at Benhaven he or she received a full diagnostic workup from the consulting psychiatrist, the staff, and any additional specialist needed. The child's level of functioning was evaluated in five areas: (1) language and speech, (2) academic skills, (3) level of socialization and gross motor skills, (4) potential for prevocational training, and (5) self-care skills. Care was taken to explore the extent and kind of possible CNS dysfunctions, particularly in the perceptual and motor sphere. The diagnostic team defined a specific set of goals for the child based on this analysis of function, and prepared a specific plan to accomplish them. All members of the treatment team who were dealing with the child reviewed his or her progress on a regular basis, at least three times a year.

Treatment at Benhaven began with a clear specification of baseline performance in a number of areas. First, a complete cataloguing of the child's self-destructive and other destructive or extremely disruptive behaviors was conducted to allow for initial and rapid behavioral control. Second, the child's speech and language abilities were assessed both by the use of standardized verbal and nonverbal intelligence tests (as appropriate) and more specialized assessment approaches such as the Illinois Test of Psycholinguistic Abilities. Third, gross motor skills, self-care abilities, and vocational or prevocational possibilities were linked to specific behaviors, indicating initial level of performance in these areas. Finally, a clear assessment of level of academic skill was made to allow for the determination of initial skill level. Each area of the child's functioning was considered important and the reader is cautioned not to take the order of establishment of the various baseline behaviors to indicate their perceived importance. Of course, behavior control at a sufficient level for academic, language, gross motor, self-care, and prevocational work is essential and is properly listed first in Benhaven's baseline establishment procedure.

To reduce the negative behavior patterns (hitting, biting, self-mutilation, head banging, and other destructive behaviors) the teachers of Benhaven employed a number of different methods, including physical restraint as well as time-out or isolation techniques. Disruptive children might also receive medication if the consulting psychiatrist judged this approach to be useful. The use of punishment was considered an ineffective means of gaining control and therefore aversive approaches were rarely employed. In addition to some physical restraint and time-out (a form of isolation), the child was introduced to a highly structured program of learning. As the baseline[3] behaviors were established and the destructive behaviors controlled, the application of Benhaven's total educational process for the individual child became increasingly well defined.

One of the primary tools used at Benhaven was the *precision teaching* approach of Lindsley, specifically adapted by the Benhaven staff. An important aspect of precision teaching is to record baseline functioning in each skill area and to chart progress. Using Lindsley's (1956) behavioral chart, Benhaven staff recorded behavior rate on log graphs. This process gave a better indication of significant changes than more conventional means of monitoring progress such as simple behavior counts on standard graph paper. In addition to precision teaching, the school relied heavily on teaching approaches used with learning-disabled and low-functioning children.

A second approach that has proved useful at Benhaven is the use of sign language and finger spelling. It is suggested that many of the children at Benhaven, if not all, have difficulty in processing information presented to them verbally, in other words, through the auditory mode. The use of sign language has allowed many of the children a means of communicating that they were formerly lacking. Roughly one-half of the thirty-nine or so children at Benhaven could communicate only through means of signing or finger spelling (Lettick, 1979). For sign language to become a communication tool the child must be able to imitate or be taught to imitate, must have or develop some internal language, must be able to learn fine motor skills, and must be able to acquire sequential memory of events.

At Benhaven, the children learned food signs first, then concrete action signs or other functional signs. According to Lettick (1979), autistic children use sign language functionally and rarely use language for pleasure. Those autistic children who initially talked, used language inappropriately before coming to Benhaven. Again, when such children are taught to use language to communicate, they generally will do so only in a functional and concrete fashion and not for pleasure.

However, *one cannot underestimate the importance of these children acquiring receptive and expressive language skills.* One of the major problems of autistic children is the communicative isolation in which they find themselves. Lettick described the joy in the face of an autistic child following a communication between that child and another human being with such force that one could almost experience what it must be like for someone who has never made contact with another human being to do so for the first time.

Another important approach is the gross motor/fine motor, perceptual/motor skill program. Each child engages in a planned set of physical activities designed to improve perceptual/motor functioning. The Kephart Walking Board, swimming, "team" sports, and other planned physical activities are used. The child's development of gross motor skills in concert with another child is a focal point of some importance in this program. Often the approach is as simple as tying two children together and getting one to move so that the other must move with or against the first child. This simple technique is another way of establishing contact, of breaking down the child's isolation. When this first "cooperative" task is accomplished, then other games requiring interaction within the context of game rules become possible. One is reminded of the sociologist George Herbert Mead's analysis of the process of socialization as one of acquiring roles or sets of interactive behaviors that follow societal expectations, or rules of the game. Within Mead's conceptual framework the "play periods" for autistic children became critical learning situations for role acquisition training.

An important program at Benhaven as the age of its population increased was prevocational and vocational training. The older children received training in taking instructions to do simple jobs and in a structured situation were trained to take on increasingly more difficult tasks as their skill levels improved. Benhaven had its own printing press and its structured living setting included farming, gardening, and florist facilities where the children could "learn by doing." Other structured vocational learning experiences were used at Benhaven but all had the same general pattern: take the child at his or her initial level of functioning, and in a highly structured situation work toward specific vocational skill development.

Autistic children, such as those at Benhaven, do not have a good prognosis for leaving a structured situation and going out into the community to function on their own. Most probably these children have central nervous system deficits, which limit the extent of their recovery. Indeed, in spite of the vast array of treatment approaches offered (including medication when required), few Benhaven children were able to cope in a nonstructured environment; however, all of these children's behavior improved markedly.

A Special Education Home-Based Behavioral Program.   Although one could argue, as we have, that severely disturbed children need total treatment, few such programs exist. It would be difficult for parents to find such a program, or if one were found, to be able to get their child into that program. Maurice, Green, and Luce (1996) responded to this need with a manual for behavioral intervention with young autistic children. Much of what they described would be effective in the treatment of other severely disturbed children. According to Green (in Maurice et al.), applied behavioral analysis is the treatment of choice in working with these children. Green held that "the behavior analytic view is that autism is a syndrome of behavioral deficits and excesses that have a neurological basis but are none the less amenable to change in response to specific, carefully programmed, constructive interactions with the environment" (pp. 29–30). Green emphasized the importance not only of a well-defined behavioral approach but also of tailoring that approach to the individual child and implementing it as early as possible. In essence, Green began by advocating approaches similar to those advocated by Lovaas and described earlier in this chapter.

Lovaas (1987) found that children diagnosed as autistic who received forty hours per week of one-to-one behavioral treatment from trained therapists showed marked improvement as compared to children who did not receive this treatment. All children began treatment before age four. Between the ages of six and seven each child's progress was evaluated. Nine children out of nineteen in the intensive treatment group were able to complete regular first grade and scored in the average or above average range on a standard intelligence test. These scores represented an average gain of thirty-seven points per child. Of the remaining ten children in the intensive treatment group, eight completed the first grade in classes for learning-disabled children. Only two children in the intensive treatment group scored in the profoundly mentally retarded range and required placement in classes for autistic and mentally retarded students. Only one child in the control groups successfully completed a regular first grade program.

Maurice et al. (1996) spelled out the methodology required to produce these results. First, the parents of the young autistic child must be willing and intellectually and emotionally able to be an active participant in the behavior program—not an easy task. Second, the parents must find a behavior specialist who can provide the training required for program implementation. Shook (1996) suggested that parents contact a professional who has received accreditation by the Association of Behavior Analysis. In essence the professional must be fully skilled in the behavioral techniques outlined in this text. Third, parents need to find teaching assistants who will aid the parents in implementing the behavior program. Scott (in Maurice et al.) placed a heavy burden on the parents both in selecting and training teaching assistants. We would suggest that a trained professional help in the beginning, both in the selection of assistants and in structuring their training.

To begin treatment the evaluator conducts an individualized behavior assessment of the child, and quantifies concrete and specific behavioral skills and deficits. For example, can the child, placed in a chair, remain seated with feet on the floor and body oriented toward the evaluator? Can the child maintain this position for fifteen seconds? The evaluator, or instructor, records the number of times a fifteen-second criterion is met during a fifteen-minute instructional period. It is clear from this one example that the process of quantification is extremely demanding. The manual produced by Maurice et al. (1996) gives specific guidance concerning what behavioral patterns need to be attended to and changed (see p. 215). Further, Anderson, Taras, and Cannon (1996) held that the assessment should include interviews with people who know the child best, direct observation of the child in the home setting, and use of formal psychological and educational testing.

Maurice et al. (1996) stated that once significant behaviors and general level of functioning are established, a plan for instruction (we would say treatment) for the child is developed. For each target behavior the instructor must define when the behavior is to be learned, give an operational definition of the behavior, indicate when training will occur, specify needed materials, structure steps in a successive approximation toward the desired behavior, and specify criteria to establish that the behavior is learned. It is also required that the instructor be precise in material presentation and clear in his or her response to either correct (usually reinforced) or incorrect (usually not attended to) responses from the child. Finally, the instructor needs to consider how to encourage generalization of correct responses. Note that the instructions given here for behavioral intervention are quite similar to those we offered earlier in this chapter.

Taylor and McDonough (in Maurice et al., 1996, pp. 63–177) detailed a step-by-step teaching program. We cannot reproduce their extensive work here, but encourage the reader to review this work. In an outline format they specified how the parent and the therapist develop a curriculum guide and identify necessary resources for the curriculum, and offered specific guidelines for charting behaviors and documenting change. After the child masters the initial tasks of imitating and attending, much of what followed, but not all, focused on language skill development.

We caution practitioners in the field and parents of severely disturbed children, particularly autistic children, not to view the home-based approach as promising uniform and unequivocal success. Many parents simply cannot effectively respond to the massive demands of the severely disturbed child. Many severely disturbed children do not respond well even to the best treatment. Even so, the approach of Maurice et al. (1996) is likely to produce significant gains for most children who experience their well-defined behavior modification methods. As we noted in our examination of Benhaven, it is our opinion that the approach of Maurice and colleagues is very likely to markedly reduce self-injurious behavior in severely disturbed children.

Controversial Approaches with Severely Disturbed Children

In addition to the time-honored behavioral and special education approaches described in this chapter, two controversial approaches have emerged: facilitated communication and auditory training. Both approaches have enthusiastic advocates and severe critics. Neither is supported by either experimental verification or a long tradition of practical application. However, when struggling to treat or teach children with pervasive development disorders, even controversial techniques require evaluation.

Facilitated Communication.   Crossley and McDonald (1980) first described *facilitated communication* (FC) as an approach to help developmentally disabled children learn to communicate. A teacher, called a facilitator, and a student or client sat side by side at a typewriter or computer keyboard. The facilitator supported the arm of the student who was asked to respond to the facilitator's questions by activating the keys. Initially the FC approach was used to aid children of normal I.Q. who had severe cerebral palsy and could not communicate verbally or through written or typed language. Despite claims by critics that the facilitator was merely guiding the child's arm, Crossley eventually convinced many skeptics. She received custody of her student who had a cerebral palsy following a legal battle. Annie McDonald is listed as Crossley's co-author on her 1980 book on facilitated communication, *Annie's Coming Out*.

Crossley (1988) suggested that facilitated communication could be a useful approach in working with children diagnosed as autistic or indeed any other child who has severe problems with communication. Biklen (1990) initially reported skepticism that such an approach could work with autistic children and then investigated Crossley's approach. He concluded that her FC approach, as part of total treatment of severely disturbed children, could be of great benefit.

Biklen and Schubert (1991) specified their FC approach (see pp. 46–47) which we have summarized as follows:

1. *Physical support.* The facilitator provides physical support under the forearm or at the hand to help the student isolate the index finger or slow the movement of the hand to a selection—for instance, a letter on the keyboard. The physical support also helps the student to initiate the action of pointing, literally to get started, and at the same time conveys emotional support. The facilitator does not assist the student in making a selection of a letter or other target such as a picture or shape.

2. *Initial training/introduction.* Students are encouraged to progress through a series of activities or choices successfully, and are pulled back from incorrect selections. The initial activities include pointing to requested pictures from among several choices (for example, "Point to the car.").

3. *Maintain focus.* The method requires the facilitator to remind the student typing or pointing to keep his or her eyes on the targets, to find a position so that pointing is relatively easy, to maintain isolation of the index finger, and to reduce extraneous actions such as slapping of objects, hand flicking, or pushing the typing device away. When students engage in extraneous actions, the facilitator ignores the behaviors and physically supports the student in redirecting typing or positioning. Similarly, if the student engages in echoed speech, the facilitator asks the student to type what he or she wants to say.

4. *Avoid testing for competence.* The facilitator is not testing the student, but merely providing support for typing or pointing.

5. *Set-work.* Students seem to have an easier time initially with set-work such as fill-in-the-blank activities, math problems, answering questions based on materials they have read, or other activities in which the answers are more predictable than in open-ended dialogue. After the

student has begun to develop fluency with the facilitated communication, personal, open-ended communication is introduced and encouraged.

6. *Fading physical support over time.* This may take a number of months or years. Given this approach, Biklen and Schubert (1991), and Biklen (1990) reported case study data to support their contention that facilitated communication was an important technique to be used with children who had severe problems with communication.

Biklen and Schubert (1991) selected twenty-one students for study to test FC. They reported that all subjects "revealed unexpected literacy and numeracy skills" (p. 46) when they participated in the program described above. Biklen and Schubert provided no statistical analysis that would allow for a more precise evaluation of their work.

Skepticism about FC's effect or lack of effect on the improvement of autistic children's language continues to be an unresolved issue. While many practitioners endorsed the method, controlled research found that the outcomes of FC rarely produced positive results (Rimland, 1993). According to Rimland's 1993 article, in twenty-six controlled studies with 218 subjects, only two studies reported positive outcomes. A controlled study meant that the facilitator could not unconsciously guide the communication. Clearly all of these studies focused on more structured FC exercises and by definition could not speak to the longer and more personal open-ended communications. Furthermore, when the facilitator has knowledge of the correct answer he or she may unconsciously guide the child's hand. In some of Lovaas's language acquisition procedures (Lovaas, 1973) prompting was part of language training. Could FC in part be the product of implicit prompting plus a gradual fading of that prompt? If so, the production of minimally facilitated, personal open-ended communications could be supported as a significant outcome. To determine what if any utility FC might have in the treatment of these children requires additional research.

Nonetheless, autistic children seemed to comply with facilitated communication procedures, which suggested that the approach at least established some contact with the person who served as a facilitating communicator. To keep an autistic child focused on any task for half an hour is very difficult. Since these children often are not responsive to attempts at physical contact or touch, the fact that they are tolerating both in the context of facilitated communication suggests there may be some value in this approach.

"Auditory Training" with Autistic Children. Stehle (1991) stated that "auditory training" was largely responsible for her autistic child's recovery and development into a young adult who may now be described as normal. Certainly one case does not establish a new treatment approach for any type

of psychosocial intervention, but when dramatic results are claimed for even one autistic child, it is useful to examine the approach.

It is well established that many autistic children are extremely sensitive to certain sensory inputs (often auditory inputs). Sensory stimulation produces no negative effect for nonautistic children, but may be extremely aversive and even intolerably intense for autistic children. Auditory training as described by Stehle (1991) seems to involve identifying frequency ranges of sounds to which the child reacts with distress. According to Stehle, Guy Berard, a French ear, nose, and throat specialist, used a technique in which bothersome frequency ranges of sounds were modified. The "treatments" were conducted twice a day, one-half hour per session, for ten days. Hearing tests were given at intervals during the treatment and if treatment was successful, hypersensitive response patterns gradually subsided. Stehle pointed out that this intervention technique did not work for all autistic children. Clearly, auditory training needs to be operationally defined and scientific research needs to be conducted to determine if this approach merits further attention.

It should also be noted that Stehle's child and family received counseling after the "auditory training" and that Stehle had sought out educational experiences for the child that were consistent with the child's increasing abilities and social skills. In essence, Stehle struggled to find a total treatment approach, which included the parent as an active participant in the treatment of her child. The book Stehle wrote stands as a testament to her perseverance and her success. We can only hope that her insights and courage will aid in developing successful programs for working with other autistic and similar children.

Overview of Treatment for Seriously Disturbed Children

Bettelheim's approach focused on the affective and emotional considerations in the treatment of seriously disturbed children. Little explicit attention was focused on behavior or cognitive intervention with these children except within the context of emotional growth. The treatment approach of Bettelheim, far from being ill-defined, was highly structured with a clear focus on initial emotional need satisfaction within the context of emotional growth.

Lovaas's approach focused on the behavior of the child with little explicit attention paid to emotional needs. Cognitive issues were considered within the context of language acquisition. Lovaas advocated many specific techniques to modify behavior but was less clear about what end point to target and how to reach it. Previously Lovaas made the critical error of recommending punishment as an essential part of modifying the behavior of autistic children. However, later work by Lovaas and his associates focused on developing an effective total behavioral repertoire and reduced emphasis on punishment, thus answering objections to their punitive technique.

The educational approach used at Benhaven focused on teaching the child a wide range of cognitive skills in language and academic subjects. The educational approach also trained the child in motor, perceptual, social, and vocational skills. The focus was on *teaching* not *treating*, and on developing the maximal coping patterns of behavior that could be achieved by each child. In 1978 the first author concluded that Benhaven did not focus on explicit approaches to deal with the emotional needs of the children. However, producing behavioral competency in social and cognitive skills may in itself be the most effective means of producing emotional growth in these children.

Conclusion

We see no reason why the theories discussed in this chapter cannot be combined to develop a balanced approach tuned to the notion that all children act, think, and feel. The insights of Bettelheim, Lovaas, and Lettick, among others, could be combined into a coherent approach to treat the whole child. In many important ways these approaches are more similar than dissimilar and complement each other in important ways. All require a highly structured treatment approach. All recognize that treatment for severely disturbed children must be long-term and intensive. Perhaps combining the treatment setting and emotional climate of the Bettelheim approach with specific behavior modification techniques and the special education techniques of Benhaven would put together the best elements of the three approaches and lead to a balanced treatment of the whole child.[4]

All three of the major approaches selected for primary focus in this chapter—psychoanalytic, behavioral, and cognitive—are represented in the treatment of severely disturbed children. We found that although the psychoanalytic approach of Bettelheim focused on emotional issues within the context of need satisfaction, it also considered cognitive and behavioral issues and interpersonal issues related to maximizing human potential. Lovaas and other behavioral and cognitive therapists did not focus either on emotional need satisfaction or interpersonal issues related to maximizing human potential. However, it is hard to read Ferster's analysis of Jean Simons's encounter with an autistic child and not see how these issues were addressed by a successful behavioral therapist/teacher. As for the Benhaven approach, cognitive, behavioral, and other methods were employed within an interpersonal context, and focused on maximizing the human potential of each child. Emotional need satisfaction was not an explicit focus, however.

When viewed as a whole, these three approaches seem to us to have more in common than their advocates would suggest. All are extraordinarily high in concrete structuring of the environment. All focus on the individual child and attempt to create a unique atmosphere and interpersonal environment in which that child's human potential will be fulfilled to the utmost. All recognize that the child must have his or her needs met, and in socially appropriate ways, if that child is to reach his or her potential as a human being.

By focusing on each of our models as applied to each of the three major approaches, these connections can be made clearer. In model one, our intrapsychic model, treatment approaches that focus on establishing basic trust, whether directly as does Bettelheim, or indirectly by increasing the intelligibility of the world as do Lovaas and Benhaven, would promise most success. Further, the treatment process would be lengthy, as our model predicts.

Model two, our interpersonal model, would describe the severely disturbed child as communicating isolation or attack, either through skeptical withdrawal from the world or through a despairing attack on that world. Such behavior until recently would have led to back-ward isolation with the child often in restraints and languishing in his or her feces and urine. Each of the above treatment approaches requires an active interpersonal role, but a rather neutral one, neither distant nor smothering but equally connected to the child's behavior. Again, a nice fit with our interpersonal model.

Finally, if one considers much of the process of socialization as the acquisition of patterns of behavior that fit with social expectations, then all approaches outlined in this chapter are clearly concerned with the child's development of appropriate patterns of behavior. Further, the negative patterns of behavior, particularly at Benhaven, are not seen as manifestations of illness but rather of inappropriate behavior—seen as violations, if you will, of reasonable expectations for the child's behavior.

NOTES

1. The term *treatment* is used here in a neutral fashion—it means any systematic psychosocial approach employed in an attempt to help the person to cope more effectively.

2. The term *mand* implies that some action be taken by the listener as, for example, in command, demand, countermand, and so forth.

3. According to Lettick (in a personal communication with the first author), if a child is busy in a productive way and not ignored, disruptive behaviors are rarely a problem.

4. It is also appropriate to include the approaches of Frieda Fromm-Reichmann (a therapist whose theoretical framework is psychoanalytic) and Virginia Axline (a therapist whose theoretical framework is Rogerian/humanistic), both of which recognize the necessity for intensive long-term and total treatment of severely disturbed children.

13 Group Treatment

Among the options to individual therapy are group approaches: group therapy, couples therapy, and family therapy. Prior to this chapter we have referred to these approaches only in the context of individual or inpatient treatments. The literature for each of these modalities is extensive, and therefore we will restrict our coverage to those group approaches for which empirical support exists and to approaches we have judged to be influential in the development of group treatment.

Group therapy was one of the first alternatives to individual psychotherapy. Pratt (1905—cited in Ettin, 1988) is generally credited with the formation of the first therapy groups (with tubercular patients), although Moreno (1953) is generally credited as the first person to use the term group therapy. According to Ettin, Pratt discovered that when his patients openly shared their distress, their outlook brightened and they followed the self-care instructions and medical guidelines much more carefully than did those patients who did not participate in groups. In addition the health of many of the patients participating in therapy group unexpectedly improved.

It was not until after World War II that group therapy became a generally accepted approach for the treatment of troubled people. The demand for psychotherapeutic treatment for returning veterans was so great that psychiatrists, most of whom used psychoanalytically oriented individual psychotherapy, could not fill the demand. Psychologists, social workers, and other mental health personnel began to practice individual psychotherapy but the demand for treatment remained too great. To satisfy the demand for psychological treatment of the veterans many mental health professionals began to use group approaches. Couples therapy and family therapy emerged somewhat later as alternative treatment modalities (Dicks, 1967; Mittleman, 1948).

The traditional therapy group was and is composed of people who did not know one another but who were troubled, had sought help, and had been selected to be members of a therapy group. The couples or marriage group is composed of the therapist and the couple and may also include a co-therapist.

As opposed to the members of a therapy group, the couples group has a prior relationship history and brings into therapy a set of issues that are in part unique to that couple. In family therapy, not only is there a prior history but also a natural power imbalance. Many couples also have power imbalance issues.

In either couples or family therapy it is common practice to require all family members to attend therapy sessions. The therapist may also see individuals or refer individuals for individual treatment. Many exceptions are made to this rule (Nichols & Schwartz, 1995). We emphasize that if one member of a couple refuses to attend the sessions then the therapist is not conducting couples therapy; such work cannot be done by proxy. In general, resistance to attending meetings on the part of any group member, partner in a couple, or family member will render treatment ineffective.

Group Therapy

Issues in Group Therapy

The first issue that distinguishes group therapy from individual therapy is the unit of analysis. In individual therapy the focus is on the individual and his or her problems. In group therapy the focus is on how people interact in the group, that is, the focus is on the group. In group therapy the interpersonal problems of group members are enacted in the here and now and it is the therapist's job to aid in the resolution of interpersonal difficulties rather than to attend to any individual's intrapsychic conflicts. To focus on an individual and his or her problems to the exclusion of others in a group setting is probably the worst blunder a group therapist can make. One of the most important therapeutic processes within the group is the development of more effective interpersonal skills. The development of such skills means that individuals learn to de-center their self-focus and begin not only to consider their impact on others but also to experience themselves as others experience them.

A second issue to consider is how one might identify different group approaches and specify which work with what specific prototypes of troubled people. Consistent with our analysis throughout the text, highly structured group treatments seem best suited as part of a total treatment approach with severely disturbed individuals (Hogarty et al., 1995). Yalom (1995) described the individuals he would choose for his intensive outpatient group as very similar to those people we have called neurotic. Yalom's approach was less structured than was Hogarty's and treatment duration was fairly long-term. Berne (1961) and Lazarus (1981) selected clients, similar to those of Yalom, and used techniques that often focused on bringing to awareness interpersonal deficits. However, Lazarus often used homogeneous groups composed of people having the same problem and employed cognitive and behavioral interventions related to these specific problems. Rogers (1967) advocated the use of *encounter groups*. These groups were unstructured and short-term and were intended to create an interpersonal climate that would allow personal growth.

To summarize, it seems to us that groups that work most effectively with severely disturbed individuals (suffering from schizophrenia, major depressions, bipolar disorders, core personality disorders, and severe substance abuse) must be highly structured, long-term, and part of a larger treatment program. Group work with people who are severely distressed requires less structure than when working with more troubled people. Treatment is likely to be relatively long-term to be effective. Finally, mildly distressed people would be good candidates for the type of group Rogers described, one in which structure is minimal and the duration of treatment is short.

Another issue of importance for group therapy is the selection and preparation of group members. In general, long-term outpatient groups do well not to mix psychotic and other severely disturbed individuals with neurotic people. Homogeneous groups of people suffering from psychosis, core personality disorders, and severe substance abuse may be effective, but as stated earlier, such group treatments often require additional psychosocial interventions. Yalom (1995) advocated selecting group members who were heterogeneous for problem type. He would omit those individuals we identified above because they would not be homogenous with respect to ego-strength, Yalom's second criterion for selection. We hold that individuals selected to participate in encounter groups should be neither severely disturbed nor severely distressed, as are neurotic individuals, particularly symptomatic neurotics. All individuals joining whatever kind of group should be screened, told what to expect in the particular group they are joining, and clearly informed of the ground rules of group psychotherapy, including confidentiality, punctual attendance, and participation in the group process.

The Encounter Group

We begin our analysis of group treatment with a discussion of encounter groups. The ancestor of the encounter group was the T (or training) Group. In 1946 the state of Connecticut commissioned Lewin, a famous social psychologist, to train people to deal with conflicts related to racial prejudice. The ultimate aim was to change attitudes through discussion in a small group format. The hope was that the principles effective in changing attitudes, discovered in small groups, could allow for the reduction of prejudice in the general population and promote fair employment practices.

To implement these objectives Lewin placed ten people together and told them to discuss an issue and reach a conclusion. No one was appointed leader. Social scientists observed the interactions and described how different individuals interacted with one another. The focus was on *process*, meaning the way people interacted, and not on the content or what was discussed. (For example: Did person B interrupt? Was person C silent?)

Following the group meeting the social scientists got together and discussed the interactional patterns. What they noted was that the group process had incredibly powerful effects on the group members. When the group rejected a member the effect on that person was devastating. Since all group members were leaders and did not know each other before the experiment, this effect was totally unexpected. Group members expressed a strong desire to attend the meetings where the social scientists discussed the group process. The group members reported that they found it very helpful to discover how they came across in the groups. Many were moved to tears and stated that the experience had profoundly changed them (Benne, 1964).

Rogers (1967) extended the T-Group concept and championed what he called the encounter group. In an encounter group there was no designated leader. Instead there was a professional *facilitator* whose task was to comment on the group's process. The facilitator would not direct the group but rather would comment on how a particular person said something or how the group as a whole was functioning. There was no preconceived goal for the group except for the ambiguous notion that the group process could foster personal growth.

Initially, encounter group interactions were characterized by what Rogers called "cocktail party talk." At some point a group member would express something personal, and there was a considerable amount of ambivalence for the other group members about what to do with this disclosure. According to Rogers (1967) the first expression of "here-and-now" feelings was often a negative comment about another group member or the facilitator. Rogers stated that after such an event it was likely that group members would begin to express important personal material. If the expression of such material proved to be safe for the members then the group could develop into one that could produce personal growth for the members.

In encounter groups there was a gradual development of immediate and personal reactivity of group members to each other. For example, if one member was critical of another member, then the second person might say, "That really hurt me." It was not the content of the criticism to which the person reacted; rather, the criticism elicited a *process* response.

As these groups developed, Rogers (1967) found that group members shared a genuine capacity to react to others' pain in helpful ways. Perhaps it is this group acceptance that allows a member to develop self-acceptance. Rogers held that self-acceptance was the beginning of change. Only when a person can experience himself or herself as he or she is does change become possible. However, it should be noted that in such groups the confrontations between group members were not infrequently brutal. We hold that such confrontations often need to be put into a different context by the facilitator if the group cannot resolve the confrontation. Rogers held that most encounter groups produced positive results although he lamented that the results often did not last.

Yalom (1995) and his associates (Liberman, Yalom, & Miles, 1973) reported that some outcomes of encounter groups were much less positive than Rogers (1967) indicated. According to Liberman et al., although the majority of Stanford students (70%) in their study reported that the encounter group experience was positive, 8% suffered psychological injury. On more objective measures of change only one-third of the participants in the Liberman et al. study improved while two-thirds did not. The investigators were able to identify the encounter group leaders who most frequently produced positive outcomes and those leaders who most frequently produced psychological casualties. Most effective were leaders who were perceived as caring and genuine, who could identify feelings in others, and who could allow others to own those feelings. Leaders who were challenging and controlling, and who were perceived as being without warmth and understanding produced the greatest number of psychological casualties.

Although Liberman et al. (1973) attributed both positive and negative results to the quality of the group leaders, they did not screen the members for psychopathology. In addition to the study's focus on the group leader we suggest participants should be screened for psychopathology before accepting them as members of an encounter group. It is possible that part of the variance in the outcomes of the Liberman et al. study was due to the effect of the encounter experience on people who were already fragile.

Berne: Transactional Analysis

Eric Berne (1961, 1964) developed one approach intended for troubled people that has been important in the development of group psychotherapy. Berne (1966) stated that his model of intrapsychic organization (*parent, adult,* and *child*) was not a metaphor for Freud's model (*ego, superego,* and *id*). In Berne's model only when a person interacts and displays behaviors that are typical of either *adults* (reality-based problem-solving behaviors), *parents* (superior and judgmental behaviors), or *children* (help-seeking and immature behaviors) are these terms appropriately used. Berne held that Freud's ego, id, and superego were not operationally defined and are therefore vague and not scientifically useful.

In spite of Berne's denial, his structural concepts can easily be framed as metaphors for Freud's concepts; that is as interpersonal translations of Freud's intrapsychic structural concepts. The *adult* is an interpersonal metaphor for the *ego,* that part of the intrapsychic structure Freud had defined as governed by the *reality principal.* The *child* is a metaphor for the *id,* the instinctual and primitive part of Freud's intrapsychic structure. The *parent* is a metaphor for the *superego,* the judgmental part of Freud's intrapsychic structure. Berne's concepts gave group therapists a ready vehicle for the interpretation of dysfunctional interpersonal interactions.

Berne named his approach *transactional analysis* and stated that pathological transactions were the subject matter of psychotherapy. This structural analysis makes transactional analysis a therapeutic approach uniquely suited to group work. According to Berne, whichever *ego state* is operative is the transactional stimulus that leads to a transactional response. Transactions are *complementary* when the response is the expected one and *crossed* when the response is not the expected one.

Berne (1961) offered four primary patterns, two complementary and two crossed transactions. In *Type I* complementary transactions, person one frames his or her communication from the *adult ego state* (asking for information, giving information, and responding as equal to equal). Person two responds by giving information or acknowledging the receipt of information, again equal to equal. *Type II* complementary communications are when one person gives a *parent* message to another person's *child*. For instance, if someone begins crying (a child response) the other could say, "There, there, it's okay," (a parent response).

Crossed transactions, *Type I*, occur when one person initiates a response in the *adult* mode and the other responds in a *child* mode. The example Berne (1961) gave was, "One day Camellia . . . announced that she had told her husband that she was not going to have intercourse with him anymore and that he could go out and find some other woman. Rosita asked curiously: 'Why did you do that?' Whereupon Camellia burst into tears and replied: 'I tried so hard and then you criticize me'" (p. 91). Berne's interpretation of this transaction is as follows. Rosita gave an adult response to which Camellia responded as a child. In *Type II* crossed communications, the initial response is an adult one but the other's response is a parent one (often critical). Complementary responses tend to be continued while crossed responses tend to terminate the conversation.

Transactional analysis per se dealt first with structural analysis—how do people in the group react? Do they respond as adults, children, or parents? What destructive transactions occur repetitively—defined by Berne as *games*? Berne referred to larger patterns of nonauthentic transactions as *scripts*. Games and scripts are identified, analyzed, and explored with the intent being to get people to give up their games and change their scripts and live authentically.

Yalom: The Traditional Outpatient Group

Although Berne was important in the development of group therapy and still has many supporters, we feel that his approach was often mechanical and was frequently reduced to one-upmanship by the therapist. We will turn to Irvin Yalom (1995) as the theorist whose approach addressed the issues of games and duplicity in interpersonal interactions but did so in a much less contrived and mechanical fashion than did Berne.

Yalom stated that psychological dysfunction is in part a function of unsatisfactory interpersonal relationships. He held that the therapeutic group is ideally suited to provide a matrix within which satisfactory and satisfying interpersonal relations can be achieved. The focus of the group is to allow individuals to become aware of their interpersonal behaviors, their impact on others, and the effect of feedback from others on each individual's sense of self and self-worth.

Yalom (1995) pointed out that the selection of group members and their preparation for participating in the group was an essential first step in creating an effective therapy group. The intent of the selection process is to ensure that the group will not be stillborn. Prospective members are asked to describe their problem and to tell what they know about therapy groups. Many misconceptions exist about such groups and their effectiveness. Often people feel that the group is a second choice and that "real" psychotherapy is done individually. Each person is informed that the group approach is just as effective as individual therapy, and in many instances is more effective.

Yalom held that there is often a fit between the kind of issues the person brings to the group and the unique opportunities for interpersonal learning that exist in the group. The potential group member is informed about how the issues that he or she described are suited for such interpersonal learning. The potential group member is informed that the group may seem unstructured and that change is often slow, and is asked to give the group about twelve weeks before deciding that it doesn't work for him or her. Ground rules are discussed, including that one come to scheduled meetings, come on time, and participate in the group discussions. Issues of confidentiality and association with fellow members outside the group are discussed. Finally the therapist emphasizes the power of the group and attempts to instill hope that the group will aid the prospective member.

Yalom stated that once group members are selected (five to ten members, with eight being optimum) an agreed-on time for regular meetings is determined and a meeting place is established. For the latter, all that is required is that the room be private with enough space for people to sit in a circle. In addition, the seating should be comfortable and there should be no table in the room. During the initial session the therapist and co-therapist (if any) introduce themselves and in general terms go over the ground rules.

After this the therapist remains quiet and, typically, a tense silence begins. Although the silence seems to last forever even to the therapist, eventually someone begins to talk. As the group interacts the therapist begins the first task: culture building. Yalom (1995) identified this process as primarily one of developing norms that would lead to the emergence of a cohesive group.

Yalom held that norms are the unwritten rules that govern the interactions within the group. If the desired implicit ground rules are developed, then the group members will increasingly accept active involvement in the group process, engage in self-disclosure, express dissatisfaction with their current modes of behavior, develop nonjudgmental acceptance of others, as well as a desire for understanding and an eagerness for change. The therapist will model these norms, an important part of the therapist's work. It is important that the therapist be active in the initial session and be ready to do so in later sessions if the circumstances require it.

After the initial session the therapist's primary function is to maintain the group. As the therapy passes through phases of group development (*forming, storming, norming,* and *performing*—Tuckman, 1965) the therapist must deal with emerging issues that threaten to destroy the group. Initially the group may opt to interact in superficial ways. The therapist must not allow such behaviors to develop as a norm or the group will not develop past banal interactions. Similarly, during the storming period negative or attacking interactions should not be allowed to go unresolved. The reader will note that these operations by the therapist are directly related to the formation of norms that will continue the development of the therapeutic group into a *cohesive* group characterized by open and helpful interactions. Later in the group's development the therapist must prevent the formation of collations, which would break the group into noncohesive parts. As the group becomes cohesive the therapist focuses on the facilitation of interpersonal learning. None of these tasks is exclusive to any one stage in the group's lifespan, although they more commonly occur in the sequence described above.

The essential task of the therapist according to Yalom (1995) is to implement the *here and now* approach to group process. When a group member does anything that diverts the interaction from what is currently going on among the group members, the therapist must return the group to the here and now. For instance, if one group member gives a recitation of his or her own personal history (a *there and then* statement, not a here and now statement) the therapist must steer the conversation back to the here and now. A typical there and then statement is, "My father never loved me." This group member has excluded the other members from the interaction and has turned the interactional pattern into a dialogue with the therapist. The therapist might respond to this remark by asking the group member, "Who in the group reminds you of your father?" This brings the group back into the interactional pattern.

The second part of the here and now intervention is to reflect back on what has just happened. This is a *process analysis* that focuses on how people are interacting *at this moment.* The therapist might say, "What do you (the person who made the there and then remark) want to say to him (the group member who reminded the 'there and then' person of his or her father) right

now." The therapist might ask the group "what just happened?", thus direct-
ing the members into discussing the current group process. Various group
members might challenge the first member's perception of the other as being
like his or her father or they might react to the first member's expressive style.
The therapist might comment on how others perceive the first member, and
explore how these evaluations impacted on that person's self-evaluation.

Within this context interpersonal learning occurs and group cohesion is
increased. Although we referred to this process as the here and now technique, we need to emphasize that it is not a mechanical device. It is a stylistic
approach sensitively keyed to the particular priority of group therapy to
remain focused on the group as a whole.

If the group has developed into an effective one, then its members will
have gained the sense that only they can change the world that they have
created, that there is little danger in doing so, that change is required to get
what they want, and that change is possible. If Yalom is right, such changes
will be structural. That is, the ex-group members will not only have changed
their behavior but will also be able to sustain those changes in the face of a
world that is often difficult. We recommend fully exploring Yalom's 1995
work on group therapy; we have only skimmed the surface of his detailed
analysis of the process of group therapy.

Lazarus: Behavioral Group Therapy

We have chosen Lazarus (1981) as an example of a cognitive-behavioral
approach to group therapy. Although Lazarus in the main worked with people
who were similar to those with whom Yalom worked, there were several
significant differences between their approaches. Lazarus insisted that behavioral and cognitive approaches and explanatory principles could account for
any and all changes that occurred in group therapy. Further, he held that
certain problems, such as lack of assertiveness, trying to stop smoking, and
trying to control weight could best be handled in homogeneous groups.

Lazarus viewed group therapy as the vehicle of choice for individuals whose primary issues were interpersonal difficulties. He used his
B.A.S.I.C.-ID analysis to make this determination (see Chapter 6 in this text).
He held that consensual validation, occasions for vicarious learning, and a
variety of modeling opportunities are unique to the group experience. He
states that cognitive and behavioral techniques such as role-playing and
behavior-rehearsal "are enhanced by the psychodramatic nuances that groups
provide. . ." (Lazarus, 1981, p. 203).

Lazarus agreed with Yalom (1995) that severely disturbed individuals
should not be accepted into outpatient groups. Once Lazarus had formed his
groups he then applied behavioral and cognitive techniques as described in
Chapter 6. He stated that the methods he used most frequently were behavior-rehearsal, praise, modeling, the empty-chair technique, and anger expres-

sion. In spite of his emphasis on behavioral and cognitive techniques, Lazarus used process material when group members were distorting the group inter-action because of "hidden agendas."

Lazarus usually limited his groups to twenty sessions. He encouraged clients who felt distressed at the end of therapy to join another group or to seek individual therapy. Following therapy Lazarus also encouraged each client to monitor his or her feelings and actions with the focus on increasing that individual's quality of life.

Couples Therapy

An important alternative to individual therapy or group therapy is couples therapy. When one's primary issues concern one's ongoing and intimate relations with another, then couples therapy is indicated. Couples literature has evolved to the point that some specification of which approaches work and with whom is possible. The seminal review of Baucom, Shoham, Mueser, Daiuto, and Stickle (1998) as well the work of Jacobson and Addis (1993), Dunn and Schwebel (1995), Snyder and Wills (1989), and Goldman and Greenberg (1992) are only a few of the publications that have made our analysis possible. As we have argued throughout this text the particular approach used in couples therapy, as in other therapies, requires the therapist to provide more structure and for the duration of the therapy to be longer as the severity of the disorder increases. To support these contentions we will examine the outcome literature of couples therapy.

Before examining which approaches work and with whom, we will describe general guidelines to help the therapist determine whether couples therapy is appropriate and what level of structure and techniques may work. The first issue is whether a couple is a couple or not. Often two people marry or live together without an emotional tie, without commitment, and without sexual interest in each other. In such circumstances, when a couple comes to a therapist often the task is to aid these two people to separate. Lazarus (1981) made a similar point when he said:

> I was once of the opinion that almost any two people could achieve happiness if they adhered to basic ground rules (such as not labeling, blaming, judging, accusing, fault finding, demanding, ignoring, or attacking, and instead praising, listening, discussing, thanking, helping, and forgiving). I have come to the conclusion that a friendly coexistence is not the same as a worthwhile marriage. This requires more than teamwork, common goals, and respectful dealings. At the very least we would add strong affection, attraction, caring and some consensus in matters of taste and interest. (p. 179)

However, no matter how dysfunctional the relationship, if the couple is committed to that relationship then the therapist begins by helping them to sustain it. The exception to this guideline is when one partner is abusing the other. Under such circumstances extreme caution is required; we do not sanction couples therapy in situations where abuse is occurring. In these cases the abused partner should be advised to contact the police and to seek a safe shelter. If the individual refuses these suggestions then he or she should be informed that the therapist must notify the proper authorities. If both partners still want to maintain the relationship, we would recommend that both people seek individual therapy as well as couples therapy. The abusing partner would need to demonstrate anger control in a series of graded exposures before the couple could resume living together. Even with these cautions the therapist is advised to be suspicious of any behavior that suggests abuse regardless of what the couple says.

The second issue that couples must face is the level of distress or disturbance that exists in their relationship for one or both of the partners. When one or both of the partners suffer from psychological problems, then individual therapy and often medication must supplement the couples therapy. When the couple's relationship is characterized by frequent and extreme confrontations, periods of estrangement, and frequent patterns of interaction that leave the partners angry and depressed, then the initial focus of the therapist is to reduce the chaos and establish some nondestructive communication between the partners.

When the two individuals are indeed a couple and the couple is not in a continuing emotional crisis, then couples work usually focuses on the partners' communication. Initially the process involves establishing accurate communication and reducing punitive and withdrawing interactions. Once partners can ask for what they want, can talk directly to their partner, have reduced punitive interactions, and are addressing the practical problems of living, then the focus shifts to issues of intimacy. Many of the approaches to facilitate the emergence of couple intimacy have already been discussed in Chapter 3 in the section Gestalt Therapy and Problems of Intimacy; we will discuss these approaches in the next section of this chapter.

Again we caution the reader not to apply what we have outlined here in a mechanical fashion. Issues that appear early in the couples therapy process may reappear later and require a return to a more structured approach. Communication may break down and often does. Crises in everyday life may lead to the reemergence of old and destructive patterns. For the therapist to exercise flexibility and accurate judgement requires frequent changes in therapeutic technique.

The first treatment approach we will consider for distressed or disturbed couples is *emotion-focused couples therapy.* According to Snyder and Wills (1989), this therapeutic approach used strategies and techniques common to Gestalt and client-centered interventions. According to Goldman and Greenberg (1992), the couples effectively treated by Johnson and Greenberg's emotion focused therapy (Johnson & Greenberg, 1985a) were less disturbed than couples in their 1992 study (Goldman & Greenberg).

An emotion-focused couples therapy approach involved nine steps (Goldman & Greenberg, 1992), which we will condense and paraphrase. First, the couple's issues were identified, explored, and defined. Specifically, the therapist focused on discovering negative interactive cycles and helping clients to both experience and accept—or own—their emotional reactions that were the causes of the automatic negative interactive cycles. The negative cycles and the emotional reactions were redefined in a more positive fashion. For instance, a partner's strident demands for support were reframed as heartfelt and legitimate expressions of need for support. The therapist also encouraged the clients to ask each other for what they wanted and to ask in a more positive fashion. Both partners must learn how to state their needs and, with the therapist's aid, find new non-punitive ways to gratify them within the context of the couple's relationship. Once these positive interactional patterns emerged the task of the therapist was to aid the clients in solidifying these gains. Specific techniques of clarification, reflection of affect, encouragement of affect expression, reframing, and certain Gestalt approaches such as the use of *I* and *thou* language (see Chapter 3) were part of the therapeutic process. Successful therapy should lead to what Bowlby (1980) called a stable attachment (see Chapter 2).

This form of couples therapy usually followed a short-term treatment format. In the Goldman and Greenberg (1992) study treatment was limited to ten sessions. Individual practitioners may require a different number of sessions but it is customary for emotion-focused couples therapy to be short-term. Significant long-term effects of this approach were found for less severely distressed clients (Johnson & Greenberg, 1985a) but not for more severely distressed clients (Goldman & Greenberg, 1992). However, Goldman and Greenberg found that emotion-focused couples therapy produced initial changes consistent with those of *systemic couples therapy* (a more directive approach that used some of the techniques of the Milan School of family therapy, in Palazzoli, Boscolo, Cecchin, & Prata, 1978—referred to in the Family Therapy section of this chapter). Providing additional structure may be an important component of the long-term efficacy of systemic couples therapy with more severely disturbed couples.

The second approach to couples therapy that we will discuss is a psychoanalytically oriented approach, *insight-oriented marital therapy* (IOMT). According to Snyder and Wills (1989), this approach has as its goals the resolution of unconscious sources of marital conflict and the facilitation of relatively conflict-free interaction between the partners. Although IOMT is less structured than cognitive or behavioral approaches to couples therapy it is more structured than emotion-focused couples therapy. For example, Snyder and Wills stated that therapy, ". . . may include instruction in listening and empathy as well as modification of grossly destructive communication patterns" (p. 39). Snyder and Wills were equally clear that neither systematic training (through modeling, feedback, and reinforcement of desired behaviors) nor structured cognitive interventions (mainly Ellis's 1968 ABC approach—see Chapter 6) were employed. Snyder has also developed specific information in the form of manuals for both insight-oriented marital therapy and the version of behavioral marital therapy approaches employed in the Snyder and Wills (1989) study.

In the Snyder and Wills (1989) study the IOMT therapists directed their attention to issues of marital conflict revealed in emotional conflicts that were not consciously known by the partners. The focus of therapy was to allow the couple to become aware of unresolved developmental issues (what we have referred to elsewhere as *fixations*) and other emotion-based issues. One example of such couples issues is the negative interactional patterns that Berne (1961) referred to as *games* and that Snyder and Wills referred to as *collusive interactions.* Another example is what Snyder and Wills called *irrational role assignments,* for example, a demand on the wife that the house must always be clean. Snyder and Wills also cited incongruent role expectations as examples of collusive interactions, such as "you must always be strong and show your feelings." Finally, Snyder and Wills identified maladaptive relationship rules, such as, "you must always do what I tell you."

Another effective approach with couples whose level of distress was similar to that of the clients in the Snyder and Wills (1989) study was the *behavioral marital therapy approach* (BMT). Baucom et al. (1998) stated that BMT refers to a group of related approaches and not to a single technique. This statement could be made for all "types" of therapy unless one is referring to a single study or a manual-driven study in which a set of protocols were closely followed. Baucom et al. held that interventions based on social learning principles could be classed under the BMT rubric. Specifically, BMT emphasized teaching couples how to negotiate (quid pro quo contracting—"if you give me this then I will give you that"), how to engage in constructive speaking, how to listen empathetically, conflict resolution techniques, and the importance of sharing recreational activities. Direct training in communication skills was also employed, with the therapist reinforcing desired responses and modeling desired behaviors. The focus of BMT was on the present, and on the problematic interactions of which the clients were aware. The clients were also asked to complete homework assignments and to apply the behavior principles they had learned in the therapy sessions. The duration of therapy was relatively short-term. For example, in the Baucom, Sayers, and Sher study (1990) the couples completed twelve sessions. For readers interested in more specific details of Baucom and associates' BMT approach, see Baucom and Epstein (1990).

This approach has been found to be effective with the category of clients whom we would call neurotic. However, the effects of BMT may not last, as evidenced by the results of the Jacobson, Schmaling, and Holtzworth-Munroe study (1987). Further, Snyder, Mangrum, & Wills (1993) reported that 38% of the couples that received BMT were divorced after four years while only 3% of those couples that received insight-oriented marital therapy were divorced after four years. Snyder et al. attributed the differences to the failure of most BMT approaches (but not all—see Baucom et al., 1990) to deal concretely with hidden and distressing emotions centrally implicated in the couples' conflicts.

Before reviewing couples work with respect to sexual dysfunctions, a few cautions are required. According to Katchadourian (1989), one-third of the cases of sexual dysfunction may have physical causes. More specifically 40% of the cases of erectile dysfunction may be caused by physical factors. Trauma, including surgery, may lead to sexual dysfunction. For instance, prostate surgery can damage nerves that supply blood to the penis, thus preventing erections. Improperly repaired damage to the vagina (such as improperly repaired episiotomies) often causes women pain during coitus, as can medications that prevent lubrication. In addition medications (including many blood-pressure medications) can cause erectile dysfunctions. These are only a few examples of the many physiologically based causes of sexual dysfunction. Before implementing any psychosocial intervention, therefore, possible biological causes should be explored and ruled out.

In addition to this caution are three others that must be employed by therapists who wish to effectively use couples therapy in the treatment of individuals who have sexual dysfunctions. First, if there are unresolved intrapsychic wounds that directly impact on sexual activity (such as childhood sexual abuse or rape), these issues must be directly addressed. Individual psychotherapy may be essential to resolve the intrapsychic conflict (Katchadourian, 1989). Second, if the couple is emotionally disengaged then it is unlikely that couples therapy will help either the relationship or the sexual dysfunction of the affected partner (Hahlweg, Schindler, Revenstorf, & Brengelmann, 1984). Finally, more severely disturbed couples are less likely to profit from couples therapy (Snyder, Mangrum, & Wills, 1993). None of these issues is unique to sexual dysfunction but apply in general to the effectiveness of couples therapy.

Couples therapy when one or both of the partners suffer from sexual dysfunction has been more successful in dealing with female sexual dysfunctions than with male sexual dysfunctions. The earlier works of LoPiccolo and Lobitz (1972) and Masters and Johnson (1970) may be considered a form of couples therapy. They reported success for treating a variety of female sexual dysfunctions, including lifelong orgasmic disorders. Both approaches included forms of direct sexual practice (for example, LoPiccolo & Lobitz, masturbation training; Masters & Johnson, partner-assisted directed practice). In addition Masters and Johnson advocated *sensate focus*. Couples are given homework assignments to give each other mutual pleasure through touch while avoiding genital touching. Partners were also told not to have sex. Esner-Hershfield and Kopel (1979) reported that LoPiccolo's *sexual skills training* was more effective when done with partners, than when done alone. In addition Zimmer (1987) used behavior marital therapy for eight weeks prior to the implementation of twelve weeks of the Masters and Johnson program. The target population of Zimmer's study consisted of couples where the women were identified as having sexual dysfunctions that were not lifelong. Also, these couples were maritally distressed in addition to having a sexual dysfunction. In this study the combined approach was superior to relaxation training program and the Masters and Johnson program or to a period of time prior to treatment referred to as a wait-list control group.

Baucom et al. (1998) were less optimistic with respect to male sexual dysfunctions, particularly erectile dysfunctions. Baucom et al. held that men may not be willing to emotionally expose themselves with respect to sexual dysfunction, which could in part account for the general lack of positive results for the treatment of male sexual dysfunctions. Baucom et al. also reported that the number of medical options for impotency problems are uncomfortable or unpleasant but allow men to avoid dealing with emotional issues related to sexual dysfunction.

Couples Assisted or Family Assisted Therapy

Baucom et al. (1998) viewed any intervention in which the primary focus was on one partner or one family member to be either couples assisted or family assisted therapy. They included couples sex therapy as couples assisted therapy. However, we restrict the modifier, *assisted therapy,* to either family or couples interventions in which the more troubled person is the primary focus of treatment. The other partner or family members are included when the pattern of interaction within the family or couple contributes directly or indirectly to the dysfunctional behavior, thoughts, or feelings of the troubled person. If the other family members or the other partner are not severely troubled they can serve as surrogate therapists or become a direct part of the therapeutic process. These couples assisted or family assisted approaches have been found useful when the troubled person is suffering from obsessive-compulsive disorder, agoraphobia, depression, alcohol abuse, or schizophrenia.

The couples assisted and family assisted approaches that Baucom et al. (1998) reviewed for the treatment of OCD and agoraphobia were assisted *exposure* and *response prevention* (see Chapters 6 and 7). In the main, no advantage was gained by teaching the nonaffected individuals to participate in exposing the troubled person to stressful stimuli or by enlisting the aid of nonaffected individuals in preventing the occurrence of the undesired response to these techniques without assistance of family members or the nonaffected partner. In particular the effectiveness of exposure and response prevention with OCD, which has proved effective in treating compulsive behavior in individual therapy (DeRubeis & Crits-Cristoph, 1998), was not aided by the assisted format. However, when the couple received communication training in addition to exposure training the agoraphobic partner reported less anxiety and was able to leave home unassisted more frequently than agoraphobic individuals who had received partner-assisted exposure and relaxation training. *Communication training* consists of teaching people to engage in constructive speaking, empathic listening, and conflict resolution (Jacobson & Margolin, 1979; Stuart, 1980).

Baucom et al. (1998) reviewed research that has demonstrated the effectiveness of couples assisted and family assisted approaches for more severely disturbed people. They reported a complex interaction with respect to couples assisted therapy in which the affected partner was diagnosed as suffering from depression. However, this approach to the treatment of depression, as was the case for families and couples in which the affected partner was suffering from alcoholism or schizophrenia, were often more successful than individual therapy or other unaided treatments.

In cases when one of the partners was diagnosed as suffering from a dysthymic disorder or a major depression, the specific couples assisted approaches cited by Baucom et al. (1998) were BMT (described in this chapter) and a couples version of interpersonal therapy (described in Chapter 10). These approaches were often compared with individual cognitive therapy (see Chapters 6 and 10). Couples assisted approaches were superior to individual therapy when marital distress preceded the onset of depression and when the couple reported that they were having interpersonal difficulties in their marriage.

Baucom et al. (1998) cited two sets of studies in which behaviorally oriented couples approaches were used as part of the comprehensive treatment of alcoholism: Azrin and colleague (Azrin, 1976; Hunt & Azrin, 1973) and O'Farrell and colleagues (O'Farrell et al., 1996; O'Farrell, Cutter, & Floyd, 1985). These two approaches went by the acronyms CRA (the Community Reinforcement approach used by Azrin) and CALM (Counseling for Alcoholic Marriages used by O'Farrell). Both included the use of disulfiram (Antabuse), a drug that makes one ill if one is taking the drug and drinks alcohol. Perhaps the encouragement of the drinker's spouse will lead to sustained disulfiram use but we are skeptical (see Chapter 9). In any event, therapists are advised to involve the drinker's spouse in the treatment as part of a more comprehensive treatment program (see Chapter 9).

We will not comment on the family assisted approaches cited by Baucom et al. (1998). The problem with Baucom et al. is that they did not cite Hogarty et al. (1995) in their review. In this study Hogarty et al. employed all of the components of the treatments of schizophrenia listed in the studies reviewed by Baucom et al. (for example, psychoeducation; the lowering of expressed emotion, particularly negative emotions; and coping-skills training). We have more fully discussed the Hogarty et al. approach elsewhere (see Chapter 11).

Family Therapy

Overview

In family therapy the family is the unit of analysis (occasionally even the extended family). Novices and inexperienced family therapists must become familiar with the technical language of family therapy. Most approaches to family share certain theoretical concepts. First, the most disturbed individual in the family is referred to as the *identified patient* (IP). The meaning of this term is that the troubled individual is a part of a family system and that his or her symptoms serve the purpose of maintaining the current dysfunctioning family system. The second commonality in family therapy approaches is that the family is viewed as a system and that all family members maintain that system with their interactional patterns serving primarily to maintain the pathology of the IP. If the family is dysfunctional (and in the heyday of family therapy, to have a disturbed family member was proof that the family was dysfunctional), then the family structure must be changed.

Early in the analysis of infantile autism many psychoanalysts held that the mother of the child caused the child's autism. Mothers of autistic children were referred to as "ice box" mothers and were said to be cold and distant from their children. However, there was little evidence to support this conjecture and a great deal of harm was done to many women whose only sin was that they had an autistic child. Similarly many family therapists held that the dysfunctional family caused schizophrenia. Hogarty et al. (1995), and a great deal of empirical evidence (see Chapter 11), place such an analysis in the same category as that in which the mother was said to cause infantile autism. Rather than try to change the family, Hogarty et al. tried to aid the family in dealing with its schizophrenic member, and suggested that the disturbed person would also need individual attention and medication in addition to family therapy. However, if the family and its structure does contribute to any family member's emotional difficulties, then family therapy can be a very useful intervention strategy.

Kazdin and Weisz (1998) stated that commonly employed family techniques were . . . "joining, reframing, enactment, paradox, and assigning specific tasks" (p. 7) (to be completed outside the therapy sessions). These techniques were borrowed from structural family therapy (Minuchin, 1974) and strategic family therapy (Haley, 1976). The focus for these techniques is on patterns of interaction within the family. The family is the unit of analysis and, as is the case for couples or group therapy, to focus on any family member to the exclusion of others is a therapeutic blunder.

According to Minuchin (1974) *joining* is the first and most important part of family therapy. It means that the therapist strives to be accepted into the family as an active participant. Further, the therapist attempts to join the family in a leadership position. One cannot effectively join a family by confronting its members, however. In fact, Minuchin often accommodated the most powerful of the hostile family members, and after he had formed a positive connection with that member he would try to engage the other family members who had been passive or withdrawn.

Barker (1986) defined *reframing* as "a process whereby new meaning is given to a behavior, a sequence of interactions, a relationship or some other feature of the current situations" (p. 73). Often this means taking a negative statement or event and redefining it in a positive way. Barker gave an example of reframing drawn from the work of Bandler and Grinder. According to Barker,

> Bandler and Grinder (1982, pp. 5–7) cite as an example the case of a woman who liked to have her carpets perfectly clean and smooth. Whenever there were any footprints on them she became upset. She was asked to imagine that the carpets were perfectly clean, fluffy and unmarked but it was pointed out to her that this meant that her loved ones were nowhere about and that she was quite alone. . . . (p. 108)

The therapist in the above example also emphasized how nice it would be for this woman to have her loved ones around her. The woman's view of carpets having to be perfect was changed to the need to be with her loved ones.

Reframing in family therapy often occurs during the implementation of an *enactment*. The therapist has observed a problematic behavior sequence. He or she then intentionally activates this sequence but intervenes to develop a new way of experiencing and attributing meaning to the behavior sequence. For example, if a mother continually picks on one child for being untidy the therapist might ask the mother to more fully describe her untidy child. If the mother berated the child the therapist might say, "Come on, Mom, he is just a little boy and he needs your help. Maybe you could praise him when he puts up a toy or puts his clothes in the dirty clothes bin." The therapist might then direct a comment to the child, "Does Mom ever praise you for cleaning up your room?"

Paradox according to Nichols and Schwartz (1995) is a controversial procedure based on encouraging undesirable behaviors (which can be referred to as symptoms). Haley (1963) held that when a troubled person employed a symptom the covert purpose was to control the others or the other with whom he or she was interacting. An example given by Nichols and Schwartz described a wife who incessantly accused her husband of various infidelities. Her anger led him to become more distant and defensive, thus further exacerbating her jealousy. The paradoxical instructions to the wife were to direct her to markedly increase her expressions of jealousy. The wife refused to hurt her husband further, thus reducing his anger and withdrawal. The quick fix or magic bullet character of this technique may seduce therapists into overusing it and lead them to become puppet masters rather than effective agents of change.

The Milan School of family therapy, a variant of Haley's strategic therapy, frequently used paradoxical interventions (Palazzoli et al., 1978). The family was to meet with the therapist once a month for ten sessions. Each session was highly structured. The therapist (or therapists) working with the family was observed by other therapists from behind a one-way mirror. During the session the observing therapists formed hypotheses about the family's problems and made decisions about the course of action to be taken. After about forty minutes the therapists working with the family and the observers met in the absence of the family and formed a course of action. The therapist (or therapists) then met with the family who received treatment. The treatment usually consisted of positive conation, reframing, and instructions to perform a ritual, usually a form of paradoxical intention. Nichols and Schwartz (1995) commented that often after the families received the treatment they did not keep subsequent appointments and did not return.

Another technique common to many family therapy approaches is to assign tasks to the family. Task assignment may take the form of developing a specific contract between family members or it may require the family members to practice behaviors modeled in the therapy session. An assigned task may also be a paradoxical task, as described in Chapter 3.

Strategic and Structural Family Therapy

Strategic family therapy owes much of its development to the work of Haley (1976). Haley felt that much of the identified patient's pathology was caused by his or her use of symptoms to control the behavior of other family members. Haley held that a great deal of the negative interactive patterns in the family could be understood in terms of power operations. Thus he described the symptoms of the identified patient as ways to control others when all else had failed. Once these sequences were identified, Haley directed interventions to interrupt the sequence.

Nichols and Schwartz (1995) gave an example of how Madanes (a longtime collaborator of Haley's) dealt with a child who was having uncontrollable temper tantrums. Madanes described the child's mother as a shy and timid person who responded by withdrawing or overreacting to her child's tantrums. Madanes asked the mother to have a temper tantrum and then to kiss her boy. The boy was asked to have a temper tantrum and then to kiss his mother. They were told to perform this act before and after school. The mother was also told to give the boy cookies and milk, depending on how well he performed his temper tantrum. Following this exercise (a form of paradoxical direction), the mother reported that she needed no more therapy and that the temper tantrums had stopped.

The other approach to family therapy that has contributed a great deal to current practices is Minuchin's structural approach (1974). According to Nichols and Schwartz (1995) there are three constructs that are basic to Minuchin's approach: *structure,* the organized pattern of family interactions; *subsystems,* collations that exist within the family; and *boundaries,* distinctions between individuals, subsystems, and the family and the outer world.

Minuchin argued that one must change the family structure if the problems of individuals are to be resolved. Of particular importance in problematic family interactions were those of cross-generational collations that undermine the mother-father unit. Getting the mother and father together in terms of their treatment of their children was one of the most frequent goals of Minuchin's approach. In addition Minuchin was aware of the notion of triangulation, in which two members of the family gang up on a third. This interactional pattern often occurs when there are cross-generational collations. He also identified troubled families as those in which the members were either enmeshed (had no clear boundaries between themselves and other family members) or disengaged (had no connection between themselves and other family members). He further noted that dysfunctional families often vacillated between these two extremes. G. R. Patterson (1992) supported this notion when he observed that aggressive children's behavior was maintained by initial parental aggressive overinvolvement and then by parental withdrawal (see Chapter 7). Minuchin's system allows the therapist to chart the family's boundary conditions, identify collations, identify triangulation patterns, and determine the extent and nature of the family's enmeshment or disengagement or both. (For a more complete analysis see Nichols & Schwartz, 1995, pp. 214–223.)

Conclusion

Our review of group approaches to psychotherapy, an enormous subject, has been limited by space demands. Indeed, we have barely touched on the vast literature of group therapy, couples therapy, and family therapy. However, it is not our intention to offer a comprehensive review of group approaches. Rather, our aim is to sensitize the student to the importance of these approaches. In addition, we hold that there is a need for more practitioners who have not only been exposed to group approaches but who have also had supervised experience in conducting the various types of group approaches.

14 Anticipations of Tomorrow

The purpose of this text is to make a case for a comprehensive system of psychosocial intervention, which includes but was not limited to psychotherapy and counseling (see Chapter 2). We have organized therapy—broadly defined to include any systematic psychosocial intervention—into two models, the intrapsychic model and the interpersonal model. We offer these models as a means of specifying the structure of therapy, the duration of therapy, and the interpersonal roles a therapist needs to portray to establish an effective therapeutic relationship. We have emphasized that effective therapy not only deals concretely with the client's behaviors but specifically with those behaviors that are violations of legitimate social role expectations. Further, the therapist must deal with those circumstances that violate the legitimate rights or needs of troubled people. Finally, we have offered specific therapeutic techniques that have been found to be effective with specific prototypes of clients.

However, problems remain with our attempt to develop a comprehensive theory. For any science, theory must clearly define the domain of interest, establish an adequate classification system, and offer a coherent and comprehensive system of causal analysis. The intent of this chapter is to specify the domain of interest for the field of abnormal psychology, define what is required beyond domain definition for an acceptable classification system in our field, and develop an etiological theory, or theory of cause. Our proposed theoretical integration is quite different from the DSM-IV and the medical model of causality.

In addition we will explore issues that we consider important to the future development of the science and art of psychosocial intervention with troubled people. The first issue concerns troubled people who do not fit into the category their initial behavior would suggest. We have discussed this issue in Chapter 7 with respect to children who were more disturbed than their initial behavior suggested. We also noted in Chapter 9 that there are people whose behavior might not lead to a diagnosis of antisocial personality disorder but who would be classified as psychopaths on the Hare Scale. A case history of a client initially diagnosed as suffering from a major unipolar depression will be given to illustrate another common problem with initial diagnoses. In this case the client was less disturbed than he originally appeared.

The second issue we will address is the identification of those characteristics that effective therapists share. In addition to techniques and general considerations of psychosocial interventions, there may be characteristics related to the therapist as an individual that determine good outcomes. Third, we will examine some of the issues in manual-defined therapy. Finally, we will consider the problem of ending therapy.

Classification and the DSM-IV

The development of an adequate classification system is essential for any science, including abnormal psychology. Although Adams and Cassidy (1993) agreed with the DSM-IV and held that classification should not be "theoretical," they did not specify how one gets started in the classification process. We argue that to develop any classification system one first make a theoretical leap.

That leap involves the definition of a domain of interest. For any classification system one must first implicitly or explicitly define one's domain of interest. We hold that patterns of acting, thinking, and feeling that are dysfunctional are a significant part of the domain of interest for abnormal psychology. The DSM-IV defined its domain of interest as *mental disorders* (we hold that this term is functionally equivalent to specific kinds of abnormality), which are characterized by "personal distress, . . . disability . . . , increased risk of suffering, death, pain, disability, or an important loss of freedom." (DSM-IV, p. xxi). In addition the DSM-IV stated that, "Whatever its original cause, it [the mental disorder] must currently be considered a manifestation of a behavioral, psychological, or biological dysfunction in the individual." (DSM-IV, pp. xxi, xxii).

In neither of these two definitions of the DSM-IV domain of interest has the critical term been defined. What defines a behavior, thought, feeling, or biological process as *dysfunctional*? We hold that patterns of thinking, feeling, and acting are dysfunctional if these patterns produce subjective distress, lead to gross distortions of reality, are dangerous to oneself or others, or are so peculiar or bizarre that they make it difficult for the individual to survive. Biological dysfunctions that contribute to these negative conditions are also part of the domain of interest. Such patterns, if made universal, would be likely to have negative consequences for the survival of the species.

It is generally agreed that an adequate category classification system generates categories that are mutually exclusive and exhaustive. To be *mutually exclusive* requires that each category stand for one and only one set of regularly occurring observations within the domain of interest. To be *exhaustive* requires that all regularly occurring observations be identified within the categories. Most classification systems are hierarchically organized. An example of a hierarchical classification is that of Lineas. In his classification system a dog is also a mammal. All dogs are mammals but not all mammals are dogs. The term dog is subordinate to the term mammal. It is possible to apply the same logic to the classification of mental disorders. One could consider schizophrenia as a subordinate type of psychosis. We would suggest that a hierarchical system is potentially very useful for the classification of mental disorders.

The DSM-IV fails to meet any of these criteria. It often requires several "diagnoses" for the same set of observations. That is, many disorders may be identified and when this occurs, the disorders are said to be co-morbid. If more than one clearly defined pattern is observed then a good case can be made for multiple labels. However, if the same or overlapping behaviors are used for different categories (or labels), then confusion in the classification is unavoidable. The awkward notion of comorbidity and the problems of reliability and validity are clear evidence of confusion within the DSM-IV (Widiger, 1993; and Carson, 1993). At present it is impossible to determine whether all regularly occurring patterns are labeled or not because of the lack of a system that allows for mutually exclusive labels. Further, the current DSM-IV system is not organized in a hierarchical fashion and with its current emphasis on the categorical medical model (Carson, Butcher, & Mineka, 1998), it cannot evolve into one.

There are many other problems with the current classification system. Among these is the use of the term multiaxial. The DSM-IV is defined as a multiaxial system. According to the DSM-IV, "A multiaxial system involves an assessment on several axes, each of which refers to a different domain of information that may help the clinician plan treatment and predict outcome" (DMS-IV, p. 25). This is a peculiar definition of the term axis. As stated earlier axis is often used as a synonym for the term dimension in psychological research. A dimension refers to more or less of something (see Chapter 7). In addition, dimensions are usually thought to be independent of one another. In this sense the DSM-IV is not an axis system; in fact the DSM-IV is a standard category system. As we shall see, this criticism of the DSM-IV is not trivial.

The DSM-IV is described as a five-axis system. Axis I refers to all mental disorders except personality disorders and mental retardation. Axis II refers to personality disorders and mental retardation. Axis III refers to medical disorders related to Axis I or Axis II disorders. Axis IV refers to the extent to which a person has been stressed in the preceding year. Axis V refers to the person's highest level of functioning in the preceding year. Axis IV and V are true dimensions but are not required for "diagnosis." Axis I, II, and III are category systems.

One means of moving the axis system of the DSM-IV toward a real axial (dimensional) system is to closely examine Axis II. In what ways are the personality disorders (or mental retardation) different in kind from Axis I disorders? In what specific ways are disorders of mental retardation the same as personality disorders? Do they belong on the same axis? We argued in Chapter 9 that there was no compelling reason for a second axis, "Neither empirical nor rational arguments indicate strong justification for separating personality disorders from other mental disorders," (Livesley, Schroeder, Jackson, & Jang, 1994, p. 6). However, one could make a strong argument that people who suffer from mental retardation are different in kind from people who suffer from Axis I disorders. There is evidence that one of the primary causes of most types of mental retardation is some form of brain damage, a physiological disorder. Under such circumstances psychosocial intervention will be limited in its utility by the extent of that brain damage.

Logic would require that in addition to mental retardation, other Axis I disorders that are known to be physiologically caused diseases (for example, dementias, personality change due to a general medical condition, some sexual disorders, and some sleep disorders) do not belong on Axis I. We suggest that these disorders be omitted from the classification system of mental disorders or be included as diseases that produce characteristic psychosocial problems requiring specific psychosocial interventions. Clearly, psychosocial treatment is required as part of the management of patients having these disorders, as we argued is the case for all chronic disorders (see Chapters 4 and 5). We would also suggest that paying attention to psychological issues is essential in the treatment of virtually all illnesses. The injunction to treat the whole patient must be more than a mantra; it must be a reality.

If the category approach of the DSM-IV is not adequate, what other alternatives exist for classification systems of mental disorders? According to Widiger and Frances (1985) there are three major approaches to the classification of abnormal behavior (we would add abnormal thinking and feeling). They are the *categorical approach,* as used in the DSM-IV, the *dimensional approach,* and the *prototype approach.* There are advantages and disadvantages to all three. Carson et al. (1998) argued that the categorical approach assumed that:

(a) all human behavior can be divided into the categories normal and abnormal, and (b) there exist discrete, nonoverlapping classes or types of abnormal behavior, often referred to as "mental" illnesses or diseases. As already suggested, many professionals believe that this approach is inappropriate for most recognizable types of mental disorder, which seem to be neither discrete (i.e., their boundaries routinely blend with those of other categories) nor always the manifestation of a common set of underlying factors. (p. 27)

If the categorical approach of the DSM-IV is critically flawed, then what about the dimensional approach? We argue that Axis I disorders could be ordered on a dimension of severity of the disorder and the number of dysfunctional patterns of acting, thinking, and feeling that are observed. Thinking and feeling dysfunction could be inferred not only from overt behavior but also from the history of the individual, his or her self-report of subjective distress, and from psychological tests. We hold that troubled individuals could be ordered from least severe to most severe and that the personality disorders from the DSM-IV would fit in this organizational scheme.

Millon and Davis (1996) held that there are three sources of data for the classification of mental disorders: *signs*, overt behavior; *symptoms*, self-report of thoughts and feelings that express subjective dissatisfaction and distress; and *traits*, inferred stable characteristics of the individual. We would agree that one must measure all three data sources but we would also allow the three measures to co-vary and would expect that regularly occurring patterns will emerge that could be ordered on a severity dimension. Millon, as one of the framers of the DSM-IV, would have us place personality traits on a separate axis (Axis II).

If one agrees that personality disorders (in our view, only core personality disorders—see Chapter 9) can be included in dimension I or Axis I, a case can be made for the necessity of including at least one other dimension for a relatively complete specification of mental disorders. We hold that there is a natural dimension, the cognitive dimension, on which could be ordered all mental disorders and many diseases that affect cognitive functioning. The ordering of individuals on this dimension would be from low-level cognitive functioning to high-level cognitive functioning. The current state of the science and art of psychological assessment allows for an extensive quantitative and qualitative description of cognitive functioning as well as use of a simple IQ score.

Finally, a medical diagnosis of physiological damage caused by the mental disorder is necessary for a complete specification of the disorder. Cirrhosis of the liver as a consequence of chronic alcohol abuse is an example of such a diagnosis. This requirement is similar to what is called an Axis III diagnosis in the DSM-IV. However, there really is no Axis III in our sense of axis or dimension; in other words, there is no dimension but rather the standard medical classification system. The requirement of a medical diagnosis for a complete classification, and an additional requirement that one must rule out physical diseases that mimic mental disorders, means that a medical examination must be a routine part of any mental disorder examination.

Although the dimensional part of our approach makes intuitive sense, there are problems with it. The most obvious is that it is hard to get people to agree on the specification of either the number of dimensions or their names. One entry in dimensional specification is the so-called Big Five Personality

Dimensions. According to Costa and McCray (1990), there are five dimensions of personality: *neuroticism, extraversion, agreeableness, openness,* and *conscientiousness.* They maintained that these are the dimensions of personality as they exist in nature.

However, Block (1995) and Eysenck (1947) questioned the number of dimensions offered by Costa and McCray. Eysenck offered three dimensions, Block offered seven, and Cattell (1966) sixteen. It seems to us that there are almost as many dimensions as there are factor analytic theorists. We hold that it is not possible to generate a convincing dimensional analysis by mechanically using any factor analytic or other statistical approach.

Another problem with dimensional analyses is determining how to establish an appropriate category or other rubric so that one can efficiently communicate one's findings. Carson et al. (1998) held that, in part, this problem could be resolved through the emergence of clusters, which are "correlated, though imperfectly, with recognizable sorts of gross behavior malfunctions, such as anxiety disorders or depression" (p. 27). However, a better solution to the problem of communicating results may lie in the third approach to classification of mental disorders suggested by Widiger and Frances (1985), the prototype approach:

> Carson et al. (1998) defined the term prototype, "[as] a conceptual entity depicting an idealized combination of characteristics, ones that more or less regularly occur together in a less than perfect way at the level of empirical reality. Recall our earlier example of the 'dogness' prototype. Prototypes, as the example demonstrates, are actually an aspect of our everyday thinking and experience. We can readily generate in our mind's eye an image of a dog, while recognizing we have never seen nor ever will see two identical dogs. Thus no item in a prototypically defined group will have all the characteristics of the defining prototype, although it will have many of the more central of them. . . . Unlike the often forced categorical separations of the DSM, the prototypes are not [intended] to be mutually exclusive." (p. 27)

Carson et al. (1998) suggested that a prototype system would combine the advantages of the categorical approach (ease of communication of findings) with those of the dimensional approach (a more complete and accurate description of the individual). At the same time the prototype approach would avoid the disadvantages of each—principally, the forced classification of people into rigid categories and the difficulty of communicating the results of dimensional analysis.

Millon (1991) has objected to this option and held that clear and unambiguous labels could not be generated using the prototype approach. On the other hand, Cantor, Smith, French, and Mezzeich (1980) maintained that some ambiguity and lack of clarity is warranted if the classification system more accurately reflects the observed realities of mental disorders. Further, although the prototype system does not provide clear boundaries between prototypes, the ambiguities produced could very well prove to be less ambiguous than those produced by the forced category system of the DSM-IV.

We would offer a combination of our dimensional model of disorder severity and suggest that there is a natural prototypical organization of these disorders (see Figure 14.1).

The prototypes given in Figure 14.1 are arranged from least severe (disorders of dissatisfaction) to most severe (psychoses). Each prototype has suggested psychosocial treatment approaches presented in the body of our text (see Chapters 3 to 12). Strictly speaking, we did not give prototypes in this text for psychosomatic disorders, disorders in the autistic spectrum, or dementias although we discussed psychosocial treatments for these disorders (see Chapters 5, 12, and 4, respectively).

We also suggest that the most severe disorders not only have more severe patterns of dysfunction than do less severe disorders, but also that the

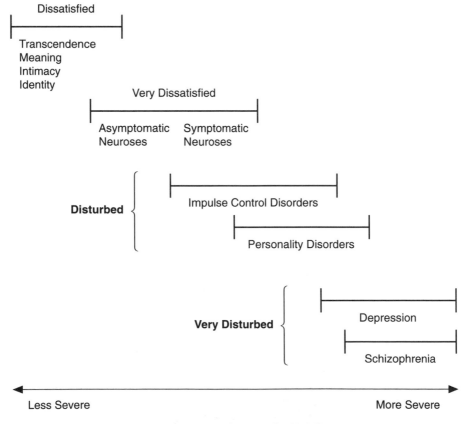

FIGURE 14.1   Prototype Definition of Mental Disorders

more severe disorders have many of the patterns characteristic of lesser disorders. For example, a schizophrenic is troubled not only by hallucinations and other characteristics of schizophrenia but frequently is also troubled by feelings of depression and anxiety. In general, our treatment approach is to deal with the most severe problems first and then with those that are less severe.

Therapy then becomes something like peeling an onion, with the outer shell representing the most severe dysfunction and each inner layer representing the next most severe dysfunction. We propose that the layers of the onion correspond to the prototypes given in Figure 14.2.

We suggest that when the most severe pattern of dysfunction a person displays has been defeated, then symptoms characteristic of less severe disorders are likely to emerge that will require treatment if the therapeutic gains are to be maintained. We are aware that this hypothesis is speculative and may not apply in every case. However, it is essential for any clinician to anticipate the appearance of problems other than those framed in the narrowly defined DSM-IV categories of mental disorders.

It is important, at this point, to offer a cautionary note to novice therapists, graduate students, and interested laypersons. Regardless of the

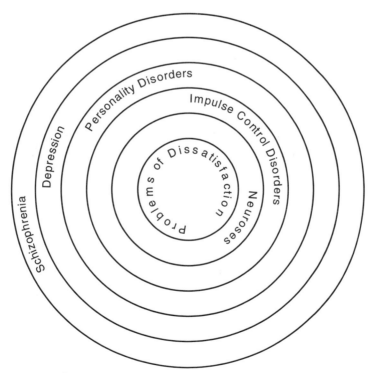

FIGURE 14.2 Peeling the Onion

theoretical soundness of the DSM-IV it is the classification system now used in the field. It must be mastered as an essential part of the training of all mental health personnel. However, we hope that our analysis will help lead to changes in the classification system.

The Medical Model, Biopsychosocial Model, and Diathesis Stress Model

The principal model in the causal analysis of mental disorders is the *medical model,* as noted earlier in this text. It is now fashionable to consider all psychological problems to be caused by some kind of brain dysfunction. The treatments for such disorders are usually some form of psychoactive medication. Although we discussed the medical model in Chapter 5, a brief exposition of its basic tenets would be useful for our analysis of causality.

In the 19th century medicine as a profession focused on the causes and cures of infectious diseases. The basic notion was that symptoms, both physiological and self-reported, were indications of an underlying disease process. If a medicine could be found that would kill the disease without killing the patient, then the disease was cured. Modern allopathic medicine has done well with this model and has extended it to traumatic injuries and disorders that can be treated but not cured at present, such as diabetes and many other chronic diseases. The medical model does less well with chronic diseases and with mental disorders probably because such disorders do not fit neatly into the model. Adherence to it may cause practitioners to ignore psychosocial factors that exacerbate or contribute to the cause of the disorder.

The uncritical application of the medical model to mental disorders is particularly unsatisfactory. In essence all mental illnesses are considered brain diseases, which are usually considered genetic disorders that cause abnormalities in neurotransmitters, which in turn cause the mental disorder. The current neurotransmitter said to cause schizophrenia is dopamine. According to this model schizophrenics have too much of this substance and antipsychotic medications are used to correct this imbalance. With respect to psychotic levels of depression, the neurotransmitters implicated are the biogenic amine neurotransmitters, and antidepressive medications are used to correct this imbalance. According to Valenstein (1998), neither of these hypotheses has been adequately confirmed by scientific research. Valenstein has stated that although mood-stabilizing medications (Lithium and others) are often life-saving for people who suffer from bipolar disorders, the physiological mechanism by which these medicines work is not known.

One option to the medical model is the *biopsychosocial model.* In this model mental disorders are considered to have complex causes. Not only are biological factors seen as causes of these disorders but also psychological and social factors are considered contributing causes. This model was proposed by A. Meyer (1948), K. Goldstein (1939), Dunbar (1943), and many others. However, this model failed to give any specific analysis of what factors actually caused a disorder or to specify treatments keyed to the total causal pattern.

A more promising model is the *diathesis stress model.* The origins of the term *diathesis* came from medical practice in 17th-century England. It referred to the individual's constitutional tendency to tolerate a disease. The notion was that some individuals had a better *diathesis* and could survive a disease that had killed others.

The model evolved and the notion that stress could overcome an adequate diathesis became a widely held belief by many 19th-century physicians. Meehl (1962) applied the diathesis stress model to mental illness. Specifically, he held that schizophrenia was caused by a constitutional weakness genetic in origin in concert with external and perhaps internal stress. Since that time this model has received increased attention.

Our extension of the diathesis stress model included Meehl's acceptance of the existence of stable characteristics of the individual (the diathesis), which would determine the individual's capacity to tolerate stress. In addition to inherited or other physiologically determined stress tolerance characteristics or both, one could also include learned stress tolerance components in the diathesis. The notion that the diathesis could contain learned components has been proposed by Parnas (1986), Metalsky and Joiner (1992), and Russo, Viatiano, Brever, Koton, and Becker (1995). The stress component of the model we refer to as stress stimuli. We hold that the sources of stress stimuli are not only physiological (pathogens, physical trauma, and so forth) but also environmental, psychological, and social.

In addition to the concepts of the diathesis, stress stimuli, and the stress response or disorder, we maintain that three additional components are required to establish an adequate diathesis stress model for mental disorders. First, troubled people often deal with stress stimuli by engaging in patterns of thinking, feeling, or acting that temporarily but ineffectively reduce the stress stimuli. Second, these defensive reactions increase the likelihood that the stress stimuli will recur, and recur with greater intensity ultimately taking the form of an automatic vicious cycle (Fenichel, 1945). Third, when the stress reaction occurs, there is likely to be feedback to both the diathesis and to the person's perception of the stress stimuli. To particularize these concepts and to further define our model, see Figure 14.3.

In Figure 14.3 SS refers to all stress stimuli perceived by the individual. If the individual responds to a stress stimulus by doing something to remove the stimulus (if hungry—eat) then the stress situation is resolved and no stress reaction (SR) occurs. If a potential stress stimulus is below threshold then no stress will be perceived.

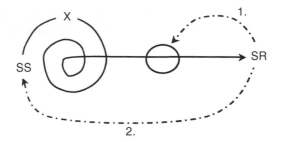

where:

SS = stress stimuli
X = defensive reactions
$\text{\textcircled{2}}$ = vicious cycle

$\bigcirc$ = diathesis
SR = stress reaction (disorders)
1. = feedback from stress reaction to diathesis
2. = feedback to stress stimuli

FIGURE 14.3   Diathesis Stress Model

However, if the individual perceives a stimulus input as stressful and unavoidable, or cannot remove or reduce an aversive stimulus through rational, problem-solving means, a defensive reaction is likely. A *defensive reaction* is defined as any irrational non-problem-solving response that temporarily reduces or removes the perception of the stress stimulus but does not lead to need satisfaction or alter the source of the stress stimulus. We consider defense mechanisms (A. Freud, 1946), as reinterpreted by Lazarus (1981), to be one kind of defensive reaction. Any other response that temporarily reduces the awareness of a stress stimulus would also be defined as a defensive reaction. For example, substance abuse, projective identification, splitting, impulsive acting out (including substance abuse), the use of people as objects for immediate gratification, hallucinations, delusions, and any other thought, feeling, or action that initially functions to reduce the awareness of stress stimuli are defined as defensive reactions.

Although the defensive reaction temporarily reduces the impact of the stress stimulus on the individual, we hypothesize that such reactions produce vicious cycles. We suggest that the *vicious cycle* paradoxically increases both the frequency and intensity of the stress stimulus (Fenichel, 1945). If one drinks to avoid the awful realities of one's life, the realities of one's life become more awful, leading to more drinking, which can lead in turn to the condition of alcoholism. We suggest that other defensive reactions produce other vicious cycles, each capable of overwhelming the individual's diathesis and producing their own characteristic stress reactions or mental disorders. If the diathesis is already weakened either physiologically or through learned maladaptive patterns, then the occurrence of the stress reaction is accelerated.

We also include two feedback mechanisms in our diathesis stress model (see Figure 14.3). One sends destructive feedback from a stress reaction directly to the diathesis either by physiologically weakening the diathesis or through new learned maladaptive patterns. The second mechanism produces an increase in the stress stimuli. For example, if a person perceives certain classes of stimuli as those that cause him or her to become anxious, then the development of a neurosis (or anxiety disorder) makes that person even more likely to overreact to these classes of stimuli.

There are immediate and important considerations that follow from this model. First, the causal pattern that produces mental disorders is complex. Second, treatment intervention can occur at any point in the causal chain. Third, it is likely that the most effective interventions will require treatment at all points in the causal chain. For example, an abused wife could be removed from circumstances—the abusing husband—in which she encountered the stress stimuli. Then the abused wife could learn that her continual excuses for her abusing husband were irrational, and an explicit attempt to defeat her defensive reaction. Therapy, supervised visitations with her husband, couples and family therapy, and other approaches could also aid in defeating this vicious cycle. There are many other points of intervention that could help the abused wife: removal from the setting within which the abuse occurred, medication if the abuse caused depression and anxiety, and so forth.

The notion of a team approach in both the assessment and treatment of mentally ill people becomes essential if our causal model is correct. When professionals act as advocates they often remove or reduce the stress stimuli or reduce disruptive feedback or both. Many social agencies also serve this function. We view intervention at the level of defensive reactions and repetitive negative patterns of thinking, feeling, and acting as typical tasks for therapists in psychotherapy and counseling. We view medications as both a means of strengthening the diathesis and reducing the effects of feedback. Psychiatrists and other medical personnel are essential at this stage of the intervention process. We think it could be helpful to particularize this multi-stage intervention approach with respect to specific disorders and specific treatment approaches.

For the lesser problems of what we have called disorders of dissatisfaction (see Chapter 3), preoccupation with issues of identity, intimacy, meaning, or transcendence are triggered by the person's perception that he or she cannot resolve these issues. Short-term humanistically oriented therapy can aid these individuals to meet their full potential. However, they can function effectively even without the aid of psychotherapy. For more severe disorders the diathesis stress pattern is more complex and increasingly complex interventions are required.

For disorders we have referred to as neurotic disorders (see Chapter 6), interventions could occur at several points in the causal chain. For whatever reason, people who are likely to develop neurotic disorders perceive many stimulus events as causing them to feel anxious or to suffer from subjective distress. These stimuli are often associated with rejections, hostility expressed toward the individual, and situations in which the individual's anticipation of failure or embarrassment is high. It is likely that he or she will invoke a defensive reaction in response to these stimuli (in this case, the defensive reaction is often one of Freud's defense mechanisms). However, such a reaction will not solve the person's difficulties. If a man's anxiety was triggered by his rejection by a woman he had hoped to date, then for him to rationalize his defensive reaction ("I really didn't want to go out with her") does not solve his problem, which is, in this case, forming a relationship.

It is likely that the man's fear of rejection will lead to more rationalization (a vicious cycle), eventually producing a neurotic reaction. Intervention for the neurosis could take place at any point in the causal chain. For example, he could be exposed to women who do not reject him. Perhaps he will then stop avoiding women and stop becoming anxious in their presence.

If an individual has severe problems—for example, compulsions, panic attacks, obsessions, or oppressive and diffuse anxieties—then antianxiety or antidepressive medications could strengthen the diathesis and reduce or eliminate the stress response or neurosis. Therapy would focus on defeating the defensive operations (see Chapter 6) and facilitating the individual's mastery of higher order mental operations to allow reality-based need satisfaction.

In the case of what we have called disorders of impulse control (see Chapter 8), often the person experiences the world as one in which he or she does not wish to live. Any frustration or conflict is likely to be perceived as yet another indication of a world in which need satisfaction is unlikely or needs can only be gratified by immediate and impulsive action. Addictive patterns are one of the most common of these disorders of impulse control. The addict experiences any block to his or her satisfaction as a reason "to make the world go away," usually by consuming as much of a drug of choice as is required to accomplish the psychological state of oblivion. Of course, when the addict recovers from the drug affect the world is still there and he or she is in worse shape than before. That the feedback weakens the diathesis is obvious. Further, withdrawal effects and drug tolerance both markedly increase the stress stimuli, thus leading to more impulsive and addictive behaviors.

As is the case with neurotic disorders, one can intervene at any point in the causal chain that produces disorders of impulse control. In general, all disorders of impulse control require external control of the impulsive behavior. For more severe disorders of impulse control initial treatment to establish control over the impulsive behavior requires institutional placement. With addicts such placement is often essential to help them in the initial process of detoxification. The psychosocial intervention strategies (see Chapter 8) focus on instituting control, defeating denial, and establishing positive behavior patterns. At present medications to treat substance abuse have not proved successful, although naltrexone and similar drugs that block the psychological effects of addictive substances and methadone maintenance programs for heroin addicts have had some success.

The application of the diathesis stress model to what we have called core personality disorders (see Chapter 9) is reasonably straightforward. Stimuli that the person perceives as being dangerous, leading to exploitation, or revealing weaknesses or vulnerability activate the stress cycle. The person who suffers from a core personality disorder is likely to react by impulsively seeking to gratify his or her needs. This gratification may be using other people as objects without regard or empathy. This individual's actions create a world that is in fact dangerous, and becomes increasingly dangerous in the escalating pattern characteristic of a vicious cycle. The perception of living in a world where it is kill or be killed drives this person's behavior. Indeed, the most dangerous of the people who suffer from core personality disorders are psychopaths who are unable to see people as other than objects for their use. To the psychopath and to some extent others who suffer from core personality disorders all people become either victims or victimizers. Such learned patterns increase the diathesis weakness and ensure destructive feedback.

It is likely that people who suffer from core personality disorders have a marked weakness in the diathesis. We would guess that in part this weakness is inherited and in part is learned. At present there are no medications that seem useful for people suffering from such core personality disorders (as narcissistic, borderline, or antisocial personality disorders). Therefore, medications are unlikely to either strengthen an individual's diathesis or reduce destructive feedback. (Occasionally antidepressive or antipsychotic medications are useful for people who suffer from borderline disorders.) It may be possible through psychosocial interventions (see Chapters 7 and 9) to defeat the defensive reaction and interrupt the vicious cycle it produces. At present our knowledge is limited concerning how to treat these troubled people except to suggest that interventions early in their lives and at all phases of the causal chain are required for effective treatment.

There are at least two distinct psychotic prototypes. First, depressive disorders indicate a clear break with reality caused by disproportionate emotional reactions. Second, schizophrenics exhibit patterns of thought and perception that grossly distort reality. In the first case almost any stimuli that could be stressful are likely to trigger feelings of hopelessness, helplessness, and worthlessness. The vicious cycle engendered could lead the individual to fall into a vegetative state of despondency and despair that would remove any obligation to solve his or her life problems. In the second case, hallucinations and delusions would be the typical reactions to stress stimuli. The vicious cycle engendered by the schizophrenic defenses could lead to the individual's total withdrawal from the world. Although such a reaction would protect the schizophrenic from his or her experience of the world as deadly, it would necessarily mean that his or her needs could not be satisfied.

For any person who is unable to function in which psychotic depression is a major factor, the first consideration in treatment is to prevent suicide. If the threat to self is imminent, then hospitalization (removal from the stress stimuli), close supervision (external controls to support a weakened diathesis), and medication (to directly strengthen diathesis) are required. Psychosocial intervention in the form of Beck's cognitive therapy, Lewinsohn's behavior therapy (to increase activity level and occurrence of reinforcing events), and Klerman's interpersonal therapy (to develop interpersonal skills necessary for effective functioning) should aid in reducing defensive operations and the vicious cycles associated with depression. The psychosocial approaches cited above should also reduce feedback from the stress response—in this case depression (see Chapter 10 for a detailed exposition of these approaches).

To treat any person whose primary problem is a flight from reality caused by hallucinations or delusions or both (primarily individuals who suffer from schizophrenia) the therapist's first consideration should be, "Can this person function outside of a protected environment?" Today HMO policies and our own inadequate systems for dealing with these patients (see Chapter 11) suggest that there may be no possible inpatient placement. Yet such placement (the removal of the person from the stress stimuli) is often required. In the absence of such placement, antipsychotic medication is now used to strengthen the diathesis and the person is maintained, either successfully or unsuccessfully, in the community. The long-term total treatment approach of Hogarty et al. (1995) cited in Chapter 11 provided intervention at all points in the causal chain.

It is hoped that our analysis will lead others to consider deeply the likelihood that the disorders we have discussed are multiply caused. If our analysis stimulates others to operationalize our speculations and to test our guesses, then our analysis will have served its purpose.

Other Important Issues

Complexities of the Learned Component of the Diathesis

The learned component of the diathesis is itself quite complex and directly related to treatment approaches. It is important to note that our analysis cannot be mechanically applied to the treatment of troubled people. We have already alluded to this issue in Chapter 7. Children often appear more normal than they are. Often a child who is highly intelligent and has mastered many of the age-appropriate cognitive and social skills has hidden, profound, early emotional problems. If these children are not treated fully and completely it is likely that they will develop severe mental disorders in adolescence.

The reader may refer to Case History 7.1 as an example of severe early emotional developmental disruption. This child was emotionally damaged by the early and severe child abuse he suffered. Although Noah merely seemed troubled at first as he approached pubescence, his behavior began to become more primitive and to exhibit self-destructive and other destructive behaviors.

We suggested in Chapter 7 that there are two learned components of the diathesis. First, there is the primary learned emotional component of each of Erikson's developmental periods (see the intrapsychic model in Chapter 2). The second component involves intellectual and social mastery. The child's primary emotional interruption, if it occurs early in life, can temporarily be masked by "normal" social and intellectual development.

In the case of Noah, intellectual and social dysfunction was minimal until the fourth or fifth grade. Short-term or supportive treatment for this child had only delayed the emergence of severe pathology. Treatment was required that was both highly structured and long-term.

Another possibility for the learned component of the diathesis exists. There are people who manifest profound disturbance but who recover in a short period of time given proper treatment, and do not further demonstrate extreme distress. The combat-fatigued veterans referred to in the Beebe and Brill study (see Chapter 2) are examples of such individuals. Note well that the posttraumatic stress disorder suffered by so many Vietnam veterans is a more serious disorder and is not what we are referring to here. The basic idea is that some people who present as severely disturbed do not have either the learned or physiological components of the diathesis suggested by the overt symptomatology. For an example of such an individual, see Case History 14.1.

CASE HISTORY **14.1**

Mr. Paul Wright

Mr. Paul Wright is a fifty-nine-year old married white male who appeared at the emergency room of his regional VA hospital complaining of lack of energy, problems sleeping, inability to work, and feelings of discouragement and inadequacy. The outpatient physician quickly determined that there were no obvious indications of physical illness and that the patient's history was consistent with good physical and mental health prior to the recent suicide of his only child, a seventeen-year-old son whose death by carbon monoxide inhalation had a devastating impact on both parents. Mr. Wright was referred to Psychology Service for profiling and treatment recommendations, with a provisional diagnosis of major depression.

During the interview Mr. Wright responded dutifully to all questions. His mood tone was consistently and severely depressed. His speech was slow but carefully organized. Although he seemed in good reality contact, his interpretations of events were self-punishing and colored by feelings of failure as a husband and father. His pervasive discouragement and self-condemnation overshadowed any personal hopes for improvement. He had sought out medical assistance because it was the responsible thing to do and not because he had any expectations of relief.

The Beck scale simply verified the interview impressions of a severe depressive episode. The subtle distortions of self-perception and predictive thinking were determined more by the patient's pervasive dysphoria than the reality factors in his accounts of recent events.

As he spoke a picture emerged of a caring, conscientious individual who came from a family with a strong tradition of service. His father was a butler who spent most of his life in service to a single wealthy family. Paul Wright grew to maturity with strong values of responsibility and duty. He took service as a chauffeur, living on the grounds of his employer's Northern Virginia estate. He married late, was utterly devoted to his wife and son, and saw his son's excellent school achievement and high moral standards as a testimony to his value as a father and as a man.

He quickly qualified this statement by pointing out how strongly he fell short of his wife's purity and virtue, expressed through her extensive involvement with her church and her lectures to and guidance of their son, whom she hoped to "shield and guide through the temptations of the world and the weaknesses of the flesh." The patient had been very pleased that his boy had followed his mother's direction, developing his own strong commitment to religion and increasing involvement in church events.

The client wondered if, had he been a more virtuous person, the tragedy might have been prevented. He saw his unending grief and depression as somehow deserved and did not blame his employer for summarily dismissing him when his emotional state interfered with his work.

The treatment approach combined cognitive restructuring with a strong, concerned, and rather directive therapist role for the initial approach. The intensity and severity of the symptoms called for immediate supportive work and the diagnostic interview was followed without a pause by a careful exploration of content that disconfirmed the self-preoccupation and irrational guilt. Mr. Wright's life of dedicated service and his unqualified affection and support for both wife and son were examined, verified, and evaluated as strongly supporting the therapist's concern and respect for the client. He was characterized as a worthwhile individual with a life of quiet achievement. This was contrasted with his employer's selfish dismissal after years of dedicated service.

Mr. Wright recognized that he had lived up to his own father's best values. He recalled that his father had often emphasized that loyalty should flow in both directions from servants to employer. By the end of the first session, the client looked less defeated and spoke of himself with neutral or even guardedly positive terms. The issue of self-harm was discussed in a forthright manner and he stated that this was not now and never would be an option. He agreed to a second session to continue the dialogue already well begun and to look at other possible treatment options.

The therapist anticipated that the content of the second session would be extremely sensitive. In order to accomplish a shift from dominant warmth and the caretaker role to nonassertive warmth and an advocate role, the therapist had to provide Mr. Wright with a reason for exonerating himself for his son's death without having to blame his wife's obsessive religiosity for the son's suicide. Therefore the second session began with a structured celebration of his son's life. As this progressed, the client began to take the lead in recounting their mutual understanding and firm friendship. Although his son revered his mother, it was to his father that he turned with problems in school, relationships, and emergent sexuality. These problems were dealt with in a caring, nonjudgmental fashion that focused on solutions and acceptance rather than redemption and restitution. A week before the suicide, his son had asked searching questions about striving for grace. Mr. Wright had answered with an endorsement of trying to live according to one's best values and regarding mistakes as acceptable human failings to be handled as lessons rather than defeats. He then looked at the therapist and asked, "Do you think what I said caused him to abandon life in the physical world for life in the spirit?" The reply came after a moment's reflection but with conviction. "Your son was one of those exceptional young people who seem somehow out of place in the brutal realities of our world. If anyone could have reconciled him to staying in the physical world and dealing with its challenges and his own natural needs and human limitations it would have been you. You passed on to him what your father gave you and nothing you've said would indicate that there was anything there to cause harm."

The client was silent for a few moments. Then he smiled for the first time, looked up, and said in a strong voice, "I'm going to be all right." In the remainder of the session it was brought out that the hardships of life built character for eternity. Mr. Wright had contributed to his son's strengths as a man.

His wife had prepared her son for life in the spirit. Both contributions were necessary and were validated by their child's life that, although short, was presented to Mr. Wright as having achieved completion of these tasks. At the end of the session Mr. Wright declined antidepressant medication, stating that he had accomplished what he needed to. He agreed to self-refer if his depressive symptoms returned and to respond to a followup call in six months. He did not request additional sessions. In the followup assessment he did confirm that he was symptom-free and content with his new job as a professional driver for a limousine leasing service.

Mr. Wright suffered severe trauma, the suicide of his son, and the abandonment of his mentor. We hypothesize that he suffered such an intense stress stimulus that he developed what appeared to be a psychotic depression. However, since it is unlikely that this client had either an inherited or learned diathesis making him vulnerable to depression, short-term therapy that focused on the stress stimuli and cognitive restructuring produced an immediate resolution of his depression.

What Successful Therapists Share

We have argued that successful therapies may very well be doing the same things with similar prototypes of disorders. For example, Beck's cognitive therapy, Klerman's interpersonal therapy, and the behavior therapy manual we have cited all employed one another's techniques (see Chapter 10). We suggest that there may be characteristics that successful therapists share regardless of their individual "theoretical" orientation or therapeutic technique.

First, successful therapists establish and maintain a working therapeutic relationship with each client. As we described in Chapter 2, that relationship is characterized by the client's perception of the therapist as caring, consistent, and knowledgeable. We hold that being perceived as caring is similar to Rogers's (1957) notion of unconditional positive regard, and that being perceived as consistent is similar to Rogers's notions of genuineness and congruence. We also hold that Traux and Carkhuff's (1967) notion of concreteness is consistent with the perception by the client that the therapist is knowledgeable. These and perhaps other therapist characteristics emphasize the importance of the therapeutic relationship. Horvath and Greenberg (1994), Bourgeois, Sabourin and Wright (1990), and Gaston, Marnsen, Thompson, and Gallagher (1988), among others, have offered empirical support for this notion.

Such perceptions are part of the second shared characteristic of good therapists, the formation of trust. However, we suggest that trust formation is in part a byproduct of the therapist's ability to engage in extensive self-examination. Certain questions are asked of themselves time and again by good therapists. For example, "Do I respect this client?", "Do I care whether he or she survives?", "Am I maintaining boundaries?", and so forth. This sort of self-examination must be engaged in if a client's trust is to be gained or maintained. This warning is similar to the old analytic requirement that the therapist should be aware of his or her blind spots. This notion has received some empirical support (Simon, 1995; Levenson, 1992; Rabinowitz, 1993).

In addition, the successful therapist must be capable of entering the client's life saga. This concept is similar to the Rogerian notion of *accurate empathy*. However, we intend for the notion of entering the client's life saga to have a grander scope. In essence the effective therapist must be able to experience this person's life from the inside. What are the life and death struggles for this person? What are his or her personal tragedies? Note how different this talk is from helping a client get rid of a particular behavior or symptom or employing a specific technique for some disorder. Our guess is that by entering a client's inner world the therapist could enlist that person's resources to prepare him or her for the inevitable losses one experiences in life. There is a great deal of strength to be gained from knowing where one has been and where one is going.

Certainly, there are likely to be many other characteristics of good therapists. However, we intend by our emphasis on the importance of therapist characteristics and the therapeutic relationship to sensitize the practitioner and student of therapy to issues other than theory and technique.

Manual-Driven Psychotherapy

At present, research on the effectiveness of psychotherapy may require any researcher to develop a treatment manual before that researcher's work will be considered for publication. The manual must specify the psychotherapeutic technique and ensure treatment consistency. Examples of manuals can be found for many different orientations to psychotherapy. For example, Beck, Rush, Shaw, and Emery (1979) offered a therapy manual for depression as did Klerman, Weissman, Rounsaville, and Chevron (1984). Luborsky and Barber (1993) wrote a manual for a modified psychoanalytic approach. Ivey, Gluckstern, and Ivey (1992) have offered a manual for an approach they called microcounseling, an approach that has many ties to Rogers's client-centered therapy.

Throughout this text we have cautioned against the application of technique in a mechanical fashion. We have argued that a therapeutic relationship is essential for effective therapy. Manual-driven approaches often either ignore this consideration or devalue its importance. In the current rush to "manualize" everything in psychotherapy, we hope that technical orthodoxy will not lead practitioners to forget or ignore the unique human being with whom they are working.

Another issue concerning manual-driven therapy could have negative implications for psychotherapy. Given the increasing influence of HMOs there could be a rush to prescribe the correct approach in order to be reimbursed. We hold that members of our profession must be reluctant to adopt any approach simply because it may be "practical" to do so.

Ending Therapy

Kupers (1988) has written extensively on issues related to ending therapy. He offered what he called a rule of thumb for determining the duration of therapy, suggesting that the more severe the disorder, the longer the therapy. We have presented evidence that the therapeutic approaches successful in the treatment of severe disorders are long-term.

Another position on when therapy should end was cited by Kupers and attributed by him to Sigmund Freud. According to Freud, therapy should end when the person is no longer suffering from symptoms and there is no indication that the symptoms will recur. Kupers also stated that Freud held that therapy should end when a conclusion can be drawn that no further progress can be made in therapy.

Research directed toward operationally defining the severity of disorders, assessing "symptom" removal, and determining when no further treatment will be beneficial is required before one can place a great deal of confidence in the correctness of the above clinical lore. In particular, the decision to terminate based on the clinician's judgment that further treatment will not be helpful is flawed. If one does not like the person one is treating, how convenient it would be to say no further treatment is needed. One could also say that the person was incurable or untreatable.

There is abundant evidence that "symptom" removal—the systematic removal of negative behaviors and the development of effective behaviors—is a good criterion for ending therapy (Lazarus, 1981). In addition, the person who is receiving therapy is often a better source about when to end therapy than the therapist (Lindner, 1954). A good hypothesis for further research would be to put these two notions together, and to specify target behaviors that need to be changed and develop a rating scale to measure satisfaction of the person receiving therapy. These measures would not only be used, as is currently the case, to determine the effectiveness of therapy but also to develop a more objective way of anticipating when to end therapy.

We would offer one more notion of when to end therapy. This is *our* rule of thumb and is not offered as a scientifically proved method. It is one that has emerged over the authors' thirty years of clinical experience. We hold that when the therapist looks forward to seeing the client it is probably time to end therapy. Therapy is not a social event but rather an intervention that serves to bring about change in the person being treated. If the person no longer represents a task for the therapist and therapy is in the process of becoming a social event (not always an obvious change), then therapy should probably end. In any event, the issue of when to end therapy is an area in which future research is essential.

Conclusion

We have offered a framework to aid clinicians in making good decisions about what psychosocial interventions are likely to work for specific troubled people. This framework supports our basic claim: that for more severe disorders the therapist must provide more structure and longer treatment will be required for successful outcomes. In general, our interpersonal model specifying therapist strategies to establish an effective therapeutic relationship was successful. Our theoretical challenge to the DSM-IV classification system and the medical model of causation is still a work in progress. However, we maintain that we have raised important questions and offered viable alternatives to the current rush to classify all mental disorders as brain diseases to be treated only, or principally, by medications.

We hold that the process of therapy requires therapists to demonstrate that they understand the person with whom they are working, that they respect the person, that they are genuine in their interaction with the person, and that the essential conditions for effective therapy are met. If the therapist selects the appropriate interpersonal role and focuses on content central to the client's problems and concerns, then the therapist has shown that he or she understands the client. If the pacing and sequencing is appropriate as indicated by the lack of long pauses and the willingness of the client to express significant and often troubling material, then the therapist has shown respect for that person. If the mutual exchange of information maintains the conditions of understanding and respect, then trust based on genuineness has developed. These accomplishments define the essential oneness of therapy in which effective technique and a therapeutic relationship have been achieved.

Our analysis has not detailed all of the critical issues therapists face today. Yet we have taken an important step toward establishing a unified theory of psychosocial intervention. We have called attention to many of the issues that remain unresolved, and critical human problems that are not being addressed by our profession or society. We hope that concern for many of these issues will transcend academic focuses and lead the reader to consider where the profession is heading and where it *ought* to be heading.

APPENDIX 1

A Modification of the LaForge 1977 Form of the Interpersonal Check List (ICL)

In the Cooper, Adams, Dickinson and York (1975) article, the ICL (Figure A.1) was not used as a self-report measure but rather as a rating scale for the client's and therapist's interpersonal behavior. Both client and therapist interpersonal roles were established after scoring the ICL (see Figure A.2) and then plotted as indicated by Figure A.3. In addition the intensity of the therapist and client roles were determined by the distance from the center of Figure A.3. See Figure A.4 for an example of the plotting procedure. The closer to the center of the figure, the less intense the interpersonal role.

In Chapter 2 we discussed the means of establishing a therapeutic relationship. By using the correct interpersonal role, the therapist can establish an emotional climate in which most of the interactions between the

FIGURE A.1 Interpersonal Check List (ICL).*

Instructions: Circle the number of each of the following words or phrases that describe the behavior of the therapist. Repeat this procedure with a second form for client behavior.

1	Able to give orders	14	Always giving advice
2	Appreciative	15	Bitter
3	Apologetic	16	Big-hearted and unselfish
4	Able to take care of self	17	Boastful
5	Accepts advice readily	18	Businesslike
6	Able to doubt others	19	Bossy
7	Affectionate and understanding with others	20	Can be frank and honest
8	Acts important	21	Clinging vine
9	Able to criticize self	22	Can be strict if necessary
10	Admires and imitates others	23	Considerate
11	Agrees with everyone	24	Cold and unfeeling
12	Always ashamed of self	25	Can complain if necessary
13	Very anxious to be approved of	26	Cooperative
		27	Complaining

Special Note: The Interpersonal Check List was specifically excluded from any copyright protection in the 1977 LaForge article (see references). The ICL and its scoring system used in this text are identical to the LaForge 1977 ICL.

Adopted from LaForge.

320

28 Can be indifferent to others
29 Critical of others
30 Can be obedient
31 Cruel and unkind
32 Dependent
33 Dictatorial
34 Distrusts everybody
35 Dominating
36 Easily embarrassed
37 Eager to get along with others
38 Easily fooled
39 Egotistical and conceited
40 Easily led
41 Encourages others
42 Enjoys taking care of others
43 Expects everyone to admire him
44 Faithful follower
45 Frequently disappointed
46 Firm but just
47 Fond of everyone
48 Forceful
49 Friendly
50 Forgives anything
51 Frequently angry
52 Friendly all the time
53 Generous to a fault
54 Gives freely of self
55 Good leader
56 Grateful
57 Hard-boiled when necessary
58 Helpful
59 Hard-hearted
60 Hard to convince
61 Hot-tempered
62 Hard to impress
63 Impatient with others' mistakes
64 Independent
65 Irritable
66 Jealous
67 Kind and reassuring
68 Likes responsibility
69 Lacks self-confidence
70 Likes to compete with others
71 Lets others make decisions
72 Likes everybody
73 Likes to be taken care of
74 Loves everyone
75 Makes a good impression
76 Manages others
77 Meek
78 Modest
79 Hardly ever talks back
80 Often admired
81 Obeys too willingly

82 Often gloomy
83 Outspoken
84 Overprotective
85 Often unfriendly
86 Oversympathetic
87 Often helped by others
88 Passive and unaggressive
89 Proud and self-satisfied
90 Always pleasant and agreeable
91 Resentful
92 Respected by others
93 Rebels against everything
94 Resents being bossed
95 Self-reliant and assertive
96 Sarcastic
97 Self-punishing
98 Self-confident
99 Self-seeking
100 Shrewd and calculating
101 Self-respecting
102 Shy
103 Sincere and devoted to friends
104 Selfish
105 Skeptical
106 Sociable and neighborly
107 Slow to forgive a wrong
108 Somewhat snobbish
109 Spineless
110 Stern but fair
111 Spoils people with kindness
112 Straightforward and direct
113 Stubborn
114 Suspicious
115 Too easily influenced by friends
116 Thinks only of self
117 Tender and soft-hearted
118 Timid
119 Too lenient with others
120 Touchy and easily hurt
121 Too willing to give to others
122 Tries to be too successful
123 Trusting and eager to please
124 Tries to comfort everyone
125 Usually gives in
126 Very respectful of authority
127 Wants everyone's love
128 Well-thought-of
129 Wants to be led
130 Will confide in anyone
131 Warm
132 Wants everyone to like him
133 Will believe anyone
134 Well-behaved

FIGURE A.1 Continued

FIGURE A.2   Scoring the ICL

After the rater completes two ICLs (Figure A.1), one for the therapist and one for the client, each ICL is scored by giving one point per category, A–P, for each item endorsed in that category. See Figures A.3 and A.4 in order to determine how to plot the results found in Figure A.1.

Interpersonal Check List Score Sheet

A	B	C	D	E	F	G	H	I	J	K	L	M	N	O	P
1	101	4	22	20	25	6	9	30	56	2	26	49	23	58	128
48	64	18	46	29	82	45	3	78	10	5	37	7	41	16	75
55	95	28	57	65	94	62	36	40	87	13	90	106	67	42	80
68	98	70	110	112	105	120	69	125	126	123	132	131	117	54	92
19	17	104	63	51	15	66	97	81	32	38	115	47	50	53	8
35	89	100	96	85	27	107	102	77	79	71	127	52	86	84	14
76	108	116	99	83	91	113	118	88	129	73	130	72	119	121	122
33	39	24	31	59	93	34	12	109	21	133	11	74	124	111	43
A	B	C	D	E	F	G	H	I	J	K	L	M	N	O	P

Place the number of items circled in each column in the corresponding lettered box at the bottom of this score sheet and do the indicated arithmetic computations.

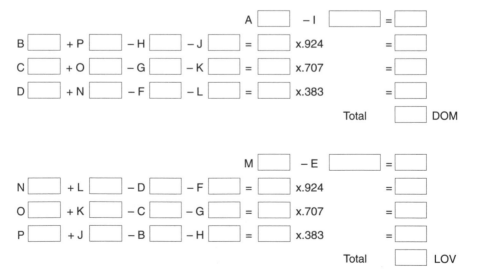

Plot DOM and LOV scores on the Interpersonal Check List on Figure A.3. Place in the appropriate interpersonal role as indicated on the Interpersonal Profile List Sheet (Figure A.3).

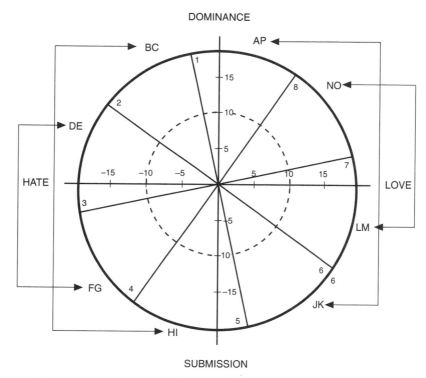

FIGURE A.3 Interpersonal Profile List Sheet.

therapist and the client are positive and the dominance patterns shift easily. If the majority of client-therapist interactions is affectively positive and dominance patterns shift often between the therapist and client, it is likely that the client will perceive the therapist as knowledgeable, caring, and consistent.

To determine the client and therapist roles during any therapy segment the rater's score of their behavior will be plotted on Figure A.3.

An example of the scoring follows. If during a therapy segment the client's score on the ICL rating of DOM was –2 and the client's score on LOV was +5, then the client's interpersonal role would be on an *LM*. If during a therapy segment the therapist's score on the ICL rating of DOM was +10 and the client's score on LOV was +10, then the therapist interpersonal role would be *NO*. In this case the *LM–NO* pattern describes an interpersonal interaction that is affectively positive. It is hoped that if other segments of the therapy session were plotted that the client role would frequently shift to the *NO* role and the therapist role would shift to the *LM* role. When the interpersonal interaction is affectively positive and the dominance patterns shift easily, it is likely that a therapeutic relationship has been established. Please see Figure A.4 to see how these scores were plotted.

Categories of Psychopharmacological Medications

Antianxiety Agents
Benzodiazepines

Brand Name (BN)	Generic Name (GN)	Common Risk Factors (CRF)	Common Side Effects (CSE)
Ativan Librium Serax Tranxene Valium Xanax	Lorazepam Chlordiazepoxide HCL Oxazepam Chlorazepate Diapotassium Diazepam Alprazolam	Benzodiazepines as a group are addictive. After addiction has occurred abrupt cessation may produce serious withdrawal effects. Anyone with a history of alcoholism is doubly at risk with benzodiazepines.	The most common side effect of benzodiazepines is sedation, which can usually be resolved by changing dosage levels. Other side effects include dizziness, weakness, and ataxia (failure of muscular coordination).

Other Antianxiety Agents

Brand Name (BN)	Generic Name (GN)	Common Risk Factors (CRF)	Common Side Effects (CSE)
Miltown	Meprobamate	Addictive; sudden cessation may produce withdrawal symptoms. Increases effect of CNS depressants.	Sedation and ataxia (loss of coordination of muscles).
Sinequan	Doxepin HCL	Severe drug interactions may occur for drugs that inhibit cytochrome P450 2 D6. Tricyclic antidepressants, seratonin reuptake inhibitors, and other drugs with similar effects should be used with caution.	Can produce anticholinergic properties (dry mouth, blurred vision, constipation, and urinary retention). Many other side effects.
Atarax	Hydroxyzine Embonate	Is dangerous when combined with alcohol or other CNS depressants.	Atarax is reported to have few side effects.
BuSpar	Buspirone Hydrochloride	Has few risk factors, but is reported to be less effective than other medications at controlling anxiety.	Headaches, nausea, among others.

Mebaral	Mephobarbital	Is addictive, as are other barbiturates. May not be given to people with porphyria (a defect of blood pigment metabolism).	Most common side effects are sedation and addiction.
Vistaril	Hydroxyzine	Dangerous when used in combination with any CNS depressants.	Few side effects reported. Dry mouth and drowsiness have been reported.

In addition to the above medications beta blockers (Atenolol) and barbiturates have been used to relieve anxiety. Beta blockets are primarily used to lower blood pressure and have many other side effects. All barbiturates have similar risk factors and side effects of mebaral.

Antidepressive Agents
Tricyclic Antidepressants

Ascendin	Amoxapine		
Elavil	Amitriptyline HCL		
Norparmin	Desipramine HCL	Tricyclics increase effects of CNS depressants; May lead to overdosing in people with suicidal tendencies.	Weight gain is common. Dry mouth is common. May increase schizophrenic reactions. Not to be used in combination with MAO inhibitors.
Pamelor	Nortriptyline HCL		
Trofanil	Imipramine HCL		
Vivactil	Protriptyline HCL		

Monoamine Oxidase Inhibitors (MAOIs)

Nardil	Phenelzine Sulfate		
Parnate	Tranylcypromine Sulfate	It is important for the patient taking MAOIs to check with his or her doctor because of serious drug interactions.	The most serious side effect of MAOIs is reactions to foods containing tyramine (red wine, aged cheeses, beer, many other foods and some cold medications).
Elderpryl	Selegiline HCL		

In the 1999 *Physicians' Desk Reference* Elderpryl is recommended at low dosage levels for Parkinson's disease but not for depression.

Selective Serotonin Reuptake Inhibitors (SSRIs)

BN	GN	CRF	CSE
Paxil Prozac Zoloft	Paroxetine HCL Fluoxetine HCL Sertraline HCL	SSRIs interact with MAOIs, producing a clinical pattern like that of neuroleptic malignant syndrome, a potentially fatal disorder.	Nervousness, sleep loss, and weight loss, among others.

Other Antidepressive Agents

BN	GN	CRF	CSE
Desyrel	Trazodone HCL	No significant risk factors mentioned in 1999 *PDR*.	Priapism (prolonged erection of the penis). Often leads to increased blood pressure. Many other side effects.
Effexor	Veniafaxine HCL	Dangerous for patients with liver or kidney disease.	Often leads to increased blood pressure. As with Desyrel may produce side effects resembling neuroleptic malignant syndrome.
Remeron	Mirtazapine	Can exacerbate both cardiovascular (heart disease) and cerebrovascular disease.	Dry mouth is common. Symptoms of apathy and depression are common.
Serzone	Nefazodone HCL	Interacts with MAOIs. May cause symptoms similar to neuroleptic malignant syndrome.	May cause vomiting, anorexia (loss of appetite), nausea, and many other side effects.
Wellbutin	Bupropion HCL	Interacts with MAOIs and may other drugs.	Seizures in patients with prior history of bulimia, seizure history, or anorexia nervosa.

Antimanic Agents

Depakote	Divalproex sodium	Should not be used with pregnant women. May cause birth defects.
Lithium Carbonate } Eskalith	Lithium Carbonate	Therapeutic doses for Lithium are just below toxicity. Dosage must be carefully monitored or death may occur.

Antipsychotic Agents
Phenothiazines

Compazine* Melloril Serentil Stelazine Thorazine Trilafon }	Prochlorperazine Thioridazind Mesoridazine Besylate Trifluopemazine Chlorpromazine HCL Perphenazine	Patients with liver disease must be closely monitored. Do not use these drugs with patients suffering from CNS depression or Parkinson's disease.

*Now rarely used as an antipsychotic medication.

Miscellaneous Antipsychotic Agents

Clozaril	Closapine	Not to be used in patients with myeloproliferative disorders (diseases involving loss of bone marrow and uncontrolled epilepsy, among other risk factors.

Hepatic failure (liver) has occurred and may be indicated by vomiting, lethargy, weakness, and other symptoms. Liver studies should be performed prior to medication and at six-month intervals.

If therapeutic levels are exceeded toxicity will occur. Virtually every organ system is affected.

Pseudo-parkinsonism, Tardive Dyskinesia, and occasionally neuroleptic malignant syndrome are common side effects. These are drug-induced, neurological disorders.

A serious side effect is agranulocytosis (a marked decrease in the number of granulocytes, which can result in frequent, chronic bacterial infections).

Miscellaneous Antipsychotic Agents (continued)

BN	GN	CRF	CSE
Haldol	Haloperidol	Should not be given to people with liver disease, among other risk factors.	Haldol shares a common side-effect profile with the phenothiazines.
Loxitane Moban Navane	Loxapine Molindone HCL Thiothixene	Similar risk factors as the phenothiazines.	Similar side effects as the phenothiazines.
Orap	Pimozide	Can lead to hyperpyrexia (abnormally high fever). No longer used for treatment of schizophrenia; now used for patients with Tourette's disorder.	Profile of side effects similar to phenothiazines.
Risperdal	Risperidone	Can exacerbate liver and kidney damage. Can lead to arrhythmias. See *PDR* for other risk factors.	Can cause Tardive Dyskinesia and Neuroleptic Malignant Syndrome.
Seroquel	Quetiapine fumarate	Similar risk factors to Risperdal.	Similar side effects to Risperdal.
Zyprexa	Olanzapine	Similar risk factors to Risperdal.	Similar side effects to Risperdal.

Note: The newer drugs used to treat schizophrenia (Seroquel and Zyprexa) not only seem to treat the negative symptoms of schizophrenia (for example, apathy) but also have fewer side effects than do other drugs used to treat schizophrenia. However, experience with these drugs is still limited and caution is advised.

Agents used in treating OCD

BN	GN	CRF	CSE
Luvox Paxil Prozac Zoloft	Fluvoxamine HCL Proxetine HCL Fluoxetine HCL Sertraline	Risk factors are the same as those listed above for SSRIs.	Side effects are the same as those listed above for SSRIs.

NOTE: Luvox is an SSRI used specifically for OCD.

GENERAL BIBLIOGRAPHY

Abrams, R. (1989, Nov./Dec.). Out of the blue. *The Sciences, 29*(6), 24–31.

Action for Mental Health. (1961). Science Editions. New York: John Wiley.

Adams, H. E., & Cassidy, J. F. (1993). The classification of abnormal behavior: An overview. In P. B. Sutker & H. E. Adams (Eds.), *Comprehensive handbook of psychopathology* (2nd ed.; pp. 3–25). New York: Plenum Press.

Aichhorn, A. A. (1935). *Wayward youth.* New York: Viking.

Alexander, F. (1950). *Psychosomatic medicine: Its principles and application.* New York: Norton.

Allen, J. A., Leonard, H. L., & Swedo, S. E. (1995). Current knowledge of medications for the treatment of childhood anxiety disorders. *Journal of the American Academy of Child and Adolescent Psychiatry, 34*, 976–986.

Almagor, M., Tillegen, A., & Walker, N. G. (1995). The big seven model—a cross cultural exploration of the basic dimensions of natural language descriptors. *Journal of Personality and Social Psychology, 69*, 300–307.

American Psychiatric Association. (1967). *Diagnostic and statistical manual of mental disorders* (2nd ed.). Washington, D.C.: Author.

American Psychiatric Association. (1980). *Diagnostic and statistical manual of mental disorders* (3rd ed.). Washington, D.C.: Author.

American Psychiatric Association. (1987). *Diagnostic and statistical manual of mental disorders* (3rd ed. rev.). Washington, D.C.: Author.

American Psychiatric Association. (1994). *Diagnostic and statistical manual of mental disorders* (4th ed.). Washington, D.C.: Author.

Analopoulos, A. D., Barkley, R. A., & Sheldon, T. L. (1996). Family based treatment: Psychosocial intervention for children and adolescents with attention deficit hyperactivity disorder. In E. D. Hibbs & P. S. Jensen (Eds.), *Psychosocial treatments for child and adolescent disorders* (pp. 267–284). Washington, D.C.: American Psychological Association.

Andersen, A. E. (1985). *Practical comprehensive treatment of anorexia nervosa and bulimia.* Baltimore, MD: The Johns Hopkins University Press.

Anderson, S. R., Taras, M., & Cannon, B. O. (1996). Teaching new skills to children with autism. In C. Maurice, G. Green, & S. C. Luce (Eds.), *Behavioral intervention for young children with autism* (pp. 181–193). Austin, TX: Pro. Ed.

Andreasen, N. C., & Black, D. W. (1991). *Introductory textbook of psychiatry.* Washington, D.C.: American Psychiatric Press.

Anthony, E. J. (1969). Research as an academic function of child psychiatry. *Archives of General Psychiatry, 21*, 385–391.

Antonuccio, D. O., & Danton, W. G. (1995). Psychotherapy versus medication for depression: Challenging the conventional wisdom with data. *Professional Psychology, Research and Practice, 26*(6), 574–585.

Apfelbaum, B. (1981). Integrating psychoanalytic and behavior therapy. *American Psychologist, 36*(7), 796–797.

Arieti, S. (1978). *On schizophrenia, phobias, depression, psychotherapy and the farther shores of psychiatry.* New York: Brenner/Mazel.

Atthowe, J. M., Jr., & Krasner, L. (1968). A preliminary report of the application of contingent reinforcement procedures (token economy) on a "chronic psychiatric ward." *Journal of Abnormal Psychology, 73*, 37–43.

Avery, D., & Winokur, G. (1978). Suicide, attempted suicide, and relapse rates in depression. *Archives of General Psychiatry, 35*(6), 749–753.

Axline, V. (1969). *Play therapy.* New York: Ballantine Books.

Ayllon, T. (1963). Intensive treatment of psychotic behavior by stimulus satiation and food reinforcement. *Behavior Research and Therapy, 1*, 53–61.

Ayllon, T., & Azrin, N. H. (1968). The token economy: A motivational system for therapy and rehabilitation.

Azrin, N. H. (1986). Improvements in the community—reinforcement approach to alcoholism. *Behavior Research and Therapy, 14*, 339–348.

Bandler, R., & Grinder, J. (1982). *Reframing.* Moab, UT: Real People Press.

Barker, P. (1986). *Basic Family Therapy* (2nd ed.). New York: Oxford University Press.

Barrett, P., Dadds, M., & Rapee, R. (1996). Family treatment of child anxiety: A controlled trial. *Journal of Consulting and Clinical Psychology, 64,* 333–342.

Barron, F., & Leary, T. (1955). Changes in psychoneurotic patients with and without psychotherapy. *Journal of Consulting Psychology, 19,* 239–245.

Bassin, A. (1968). Daytop village. *Psychology Today, 2,* 27–37.

Bateson, G. (1971). *Steps to an ecology of mind.* New York: Ballantine.

Baucom, D. H., & Epstein, N. (1990). *Cognitive behavioral marital therapy.* New York: Brunner/Mazel.

Baucom, D. H., Sayers, S. L., & Sher, T. G. (1990). Supplementing behavioral marital therapy with cognitive restructuring and emotional expressiveness training: An outcome investigation. *Journal of Consulting and Clinical Psychology, 58,* 636–645.

Baucom, D. H., Shoham, V., Mueser, K. T., Daiuto, A. D., & Stickle, T. R. (1998). Empirically supported couple and family interventions for marital distress and adult mental health problems. *Journal of Consulting and Clinical Psychology, 66,* 53–88.

Baumeister, R. F., Smart, R., & Boden, J. M. (1996). Relation of threatened egotism to violence and aggression: The dark side of high self esteem. *Psychological Review, 103,* 5–33.

Baxter. I. M., Schwartz, J. M., Bergman, K. S., Szuba, M. P., Grunz, B. H., Mazzio, I. C., Alazalei, A., Selin, C., Freng, H. K., Minford, P., & Phelps, M. (1992). Caudate glucose metabolic rate changes with both drug and behavior therapy for obsessive-compulsive disorder. *Archives of General Psychiatry, 45,* 1117–1119.

Beck, A. T. (1967). *Depression: Clinical, experimental, and theoretical aspects.* New York: Hocker.

Beck, A. T. (1976). *Cognitive therapy and the emotional disorders.* New York: International Universities Press.

Beck, A. T. (1983). Cognitive therapy of depression: New perspectives. In P. J. Clayton & J. E. Barrett (Eds.), *Treatment of depression: Old controversies and new approaches* (pp. 265–280). New York: Raven Press.

Beck, A. T., Rush, J., Shaw, B., & Emery, G. (1979). *Cognitive therapy of depression.* New York: Guilford Press.

Becker, M. H., & Rosenstock, J. M. (1984). Compliance with medical advice. In A. Steptoe & A. Mathews (Eds.), *Health care and human behavior* (pp. 175–208). London: Academic Press.

Becker, R. E., Heimberg, R. G., & Bellack, A. S. (1987). *Social skills training for depression.* New York: Pergamon Press.

Benjamin, L. S. (1994). SASB: A bridge between personality theory and clinical psychology. *Psychological Inquiries, 5,* 273–316.

Benne, K. (1964). History of the T-Group in the laboratory setting. In L. Bradford, J. Gibb, & K. Benne (Eds.), *T-group theory and laboratory methods* (pp. 80–135). New York: John Wiley.

Bergin, A. E., & Garfield, S. L. (Eds.). (1971). *Handbook of psychotherapy and behavior change.* New York: Wiley.

Bergin, A. E., & Garfield, S. L. (Eds.). (1994). *Handbook of psychotherapy and behavior change* (4th ed.). New York: Wiley.

Bergin, A. E., & Lambert, M. J. (1978). The evaluation of therapeutic outcomes. In S. L. Garfield & A. E. Bergin (Eds.), *Handbook of psychotherapy and behavior change* (2nd ed.; pp. 139–189). New York: Wiley.

Berne, E. (1961). *Transactional analysis in psychotherapy.* London: Souvenir Press Ltd.

Berne, E. (1964). *Games people play.* New York: Grove Press.

Berne, E. (1966). *Principles of group treatment.* New York: Oxford University Press.

Bettelheim, B. (1950). *Love is not enough.* New York: Free Press.

Bettelheim, B. (1967). *The empty fortress.* New York: Free Press.

Bettelheim, B. (1973). Psychotherapy and psychopedagogy. *Psychotherapy and Psychosomatics, 20,* 45–55.

Bettelheim, B. (1974). *A home for the heart.* New York: Knopf.

Biklen, D. (1990). Communication unbound: Autism and praxis. *Harvard Educational Review, 60,* 291–313.

Biklen, D. and Schubert, A. (1991). New words: The communication of students with autism. *Remedial and special education, 12,* 46–57.

Bjorkqvist, S. E. (1975). Clonidine in alcohol withdrawal. *Acta Psychiatrica Scandinavica, 52,* 256–263.

Block, J. (1995). A contrarian view to the five-factor approach to personality description. *Psychological Bulletin, 177,* 187–213.

Boddington, S. J. A., & Lavender, A. (1995). Treatment models for couples therapy: A review of the literature and the Dodo's verdict. *Sexual and marital therapy, 10,* 69–81.

Borduin, C. M., Mann, B. J., Cone, L. T., Henggeler, S. W., Fucci, B. R., Blaske, D. M., & Williams, R. A. (1995). Multisystemic treatment of serious juvenile offenders: Long-term presentation of criminality and violence. *Journal of Consulting and Clinical Psychology, 63,* 569–578.

Bourgeois, L., Sabourin, L. S., & Wright, J. (1990). Predictive validity of therapeutic alliance in group marital therapy. *Journal of Consulting and Clinical Psychology, 89,* 181–193.

Bowlby, J. (1951). Maternal care and mental health. *World Health Organization Monograph.* (Serial No. 2).

Bowlby, J. (1958). The nature of the child's tie to his mother. *International Journal of Psycho-Analysis, 39,* 1–23.

Bowlby, J. (1960). Grief and mourning in infancy and early childhood. *The Psychoanalytic Study of the Child, 15,* 3–39.

Bowlby, J. (1969) *Attachment and loss, Vol. 1: Attachment.* New York: Basic Books.

Bowlby, J. (1973). *Attachment and loss, Vol. 2: Separation.* New York: Basic Books.

Bowlby, J. (1980). *Attachment and loss, Vol. 3: Loss, sadness and depression.* New York: Basic Books.

Bowlby, J. (1988). *A secure base: Parent-child attachment and healthy human development.* New York: Basic Books.

Bretherton, I. (1992). The origins of attachment theory: John Bowlby and Mary Ainsworth. *Developmental Psychology, 28,* 759–775.

Breuer, J., & Freud, S. (1955). Studies on hysteria. In standard edition of *The complete works of Sigmund Freud* (Vol. 2). London: Hogarth. (Original published in 1895)

Brill, N. D., & Beebe, G. W. (1955). *Washington Veterans Administration Medical Monograph.*

Brink, R. L. (1979). *Geriatric psychotherapy.* New York: Human Sciences Press.

Brody, N. (1990). Behavior therapy versus placebo: Commentary on Bowers and Clum's meta-analysis. *Psychological Bulletin, 107,* 106–109.

Bromfield, R. (1995). The use of puppets in play therapy. *Child and Adolescent-Social Work Journal, 12,* 435–444.

Brown, G. W., Birley, J. L. T., & Wing, J. K. (1972). Influence of family life on the course of schizophrenic disorders: A replication. *British Journal of Psychiatry, 121,* 241–258.

Bruch, H. (1978). *The golden age: The enigma of anorexia nervosa.* Cambridge, MA: Harvard University Press.

Burchard, J. D. (1967). Systematic socialization: A programmed environment for the habilitation of antisocial retardates. *Psychological Record, 17,* 461–476.

Burnside, I., & Haight, B. (1994). Reminiscence and life review: Therapeutic interventions with older people. *Nursing Practice, 19*(4), 55–61.

Cantor, N., Smith, E., French, R. D. S., & Mezzich, J. (1980). Psychiatric diagnosis as prototype categorization. *Journal of Abnormal Psychology, 89,* 181–193.

Carson, R. C. (1993). Can the big five help salvage the DSM? *Psychological Inquiries, 5,* 317–319.

Carson, R. C., Butcher, J. N., & Mineka, S. (1998). *Abnormal psychology and modern life.* (10th Ed.). New York: Longman.

Cath, S. H., & Sadavoy, J. (1991). Psychosocial aspects. In S. Sadavoy, L. W. Lazarus, & L. F. Lissey (Eds.), *Comprehensive review of geriatric psychiatry* (pp. 79–116). Washington, D.C.: American Psychiatric Press.

Cattell, R. B. (1966). *The scientific analysis of personality.* Chicago: Aldine.

Chambless, D. L., & Hollon, S. D. (1998). Defining empirically supported therapies. J*ournal of Consulting and Clinical Psychology, 66,* 7–18.

Chic, J., Gough, K., Falkowski, W., & Kernshaw, P. (1992). Disulfiram treatment of alcoholism. *British Journal of Psychiatry, 161,* 84–89.

Ciaccio, N. V. (1971). A test of Erikson's theory of ego epigenesis. *Developmental Psychology, 4,* 306–311.

Cleckley, H. (1954). *The mask of sanity.* St. Louis, MO: Mosby.

Coleman, J. C., Butcher, J. N., & Carson, R. C. (1984). *Abnormal psychology and modern life.* Glenview, IL: Scott, Foresman.

Finch, A. J., Nelson, W. M., & Ott, E. S. (1993). *Helping the noncompliant child: A practical guide.* Needham Heights, MA: Allyn & Bacon.

Finckenauer, J. O. (1984). *Juvenile delinquency and corrections. The gap between theory and practice.* Florida: Academic Press.

Fischer, K. W. (1983). Developmental levels as periods of discontinuity. *New Directions for Child Development, 21,* 5–20.

Foa, U. G. (1961). Convergence in the analysis of the structure of interpersonal behavior. *Psychological Review, 68,* 341–353.

Folks, D. G., & Kinney, F. (1992). The role of psychological factors in dermatalogic conditions. *Psychosomatics, 33,* 45–54.

Folsom, J. C. (1968). Reality orientation for the elderly mental patient. *Journal of Geriatric Psychiatry, 1,* 291–307.

Fowler, R. D. (1996). *American Psychologist, 51* (10).

Foxx, R. M., & Azrin, N. H. (1973). Dry pants: A rapid method of toilet training children. *Behavior Research and Therapy, 11,* 435–442.

Frances, A. (1980). The DSM-III personality disorders section: A commentary. *American Journal of Psychiatry, 137*(9), 1050–1054.

Frances, A., Widiger, T., & Fryer, M. R. (1990). The influence of classification methods on comorbidity. In J. D. Maser & C. R. Clonginer (Eds.), *Comorbidity of mood and anxiety disorders* (pp. 42–59). Washington, D.C.: Psychiatric Press.

Frankel, F. H., & Zamanbsky, H. S. (Eds.). (1978). *Hypnosis at its bicentennial.* New York: Plenum.

Frank, J. D. (1961). *Persuasion and healing: A comparative study of psychotherapy.* New York: Schocken.

Frankl, V. (1960). Paradoxical intention: A logotherapeutic technique. *American Journal of Psychotherapy, 14,* 520–535.

Frankl, V. (1963). *Man's search for meaning: An introduction to logotherapy.* New York: Pocket Books.

Frankl, V. (1965). Fragments from the logotherapeutic treatment of four cases. In A. Burton (Ed.), *Modern psychotherapeutic practice* (pp. 365–367). Palo Alto, CA: Science and Behavior Books.

Freedheim, D. K. (Ed.). (1992). *History of psychotherapy: A century of change.* Washington, D.C.: American Psychological Association.

Freedman, A. M., Brotman, R., Silverman, I., & Hutson, D. (Eds.). (1986). *Issues in psychiatric classification.* New York: Human Sciences Press.

Freidman, L. (1997). Ferrum, ignis, and medicina: Return to the crucible. *Journal of the American Psychoanalytic Association, 45*(1), 21–78.

Freidman, M. (1969). *Pathogenesis of coronary artery disease.* New York: McGraw-Hill.

Freud, A. (1946). *Ego and the mechanisms of defense.* New York: International Universities Press.

Freud, A. (1976). Changes in psychoanalytic practice and experience. *International Journal of Psycho-Analysis, 57,* 257–260.

Freud, S. (1901, 1961). *Interpretation of dreams* (J. Strachey, Trans). New York: Science Editions.

Freud, S. (1964). *An outline of psychoanalysis* (J. Strachey, Trans.). London: Hogarth.

Fromm, E. (1941). *Escape from Freedom.* New York: Holt, Rinehart and Winston.

Fromm, E. (1947). *Man for himself.* New York: Rinehart.

Fromm, E. (1955). *The sane society.* New York: Rinehart.

Fromm, E. (1956). *The art of loving.* New York: Harper and Row.

Fromm, E. (1973). *The anatomy of human destructiveness.* New York: Rinehart and Winston.

Fromm-Reichmann, F. (1950). *Principles of intensive psychotherapy.* Chicago: University of Chicago Press.

Garfield, S. L., & Bergin, A. E. (Eds.) (1978). *Handbook of psychotherapy and behavior change* (2nd ed.). New York: Wiley.

Gaston, L., Marnsar, C. R., Thompson, L. W., & Gallager, D. (1988). Relation of patient pretreatment characteristics to the therapeutic alliance in diverse psychotherapies. *Journal of Consulting and Clinical Psychology, 56,* 483–489.

Gidron, Y., & Davidson, K. (1996). Development and preliminary testing of a brief intervention for modifying CHD—predictive hostility components. *Journal of Behavioral Medicine, 19,* 203–220.

Gilliand, B. E., James, R. K., & Bowman, J. T. (1994). *Counseling and psychotherapy.* Needham Heights, MA: Simon and Schuster.

Glasser, W. (1965, 1975). *Reality therapy: A new approach to psychiatry.* New York: Harper and Row.

Glassman, H. H., Jackson, W. K., Walsh, B. T., & Roose, S. P. (1984) Cigarette craving, smoking withdrawal, and clonidine. *Science, 226,* 864–866.

Glickauf-Hughes, C., Wells, M. C., & Genirberg, R. (1987). Psychotherapy of gifted students with narcissistic dynamics. *Journal of College Student Psychotherapy 1*(3), 99–115.

Glueck, S., & Glueck, E. (1950). *Unraveling juvenile delinquency.* Cambridge, MA: Harvard Commonwealth Fund.

Gold, M. S., Pottash, A. C., Sweeney, D. R., & Kleber, H. D. (1980). Opiate withdrawal using clonidine. *Journal of the American Medical Association, 243,* 343–346.

Gold, M. S., Redmond, D. E., & Kleber, H. D. (1978). Clonidine in opiate withdrawal. *Lancet, 1,* 929–930.

Golderson, R. M. (1970). *The encyclopedia of human behavior* (Vol. 2). Garden City, NY: Doubleday.

Goldfarb, W. (1945). Psychological privation in infancy and subsequent adjustment. *American Journal of Orthopsychiatry, 15,* 247–255.

Goldman, A., & Greenberg, L. (1992). Comparison of integrated systemic and emotionally focused approaches to couples therapy. *Journal of Consulting and Clinical Psychology, 60,* 962–969.

Goldstein, D. (1983). *Pharmacology of alcohol.* New York: Oxford University Press.

Goldstein, K. (1939). *The organism.* New York: American Book Co.

Gossette, R. L., & O'Brien, R. M. (1992). The efficacy of rational emotive therapy in adults: Clinical fact or psychometric artifact? *Journal of Behavioral Therapy and Experimental Psychiatry, 23*(1), 9–24.

Gossette, R. L., & O'Brien, R. M. (1993). The efficacy of rational emotive therapy (RET) with children: A critical re-appraisal. *Journal of Behavioral Therapy and Experimental Psychiatry, 24*(1), 15–25.

Gottesman, I. I., & Shields, J. (1972). *Schizophrenia and genetics: A twin study vantage point.* New York: Academic Press.

Gough, H. G. (1957). *Manual for the California psychological inventory.* Palo Alto, CA: Consulting Psychologists Press.

Grandjean, P., & York, M. W. (1979). The police and psychological disturbances. In R. E. Farmer (Ed.), *The police and social problems: The grey areas* (pp. 95–113). New Haven, CT: University of New Haven: Criminal Justice Monograph Series.

Greenwald, H. (1967). *Active psychotherapy.* New York: Atherton Press.

Gronfein, W. (1985). Psychotropic drugs and the origins of deinstitutionalization. *Social Problems 32*(5), 437–454.

Gunderson, J. G. (1975). A spectrum of modalities for treating schizophrenia. *Hospital and Community Psychiatry, 26*(2), 332–341.

Gunderson, J. G. (1978). Patient-therapist matching: A research evaluation. *American Journal of Psychiatry, 135,* 1193–1197.

Gunderson, J. G. (1988). Narcissistic traits in psychiatric patients. *Comprehensive Psychiatry, 29,* 545–549.

Gurman, A. S., & Messer, S. B. (Eds.). (1995). *Essential psychotherapies.* New York: Guilford Press.

Haas, K. (1965). Directions of hostility and psychiatric symptoms. *Psychological Reports 16*(2), 555–556.

Hahlweg, K., Schindler, L., Revenstorf, D., & Brengelmann, J. C. (1984). The Munich marital therapy study. In K. Hahlweg and N. S. Jacobson (Eds.), *Marital interactions: Analysis and modification* (pp. 3–26). New York: Guilford Press.

Haley, J. (1963). *Strategies of psychotherapy.* New York: Grune and Stratton. San Francisco: Jossey-Bass.

Haley, J. (1976). *Problem-solving therapy.* San Francisco: Jossey-Bass.

Hall, C. S., & Lindzey, G. (1970). *Theories of personality* (3rd ed.). New York: Wiley.

Hallowell, E. M., & Ratey, J. J. (1994). *Driven to Distraction.* New York: Touchstone.

Hannacheck, D. (1990). Evaluating self-concept and ego status in Erikson's last three psychosocial stages. *Journal of Counseling and Development, 68,* 677–683.

Hare, R. D., Hart, S. D., & Harpur, T. J. (1991). Psychopathology and the DSM-IV criteria for antisocial personality disorder. *Journal of Abnormal Psychology, 100,* 391–398.

Harlow, H. F. (1961). The development of affectional patterns in infant monkeys. In E. M. Foss (Ed.), *Determinants of infant behavior* (pp. 75–97). London: Methuen.

Kernberg, O. F. (1975). *Borderline conditions and pathological narcissism.* New York: Jason Aronson.

Kernberg, O. F. (1976). *Object relations theory and clinical psychoanalysis.* New York: Jason Aronson.

Kernberg, O. F. (1985). *Borderline conditions and pathological narcissism.* Northvale, NJ: Prentice Hall.

Kessler, J. W. (1966). *Psychopathology of childhood.* Englewood Cliffs, NJ: Prentice Hall.

Klerman, G. L., & Weissman, M. M. (Eds.). (1993). *New applications of interpersonal psychotherapy.* Washington, D.C.: American Psychiatric Press.

Klerman, G. L., Weissman, M. M., Rounsaville, B. J., & Chevron, E. S. (1984). *Interpersonal psychotherapy of depression.* New York: Basic Books.

Kohlberg, L. (1963). The development of children's orientations toward a moral order. I. Sequence in the development of moral thought. *Vita Humana, 6,* 11–33.

Kohlberg, L. (1981). *Essay on moral development: Volume I. Moral stages and the idea of justice.* San Francisco: Harper and Row.

Kohut, H. (1971, 1977). *The analysis of self.* New York: International Universities Press.

Kozel, N. J., & Adams, E. H. (1986). Epidemiology of drug abuse: An overview. *Science, 234,* 970–974.

Kronenberger, W. G., & Meyer, R. E. (1996). *The child clinician's handbook.* Needham Heights, MA: Allyn & Bacon.

Kupers, T. A. (1988). *Ending therapy.* New York: University Press.

LaForge, R. (1977). Interpersonal Check List (ICL). In J. E. Jones & W. J. Pfeiffer (Eds.), *The 1977 annual handbook for group facilitators* (6th annual ed., pp. 89–96). LaJolla, CA: University Associates.

Laing, R. D. (1959). *The divided self.* London: Tavistock.

Lambert, M. J., Shapiro, D. A., & Bergin, A. E. (1986). The effectiveness of psychotherapy. In S. L. Garfield & A. E. Bergin (Eds.), *Handbook of psychotherapy and behavior change: An empirical analysis* (3rd ed., pp. 157–211). New York: Wiley.

Lazarus, A. A. (1971). *Behavior therapy and beyond.* New York: McGraw-Hill.

Lazarus, A. A. (1977). New methods in psychotherapy: A case study. *South African Medical Journal, 32,* 660–664.

Lazarus, A. A. (1981). *The practice of multimodal therapy.* New York: McGraw-Hill.

Lazarus, L. W., Sadavoy, J., & Langsley, P. R. (1991). Individual psychotherapy. In J. Sadavoy, L. W. Lazarus, & L. F. Jarvik (Eds.), *Comprehensive review of geriatric psychiatry* (pp. 487–512). Cambridge, MA: Quantum Books.

Leary, T. (1957). *Interpersonal diagnosis of personality.* New York: Ronald Press.

Lee, R. (1994). Couples shame: The unaddressed issue. In G. Wheeler & S. Backman (Eds.) *On intimate ground: A Gestalt approach to working with couples* (pp. 262–290). San Francisco: Jossey-Bass.

Lief, A. (1948). *The commonsense psychiatry of Dr. Adolf Meyer.* New York: McGraw-Hill.

Lettick, A. L. (1979). *Benhaven at work (1978).* East Haven, CT: The Benhaven Press.

Levensen, E. A. (1992). Mistakes, errors, and oversights. *Contemporary Psychoanalysis, 28,* 555–571.

Levinson, D. J. (1978). *The seasons of a man's life.* New York: Alfred A. Knopf.

Levitsky, A., & Perls, F. S. (1970). The rules and games of gestalt therapy. In J. Fagan & I. L. Shepard (Eds.), *Gestalt therapy now* (pp. 140–149). Palo Alto, CA: Science and Behavior Books. Quoted in Patterson, C. J., & Watkins, C. E. (1996). *Theories of psychotherapy* (5th ed., p. 370). New York: HarperCollins.

Lewin, J., & Lewis, S. (1995). Organic and psychological risk factors for duodenal ulcer. *Journal of Psychosomatic Research, 39,* 531–548.

Lewinsohn, P. M. (1974). A behavioral approach to depression. In R. J. Friedman & M. M. Katz (Eds.), *The psychology of depression: Contemporary theory and research* (pp. 157–186). Washington, D.C.: Winston.

Lindner, R. (1944). *Rebel without a cause—the hypnoanalysis of a criminal psychopath.* New York: Grune and Stratton.

Lindner, R. (1954). *The fifty-minute hour.* New York: Holt, Rinehart, & Winston.

Lindsley, O. R. (1956). Operant conditioning methods applied to research in chronic schizophrenia. *Psychiatric Research Report, 5,* 118–139.

Linehan, M. M. (1993). *Cognitive-behavior treatment of the borderline personality disorder.* New York: The Guilford Press.

Linn, L. S. (1970). State hospital environment and rates of patient discharge. *Archives of General Psychiatry, 23*(4), 346–351.

Lipsey, M. W., & Wilson, D. B. (1993). The efficacy of psychological, educational, and behavioral treatment: Confirmation from meta-analysis. *American Psychologist, 12,* 1181–1209.

Lipsey, M. W., & Wilson, D. B. (1995). Reply to comments on Lipsey and Wilson. (1993). *American Psychologist, 50,* 113–115.

Livesley, W. J., Schroeder, M. L., Jackson, D. N., & Jang, K. L. (1994). Categorical distinctions in the study of personality disorders: Implications for classifications. *Journal of Abnormal Psychology, 103,* 6–17.

Lloyd, K. E., & Abel, L. (1970). Performance on a token economy psychiatric ward: A two year summary. *Behavior and Research in Therapy, 8,* 1–9.

Loevinger, J. (1966). The meaning and measurement of ego development. *American Psychologist, 21,* 196–206.

London, P. (1972). The end of ideology in behavior modification. *American Psychologist, 27,* 913–918.

LoPiccolo, J., & Lobitz, W. C. (1972). The role of masturbation in the treatment of orgasmic dysfunction. *Archives of Sexual Behavior, 2,* 163–171.

Lorr, M., & McNair, D. M. (1965). Expansion of the interpersonal behavior circle. *Journal of Personality and Social Psychology, 2,* 823–830.

Lovaas, O. I. (1973). Behavioral treatment of autistic children. *University programs modular series.* Morristown, NJ: General Learning Press.

Lovaas, O. I. (1987). Behavioral treatment and abnormal education and intellectual functioning in young autistic children. *Journal of Consulting and Clinical Psychology. 55,* 3–9.

Luborsky, L. (1995). Are common factors across different psychotherapies the main explanation for the dodo verdict that "Everybody has won so all shall have prizes"? *Clinical Psychology Science and Practice, 2,* 106–109.

Luborsky, L., & Barber, J. P. (1993). Benefit of adherence to psychotherapy manuals and where to get them. In Miller, N. E., Luborsky, L., Barber, J. P., & Dockerty, J. P. (Eds.), *Psychodynamic treatment research* (pp. 211–226). New York: Basic Books.

Maduro, R. J., & Wheelwright, J. B. (1977). Analytical psychology. In R. J. Corsini (Ed.), *Current personality theories* (pp. 83–124). Itasca, IL: F. E. Peacock.

Mahler, M., McDevitt, J., Setflage, C. (1971). *Separation-individuation: Essays in honor of Margaret S. Mahler.* New York: International Universities Press.

Maier, S. F., Watkins, L. R., & Fleshner, M. (1994). Psychoneuroimmunology: The interface between behavior, brain, and immunity. *American Psychologist, 49,* 1004–1017.

Mann, B. J., Borduin, C. M., Henggeler, S. W., & Blaske, D. M. (1990). An investigation of systemic conceptualizations of parent-child coalitions and symptom change. *Journal of Consulting and Clinical Psychology, 58,* 336–344.

Mann, G. A. (1979). *Recovery of reality: Overcoming chemical dependency.* San Francisco: Harper and Row.

March, J. S., & Mille, K. (1996). Banishing *OCD*: Cognitive-behavioral psychotherapy for obsessive-compulsive disorders. In E. D. Hibbs & P. S. Jensen (Eds.), *Psychosocial treatments for child and adolescent disorders* (pp. 83–102). Washington, D.C.: American Psychological Association.

Marston, W. H. (1928). *Emotions of normal people.* New York: Harcourt, Brace & Company.

Maslow, A. H. (1970). *Motivation and personality* (rev. ed.). New York: Harper & Row.

Masson, J. M. (1988). *Against therapy: Emotional tyranny and the myth of psychological healing.* New York: Atheneum.

Masters, W. H., & Johnson, V. E. (1970). *Human sexual inadequacy.* Boston: Little, Brown.

Maurice, C., Green, G., & Luce, S. C. (Eds.). (1996). *Behavioral intervention for young children with autism.* Austin, TX: Pro. Ed.

May, R. (1950). *The meaning of anxiety.* New York: Ronald Press.

May, R. (1961). *Existential psychology.* New York: Random House.

May, R. (1972). *Power and innocence: A search for the sources of violence.* New York: Norton.

McCord, W. (1985). The effectiveness of milieu therapy with psychopaths. *Milieu Therapy, 4,* 29–40.

McCord, W., & McCord, J. (1956). *The psychopath: An essay on the criminal mind.* New York: Grune and Stratton.

McEachlin, J. J., Smith, T., & Lovaas, O. I. (1993). Long term outcome for children with autism who received early intensive behavioral treatment. *American Journal on Mental Retardation, 4,* 359–372.

Meany, M. (1998, March). *Stress and disease.* Paper presented at Mind Matters Seminar, Schubert Theater, New Haven, CT.

Mechanic, D. (1987). Correcting misconception in mental health policy: Strategies for improved care of the seriously mental ill. *The Millbank Quarterly, 65,* 203–230.

Meehl, P. E. (1962). Schizotaxia, schizotypy, schizophrenia. *American Psychologist, 17,* 827–838.

Meichenbaum, D. (1977). *Cognitive behavior modification.* New York: Plenum Press.

Melnick, J., & Nevis, S. M. (1994). Intimacy and power in long term relationships: A Gestalt therapy systems perspective. In G. Wheeler & S. Bachman (Eds.), *On intimate grounds.* San Francisco: Jossey-Bass.

Meltzoff, J., & Kornreich, M. (1970). *Research in psychotherapy.* New York: Aldine.

Metalsky, G. I., & Joiner, T. E. (1992). Vulnerability to depressive symptomatology: A prospective test of the diathesis-stress and causal mediation components of the hopelessness theory of depression. *Journal of Personality and Social Psychology, 63,* 667–675.

Meyer, C. B., & Taylor, S. E. (1986). Adjustment to rape. *Journal of Personality and Social Psychology, 50,* 1226–1234.

Meyer, R. G. (1989). *The clinician's handbook* (2nd ed.). Needham Heights, MA: Allyn & Bacon.

Miller, N. E., Luborsky, L., Barber, J. P., & Dorherty, J. P. (Eds.). (1993). *Psychodynamic treatment research: A handbook for clinical practice.* New York: Basic Books.

Millon, T. (1991). Classification in psychopathology: Rationale, alternatives and standards. *Journal of Abnormal Psychology, 100,* 245–261.

Millon, T., & Davis, R. O. (1996). *Disorders of personality: DSM-IV and beyond* (2nd ed.). New York: Wiley.

Minuchin, S. (1974). *Families and family therapy.* Cambridge, MA: Harvard University Press.

Mittleman, B. (1948). The concurrent analysis of married couples. *The Psychoanalytic Quarterly, 17,* 474–491.

Monahan, L. H. (1977). Diagnosis and expectation for change: An inverse relationship? *Journal of Nervous and Mental Diseases, 164,* 214–217.

Moreno, J. (1953). *Who shall survive?* New York: Beacon House.

Mosher, L. R. (1974). Psychiatric heretics and the extra-medical treatment of schizophrenia. In R. Cancro & N. Fox, (Eds.), *Strategic intervention in schizophrenia* (pp. 279–302). New York: Behavioral Publications.

Mosher, L. R., Menn, A., & Matthews, S. M. (1975). Soteria: Evaluation of a home-based treatment for schizophrenia. *American Journal of Orthopsychiatry, 45,* 455–467.

Mowrer, O. H. (1960). *Learning theory and the symbolic processes.* New York: Wiley.

Mowrer, O. H. (1961). *The crisis in psychiatry and religion.* New York: D. Van Nostrand Press.

Mrazek, D. A. (1993). Asthma: Stress, allergies and the genes. In D. Goleman & J. Gurin (Eds.), *Mind body medicine* (pp. 193–206). Yonkers, NY: Consumer Reports Books.

Myers, I. (1962). *The Myers-Briggs type indicator.* Princeton, N.J.: Educational Testing Service.

Newman, M. G., & Cates, M. S. (1977). *Methadone treatment in narcotic addiction.* New York: Academic Press.

Nichols, M. P., & Schwartz, R. C. (1995). *Family therapy concepts and methods* (3rd ed.). Boston: Allyn & Bacon.

Nietzel, M. T., Speltz, M. L., McCauley, E. A., & Bernstein, D. A. (1998). *Abnormal psychology.* Needham Heights, MA: Allyn & Bacon.

Nirenberg, T. D. (1983). Treatment of substance abuse. In C. E. Walker (Eds.), *The handbook of clinical psychology,* (Vol. 2, pp. 633–665). Homewood, IL: Dow Jones-Irwin.

O'Brien, W. B., & Biase, V. D. (1984). The therapeutic community: A current perspective. *Journal of Psychoactive Drugs, 16,* 9–21.

O'Farrell, T. J., Choquette, K. A., Cutter, H. S. G., Brown, E. D., Bayog, R., McCourt, W., Lowe, J., Chan, A., & Deneault, P. (1996). Cost-benefit and cost effectiveness analysis of behavioral marital therapy with and without relapse-prevention sessions for alcoholics and their wives. *Journal of Studies on Alcohol, 54,* 652–666.

O'Farrell, T. J., Cutter, H. S. G., & Floyd, F. J. (1985). Evaluating behavioral marital therapy for male alcoholics: Effects on marital adjustment and communication before and after treatment. *Behavior Therapy, 16,* 147–167.

Orlofsky, J. L. (1976). Intimacy status: Relationship of interpersonal perception. *Journal of Youth and Adolescence, 5,* 73–88.

Ornish, D. (1982). *A lifetime program for healing your heart without drugs or surgery.* New York: Signet.

Palazzoli, S., Boscolo, M., Cecchin, L., & Prata, G. (1978). *Paradox and counterparadox.* New York: Jason Aronson.

Paris, J. (1973). Psychiatry and ideology. *Canadian Psychiatry Association Journal, 18*(2), 147–151.

Parnas, J. (1986). Risk factors in the development of schizophrenia: Contributions from a study of schizophrenic mothers. *Danish Medical Bulletin, 33,* 127–133.

Parr, A. E. (1977) Preparing for the future: Art, heart, and habitat. *Occasional Stiles,* 25–29.

Parsons, F. (1909). *Choosing a vocation.* Boston: Houghton Mifflin.

Patrick, J. (1986). Therapeutic response to rage reactions in the treatment of severely disturbed narcissistic personality disorders. *Dynamic Psychotherapy, 4*(2), 151–158.

Patterson, C. H. (1989). Eclecticism in psychotherapy: Is integration possible? *Psychotherapy, 26,* 157–161.

Patterson, C. H., & Hidork, S. C. (1997). *Successful psychotherapy: A caring, loving relationship.* Northvale, NJ: Jason Arousn.

Patterson, C. H., & Watkins, Jr., C. E. (1996). *Theories of psychotherapy* (5th ed.). New York: HarperCollins.

Patterson, G. R. (1982). *Coercive family process.* Eugene, OR: Castalia Press.

Patterson, G. R. (1984). Siblings: Fellow travelers in the coercive family process. In B. J. Blanchard & D. C. Blanchard (Eds.), *Advances in the study of aggression* (pp. 174–213). New York: Academic Press.

Patterson, G. R., Dishion, T. J., & Chamberlain, P. (1993). Outcomes and methodological issues relating to treatment of antisocial children. In T. R. Giles (Ed.), *Handbook of affective psychotherapy* (pp. 43–88). New York: Plenum Press.

Patterson, G. R., Reid, J. B., & Dishion, T. J. (1992). *A social learning approach: IV. Antisocial boys.* Eugene, OR: Castalia.

Paul, G. L. (1967). Strategy of outcome research in psychotherapy. *Journal of Consulting Psychology, 3,* 109–118.

Paul, G. L., & Lentz, R. J. (1977). *Psychosocial treatment of chronic mental patients: Milieu versus social-learning programs.* Cambridge, MA: Harvard University Press.

Pavlov, I. P. (1927). *Conditioned reflexes: An investigation of the physiological activity of the cerebral cortex* (G. V. Anrep, Trans.). London: Oxford University Press.

Pavlov, I. P. (1928). *Lectures on conditioned reflexes* (W. H. Gantt, Trans.). London: Lawrence and Wishart.

Peele, S. (1989). 'Ain't Misbehavin': Addiction has become an all purpose excuse. *The Sciences, 29,* 14–21.

Perls, F. S., Hefferline, R. F., & Goodman, P. (1951). *Gestalt therapy.* New York: Dell.

Piaget, J. (1952). *The origins of intelligence in children.* New York: International University Press.

Powers, E., & Witmer, H. (1951). *An experiment in the prevention of delinquency.* New York: Columbia Press.

Price, V. A. (1982). *Type A behavior pattern: A model for research and practice.* New York: Academic Press.

Pritchard, J. C. (1835). *A treatise on insanity.* Philadelphia: Barrington and Haswell.

Rabinowitz, J. (1993). Pitfalls of decision making in mental health practice. *Megamot, 34,* 600–622.

Rachman, S., & Eysenck, J. J. (1965). *The causes and cures of neuroses.* New York: Robert E. Knapp Publ.

Rapoport, R. N. (1960). *Community as doctor: New perspectives on a therapeutic community.* Springfield, IL: Charles C. Thomas.

Redl, F., & Wineman, D. (1951, 1954). *Children who hate.* Chicago, IL: Free Press.

Rees, L. (1964). The importance of psychological, allergic and infective factors in childhood asthma. *Journal of Psychosomatic Research, 7,* 253–262.

Reid, W. H. (1989). *The treatment of psychiatric disorders.* New York: Brunner/Mazel.

Rice, M. E. (1997). Violent offender research and implications for the criminal justice system. *The American Psychologist, 52,* 414–423.

Rice, P. K. (1969). *The modification of interpersonal roles.* Unpublished doctoral dissertation, West Virginia University.

Richelsen, E. (1993). Treatment of acute depression. *Psychiatric Clinics of North America, 16,* 461–478.

Riesman, D., Glazer, N., & Denney, R. (1950). *The lonely crowd.* New Haven: Yale University Press.

Rigazio-DiGilio, S. A., Goncalves, O. F., & Ivey, A. E. (1996). From cultural to existential diversity: The impossibility of psychotherapy integration within a traditional framework. *Applied and Preventive Psychology, 5,* 235–247.

Rimland, B. (1964). *Infantile autism.* New York: Meredith.

Rimland, B. (1993). Facilitated communication update: The paradox continues. *Autism Research Review International, 7,* 9–10.

Robbins, L. N., Helzer, J. E., Weissman, M. M., Orvaschel, A., Gruenberg, E., Burke, J. D., & Regier, D. A. (1984). Lifetime prevalence of specific psychiatric disorders in three cities. *Archives of General Psychiatry, 41,* 949–958.

Roethlisberger, F. J., & Dickson, W. J. (1939). *Management and the worker.* Cambridge, MA: Harvard University Press.

Rogers, C. R. (1942). *Counseling and psychotherapy; newer concepts in practice.* Boston: Houghton Mifflin.

Rogers, C. R. (1951). *Client-centered therapy: Its current practice, implications, and theory.* Boston, MA: Houghton Mifflin.

Rogers, C. R. (1957). The necessary and sufficient conditions of therapeutic personality change. *Journal of Consulting Psychology, 21,* 95–103.

Rogers, C. R. (1961). *On becoming a person.* Boston: Houghton Mifflin.

Rogers, C. R. (1967). *The therapeutic relationship and its impact: A study of psychotherapy with schizophrenics.* Madison, WI: University of Wisconsin Press.

Rogers, C. R. (1967). The process of the encounter group. In Bugental, J. F. (Ed.), *Challenges of humanistic psychology* (pp. 263–272). New York: McGraw-Hill.

Rogers, C. R., & Dymond, R. F. (1954). *Psychotherapy and personality change.* Chicago: University of Chicago Press.

Rosen, J. N. (1947). The treatment of schizophrenic psychosis by direct analytic therapy. *Psychiatric Quarterly, 21,* 117–131.

Rosen, J. N. (1953). *Direct analysis: Selected papers.* New York: Grove.

Rosen, J. N. (1962). *Direct psychoanalytic psychiatry.* New York: Grune and Statton.

Rosenhan, D. L. (1973). On being sane in insane places. *Science, 179,* 250–258.

Rosenhan, D. L., & Seligman, M. E. P. (1995). *Abnormal psychology* (3rd ed.). New York: Norton.

Rosenman, R. H., Brand, R. J., Jenkins, C. D., Friedman, M., Straus, R., & Wurm, M. (1975). Coronary heart disease in the Western Collaborative Group Study: Final follow-up experience of $8\frac{1}{2}$ years. *Journal of the American Medical Association, 233,* 872–877.

Russell, E. W. (1974). The power of behavior control: A critique of behavior modification methods. *Journal of Clinical Psychology, 30*(2), 111–116.

Russo, J., Viatiano, P. D., Brever, D. D., Koton, W., & Becker, J. (1995). Psychiatric disorders in spouse caregivers of care recipients with Alzheimer's disease and matched controls: A diathesis-stress model of psychopathology. *Journal of Abnormal Psychology, 104,* 197–204.

Sadavoy, J., Lazarus, L. W., & Javik, I. F. (Eds.). (1991). *Comprehensive review of geriatric psychiatry.* Cambridge, MA: Quantum Books.

Sahakian, W. S. (1976). *Psychotherapy and counseling.* Boston: Houghton Mifflin.

Salter, A. (1949). *Conditioned reflex therapy.* New York: Farrar.

Sanders, M. R., & Dadds, M. R. (1993). *Behavioral family intervention.* New York: Pergamon Press.

Sarafino, E. P. (1994). *Health psychology: Biopsychosocial interactions* (2nd ed.). New York: Wiley.

Sartre, J. P. (1956, 1974). *Being and nothingness* (H. E. Barnes, Trans.). New York: Citadel Press.

Scanland, S. G., & Emershaw, L. E. (1993). Reality orientation and validation therapy: dementia, depression, and functional status. *Journal of Gerontological Nursing, 19,* 7–11.

Schaefer, E. S. (1959). A circumflex model for maternal behavior. *Journal of Abnormal and Social Psychology, 59,* 232.

Schatzberg, A. F., & Cole, J. O. (1991). *Manual of clinical pharmacology* (2nd ed.). Washington, D.C.: American Psychiatric Press, Inc.

Schmideberg, M. (1945). The analytic treatment of major criminals: therapeutic results and technical problems. Psychology and treatment of criminal psychopaths. *International Journal of Psychoanalysis, 30,* 197.

Seligman, M. E. (1995). The effectiveness of psychotherapy. *American Psychologist, 50,* 965–974.

Shadish, W. R., Montomery, L. M., Wilson, P., Wilson M. R., Bright, I., & Okwambra, T. (1993). Effects of family and marital psychotherapies: A meta-analysis. *Journal of Consulting and Clinical Psychology, 61,* 992–1002.

Sherman, E. (1981). *Counseling the aging: An integrative approach.* New York: The Free Press.

Shook, G. L., & Favell, J. E. (1996). Identifying qualified professionals in behavioral analysis. In C. Mauruce, G. Green, & S. C. Luce (Eds.), *Behavioral intervention for young children with autism* (pp. 221–229). Austin, TX: Pro. Ed.

Shows, W. D. (1977). A psychological theory of later years: C. G. Jung. In W. D. Gentry (Ed.), *A model of training and clinical service.* Cambridge, MA: Ballinger Publishing Co.

Shure, M. B. (1992). *I can problem solve (ICPS): An interpersonal cognitive problem solving program.* Champaign, IL: Research Press.

Silverman, W. H. (1996). Cookbooks, manuals, and paint by numbers: Psychotherapy in the 90's. *Psychotherapy, 33,* 207–215.

Simon, R. I. (1995). The natural history of therapist sexual misconduct: Identification and prevention. *Psychiatric Annals, 25,* 90–94.

Singer, J. (1974). *Imagery and daydream methods in psychotherapy and behavior modification.* New York: Academic Press.

Skinner, B. F. (1953). *Science and human behavior.* New York: Macmillan.

Skinner, B. F. (1959). *Cumulative record.* New York: Appleton-Century-Crofts.

Skinner, B. F. (1961). *The analysis of behavior: A program for self-instruction.* New York: McGraw-Hill.

Skinner, B. F. (1966). An operant analysis of problem solving. In B. Kleinmuntz (Ed.), *Problem-solving: Research, method, and theory* (pp. 225–257). New York: Wiley.

Skinner, B. F. (1971). *Beyond freedom and dignity.* New York: Alfred Knopf.

Smith, M. L., & Glass, G. J. (1977). Meta-analysis of psychotherapy outcome studies. *American Psychologist, 32,* 752–760.

Snyder, D. K., Mangrum, L. F., & Wills, R. M. (1993). Predicting couples' response to marital therapy: A comparison of short- and long-term predictors. *Journal of Consulting and Clinical Psychology, 61,* 61–69.

Snyder, D. K., & Wills, R. M. (1989). Behavioral versus insight oriented marital therapy: Effects on individual and interpersonal functioning. *Journal of Consulting and Clinical Psychology, 57,* 39–46.

Sobell, M. B., & Sobell, L. D. (1978). *Behavioral treatment of alcohol problems: Individualized therapy and controlled drinking.* New York: Plenum.

Sohn, D. (1995). Meta-analysis as a means of discovery. *American Psychologist, 50,* 108–110.

Spitz, R. A. (1946). Anaclitic depression. *Psychoanalytic Study of the Child, 2,* 313–342.

Stehle, A. (1991). *The sound of a miracle.* New York: Doubleday.

Stern, D. A., Fromm, M. G., & Sacksteder, J. L. (1986). From coercion to collaboration: Two weeks in the life of a therapeutic community. *Psychiatry, 49,* 18–32.

Stevenson, J. (1999). The treatment of the long term sequelae of child abuse. *Journal of Child Psychology and Psychiatry and Allied Disciplines, 40,* 89–111.

Stipek, D., & Hoffman, J. (1980). Children's achievement related expectancies as a function of academic performance histories and sex. *Journal of Educational Psychotherapy, 72,* 861–865.

Stone, A. A., Reed, B. R., & Neale, J. M. (1987). Changes in daily event frequency precede episodes of physical symptoms. *Journal of Human Stress, 13,* 70–74.

Strupp, H. H. (1993). The Vanderbilt psychotherapy studies: Synopsis. *Journal of Consulting and Clinical Psychology, 61*(3), 431–433.

Strupp, H. H. (1996). The tripartite model and Consumer Reports study. *American Psychologist, 51,* 1017–1024.

Strupp, H. H., & Bergin, A. E. (1969). Trends in research in psychotherapy : A critical review of issues, trends, and evidence. *International Journal of Psychiatry, 7,* 2–37.

Stuart, R. B. (1980). *Helping couples change: A social learning approach to marital therapy.* New York: Guilford Press.

Stubbs, J. P., & Bozarath, J. D. (1994). The Dodo bird revisited: A qualitative study of psycho-therapy efficacy research. *Applied and Preventive Psychology, 3,* 109–120.

Sue, P., & Sue, E. (1990). *Counseling the culturally different* (2nd ed.). New York: Wiley.

Sullivan, C. T. (1967). Recent developments in "direct psychoanalysis." In H. Greenwald (Ed.), *Active psychotherapy* (pp. 90–107). New York: Atherton Press.

Sullivan, H. S. (1948). The meaning of anxiety in psychiatry and life. *Psychiatry, 11,* 1–13.

Sullivan, H. S. (1954). *The psychiatric interview.* New York: Norton.

Szatmari, P., Bremner, R., & Nagi, J. (1989). Asperger's syndrome: A review of clinical features. *Canadian Journal of Psychiatry, 34,* 554–560.

Tarnoski, K. J., Simonian, S. T., Beckley, P., & Park, A. (1992). Acceptability of interventions for childhood depression. *Behavior Modification, 16,* 103–117.

Taulbee, E. S., & Folsom, J. C. (1973). Attitude therapy: A behavior therapy approach. In R. R. Juryevich (Ed.), *Direct therapy.* Coral Gables, FL: University of Miami Press.

Thoresen, C. E., Friedman, M., Powell, L. H., Gill, J., & Ulmer, D. K. (1985). Altering the type A behavior pattern in postinfarction patients. *Journal of Cardiopulmonary Rehabilitation. 5,* 258–266.

Tillich, P. (1952). *The courage to be.* New Haven, CT: Yale University Press.

Toder, N. L., & Maria, J. E. (1973). Ego identity status and response to conformity pressure in college women. *Journal of Personality and Social Psychology, 26,* 287–294.

Traux, C. B., & Carkhuff, R. R. (1967). *Toward effective counseling and psychotherapy.* Chicago: Aldine.

Traux, C. B., & Mitchell, K. M. (1971). Research on certain therapist interpersonal skills in relation to process and outcome. In A. E. Bergin, & S. L. Garfield (Eds.), *Handbook of psychotherapy and behavior change* (pp. 299–344). New York: Wiley.

Tuckman, B. W. (1965). Developmental sequences in small groups. *Psychological Bulletin, 63,* 384–399.

Uchino, B. N., Cacioppo, J. T., & Kiecolt-Glaser, J. K. (1996). The relationship between social support and physiological processes: A review with an emphasis on underlying mechanisms and implications for health. *Psychological Bulletin, 119*(3), 488–531.

Urban, H. D., & Ford, D. H. (1971). Some historical and conceptual perspectives on psychotherapy and behavior change. In A. E. Bergin, & S. L. Garfield (Eds.), *Handbook of psychotherapy and behavior change* (pp. 3–35). New York: Wiley.

Valenstein, E. S. (1998). *Blaming the brain.* New York: The Free Press.

Valliant, G. E. (1977). *Adaptation to life.* Boston: Little, Brown.

Valliant, G. E., & Valliant, C. O. (1990). Natural history of male psychological health. XII: A 45-year study of predictors of successful aging at age 65. *American Journal of Psychiatry, 147*(1), 31–37.

VandenBos, G. R. (Ed.). (1996). Outcome assessment of psychotherapy: A special issue. *American Psychologist, 51*(10).

Van de Water, D. A., & McAdams, D. P. (1989). Generativity and Erikson's "belief in the species." *Journal of Research in Personality, 23,* 435–449.

Wachtel, P. L. (1977). *Psychoanalysis and behavior therapy: Toward an integration.* New York: Basic Books.

Wachtel, P. L. (1994). Clinical process in personality and psychopathology, *Journal of Abnormal Psychology, 103,* 51–54.

Walder, L. (personal communication, March 18, 1964).

Walker, E. F., Newman, C. C., Baum, K., & Davis, D. M. (1996). The developmental pathways to schizophrenia: Potential moderating effects of stress. *Development and Psychopathology, 8,* 647–665.

Walker, N. (1957). *A short history of psychotherapy in theory and practice.* London: Routledge and Kegan Paul Ltd.

Walker, P. Luther, J., Samloff, I. M., & Feldman, M. (1988). Life events and psychosocial factors in men with peptic ulcer disease. II. Relationship with serum pepsinogen concentrations and behavioral factors. *Gastroenterology, 94,* 323–330.

Wallace, J. (1989). A biopsychosocial model of alcoholism. *Social Casework: The Journal of Contemporary Social Work. 70,* 325–332.

Wallerstein, R. S. (1963, May 23). *Reconstruction and mastery in the transference psychosis.* Paper presented to the Topeka Psychoanalytic Society, Topeka, KS.

Watson, J. B. (1914). *Behavior: An introduction to comparative psychology.* New York: Holt.

Watson, J. B. (1916). The place of the conditioned reflex in psychology. *Psychology Review, 23,* 89–116.

Watson, J. B. (1925). *Behaviorism.* Chicago: People's Institute Publishing Co., Inc.

Watson, J. B. (1928). *Psychological care of infant and child.* New York: W. W. Norton.

Weinstein, K. A., Davison, G. C., DeQuatro, W., & Allen, J. W. (1986). *Type A behavior and cognitions: Is hostility the bad actor?* Paper presented at the 94th Annual Convention of the American Psychological Association, Washington, D.C.

Werner, H. (1957). *Comparative psychology of mental development.* New York: McGraw-Hill.

Wheeler, G., & Backman. (Ed.). (1994). *On intimate ground—A Gestalt approach to working with couples.* San Francisco: Jossey-Bass.

Whitehead, W. F. (1993). Gut feelings: Stress and the GI tract. In D. Goleman & J. Gurion (Eds.), *Mind body medicine* (pp. 161–176). Yonkers, NY: Consumer Reports Books.

Whitehorn, J. C., & Betz, B. J. (1960). Further studies of the doctor as a crucial variable in the outcome of treatment with schizophrenic patients. *American Journal of Psychiatry, 117,* 215–223.

Widiger, T. A. (1993). The DSM-III-R categorical personality diagnoses: A critique and alternatives. *Psychological Inquiries, 4,* 75–90.

Widiger, T. A., & Frances, A. (1985). Axis II personality disorders: Diagnostic and treatment issues. *Hospital and Community Psychiatry, 36,* 619–627.

Williams, M. E. , Davison, G. C., Nezami, E., & DeQuattro, V. (1992). Cognition of type A and type B individuals in response to social criticism. *Cognitive Therapy and Research, 16,* 19–30.

Williams, R. B., Suarez, E. C., Kuhn, C. M., Zimmerman, E. A., & Schanberg, S. M. (1991). Biobehavioral basis of coronary-prone behavior in middle-aged men. Part I: Evidence for chronic SNS activation in type A. *Psychosomatic Medicine, 53,* 517–527.

Wing, J. K. (Ed.) (1966). *Early childhood autism: Clinical, educational, and social aspects.* New York: Pergamon Press.

Wishnie, H. (1977). *The impulsive personality: Understanding people with destructive character disorders.* New York: Plenum Press.

Wolf, M. M., Phillips, E. L., & Fixsen, D. C. (1975). *Achievement place phase II: Final report.* Lawrence, KS: Department of Human Development, University of Kansas.

Wolf, S., & Wolff, H. G. (1947). *Human gastric function* (2nd ed.). New York: Oxford University Press.

Wolpe, J. (1958). *Psychotherapy by reciprocal inhibition.* Stanford, CA: Stanford University Press.

Yablonsky, L. (1965). *The tunnel back: Synanon.* New York: Macmillan.

Yalom, I. D. (1980). *Existential psychotherapy.* New York: Basic Books.

Yalom, I. D. (1995). *The theory and practice of group psychotherapy* (4th ed.). New York: Basic Books.

Yates, A. J. (1970). *Behavior therapy.* New York: Wiley.

Yontef, G. M. (1995). Gestalt therapy. In A. S. Gurman & B. Messer (Eds.), *Essential psychotherapies: Theory and practice* (pp. 261–303). New York: Guilford Press.

York, M. W. (1994). Review of *Thus Spoke Zarthustra for Choice.*

York, M. W., Bradberry, S., Karis, M., Burdick, K. P., & Menore, G. (1996). *The relationship between certain personality variables and the report of symptoms suggestive of coronary heart disease, asthma, and gastrointestinal disorders.* Unpublished manuscript, University of New Haven, West Haven, CT.

York, M. W., Burdick, K. P., Tyson, S. S., Sozewska, S. A., & Rabinowitz, J. A. (1992, April). The nonverbal portrayal of interpersonal roles. Paper presented at the Eastern Psychological Association Meeting, Boston, MA.

York, M. W., Wilderman, S. K., & Hardy, S. T. (1988). Categories of implicit interpersonal communication: Cross cultural responses. *Perceptual and Motor Skills, 67*(3), 735–741.

Zimmer, D. (1987). Does marital therapy enhance the effectiveness of treatment for sexual dysfunction? *Journal of Sex and Marital Therapy, 13,* 193–209.

Zoccoliollo, M., Pickles, A., Quinton, D., & Rutter, M. (1992). The outcome of conduct disorder: Implications for defining adult personality disorder and conduct disorder. *Psychological Medicine, 22,* 971–986.

Zvi, G. (1975). *Psychopathology: A cognitive view.* New York: Gardner Press.

INDEX